DEMOCRATIC POLICING IN A CHANGING WORLD

WITHDRAWN

DEMOCRATIC POLICING
IN A
CHANGING WORLD

Peter K. Manning

Paradigm Publishers
Boulder • London

All rights reserved. No part of the publication may be transmitted or reproduced in any media or form, including electronic, mechanical, photocopy, recording, or informational storage and retrieval systems, without the express written consent of the publisher.

Copyright © 2010 Paradigm Publishers

Published in the United States by Paradigm Publishers, 2845 Wilderness Place, Boulder, CO 80301 USA.

Paradigm Publishers is the trade name of Birkenkamp & Company, LLC, Dean Birkenkamp, President and Publisher.

Library of Congress Cataloging-in-Publication Data

Manning, Peter K.
 Democratic policing in a changing world / Peter K. Manning.
   p. cm.
 Includes bibliographical references and index.
 ISBN 978-1-59451-545-3 (hbk. : alk. paper)
 ISBN 978-1-59451-546-0 (pbk. : alk. paper)
 1. Police. 2. Conflict management. I. Title.
 HV7921.M36 2010
 363.2'3-dc22

                                                              2009031080

Printed and bound in the United States of America on acid-free paper that meets the standards of the American National Standard for Permanence of Paper for Printed Library Materials.

Designed and Typeset by Straight Creek Bookmakers.

15 14 13 12 11   2 3 4 5

Contents

Preface

Policing in the United States and among the Western democracies is assumed to be democratic in theory and practice. This assumption raises a number of questions about the role of policing worldwide. Close examination of the role of the police and policing in democracy and the shaping of policing by democratic polities remains undone. The police as an organization and policing as a practice are embedded in the supporting institutions of a democracy, and can sustain or erode the quality of democratic life. Police in democratic societies can and do carry out nondemocratic policing and employ practices that are designed to increase inequalities. Police in nondemocratic or authoritarian societies can also act democratically. The idea that democratic societies must or do have democratic policing is a circumlocution, a rhetorical tactic. While some scholars have struggled to explicate the connections between policing, democracy, and democratic institutions, the family of terms *democratic, the police, policing* and even the context of their use are left unexplored. This semantic confusion is only amplified by the recent attempts to commodify and export "community policing." The origins and tacit expectations of democratic policing even in the restricted set of Anglo-American societies (England, Australia, New Zealand, Canada, and the United States), until recently, have been rarely explored. Democratic police systems are usually seen as natural developments, the result of a salutary yet unexplicated process. An analysis of the role of democratic police, and policing, a powerful agency with almost unlimited access to tools, including gas, automatic weapons, tanks, and readily accessible nonlethal tools, requires a consideration of the moral, political, and ethical limitations upon it.

A vague and assumed connection is also drawn between policing and justice, although each remains an undefined and fuzzy concept. Pragmatic, technique-based studies, focusing on epiphenomena like arrests, changes in the official crime rate, or clearances, fail to address the deeper questions of democracy and governance that police actions reflect. This pragmatism smothers scholarly creativity and obscures the question of the consequences of meaning of alterations in "crime" or other measures of the quality of life. Modernity has altered the bases of police legitimacy as traditional beliefs and local conventions decline while mobility, mass communications, and the globalization of industry and commerce have swept over industrialized societies. The police mandate is affected by global political and economic dynamics. It is too soon to know how 9/11 and its aftermath have affected democratic police practices.

Given these sociocultural limitations, this book presents a theoretical framework for understanding the nature and function of democratic policing with special emphasis on Anglo-American policing and its impact on social order in modern Western democratic societies. The philosopher R. G. Collingwood claims that the value of an inquiry should be judged not by the answers provided or imagined but by the *questions posed*. Using a modified version of Rawls's political liberalism, I pose a series of questions that animate this inquiry: What are police good for? How can we know and evaluate democratic policing? What is known about such policing in Anglo-American democracies? If a democracy rests on equality, justice, and basic rights and responsibilities, what role do the police play in shaping them? How and in what ways does policing sustain notions of equality and a sense of justice or enhance (or at least not erode) citizens' quality of life? Taking a longer view, can we establish the extent to which policing increases or decreases the vast structural inequalities and differences in life experiences that sustain such inequalities? Do the police singularly and collectively contribute to the sense of justice? Is this sense of justice differential by ethnicity, age, class, and other indicators of stratification? To address these questions, it is necessary to come closer to social life and interrogate plainly the matter of justice and why it is a collective concern. Only then can the matter of policing practices be addressed. That is my aim in this book. The first question then is of justice and its role.

THE MATTER OF JUSTICE

Justice, used here to refer to what might be called a sense of justice or natural justice, is assumed to shape policing practices. What is "just" in regard to policing? This question has been submerged frequently and confounded with matters of legal procedures, awkwardly queried as a result of violent and somewhat rare events, and generally assumed. Justice has not been held out anywhere or by any scholar as an explicit and enduring standard for policing. It is, however, implied in the masterful *Report of the Independent Commission on Policing for Northern Ireland*, the Patten Report (1999). The matter is challenging and left to political philosophers. Here, I want to argue for the relevance of justice as fairness as a standard when combined with matters closer to police practice. This is because any surface feature of policing offered as a standard, be it "efficiency," "accountability," "crime control," "smart management," or "what works?" begs the question of for what purpose and why? Decline in crime as shown in officially kept police statistics is not only largely irrelevant to justice but profoundly distracting as a surrogate for policing effects. Can justice be "managed" or made "smart"? Compared to what? It would seem to be self-evident that if the police are any or all of these things yet fail to meet the justice standard, they can be said to have failed. They are generally failing since the job deals with social and political failures, but that having been said, behind my formulation is a more tendentious assertion: to produce justice, one must pursue and defend equality. At least one should expect that like physicians, police should leave the society no less troubled than before. "Do little harm" has never been a police slogan, mission statement, or stated principle. They should maintain civility and restraint. Order absent justice is a dubious and undesirable facade. Disorder is in the weave and woof of everyday life and an aspect of its charm and nuance. In recent years, disorder in and of itself is said to be undesirable per se. Life may appear chaotic on the surface, unless ordering is understood. The need to emphasize the salience of justice in social science and specifically in the field of criminal justice is ample evidence of regrettable circumstances.

As an opening consideration of justice, I shall rely on Alan Ryan's introductory essay to a collection of classic papers aptly entitled *Justice*. His essay, while succinct, provides a most persuasive rationale for the importance of the justice standard in assessing matters of concern to social sciences. Ryan outlines basic propositions about the importance of the concept of justice. Justice is the "most political or institutional of the virtues," he argues, because the legitimacy of the state rests on its claim to do justice (1993, 1). Justice in action is also stringent in its demands—it trumps other demands (ibid., 2) because it is seen as a high virtue in civilized societies. It requires consistency of application (ibid.), and only exceptions of an unusual kind can be considered truly acceptable. Justice is intimately connected to respect for other rights and indeed could be said to be the grounding of other citizens' rights (ibid.). (I would argue it is also connected to basic self-respect.) Ryan draws on the lucid and persuasive work of John Rawls. According to Rawls (1971, hereafter cited as TJ, as quoted in Ryan 1993, 3), observing the principles of justice gives rise to corollaries—those from which "rights" are derived. It is not easy to be just or to observe the principles it implies. Justice is a virtue but may not be "soft" or malleable; it may be "hard" or require diligence of application and willingness to be sensible as well as just. Penultimately, justice is basic to human interactions and reciprocity—it is fundamental. Justice does not stand alone: justice may be in conflict with utility or pragmatism because the current inequities sustain the inability of some to receive justice "equally" and because the series of decisions accruing to "the greatest good" damages some perhaps mortally, that is, they may be executed (TJ, 5). The dialectic perhaps between utility and justice remains an important one since the balance of general well-being and the individual's well-being is not isomorphic (Rawls and Kelly 2001, hereafter cited as JF, 20). Rawls articulates the need to understand the workings of distributive justice. I seek to extend these ideas to query the role of the police in distributing rights and sanctioning obligations. On the other hand, allocative justice reproduces present inequalities and in fact adds to them inevitably. In this sense, it sustains injustice and privilege. Modern societies, stripped of traditional religious beliefs, absent binding historical memories that constrain, and powerful mythopoetic enactments, require equality as a principle. These remarks frame my central argument.

The most persuasive and important statement of the implications and require-ment of justice, and a text from which Ryan's argument is drawn, is work by the late American philosopher John Rawls. Rawls argues in *Justice as Fairness* (JF), a synoptic version of his classic *Theory of Justice* ([1971] 1999 [TJ]),[1] for a "pure theory" of justice. He seeks to avoid the institutional impediments, prejudices, preset ideas and preferences, and current maladies of practice and operation and assumes that achieving the good is possible—both in actions directed toward others and actions taken on behalf of others. This purity is signified by his adopting the original posi-tion, the veil of ignorance and other moves that obviate the sociological realities that might prevent consideration of the principles advanced. This thesis also requires making assumptions about citizens. The actions and trust of the citizen at large is a central connection between just actions and a just society. The person within the structure of liberal democracy is characterized by Rawls as having reasonable and rational trust (TJ, 196; what follows is my paraphrase). The citizen is assumed to have a capacity to be both reasonable and rational and a willingness to believe in the justness of institutions. This should in turn be reciprocated by others—sustained by a belief that others are willing to do their parts as well. This is a reciprocated sense of trust in Rawls's terms. When others with evident intention do their part in just or fair institutions, then citizens tend to develop trust and confidence in them. There is a dynamic in this and a degree of reflexivity. People should manifest a will-ingness to further invest trust. Trust and confidence grow stronger when a sense of cooperative arrangements is sustained and when basic institutions framed to secure fundamental interests (for example, the basic rights and liberties) are more willingly and steadfastly recognized in public political life. There cannot be a more elegant statement of requirements.

This institutional sketch is complemented by a parsimonious characterization of the citizen in a democracy. It is a contractarian formulation. Absent a generalized sense of trust by citizens of the state, no democratic polity can long operate. The role of the person is embedded in two great ideas that are the heart of his theory of justice. Rawls argues that conditions of a well-ordered society include notions about citizens, their commitments, and their beliefs in an ordered society. Citizens act justly and do their part in upholding just institutions, strictly complying with the demands of justice and honoring their duties and obligations toward fellow citizens; they act within a system of public law that ensures citizens that they are asked no more than others and can expect to be affected if they violate they law, and if so, they are treated consistently and similarly as cases of a similar sort. The assump-tions of the citizen are that the society is just, and the tacit basis of this constitutes a system of background expectations. It is essential, Rawls argues following H. L. A. Hart, that the system of laws should be public, well expressed, and well defended and that this public face is essential to sustaining a shared belief in its fairness. In this sense, a dramaturgical view of law, encompassing both its instrumental and its symbolic or expressive effects, must be appreciated. That is, laws selectively elevate or suppress symbols that represent groups' collective interests; the enforcement or lack of enforcement of these laws in turn represents the erosion or enhancement of the social fate of groups. This is a part then of the re-representation of fairness. I quote here by way of summary from Rawls's *Justice As Fairness* (JF, 42–43):

1. Each person has the same indefeasible claim to a full, adequate scheme of equal basic liberties, which scheme is compatible with the same scheme of liberties for all; *and*
2. Social and economic inequalities are to satisfy two conditions: first, they are to be attached to offices and positions open to all under conditions of fair equality of opportunity; and second, they are to be to the greatest benefit of the least-advantaged members of society (the difference principle).

The first principle is prior to the second and is essential to its attainment. I adopt these principles as standards, in spite of the empirical realities of the present welfare capitalistic state that does not respect "all the main political values expressed by the two principles of justice" (ibid., 134). In a sense, this outline of *principles* is a thought experiment intended to guide investigation. As Rawls explains at some length, this formulation assumes that inequality exists along many dimensions (education, income, lifestyle, extant social capital such as savings and assets) *and* that any framework that assumes equality of choice or action available to all choosers (e.g., rational choice theories) is misleading.[2] The current vast inequality in the distribution of wealth, talent, and various forms of social capital makes the notion of free "rational" choice as a basis for social order a nonsense. It is a nonsense on stilts for well-known reasons. The constraints on choice, the range of present and future options, unequal resources, material and symbolic, and the tactical advantages and the competence to utilize these will pattern any choice. We are ultimately hostage to others. In that sense no choice can be called "free" or even "optimizing." The latter assumes that knowledge is equally and fairly distributed and that the future consequences of actions can be anticipated and integrated with current options and understandings. Therefore, mere palliative, allocative moves that assume that the market or other "natural forces" (intelligence, class, gender) sustain, or will eventually produce, democratic order will not do so; *they merely dramatize and may increase the present inequalities.* Justice, as Rawls has so eloquently stated, requires a distributive approach, not a merely allocative approach. To allocate further to those who already have ultimately destroys the necessary commitment of citizens to work and to sustain the economy. In a final move, Rawls argues for a constant reconsideration of the workings of this assemblage—the process should be subjected to frequent reflexive reassessment (TJ, 579).

The question arises: what now of the police? The role of the police qua institution is only imaginable, an inference, rather than a function stated by Rawls. Rawls assumes for purposes of the argument in JF that agents of the law and those who create it are acting in good faith, attempting to clarify the meaning of rules, and treating crime as criminal and treating similar cases similarly. That is, democratic policing would be that which does not violate these tacit assumptions or background expectations, because if it did repeatedly, the stability issuing from a shared sense of justice would be threatened (TJ, 453ff). To further pursue this point, the imposition of harsh laws, punishments, and other fictional attempts to punish criminals cannot alone sustain stability based on justice. As Rawls subtly argues in "Two Concepts of Rules" (1955), there is no rational threshold or rule that might guide what is a rational level of punishment. All punishment can only be seen constitutively. If the agents of the justice system repeatedly punish those who have not committed crimes, and these punishments are cumulative, the consequences serve to further undermine compliance. This a great harm—the exploitation and punishment of the innocent. By implication, at least short-term variations in officially recorded crime have a moot role. In effect, the agents of governmental institutions have a more binding obligation to carry out justice. This obligation exceeds others. Rawls writes:

> The thing to observe here is that there are several ways in which one may be bound to political institutions. For the most part the natural duty of justice is the more fundamental, since it binds citizens generally and requires no voluntary acts in order to apply. The principle of fairness, on the other hand, binds only those who assume public office, say, or those who, being better situated, have advanced their aims within the system. There is, then, another sense of *noblesse oblige*: namely, that those who are more privileged are to acquire obligations tying them even more strongly to a just scheme. (TJ, 116)

Rawls's concerns are with the *sustaining institutions* that provide a structure of orderly life, not with their operations, or the differential consequences of their operations. The police are a part of what Rawls terms the "basic structure" (JF, 10), institutions that affect the life circumstances of all citizens. *They have an obligation to act justly.* Clearly, as we shall see in later chapters, the criminal justice system distributes sanctions, most of which are negative marks that can dramatize, stigmatize, isolate, and destroy people. They also facilitate the success of others by the patience, compromise, and willingness to overlook offenses. While Rawls does not concern himself directly with the criminal justice system or with negative delicts, crime is a form of inequality that is punished. In this sense, policing is an aspect of formal social ordering and in the sense that it *operates as an agency for the redistribution of life chances in a population* (an inference from JF, 50–52). If status orders are both horizontal (lifestyles, consumption patterns, groups of occupations) and vertical (based on income, ethnicity, and occupation), then penalties assessed by police *directly* such as traffic stops, interrogations, searches, surveillance, raids, violence, and arrests, as well as *indirect costs* resulting from the previous direct police actions such as court-ordered fines, jail or probation, community service, or prison, alter the life prospects of those encountering the police routinely. The benefits and costs are both direct and indirect. While this general well-being or ability to thrive is not usually measured in studies of collective efficacy and neighborhood trust of the police, it is a measurable feature of a neighborhood. On the other hand, there is a "law enforcement bonus" associated with fewer traffic stops, searches, misdemeanor arrests particularly, and absent surveillance by various forms of policing. While this distributional function can be said of government as a whole, the role of the police is fundamental both symbolically and instrumentally—they represent trustworthiness and exercise violence. They are the immediate face of government. This view of policing is intended to avoid the debilitating arguments from utilitarianism, on the one hand, that ascribe the greatest good to the choices made regardless of the present and current constraints of iniquitous conditions, and from social theory, on the other, that is, explaining the factual state of current social relations (large inequities based on genetic, class, education, and other bases for "social capital") as inevitable, determined, and determinant.

What do police do? The police, by surveillance and tracking of selected groups of people and known suspects, making arrests, traffic stops, and sweeps of areas, keeping a jail, and applying street justice under the guise of "discretion," can radically alter life chances, enhancing some, and rarely even ending life. They act as a redistribution mechanism in the context of the present inequalities of even a wealthy society. If we are to hold to the Rawlsian difference principle simply put, it would require that nothing be done by formal agencies of the state that increase present known inequalities on the basis of policy and or practice. The actions of officers with original authority can be assumed to balance the risks they produce, given reasonable training and recruitment. In my view, the difference principle as a frame of reference for considering consequences should govern police actions. That is, given the current range of inequalities in education, opportunity, income, and skills, any police practice, especially that driven and shaped by policy, should not further increase extant inequalities.[3] In practical terms, this means, on the one hand, that they should attend to civilities and observe procedural justice, avoiding damage to present collective capacities. On the other hand, efforts to build communities, partnerships, and other forms of community policing are inconsequential. Since they do little harm, they cannot be discounted. Popular, short-term dramatic, and perhaps policy-driven operations, "hot-spot" policing, targeting "gangs" and neighborhoods because of their class and/or ethnic composition, sweeps, crackdowns, or raids of areas or groups, violate the equally shared rights required by the application of the difference principle (JF, 51). They can be seen at the extreme as governmentally sponsored terrorism actions taken unannounced with targeted groups as the rationale aimed to instill fear and a sense of trepidation, and for which few remedies, civil or criminal, are available. In particular, "militaristic" operations based on categorical thinking—raids on "terrorists," "gang members," "drug dealers," the homeless or mentally ill—are inconsistent with procedures that emphasize behavior, not color, thoughts, intentions, plans, or mischievous wishes. The present inequalities are unlikely to be reduced by any current policing practice, but what is done now surely increases them. Insofar as systematic crime-control efforts do not radically increase inequalities—for example, by arresting the innocent, harassing the young, insulting and disrespecting people stopped—they are needed periodically. Insofar as crime suppression via arrests sustains order and trust, it is essential; however, if communities lack social integration, police efforts may be palliative at best. On the one hand, raids and the like instill a sense of distrust of authorities as they are not announced, affect all, innocent and guilty alike, and create chaos in neighborhoods so affected. On the other hand, evidence suggests that the police when concerned about matters of collective efficacy or social integration in neighborhoods or beats tend to focus on those areas where it is in fact high (Skogan et al. 1999). Whether these police activities will increase community well-being in any significant and lasting fashion is yet unknown.

These rules of thumb do minimally constrain local communities and individual officers. Locally marked and accepted standards, especially when dramatized by the police, are of considerable value in sustaining order (Ellickson 1991; Meares and Kahan 1998). Practices vary, and cannot be collapsed by use of summary rules that are mere generalizations about means, modes, or the like, as John Rawls argues in the brilliant article "Two Concepts of Rules" (1955). They are made meaningful by context, and this gives them their character and meaning. Clearly, the police, formally and informally, within the law and outside of it, engage daily in the redistribution of rights, duties, obligations, and privileges. They enact the circumstances of everyday justice. They mediate the forces of law and those of revenge, self-help, and local terrorism by groups (represented by hate crimes and the like). They are symbols, icons of order, not of equality. They manage the aesthetics and politics of appearances. The question of the role of police actions in democratic societies requires a step back into the origins and patterns of policing as well as current practices.

One difficulty in making a theoretical connection between democracy and policing is that the signifier "police" has been variously defined, as I explore below. Several important qualifications and specifications have arisen in the past twenty years. It is now recognized that "police" are both public and private, only the public police having access to the criminal justice system via arrest, variously in competition with each other and other nonpolicing agencies, and both locally and nationally legitimate. They are intertwined into networks. They work via patrol, surveillance, tracking, and arrest. They are constrained by law, but in fact they work by exception or the capacity to pragmatically respond to uncertainties. Any effort to restrict their functions to "law enforcement" is thus misleading, and the imputation that they either create or sustain order is dubious. They react to failures. The functions of domestic or low policing are always accompanied to a lesser or greater degree by matters of national security. Concern for national security varies over time and among nations (Weitzer 1990).

Finally, a note on modernity. The idea of modernity and perhaps the high modernity of the present has overwhelmed writers in many fields, but it has had little if any influence on the fields of criminology and criminal justice. The theories and concepts still applied are those of the late nineteenth century, and crimes of concern of early modernity and industrialization. These are no longer the fundamental problems gripping modern societies. They are quickly being overshadowed by crimes against nature, the environment and its species, crimes that manifest deep violations of public trust such as the market crash of late 2008 and 2009. As Durkheim (1961) points out, modernity, with the fragmentation of religious beliefs, the growth of individualistic capitalism, and industrialization and urbanization, requires a foundation of justice and equality. The public police are an antiquated early-nineteenth-century idea that was born in the crucible of urbanization, empire building, and the rise of the working classes (Palmer 1988). It has little changed since then. Police service is done more quickly. On the other hand, modernity is shaping policing. Efforts to understand the role of policing in democracies require an understanding of the postmodern world, one in which rapid communication, displacement of time and space relevant to interactions, and cheap worldwide transportation impact policing. In many respects, this change produces displacement and distrust across national and cultural boundaries, even as states grow weaker, and the local nature of policing comes into question. Insofar as policing is a means for coping with uncertainty and reducing distrust, it faces new challenges from uncertainties produced by the media, the law, untoward events, internal command and control issues, fading jurisdictional borders, and variations in officially recorded crime, and each new adaptation to these changes and uncertainties produces a new set of conditions connoting uncertainty.

OVERVIEW OF CONTENTS

This preface and the first three chapters constitute part 1 of the book. They set out the philosophical grounding for the consideration of democratic police. They concern the interweaving of justice and policing. Chapter 1, "Defining Democratic Police and Policing," seeks to ground policing with reference to democracy in modern urban societies in the English-speaking world (termed here the Anglo-American world of the United States, United Kingdom, Canada, New Zealand, and Australia, what I refer to as the AADP nations). There are at least seven versions of democratic policing advanced by scholars (Bayley; Berkeley; Sklansky; Loader and Walker; Shearing and colleagues; Liang; and Newburn, Smith, and Jones). Unfortunately, they do not specify practices that might translate the ideas into action or the practices that characterize AADP nations. Five modes of definition have been advanced—historical, textbooklike, analytic, typological, and context sensitive; most of these are based on variations of Bittner's classic definition. The outline of requirements from the historian Liang includes five features: guided legalistically, absent torture, counterterrorist activities, addressing civilities, and focus on individuals, not groups. He argues further that the tacit values of citizens should guide policing. These are useful guidelines.

Chapter 2 considers dimensions of democratic policing. These include its mode of emergence; collective orientation, democratic versus nondemocratic features, commitment to fairness and sustaining trust; its features that are seen as both sacred and profane; mode of centralization; imagery; place within a competitive field; and its mandate. While it is a kind of magic, its sacred canopy obscures its violence, its archaic bases, and its early modern origins.

Chapter 3 revisits the Rawlsian principles. I argue for policing as a matter to be assessed by the criteria suggested by Rawls's difference principle. This pertains to the obligation of those in public office to refrain from doing injustice via stated policies or a pattern of concerted action. I then refine my definition of policing and proceed to provide some elaboration and tessellation upon it.

Part 2 of the book concerns the police as an institution. Chapter 4 discusses the beginnings of research on AADP nations and the structural features of such policing. It concludes with a characterization of police studies as a paradigm that highlights and dramatizes selectively certain aspects of policing and its effects and ignores or reduces in salience others. In many respects, policing as a field of study mirrors the occupational concerns of the police and in that sense is oriented to a sociology *for* the police rather than a sociology *of* the police.

The fifth chapter outlines the structural features of American policing. This emphasizes the decentralized, diverse-in-size, locally funded, politically sensitive nature of policing in America. The other features are direct consequences of the decentralized local system. There is no academy or training center for state or local police and several federal training centers. The policing of the United States, more than any other Anglo-American society, is done by layered and competing agencies—city, county, township, state, and federal agencies. The state police are not gendarmerie except perhaps at the state level. The specialization and centralization of control found in English, French, and German policing, in large part driven by concerns for crime prevention and antiterrorism policing, have not been accepted in the United States and Canada. They remain localistic and decentralized in focus and spirit.

Chapter 6, a key transitional chapter between analytic definitions and policing as an activity, begins with a discussion of the failure to produce a coherent analytic conception of policing. Police studies as a field reflects the commonsense version of policing—its central occupational ideology. What passes for "theory," the broken-windows thesis, is an articulated version of the convictions of the police. The only acknowledged framework used to describe policing in somewhat abstract terms is an essay written for an eastern literary magazine. An examination of the results of research show that the supporting empirical evidence is at best mixed. Its impacts, carried to logical conclusion, would increase inequalities, reduce trust in the police among the less fortunate, and perhaps increase social distance between the police and the majority of those they serve daily. It could and does stimulate nondemocratic policing practices.

The final chapter in part 2 concerns efforts to reform policing in the past twenty-five or so years. These include community policing, problem-solving policing, hot-spot policing, and crime analysis and crime mapping. Attempts to reform police have been frequent, the purposes unclear because the purpose is obscured, unstated, or mistaken. No underlying principle guides these efforts at change: community policing aims at partnerships, reducing social distance with communities, and making police more visible and present in the minds of the citizens; crime mapping and analysis and crackdowns are clearly and directly crime oriented and inwardly aimed at better management and accountability of middle managers within large police departments; and problem solving has shown no measurable results when it has been used. These reforms have had little operational or structural impact in spite of the widespread publicity and funding they have generated.

Part 3 concerns police practices and their consequences. Chapter 8 concerns what might be called tactical poetry—the nature of policing—and chapter 9 outlines the police métier, standard police practice. Efforts at reform have little altered this basic *police métier,* and chapter 10 shows the faults of nondemocratic policing. Crackdowns and waves of arrests have resulted in a race-based view of policing, a spiraling upward of jail and prison populations, a crushing pressure on low-income neighborhoods as a result of returning ex-offenders, and great ambivalence among lower-class people about the validity and reliability of police efforts. It is striking that the conventional view of policing found in the journals in the field of police studies, with the exception of papers on "corruption," rarely includes specification of the negative consequences of routine policing as seen from the perspective of those policed.

The distilled empirical materials I rely on here derive from my recent research on homeland security, policing massive public demonstrations such as the Democratic National Convention in Boston, crime analysis and crime mapping, and the role of information technology in shaping policing. These studies are reported in later chapters. They are ethnographically informed studies based on observation, interviews, and documents, and include fieldwork in Washington, D.C., Boston, and a midwestern city.

Acknowledgments

Any book is composed in, of, and by fragments, movements, losses, travels, and adventures. Some things lost are found in the text as it unfolds; some are lost forever. I used to wander in the Oxford Parks, in Headington outside Oxford, amble along the Banbury and Woodstock Roads, and sit by the Cherwell. Those days are gone. I once imagined the long structure of a book in the sky over the parks. I cycled at night on the Cowley Road up to Junction Road. My clothes, books, papers, and computers, even loved memorabilia, were abandoned repeatedly, thrown out with other emotional baggage. Left. I littered many streets with black plastic bags left for collection—filled with once treasured bits: fragments, pictures, postcards, diaries, journals, *memento mori*. My possessions—except my books—were once contained in a single airplane-ready cardboard box. I have been reading *Ulysses* while I make the final edits of this book. Bloom wandered too.

Portions of chapters 1 and 5 were rehearsed in *Policing Contingencies* (2003), while chapter 3 was presented first to an international police conference held at the College of Criminal Justice and Safety, Eastern Kentucky University, Richmond, Kentucky, June 12–15, 2003. It was published in a condensed and considerably revised form in Spanish in *Revista Cennipec* (Universidad de los Andes, Merida, Venezuela) and subsequently in *Police Quarterly* 8 (March 2005): 23–43. Chapter 4 is a much revised version of a chapter published in Trevor Jones and Tim Newburn, eds., *Plural Policing* (2006).

Any book is an emblem of the patience and understanding of others. I thank my families, children and grandchildren, for their tolerance over time, in two countries, and in several cities. I learned and grew in Oxford long ago, in Merida and Caracas, Venezuela, with my friends there, democrats all. On several marvelous visits to the Andean city of Merida, I spoke about democratic policing, watched the clouds gather around the peaks of the Andes in the late afternoon, wandered in the mist on excursions with friends, attended a fiesta at El Salmon, and saw the *trucha*, the pigs, and the rows of harvested potatoes tattooed on the barren hills. I sailed, too, in the Caribbean, because a bank could not pay us for consulting, and I watched the burning sun. I thank Chris Birkbeck and family, Luis Gerardo, Yoana, Reynaldo, and colleagues in the Centro de Investigaciones Penales y Criminológicas at the Universidad de los Andes, Merida, Venezuela. The College of Criminal Justice at Northeastern University and the facilities provided by the endowed Brooks Chair financed much of the travel and writing associated with this book. In the final stages of writing, I benefited from the penetrating insights and questions of Michael W. Raphael. He has been a good colleague in difficult times. He produced the reference list with consummate skill. Rebecca Pfeffer good-humoredly worked on the bibliography. The book is better as a result. Closer to home, around the corner, I thank Conor, Brett, Justin, Chris, Ashleigh, and Matty P. at Conor Larkin's and "Benko," at Our House East. Joe L. asked me to mention his name, too. Bobby has been a good friend. All of them laughed, listened, and talked with me.

What I took to be my life changed abruptly when I moved to Boston and was named to the Elmer V. H. and Eileen M. Brooks Professorship in the College of Criminal Justice at Northeastern University. I moved my heart, and my heart moved me. This book, like the last, is dedicated once more to my friend and colleague Anne Warfield Rawls. It is just possible I might have written it without her. Probably not....

Peter K. Manning
Boston, Salisbury Beach, and Newburyport, Massachusetts
June 2008

PART ONE

The Necessity of Justice

CHAPTER ONE

Defining Democratic Police and Policing

Democracy and policing are intimately related, but the nature of this intimacy is not clear. The ideas of John Rawls, a version of a pure democratic theory, inspires the theory that policing is a kind of redistributive mechanism resting on notions of trust, equality, and legitimacy. It fits well with the notion of high modernity in which strangers must interact repeatedly in some civilized manner. Policing is about the management of uncertainties and rests on compliance and mutual trust.

This chapter is an exercise in articulating the role of policing in a democracy. Here I primarily, though not exclusively, reference English-speaking countries or Anglo-American societies (North America, the UK, Australia, and New Zealand). I refer to them as AADP nations. They are the bearers of the Peel legacy—the notion of a visible, reactive, bureaucratically organized means of state-based resolution of conflict with minimal force. It is a mode of governmental control and governance. I draw on the ideas of scholars who have combined an empirical research-based interest in policing with a theoretical zest and diligence that include concerns for democratic practice. The presence of democracy, as ideology and practice, shapes what is expected implicitly of police. But the family of ideas that "democracy" connotes has not been well connected to the objects "police" and "policing." In order for policing to possess social reality and presence, it must have a role in everyday life and the politics of everyday life. Clearly, this reality is heterodox, multifaceted, and ambiguous because the police are not a thing, an abstract absence or a constant presence. They are a conception or illusion of presence as well as a presence.

Seven versions of the idea of democratic policing, stated in various degrees of complexity and detail and arising from historical, jurisprudential, and sociological perspectives, are discussed in this chapter. I summarize those who have explicitly linked democracy and police, namely, George Berkeley; David Bayley; Trevor Jones, Tim Newburn, and David Smith; Clifford Shearing; David Sklansky; Ian Loader and Neil Walker; and Hsi-Huey Liang. These are arrayed somewhat chronologically, although Bayley's work has evolved from 1969 to the present. Liang's work, even though published in 1992, is considered last because his ideas are most explicit with democratic policing and its limits. The elegant and compelling definition of Egon Bittner requires special and detailed examination. I conclude with a consideration of five modes of defining police. A formal synthetic definition is presented in chapter 3.

DEMOCRACY AND POLICING: SEVEN VERSIONS

Democracy as a system of elements and institutions requires compromise in policing as in other aspects. Theories of the origins, strengths, and weaknesses of democracy and its realization cover a vast intellectual territory, as do theories of justice associated with a democratic polity. The idea in this chapter is to locate the essential aspects that link a democratic polity to a democratic police. Democratic policing can be carried out in nondemocratic nations if it meets the principles governing it analytically. It is carried out in rather diverse functional, structural, and image-based fashion (Bayley 1992), suggesting there is something deeply rooted in the practices and ensemble rather than the structure and function. That is, it would appear that restraint and responsiveness to citizen demand guide democratic policing more than other factors (Clark and Sykes 1974, 460–65; Bayley 1979, 120–21). Structural and functional variables do not account for this feature. All policing requires some attention to the difference principle, to the redistributive aspect, and to fairness, because, short of totalitarian governments and the reign of terror, all policing requires extended and consistent compliance from the public. The notion that law is rationed in some sense and that discretion at the bottom accounts for the flexibility and survival of democratic policing misses the larger and more significant point about compromise and tolerance of minorities (of whatever sort). As an organization, the democratic police are linked in both direct and indirect fashion with the vague expectations of citizens in a democratic society. As Bayley (1969, 409–10) first articulated, the police affect democracy (and democracy affects policing) in what functions they carry out, how they carry them out (and what they represent), and how they are treated as personnel. Unfortunately, Bayley, like other scholars, does not tell us how to judge the extent to which any of these features obtains. The criteria advanced assume a democratic polity and historical legitimacy. Let us now consider the core ideas of scholars who have articulated the vital connections between democracy as a system of elements and the police as an organization. This exercise assumes a general notion of democracy rather than a precise definition.

George Berkeley

George Berkeley's *Democratic Policeman* (1969) was the first clear statement of the place of policing in a democracy. It is written in a readable, almost journalistic, fashion and places the questions of interest in the broad context of public policy. He addresses the character of democratic policing directly. It is an essay in comparative public administration based on research, primarily interviews, done in France, Sweden, Germany, England, and the United States. Unfortunately, it does not include a discussion of the origins of democratic policing, definitions of policing, democratic policing, or the requirements for sustaining it. These elements are there by implication only. He argues that the desired or preferred democratic organization (for it is not about the policeman at all but rather the police organization as an administrative entity) has a bureaucratic form that provides standardization of rules and procedures, opportunities for mobility (horizontal and vertical within the organization), and employee participation in decision making. This focus on the internal facets of a democratic organization is a unique contribution of the book. He points out, as do David Bayley and David Sklansky (discussed below), the relationship between internal procedures and treatment and the expectations of civil and restrained interactions with the public. How is it possible to treat citizens equally and reasonably when the police organization is capricious and often mysterious in its own sanctioning, reviews, promotions, and rewards? His conception favors a kind of liberal policing based on equality, political participation of the police, centralized administration, and restrained, legalistic practice and focuses on ways to produce a "democratic police officer" based on sound education, training, and supervision. His most striking admonition is urging police leadership to make the police organization less punitive and more egalitarian and fair and urging the police into politics internally and in the polity more generally. His position is clearly in favor of both constraint and restraint: "The more active the policeman, the more he tends to erode the foundation of democratic society" (1969, 4). This is striking given the current emphasis in the United States on active intervention to reduce crime and disorder and the elevation of "crime fighting" as the principal role of the police. Since he urges police to be active in crime prevention and sees it as an important facet of democratic policing (ibid., 205), it is perhaps fair to see his restrained officer as operating in a reactive, crime-focused manner while actively promoting crime prevention in its many forms. "Crime prevention" for him refers to the broad service and caring functions of policing that directly or indirectly reduce officially recorded crime, not those matters intended, for example, by use of the arrest sanction. On balance, his principled view of restraint and civility is consistent with the Rawlsian notions of the limited damage via policing guided by the difference principle.

David Bayley

David Bayley, during his long and distinguished career, has consistently questioned the role of the police in a democracy. He has approached this question historically and cross-culturally and through rich empirical studies of policing. In the late sixties, after returning from an extended period of research in India, Bayley outlined how police could shape political development. It is a clear, prescient, and reasonable model of political philosophy combined with detailed ethnographic work. His principal interests at this time were the ways in which the police can affect political development in a democracy. This was a unique and significant question. He argued that police affect political development by *what they do in the polity at large*: by maintaining stable conditions of social life, by activity in the political life of a nation, by the degree to which they use force or not, by their direct and indirect participation in political life, and by supporting police and law enforcement practices. They also carry out administration and enforce regulations (or not). They deal with the public and alter the scope and kind of enforcement they carry out in critical situations. He makes a brilliant, almost epigrammatic, remark concerning the role of the law and law enforcement in AADP nations, stating that police officers in these countries are "uniformed technicians in enforcing the law" (1969, 18). Bayley also notes a second set of *specific, variable role functions* that are possible by the police in a democracy. These include whether they are active or passive, including the extent of responsiveness to citizen demand; how secretive they are; how they treat individuals; and how impartially they act (ibid., 23). A third set of activities concerns what the police are or how they are seen. This might be called the *imagery of the police*. They have a role in promoting innovation and consumption of materials related to crime and order, including education and technological innovations, and they possess an imagery that resonates with members of the society. Finally, Bayley proposes that how the police treat themselves—their social composition, their occupational culture (my terms), and their promotion and hiring and firing policies—reflects at best democratic principles. In this last set, Bayley turns his attention to how the police represent a society, both symbolically and in respect to the kinds of people (their ambitions, aims, and beliefs) they recruit and maintain.

Bayley then takes a striking and important turn and asks what, in ideal terms, police could or should contribute to a democratic polity. The police should:

- Strive to be studiously nonviolent
- Reflect what people want them to enforce
- Close the gap between those who enforce the law and those against whom it is enforced
- Recruit widely from various regions, groups, and social segments in the population
- Become a part of a growing economy, contributing knowledge and skills (ibid., 28)

Bayley's Indian research includes historical materials and a large social survey of attitudes toward the police. His assessment (see Chapter 16, "Conclusions") of the extent to which Indian police at the time fulfilled the expectations set out above is rather limp and vague, concluding that they did well given limited public trust, political corruption, the occasional bit of malfeasance and violence, a lack of resources, and division of policing functions. The conclusion he draws is that the traditional mode of politics, "corruption," limited the capacities of the police to facilitate democracy in India but had nevertheless not been entirely a hindrance.

Thirty-two years later, the most dramatic, well-written, and well-presented argument concerning the requirements for democratic policing is again David Bayley's. It is found in a U.S. Department of Justice publication (Bayley and National Institute of Justice 2001) and later in a revised form in a book, *Changing the Guard* (2006). In spite of arguing consistently for more than thirty years that structure and function alone cannot account for the outcomes one associates with democracy, he now recasts his argument, asserting that some policing principles can be held out in theory. Although democratic government is necessary for democratic policing, Bayley states some hopeful categorical principles for guiding police if they are to be levers of democracy. This is an emergent concern for students of the police except those concerned with the contours of transnational policing of various sorts. He does not discuss the extent to which these factors obtain in the United States at the dawning of the twenty-first century. Bayley's are the only research-based arguments for a set of guiding norms for policing in democracy.[1] As such, his work is an important landmark in scholarship, and the limits and strengths of these tenets must be addressed prior to further discussion of democratic policing. He argues in the 2001 document that democratic policing should be guided by the following principles or priorities. The police organization should:

- Give top operational priority to serving the needs of individual citizens and private groups
- Be accountable to the law rather than to the government
- Protect human rights, especially those involving unfettered political activity, which is the hallmark of democracy
- Be transparent in its activity

In Bayley's 2006 version of this list, he omits transparency and argues for "responsiveness"—serving the needs of individuals and private groups. The terms *must* and *should* are interchangeable in his discourse.

Such lists rest on assumptions about policing as an organization within a democratic society, assuming that there is a degree of independence in the actions of police apart from the supporting legitimacy of other institutions. It assumes cultural, social, and political differentiation of function. The idea that police should be the leaders—that they can somehow encourage, create, sustain, strengthen, or otherwise be a part of producing a democratic state—is getting the entire argument backward. It is a democratic state and culture that produce democratic policing, and there is no evidence that the contrary can result. In fact, in Ireland, the English police and militias long prevented the mergence of any sort of democracy (Palmer 1988). Bayley describes briefly his fieldwork in four countries (Bayley and National Institute of Justice 2001, 3–6, 15) but does not employ or quote from these data in his essay. He is concerned with the impetus for policing efforts abroad, their rationale and costs, and to some degree their political warrant. He also includes a kind of strategy for producing democratic policing—a list of hopes (ibid., 49). His broadest aim is to argue for policing as one means by which democratic modes of governance can emerge.

There are serious limitations to the 2001 Bayley list. The police cannot serve individual needs and requests for service and those of private groups whose interests often are at odds with those of both the police and the government of the day. Elites, often in complex fashion and indirectly, shape policing and set policing priorities via the political process. The order obtained is more often than not the order preferred by the elites, not those politically marginal but directly subject to the consequences of the politics of order. Aggregated demand is not a surrogate for political legitimacy or political group power. Would any observer equate calls for service in a large city with political power or see them as an index of political power? Quite the contrary, I believe. Clearly, aggregated demand is the best indicator of the absence of other resources and capacities. The police do not serve equally "the people"; they serve the state in third-party conflict resolution. They act neutrally on behalf of the state. The collective good as aggregated individual demand is the guiding beacon for police actions. That is, individual aggregated demand indexed by calls for service is not a surrogate for "meeting needs." These needs are elastic and open-ended. As any close analysis of police actions in massive public demonstrations or rebellious activities reveals, the police are constantly weighing the legality of their planned actions against and their sense of their obligations to the government of the day. They are, after all, the arm of the executive branch of government. The "law" and its relevance in any case require constant interpretation in the event of application of police force (Stenning 2008). The role of the police as protectors of human rights connected with political activity is equally a slogan, a caution if interference is noted, not a guide to how to do so. The term *transparent* is a miraculous buzzword when applied to an organization whose root and foundation are secrecy, misdirection, dissembling, and lying in the interest of order maintenance. While it is somehow linked to accountability, review, and complaints, transparency is meaningless in an organization in which virtually all the directly affecting decisions are made invisibly, a reflection of patterns of policing, and rarely reviewed even if a record is available (Reiss 1974).

Let us consider these ideas in a slightly broader political context. The focus of this list is individualistically defined and generated needs, demands, rights, and duties implied by a state governed by democracy, a constitution, laws, voting, and mechanisms for balancing power and authority among segments of the government of the day. Individualism is of course culturally and socially defined and is a product of long development based on emerging capitalism, Protestantism, and its concern for individual self-determined fate, status differentiation, and vertical differentiation of function (the division of labor in an advanced country) and in every way precedes the emergence of a differentiated, legally constituted representation of state authority. The extent of differentiation of legal force from cultural and social assumptions is contextual and historic, as Bayley has argued (1975, 1985). The detachment of legal authority from religious, kin, and local authority has not been established in any country in which U.S. programs are involved. If these clustering and undifferentiated modes of authority exist, the distinctive force of law as an entity cannot emerge. Law is, as Black (1976) has correctly argued, inversely related to other modes of social control. Human rights, legal rights, and the like have no reality in nation-states where law is a secondary or tertiary shadow on everyday life. These "rights" cannot be protected or engaged if they do not exist. Strategies for reform (see chapter 4) are reasonable, given a democratic infrastructure, traditions, and legal framework, little of which exists in the countries studied. The sequence described has not taken place in the countries studied, and in any case the police are at the far end of an evolutionary process. Finally, if my arguments in this book are at all viable, the basis for the emergence of police is trust in impersonal authority generally. Absent trust, nothing follows, which in turn means that "democratic policing" by definition cannot be imposed by bribes, law, conquest, or war.

Bayley has been a notable federally funded expert in the export of policing. The recent explosion of policing abroad under the umbrella of UN-based police actions, "rule of law funding" (Bayley 2001, 4), peacekeeping, training foreign police, and combating transnational crime (ibid., 5) is striking. As Bayley notes, it is impossible to ascertain precisely the extensive expenditure of the United States in "policing" in its several forms abroad, but he estimates that some several billion dollars have been processed, funded, or directed by the United States through a variety of federal agencies, including the CIA, DEA, FBI, Departments of Defense and State, and others (2006, 41–43).[2]

The notion of creating "democratic police" in Bosnia and Kosovo and the experiments in Haiti and elsewhere, for example, are truly anomalous cases, since there was neither police nor democracy there. These organizations cannot be considered democratic police, for they operate in an institutional and cultural structure that does not possess or support democratic policing. Policing rests on institutional structures, requires symbolic and cultural capital to work, and thus cannot be a *commodity* exported, given, bought, or sold to another nation (Brogden and P.Nijhar 2005). In this case, the idea, much like community policing (CP), exists in name only, absent the tacit expectations and assumptions in which police practice is embedded. The culture that fosters individual rights, constraints on the state by law, the permission of those who are governed to be governed by laws, and a language reflecting individuals and selves, not tribal obligations and loyalties, supports a democratic police structure. The professionalization, specialization, and bureaucratic elaboration of the police are based on these notions and cannot create them. The direction of causality works in only one direction. Designating police functions absent the institutional structures leads to logical contradictions (Bayley 2006, 15)—one cannot serve individuals in societies in which classic Western European notions of the individual, individualism, and individual rights and legal safeguard in the law have no place.

In an unpublished version of his conception of democratic policing (presented at American Society of Criminology in November 2005), Bayley returned to a more conservative view, arguing for the value of traditional policing practices in the context of political pressures for domestic police to engage in antiterrorism. Calling this the Peel model, Bayley urged considering these traditional practices as fundamental to democracy. He presented reactive policing rather than anticipation and active, interventionist policing; a focus on events and places, not persons; a public, not private, basis for policing; fixed strategies (those maintained since the mid-twentieth century, such as random patrol, response to calls for service, and investigation of reported crime); general duty officers as the standard; and operations that are closely regulated by law. These notions echo Liang (discussed below) and question the extent to which domestic police should shift their strategies and practices in line with the new rhetoric of fear and terrorism. This version of democratic policing strongly supports the separation of the police from the pressures and concerns of the government of the day and their obligation to civil government rather than to "politics." Yet, in many respects, policing plays on the cultural, political, and symbolic capital available to it much more than producing such capital in the course of its activities.

Trevor Jones, Tim Newburn, and David Smith

Trevor Jones, Tim Newburn, and David Smith (1996) set out to address the tenets underlying democratic policing. One of the few efforts that is grounded in an examination of democracy itself as a source of the ideas on which democratic policing might be based, their work is a rather painful effort at clarification. After wrestling with the idea of democracy as it applies to policing and searching for solutions in previous published work, they advance seven abstract criteria for judging the quality of police governance in a democracy: equity, delivery of service, responsiveness, distribution of power, information, modes of redress, and participation. They are listed in order of priority for democratic policing. The authors hope for policies that might ensure or increase the possibility of their criteria's being met but note that police policies are rare, often violated or bent, and very unpopular with the rank and file and most administrators. They are singularly pessimistic about equity being achieved but suggest something like an audit of the impact of policing (ibid., 191) as a rough index of success in this regard. They suggest that service ought to be provided to citizens in general on the basis of needs and that arrests ought to be proportionate to the number and severity of offenses. They argue that "the principle of effective service flows from the principle of equity" (ibid.).[3] It is vexing to attempt to produce equal service in an unequal society. Power, undefined, is best distributed rather than highly centralized if democratic policing is to be viable. Information on performance is one aspect of needed information, but the authors are moot on what is needed in this regard. Redress is necessary for righting wrongs and appeals against malevolent management. Citizen participation in police governance is lightly regarded by the authors, perhaps reflecting the failure of community watch, advisory boards, and the like to influence in advance any policing decisions or policies. In the final section of the paper, the authors attempt to identify aspects of English law and policy that might be in line with these criteria.

These features are important and begin with the idea of equity and entertain the notion of distributive justice in reference to service. In large part, with the exception of the service delivery criteria, these are *managerial criteria* that ignore the needs and demands of the publics coerced and served. The remedies are policy-like, refer to governance of the police organization, and have little or at best vague reference to principles that might guide policing on the ground. The role of the preferences and priorities of the public are not considered, as the police-as-organization again reigns as the focus of attention. There is no direct discussion of police practice.

Clifford Shearing

Clifford Shearing, especially in recent years (Shearing and Johnson 2003; Shearing 2003), has adumbrated a conception of democracy and social control that has significant implications for our expectations and demands of public policing. He does not begin with a specific conception of democratic theory but sketches out a new, rather broad, notion concerning social control and security. Security and governance feature prominently is his framework. In perhaps the broadest and at the same time most succinct statement of his ideas (2006), he rejects the notion of a top-down, state-oriented, and traditional sociological view of the state and social control that he traces to Weber via Maitland and Hobbes. This traditional view, his straw person, is a rather ill-formed contract theory in which the people, having given authority to a sovereign government, are subject to it and its exclusive control of legitimate force. Given this umbrella of authority, other pockets of authority are seen to exist but are the source of compliance, while the legitimate government directs, controls, and otherwise shapes social life. Shearing argues that this view obscures the multiple sources of order and ordering in modern societies and that research has been blind to the complexity that in fact exists. He raises to high significance the question of the sources of legitimate authority in postmodernity (my terms). Shearing urges us to see complexity: many groups with diverse goals, values, and overt concerns and beliefs, in association, are sources of order or policing. Local, regional, national, international, and transnational forces compete. These groups might be said to negotiate security in the shadow of the government, morality, and the law. In his scheme, primacy is not granted to the formal central public sources of authority. He advocates "nodal governance" with several power centers contesting and possessing overlapping legitimate authority. For Shearing, the role and consequences of a state with centralized, massive, and uncontested authority are those imagined by Rousseau and later by Chomsky: rule by force, fraud, and violence by the powerful and wealthy and regulation via the law for the poor and the marginalized within the society.

Security in this conception is a reflection of many forces, a network of interconnected but not coordinated sources, and a variously fragile and strong set of nodal points (private associations, private security companies, government and semigovernmental agencies such as municipal police groups in the UK) acting and interacting to sanction behavior. In effect, the sovereignty remains with the people in their various associations, some of which are formal and bureaucratic. This is again Rousseau speaking softly. "Security" (undefined) is something of an amalgam or configurative idea, symbolized by various groups and originally sourced in the people in some unarticulated fashion. The notion that communities have self-interests, self-governing properties, and resources to self-govern is salient in all of his writings (with associates Kempa, Johnston, Wood, and Dupont, among others). Security would appear to refer to the configuration of forces that through interplay, conflict, and competition produce a layering of formal order in the society. The whole is a function of the parts, variously coordinated. The central role in civilized societies of violence and its control are not well expressed. The distinction between violence as an immediate effort at control in the short term, and power as the capacity to coerce to ensure compliance, and legitimate authority is not made. The network of forces or groups somehow negotiates order, and the key lies in dispute resolution at the local level. The grounding of the system appears to be in fundamental local orders, and there is little stated concern for broader conceptions of justice. Bayley and Shearing, in a significant contribution to police scholarship, write, "Our focus is the self-conscious process whereby societies designate and authorize people to create public safety" (1996, 586). This could be seen the other way around, of course: it is not the designates who create order but stand for the order presumed by those who designate them. Public safety as an organized matter, not an individual role or obligation, is not distinguished from security, and is an oxymoron if the aim is to discuss all the modes of policing available. Some policing agencies concern themselves not at all with "public" safety but rather, as they say later in the article, "communities of interest."

In other publications, Shearing (with Johnston 2004) argues that what he calls *police* (it is the uniformed, publicly paid, visible low or domestic public police to which he refers here) has been mistakenly seen as the only kind of police. While *policing* is done by many agencies with many sanctions, *police* here would appear to be public police with a criminal sanctioning capacity, public validated mandate, and related functions, while policing is the enactment of sanctions associated with various formally constituted agencies. Bayley and Shearing write that their concern is with all explicit efforts to create visible agents of crime control (1996, 586). The role of the public police assumes a kind of default position theoretically; that is, whatever its empirical role, it is only one among many sources and instrumentalities for ordering deviance. There may be a tension between the philosophic, the institutional, and the empirical, and reform efforts try to keep them separate.

The most precise statement of Shearing's emerging vision is found in an article in *Police Quarterly* (2005).[4] Here, Shearing argues that this is the age of diversity in policing—that there are new mentalities (a concept borrowed from Foucault), new institutions, and new technologies that have produced a new set of police practices. This set of intertwined concepts is central to his ideas because the idea is a *configuration*: not a set of organizations, groups, or political interests but intertwined processes. It might be possible, for example, given this scheme, to begin with targets and move out to discover what aspect of the nodal is "policing" such, rather than beginning with the agency and attempting to chart its functions and duties. Augmenting this diversity are new modes of policing that have emerged and clustered to form policing assemblages. These nodes, in turn, have produced a second set of new mentalities, institutional arrangements, and technologies. He is generous in his vision and sentiments: he sees various forms and nodes interacting and mutually shaping each other to yield new policing styles and practices. The term *practice,* unfortunately, is left undefined, perhaps because of the brevity of the paper, and examples of nodes are offered later—the military and private police. This process has (my paraphrase) influenced where and how policing gets done by whom, who authorizes what gets done, and to whom accounts are given (ibid., 58). These changes make public police less powerful and perhaps, he argues, put them into a crisis mode. He correctly notes that the police have no monopoly on any function that is not being done by others (agencies) somewhere. He believes the reduction in the public police role may not prove to be a bad thing and further argues that the central political question is how to integrate and coordinate various modes of security governance and how this should be funded (ibid., 61).

This conception of crime control raises the question of whether Shearing and others have identified and defined a new complexity now captured in their work or whether the actual changes in social structure have been there while others have been unable to adequately capture their nuanced appearance. It is doubtless both. Security is a social concept to which police, among others, contribute. They do not create it, but surely they can damage it. The overemphasis on police as a source or cause of security is corrected in recent work by Shearing and colleagues Loader and Walker (2007). They argue that security is a "bottom-up" process, not a top-down one.

It would appear, given this conception, that the public police have no necessary role in sustaining democracy, even if they have not been so placed in other writing. By implication, they could be a detriment to democratic policing if they should act to reduce the power and authority of the other nodes or segments in a network of control. This has certainly been the case in totalitarian states such as Russia under Stalin and Germany under Hitler in which the police become the proximate instrument of terror (Arendt 1985). In Shearing's and others' conception of democratic policing, legitimate government does not accommodate, steer, or interact with "private" forms of control; it is but one node of many forms of control. It would also appear that Shearing would prefer that public policing be tertiary to other less formal and perhaps less violent modes of control. Although Shearing and associates imply that a diminution in the power of the public police is needed, they still define the job of concern as crime control. This quite wrong view of policing, rejected by Shearing in other publications, elevates a single form of sanctioning as the basis for concern, whereas the network idea must by definition include a variety of other functions (as do the public police themselves). There is a suggestion in this that the reduced capacity of the public police, real or imagined, now or in the future, is welcome. The network metaphor implies equality in some sense of functions and practices consistent with the lessened role of the public police. A node or entanglement would appear to be the unit of analysis, not an organization, and would somehow be a collocation of similar practices surrounding the notional idea of crimes (only the public police can formally sanction "crime," and even then it is subject to review by supervisors in police, district attorneys, and the procurator fiscal in Scotland). Governance, in turn, would appear to be the generation and sustaining of compliance. In this contested arena of control, crime remains the centerpiece, and the public police have the access to the most common source of criminal disputation when the state takes up the dispute on behalf of the citizen. The civil law system remains open as always in Anglo-American societies to cases: citizens can go to the law. The criminal justice system restricts the right to enter a case to its agents, the police. It is assumed that the public police are no less democratic or menial than other police and that the networks of control are more benign than those with centralized processes based on common-law procedures.

The underlying dynamic, unexplicated spirit moving the configuration, in the Shearing nodal model of control, is the reaction of organizations to new challenges in the environment—for example, white-collar crime, cyber crime, identity theft, terrorism, or the electronic tracking of citizens—and they innovate with specialization, new police (used generically) practices, or both. These challenges require rethinking the object "policing." In this conception, Shearing moves away from the conventional thought about policing—a publicly funded conservative organization—to a process-shaped responsive configuration of policing. These challenges in turn create new interorganizational relationships such as task forces and new centers for research (money laundering, terrorism, and risk management and assessment in the private sector), and a new node appears. These nodes or clusters of practices, mentalities, resources, and technologies are part of an emerging collection of policing practices. These configure the modes of policing noted above (who gets what, when, and how). None of this bears on the question of justice or fairness in respect to the question of either inequality or reducing social capital (Rawls's second proposition). It must be said, however, that the implication of a configuration conception of social control is that competition and conflict among agencies expand liberties rather than reduce them.

David Sklansky

Some of the salient interconnections between policing as an institution and organization and democratic theory are summarized quite succinctly by legal theorist David Sklansky in a series of papers (edited into a book published in 2007). He summarizes initially changing modern theories of democracy because at least implicitly they imagine the police and their function quite differentially. He argues that a pluralistic theory of democracy rests on a notion of elites as deciders, a rather disinterested political mass, competition among interests and interest groups, and a kind of "good chaps are negotiating" as the model of democratic politics. A participatory theory, more popular in recent years, emphasizes the wide participation of many publics, especially the once marginal community involvement in politics and political decisions, and a model of deliberation and consensus seeking. These features, of course, complement the presumed ambit of meaning of the contested concept itself, that is, how to achieve "democracy" in practice.

Sklansky asserts correctly, in an idea that has shaped my arguments, that "few discussions of policing draw explicitly on democratic theory" (2003, 1702). The interconnection of policing to broad questions of equality, security, opportunity, and access to collective goods is generally unexamined (see, however, the arguments in Loader and Walker 2007). As Sklansky notes almost in passing, policing is a form of redistribution or costs and benefits to given social strata, and in that sense it has an obligation to resist domination by powerful groups, not to act exclusively on the behalf of the powerful, and to act, on the other hand, as an "unthreatening as possible as a tool of official domination" (2003, 1809). This is a fundamental point of the greatest importance. It parallels Berkeley's ideas. Of course, the actual extent to which police are engaged in redistribution of rights, goods, and services is an empirical question. It is not clear what precise good they do since they are not judged by these criteria.

In an expanded overview of the requirements for a democratic police, Sklansky suggests that it entails:

- Participation of citizens in some form that augments accountability of police to the people
- Transparency of actions and decisions
- Workplace democracy in police organizations
- Concern for equality of service
- Restraint in regard to actions that increase inequality
- Concern for the risks entailed by the privatization of police services (2003, 2005 draft; my paraphrase and summary)

The accountability and transparency issue, noted here, is treated very widely in the literature. Most view police accountability hopefully yet are aware it has been developed in every way weak, erstwhile, and ineffectual, whether coming from inside sources or outside agencies (see Bayley 1979, 130–35; and Walker 2005). Transparency seems a dubious value insofar as the police are based ultimately on secrecy and cunning. The term *transparency* seems to have taken on coloration by association with the notion of ability to account for or rationalize decisions made rather than to produce in advance explanations such that debate can ensue (Stenning 1995). In other words, the ability to explain after the fact the organizationally grounded reasons for a decision or policy is quite different from a public statement in advance of a policy or position. Institutional accounts or rhetoric, dramatized after the fact to suit the audience and serve the interests of the organization, are obliquely related to what is done and why. Perhaps it must be so. The issue of democracy *within* the police, as noted above, has rarely been of concern. It is striking that except for a small interchange on democracy in the workplace in the 1970s (Angell 1975; Guyot 1979), the capricious pseudo- or mock bureaucracy of the police, punitive and focused on the patrol officer, has been of little interest to scholars (Bittner 1972; Manning 1997, chap. 6). Sklansky argues with data that the police have made major efforts successfully to increase diversity, especially at the higher levels of command (2008, chap. 7). The role of unions is rarely examined, and democracy in the workplace has not been explored (Sklansky 2005). The question of the role of policing in the principled avoidance of amplification of inequality is raised in this Sklansky article, but he offers no suggestions in this regard, although he notes the efforts of Meares and Kahan (1998) to elevate local norms over higher judicial rulings and doctrines. Conservative arguments that take up equity and equality explicitly and directly eschew the quest for equality of service. Wilson (1975) and Wilson and Kelling (1982), for example, state that some areas are beyond salvation and that only selected areas should be given police attention to reduce disorder (see chapter 6). Only recently in this country have the private police been of concern—affluence has made it a moot point—but clearly a theory of policing must take into account the range of types and kinds of police and policing present (Klockars 1985; Bayley and Shearing 1996; Forst and Manning 1999). Like Bayley and Shearing (1996), Sklansky sees that unfettered growth in the private security industry would diminish the level and perhaps the quality of services available to those less able to pay. Like others, his concern is police and organization focused and has little to say about the obligation to sustain trust and compliance—the view of the citizen as opposed to the view of the police or the police-reformer. He argues for the virtues of equal opportunity in hiring, firing, and promotion in police organizations; he is almost alone in this concern. In these important papers, Sklansky presents a powerful and penetrating jurisprudential sketch of policing as imagined in the context of democracy.

Ian Loader and Neil Walker

Ian Loader, and his sometimes coauthors Aogan Mulcahy and Neil Walker, has outlined a subtle and compelling conception of democratic policing in several recent publications (Loader and Mulcahy 2006; Loader and Walker 2007, Loader 2006). His 2007 publication with Walker, a detailed exposition in sociologically grounded political philosophy, sets a new vision and tone and is discussed below. It appears that "policing" is a background function contingent upon a thick sense of security. To simplify in the interests of complexity, I would assert that thick security is both enhanced and eroded by policing in democracies and that, metaphorically speaking, to foreground police is to background thick security. Rather than placing more police and more policing as implicit requirements for security, Loader and Walker suggest that the role of the police is in every way secondary to the state's obligations not to reduce security and to seduce citizens into perhaps overlooking the potentially negative consequence of more policing and reliance on it for order and security. But I am getting ahead of their arguments and evidence. The most important notion is that policing as a practice and as an institution is embedded in a "culture of policing" that includes sentiments, beliefs, memories, and symbolization. It is not just an agency engaged in "law enforcement." The word *policing* compacts symbolization and is multifaceted.

Articulating the role of culture in connection with the questions of what is policing and what is its relation to democratic government is the aim of Loader and Mulcahy in their book *Policing and the Condition of England* (2003). They dramatize their focus with a quote from Durkheim that asserts that a state should be known not by pride or for being the greatest or the wealthiest but as the most just. This, of course, would be consistent with Rawls's position, I would argue, should he be concerned with particular institutional arrangements. They approach this question with archival research and long interviews with citizens, police officers of various ranks, chief constables and top command, members of police unions, and various high civil servants. They conclude that post–World War II England now envisions its police as an embodiment, representative, evocative icon, and symbol of the best of British-ness. Thus, the degree of social change is a salient variable shaping the presentation of policing to itself and to the public. They place their analysis in a sociocultural arena in which the police are one institution among many, both standing outside the others and being a selective representative of those others—church, state, local politics, and the family. They are perhaps the most visible part of a cultural edifice or configuration. The authority of the police in post–World War II England is dif-ferent, perhaps diminished, but it is different because English society and culture are now different. The book is about what the police represent, not what they do. They ask, as does the first chapter in this book, what modernity and postmodernity have to do with policing, that is, its representations and its manifestations.

Here is a challenging and subtle depiction of the relationships between "polic-ing" as a signifier or an expression and its content. Once unarticulated sentiments are attached to the symbol and icon of the police, especially the individual bobby on the beat, they later resonate in various multifaceted polymorphic and condensed narratives. These narratives place the police in a sociohistorical context. The idea of policing and stories about it stand for structures of sentiment and evoke them. The police are *tokens* in this precise Durkheimian sense: they remind us of what they stand for. They are minders and reminders. Memory, narrative, feeling, and self are the *tacit backdrop* for discourse about the present, illustrating not a decline in police power or the centrality of the symbols but the tension in modern societies between the sacred and the secular, the traditional and the modern, the collective and the individual. They claim research should focus on the meanings of security and in that sense should not bind itself to the most visible and dramatic facet of policing, the "police occupational culture," but the culture of policing and the policing of culture. The culture of policing is an amalgam of what is thought about police, what feeling they evoke and elevate, and how this sentient nexus connotes order. In this work, Loader and Mulcahy emphasize that the police represent democratic thinking, are a symbol, and do not in themselves create order, or indeed feel they can. Insofar as the society respects notions of equality and justice, these will be reflected in social notions about policing and perhaps their practices. The police are one facet of a culture: they are in every way a dependent, reactive, responsive force.

Loader and Walker's argument (2007), on the other hand, focuses on the ways in which the public police represent and should or might sustain equality, order, and the rights of the marginal and minority peoples. While their notions stand above practices and actions, they attribute to the public police a central or core role of best expressing and representing in everyday life the arena in which the society affirms itself. Legitimate authority is in some way the least-worst option when contrasted to the two oppositional conceptions they discuss: the nodal network security concep-tion of Shearing (discussed above), on the one hand, and the idea of reassurance policing associated with Martin Innes (2003), on the other. Their advocacy of public policing rests on the assumption of diversity of populations with various life chances, inequality, and differential demand for order and service.

The primary argument could be seen as a defense of public police, this body as a reactive, accountable organization that best sustains the collective will as seen in the idea of "thick public good." By seeing police as reactive and in effect the last resort, they echo the importance of the collective or general will, the grounding sentiments that sustain society, not the police. The police are not a machine to satisfy demand. What policing represents is both instrumental in the sense of protecting public safety and symbolic insofar as it constitutes what is seen as the source of safety and well-being. The connection, between the instrumental and the expressive or symbolic, sustains the individual well-being or "ontological security" (following Giddens, 1991). The police are, however, not expected to be responsive to raw demands and priorities of the public as an aggregate in part because they might produce further marginalization and inequality of the now marginal and powerless and in part because it reduces security to a marketable commodity. By responding to market demand, the police may well send exclusionary signals to the less powerful. These signals, in part, would serve to isolate and exclude rather than to sustain and include.

Security, according to Loader, has to do with "the resources individuals and groups possess for managing the unease and uncertainty that the risks present in their environment generate—and these resources differ in amount according to people's sense of their place within that environment" (2006, 210). Here, security is a *capacity,* something like collective efficacy or social capital, rather than a visible, erstwhile, and dramatic action such as "crime control," suppressing crime or arresting offenders. Police are creators of meanings about crime, deviance, and so forth; as I noted above, they are minders and reminders; they stand for culture indirectly in its sustaining fashion. Tacit confidence in police means that they are the "limited, rights-regarding, constrained, reactive agencies of last resort" (ibid., p. 204; quoting Baldwin and Kinsey 1982). The idea of police as "backstop" or secondary or tertiary is, of course, obvious, since all other forms of control—individual, group, and associational—have been compromised in some sense if police action is mobilized.[5] Loader, following the notion of police as constrained and an agency of last resort, cautions against two spirals that might result from a more market-based (and perhaps media-driven) policing—one leading to greater and greater police suppression of crime, the authoritarian spiral, and the other, the fragmentation spiral, leading to net widening and less collective identification. Loader concludes, "The state is best equipped ... to act as a meta-authority over what has today become a diverse range of public, commercial and citizen policing actors in ways that coordinate the allocation of policing resources, ensure that all policing agencies answer to democratically negotiated priorities, and call such agencies to account for their performance" (ibid.).

Loader and Walker's broad attempt to theorize policing and the state is unique and deserves further comment. They argue for a thick concept of security that is a combination of personal security and relational security. This is a kind of spiraling of effects from individual social relations to a shared sense of mutual trust to a kind of reflexive understanding about such a condition (2007, 145). This is the "civilized security" they favor and that the state provides the best conditions for, not the market, and in effect is watched over by the police. The police in a limited fashion both stand for and sustain security. Beneath the state's powers and the legitimacy of the police is trust, which, like security itself, is an undefined base concept in their argument. They correctly argue that security is a moral category (ibid., 18) and note that the modern state has both gained in strength and weakened in its capacity to maintain a monopoly on violence and order maintenance. They note important changes in the configuration of forces that surround security in the modern state (most of which are dealt with in the following chapter), conceptions of the state, and for the preeminence of the state in producing order. The connections between the police and the state are well discussed. The book is an important contribution to understanding democratic policing. Unfortunately, although they argue for a strong and regulated democratic state, with the police as a kind of mediator between what might be called politics and the collective good, they provide no criteria by which the police could be judged in this regard. In general, their conception of policing is based on a kind of restrained/restraint model without presenting what the criteria of this model might be. The central point here is that Loader and Walker have attempted to outline the role of the democratic state, the police function in this context, and the necessary conditions under which "thick security" is at least not damaged. In many respects, I want to locate the police in the political economy of the democratic state. Police practice is more or less a cautionary matter insofar as it might reduce liberties by excess, and by ratcheting up control, they will focus on minorities. Criteria by which one might judge competent police (organizational) performance are absent.

Hsi-Huey Liang

An eminent historian of policing, Hsi-Huey Liang (1992, 2) places the idea of democratic policing elegantly within the context of Western European history from 1818 to World War II. This work is comparative, cross-cultural, and historical and draws on original documents.

What is expected of policing, he argues, is embedded in *nonstated values* that shape their actions and intentions. Whatever the structure and degree of specialization of democratic police, they are restrained by social matters other than law and custom and are embedded in more than local traditions. These resources are tacit rather than known and present, and they do not lie within the heads or hands of the police. The police represent these ideals.

Liang develops his ideas in the context of the historical development of European democracies, and he contrasts the actions of democratic and nondemocratic regimes to great benefit. He argues in sum that democratic police should be legalistically guided, focus on individuals and not group politics, eschew terrorism (and counterterrorism) and torture, and strive to ensure minimal damage to civility. I have somewhat shortened his list for this analysis. Let us look at these features *seriatim*.

The value of highlighting *legalistically guided* is that although it cannot guide choice prospectively, it provides remedies, both civil and criminal, for excessive violent actions. It holds out the possibility of appeal, redress, and complaint. The *focus on individuals* is consistent with common-law notions of innocence and the obligation of the state to prove contentions or allegations of guilt. Setting out categories of people, such as "Cape Verdean neighborhoods" in Boston, "gangs," "drug users," "terrorists," or "white people," should not be the basis for policing. People should not be uniformly targeted, watched, and tracked because of their affiliations, color, or beliefs. In totalitarian societies, as Hannah Arendt points out, though everyone is innocent of particulars, they are all subject to terror as citizens. In the extreme, caution, fear, or self-protection cannot insulate or protect one, because "terror chooses its victims without reference to individual actions or thoughts, exclusively in accordance with the objective necessity of the natural or historical process" (1985, 467). Whereas terror ratchets up obedience and retreat, democracy credits individual rights and duties.

This prohibition on categorical policing is associated with the long-standing hesitation of Anglo-American societies to prosecute domestically based conspiracies (Epstein 1990). Police use of terrorism against individuals or groups invites retaliation on the same terms and ignites a cycle of violence. Thus, local domestic police should eschew terrorism and counterterrorism. This may be necessary at the national level with coordinated actions directed outside the domain of domestic national law. These functions, in turn, are best performed by protected centrally controlled agencies such as the former MI5 and the CIA. Historically, the Royal Ulster Constabulary (RUC) response to the Irish Republican Army (IRA) and others in Northern Ireland shows that *terrorism and torture begot more of the same* from those initially targeted (Taylor 1980; Mulcahy 2005; Lafree, Dugan, and Korte 2008). The eschewal of torture has historical precedents usually associated internationally with conditions of war and with the stipulations of the Geneva Convention. North American police forces have not been faced with the dilemma confronting the Metropolitan Police in the UK, the RUC in Northern Ireland, and the Gardai in the Republic of Ireland. Domestic security was threatened and torture easily rationalized by the forces. Abundant evidence is available that torture as defined by the convention was used against "unlawful participants," an Orwellian perversion of language that covers anyone captured by American troops post-9/11 in several fields of combat (Hersh 2004). Torture not only is ineffective but escalates violence in enforcement rather than reduces it, and it typically is applied to those least able to appeal or to resist confession or admission of crimes. *Minimal damage to civility* is a direct analogue of the difference principle. While little can be done to elevate civility, active, direct interventions do reduce civility rather than increase it. There is no evidence whatsoever that reduced officially recorded crime in and of itself increases quality of life. Since high crime is a symptom, and not a cause of, reduced quality of life, symptomatic treatments cannot succeed. Arguments that advocate crime control alone are thus deeply flawed and contribute to the malaise and do not reduce it (e.g., the admonishing in Sherman 2005).

These explicit features of Liang's term, *democratic policing*, whether such standards are met or not, allows Liang to suggest the importance of the penumbra of policelike activities that shadow his definition and make democratic policing possible. I share this view. The periphery sustains the core. These "policelike" activities include the existence of high or political police, self-policing or what might be called, following Black (1983), self-help, and central state police, or a kind of gendarmerie. These functional alternative modes of dispute resolution are necessary in a democracy because without resistance, serious crime control may fade and the public police may gain a hegemony that borders on a monopoly of force. This total control by law is what Black (1976) calls an anarchy produced by excessive centralized control. Liang argues quite persuasively on historical evidence that it is through citizen resistance and parallel and counter police forces that a restrained democratic police is sustained. Private state security police, the high police, and the various self-policing forms sustain the tension that permits the general strategies of democratic Western European police to work. Liang sees these alternatives, as I do, as the result of competition and restriction of public police by conventions, local traditions, law in action, and limited resources. On the other hand, the *strategies* he includes as necessary for the survival of the democratic police include using the threat of potential violence; moves to divide and conquer opposition prior to confrontation; using force, violence, and deceit; and developing credible mythmaking over long periods of time (1992, 14–17). The mythmaking aspect is conjoined to the quasi-sacred aspect of democratic policing— their distance, awesome features, mystery, and inscrutability.[6] Their unpredictable appearance is in fact a part of their mystification and power. These requirements and constraints become paramount in times of "crisis" when national security easily trumps individual rights and fascism lurks in each new initiative of the government to provide "homeland security." Liang has tried to penetrate the everyday assumptions of policing and go beyond mere observation of practices.

In summary, these seven conceptions variously explicate the role of the police in democracy and show some interest in the role of police and policing. Each is lacking. None outlines the necessary features of democratic policing as a practice. Most consider the role of democratic government and implicitly the limited role of the police in creating or sustaining democracy. Bayley and Loader emphasize what should not be done, that is, those actions that would reduce democratic participation, involvement, and commitment to the social order. When noted, the requirements are general and abstract, such as transparency and accountability. Berkeley and Sklansky raise the profound question of fair treatment within the police organization of officers and employees as a necessary condition for fair treatment of citizens. All these suggest the importance of an undefined operator, "restraint," and the police as a "last resort." The idea of legal and procedural protections is also embedded in the idea of constraint (cf. Chevigny 1995). But the role of law is a shadow, an assumed effect that as much as anything is something that can be rationed, limited in application, and more honored in the breach than in application. Bayley, Sklansky, and Jones, Newburn, and Smith call for some form of accountability, while Shearing would find this in the local nature of the policing organizations, and therefore some form of meta-accountability to the state would be unnecessary. All save Shearing and associates urge explicitly and implicitly the reeminence of the prestige, resources, coordinative capacity, and stated disinterest of the public police and express concerns about the growing power and perhaps prestige of the private police and enclaves of protected high-status citizens. Ironically, none argues for reform along the lines of "community policing," collective efficacy, or positive efforts of the police to reduce inequalities. Liang alone makes the case for explicit matters to be excluded and dramatizes the relevance of the nonpublic police as counterbalancing and necessary to modify the authority of state-sponsored police. The police are seen as a needed risk, and the wish is that they do no further harm to liberties, security, and material well-being. The origins of the police in England suggest that there was great awareness of their potential for creating havoc and crushing dissent as well as protecting property and life (1988). The most explicit treatment of the "risks" of the public police is in Loader and Walker's *Civilizing Security* (2007) in which they caution against the state and the police as either a partisan (conservative on behalf of the powerful), a meddler (in neoliberal terms), or an idiot (unable to gather analyze and apply information to provide security). They reject each of these self-produced caricatures in favor of thick security, as discussed above.

This review of some seven carefully crafted ideas about democratic policing suggests the following working notions or constraints on the consideration of democratic policing. Here, as a working notion, I argue it should not be studied as a "system" of abstract principles, strategies, or aims designed for political change. It should not be, but it can be, the basis for an ideologically derived policy of imposed social change from "above." It must be assumed that the evolutionary elements that produce and were amplified by democratic police practices remain at the heart of the idea. It is their constitutive practices that sustain democratic policing. The kind of policing that is suggested by the notion is not a type, not an abstract notion. It is an ensemble of practices based on a set of general principles. The ideas are interwoven with policing practice.

FIVE MODES OF DEFINING POLICING

The conceptions addressed above are loosely related to definitions current in the literature. They take for granted the cultural and political environment, assume a stable and reasonably consensual political state of affairs, and imagine a force restrained by tradition, law, socialization, and good sense. None address how centralized governments of bad faith might "capture" policing or collapse it with the military, and few address the question of complicity of the domestic police with totalitarian regimes and the role of the police in conquered countries such as Vichy France or Shanghai prior to World War II. The "nested" aspect of policing functions, in periods of war, conquest, rebellion, and the mergence of colonies into nation-states, has not been well studied. By isolating policing from a sociopolitical context, social scientists have reduced the multidimensionality of policing. Let us now examine the several types of definitions of policing available. They are all flawed to some degree.

Historical-Descriptive

The first mode is what might be called *historical-descriptive* approaches. These works assume policing exists as a manifestation of the development of the capacity of society to provide security consistent with the cultural configuration of the society or nation-state. The best known are the studies of the emergence of the modern British police. These include the works of Reith, Critchley, Lee, Jennifer Hart, and to a lesser extent the more recent historically informed work of Emsley (1996, 2002). The discussions are organized chronologically, assume a developmental and cumulative character, focus on the public police and their links to elites and legislative actions (acts of parliament in particular), and apply them to a period-organized (periods defined by calendar years) textual analysis. On the whole, these works do not attempt definitions but use rather general terms and play on taken-for-granted meanings of modern police and policing. That is, they highlight and discuss those aspects of the present policing that emerged at given periods as evidence of the evolutionary aspect of policing. There is a certain tautological quality in these arguments because it is implied that the police at present evolved as they did to emerge as the present democratic police. This sort of definition is often accompanied by flattering positive adjectives such as *fair, just, democratic,* and the like without definition of the terms. Broad attempts at explanation of the rise of the public police, consistent with the explanations for the rise and diffusion of democratic policing in and from the United Kingdom, are few (see, however, Brogden 1987; and Palmer 1988). Materials on the rise of policing are less available than materials on given departments (in English, namely, studies of large North American or English cities), and the variety of modes of policing are quite wide and are present from tribal societies such as the Cheyenne to the present (see Black 1976).

Textbook Definitions

A second mode of approaching policing, equally vague and the most common, is nondefined or *textbook definitions.* A common approach in police studies and criminology textbooks is to offer no definition (e.g., Siegel 2006), reduce policing to functions (LaFave 1965; Siegel 2006, 507–8), or rely on commonsense categories such as "county sheriffs" and "local police" to create tables and array statistics (Reeves and Goldberg 1996). Such definitions are accompanied by a description of stages of development or brief histories, including some reference to Robert Peel and the invention of the 1829 London police. The usual move is to collapse law enforcement, public security, order, and crime control as embodied by the local police force. The complexity of the institutional role is not discussed.

Typological

A third approach is *typological*. These works are the result of organizing and arraying idealized, abstracted, selective, and theoretically derived concepts that are then used to order data. The police as an abstract, selective, idealized, and constructed ideal (following Weber 1947) are not a body of people but an idea. Policing, in turn, is a practice, not a thing. As a way of discussing this approach, one I use in my own work, I propose to outline a somewhat synthetic array, based on the work of Klockars (1985) and consistent with my definition in the next chapter of police and policing.

Informal policing. The dimensions involved here are the extent to which the participants are required generally or specifically or whether they volunteer. In some sense, the sequence from occasional to voluntary reflects the routinization and formalization of policing as a function.

1. Occasional (ad hoc, hue-and-cry, and other undefined obligations of citizens to respond to and organize against violations of a local order). At the lowest level of organization, this is what Black (1983) terms "self-help" and is characterized by a mixture of retaliation, revenge, and neutral punishment based on rules and principles.
2. Obligatory (posses, vigilante groups).
3. Voluntary (militias, police auxiliaries, reserves, local self-help associations, Texas Rangers). These can be divided further into those militias that are privately funded, such as the original twentieth-century militia formed in Northern Ireland in 1913 (Farrell 1983), and those publicly funded militias and gendarmerie that go back to the early seventeenth century.

Although these examples are drawn from societies with democratic policing, the analytic framework is adequate for examples drawn from other societies.

Since full-time democratic policing is my subject here, the notion of an ideal type can be illustrated with reference to avocational types of policing. The primary point here is that they loosely affiliate with central state power; are occasional, unpaid, or modestly paid on the occasion of their use; and may or may not be visible and uniformed. They cannot be fired, as they are semivoluntary. These types of policing are not accountable to any body, are unpaid, and are difficult to supervise, direct, or dismiss. They are a contrast to vocational public policing, my focus later in the chapter. An earlier emergent example of avocational policing is the Texas Rangers prior to 1901 when they nominally became a state police under the governor (Webb 1965; Robinson 2000; Utley 2002, 2007). They are a provocative example in part because they are part of the mythology of the American West and in part because they functioned as state police, militia, and the army of Texas as a republic and as a state.

The Texas Rangers were begun around 1821, in response to the threats of Indian attack on settlers and newly developed businesses. From the period 1823 to

1836 they were an amorphous ad hoc group, but during the war with Spain in 1836 they were mobilized to guard the frontiers of the republic. They were semivoluntary, partially self-supporting small groups of semisupervised "officers," usually formed into groups of around one hundred men. Until 1874, when they became a state police of sorts, the Rangers acted in part as police and in part as a kind of national guard or militia (Robinson 2001, 160). Robinson, an acute observer, writes that by 1881 "the days of the traditional Rangers were over" (2001, 244). As local police organizations grew, the Rangers shrank in political and legal power. Their police powers were reduced (only command officers could make arrests) in 1900, and they were reduced to about eighty men. In 1935 they became part of the state police with specialized functions and units spread throughout the state. This is still their status—an elite aspect or element of the state police.

Formal policing. Policing may be publicly or privately funded. The distinction here arises when officers are uniformed, paid, full-time functionaries who can be fired and who hold a role or position in some loose organization. The key difference, it can be argued, is that *with the development of truly formalized public policing, the criminal sanction can be employed and cases can be entered into the criminal justice system.* The capacity to enter a case into the criminal justice system, that is, to shape it to legal procedures, works in two directions—it makes the case actionable as it moves forward toward resolution and "backward" to establish the grounds for the arrest. This access is restricted to all other citizens, unlike the right to bring a suit in civil court in common-law countries. There are (at least) four subtypes of formal policing using the criterion found in the legal system: the degree to which the rights of individuals and procedural guarantees are weighed in favor of the citizen as opposed to the state. Although this theory is arguable, one can order the sequence as follows:

1. Religious systems based on Islamic law (most of the Middle East and Indonesia).
2. Nondemocratic systems based on totalitarian regimes (Stalin, Mao, Hitler) and those embedded in conquered states (France and Western Europe under the Nazis, Eastern Europe until the late 1980s).
3. Civil law–based systems of policing (Western Europe outside of Ireland and the United Kingdom, Latin America).
4. Common law–based systems (classically the AADP countries described above and further characterized by the features outlined later in this book. In broad terms, this policing can be divided into low policing based on crime and domestic order with the background of surveillance and coercion and high policing, which is secretive and invisible, relies on informants, and tends toward totalistic concern with the citizens' actions and thoughts rather than narrowly concerned with criminal behavior).

We are concerned henceforth and herewith with formal common-law vocational policing in *democratic systems*. To move to a slightly more abstract level, this type of policing has a stated purpose or mission, a mandate, legitimacy with respect to the polity, somewhat defined strategies and tactics, and some territorial range, that is, a spatial or symbolic limit (private spaces, corporations with private laws) on legal policing actions. Vocational policing can be either privately funded (e.g., mercenaries, bounty hunters, private investigators, corporate or in-house security, and contract security) or publicly funded. Klockars (1985), as noted above, argues that vocational police organizations must meet two criteria. First, police agents must be vulnerable to being fired, forced to resign, or otherwise terminated. This serves to distinguish "police" from actors in other semiformal associations (vigilantes, posses, neighborhood watch groups, and the like). The second feature is that they are directly responsible for their actions and the consequences of their actions. This has changed in the past thirty years as suits against individual officers and departments and criminal actions have been permitted. On the other hand, the courts are extremely tolerant of a wide range of police actions. Economists call the problem of holding responsible those who act as agents by contract the "agency problem." It is in part a function of the fact that there are always "non-contractual elements of contracts" (Macaulay 1963). This problem is perhaps best dramatized by the use of hired interrogators at Abu Ghraib in Iraq and Bagham prison in Afghanistan and the contracting out of prisoners to other nations by the CIA. Their responsibilities are limited even if they, as they did, torture prisoners. This problem also applies to the use of corporate warriors and services in Bosnia and Kosovo and other contractors and subcontractors of U.S. government who are employed through individual contracts to private corporations who are in turn contractors with the U.S. government (Scahill 2007). Neither the organizations nor the agents are publicly or legally accountable (Singer 2004). By these two broad criteria it is clear that the assumed loyalty of the police officer is to the state, that his or her commitment must exceed routine obligations to enforce the law, and that any identification of the officer with the particular interests of the government of the day or personal political attitudes toward groups and the principles and political activities must be neutralized or, at best, set aside.

Liang, reviewed above and later in this chapter, suggests several useful distinctions. He argues that police can be divided into security or high police (more like secret police); gendarmerie or sherifflike officers; domestic or "low" police; and those that are not public, that is, international and parallel or oppositional types of police (arising from resistance of the citizen to the public police).[7] In these taxonomies, the base or original state is self-help or semiformal, semiorganized acts of revenge, self-defense, or using police to accomplish acts or revenge or control (see also Black 1983). In these schemes, there is a notion of evolution and development in that they value the present systems and argue that its emergence is a sign of civilization, but neither author denies the constant presence of all the types noted in modern societies.

R. I. Mawby (2003) has made an important point in his review of world systems of policing. He argues that typological distinctions are confounded by several recent trends: the homogenization and democratization of policing in the former communist and Eastern European nations; the movement toward transnational policing in the

European Union through joint agreements, task forces, and transnational conventions and organizations (Deflem 2004); the overlay of colonial or ethnic models of policing on semi-indigenous modes of ordering policing in the developing world (Enloe 1980a, 1980b; Lia 2006); and the confounding of peacekeeping (political ordering—see below) and war making (controlling a territory and eradicating the enemy's will to resist).

The most important specification of the democratic policing type is made by Weitzer (1990, 1995) based on his work in Zimbabwe and Northern Ireland. He argues that settler states—those in which the minority dominates a majority, is focused more on security to maintain than superiority, and shades toward nondemocratic measures to remain in power—are a special type of democratic policing. I consider them "quasi-democratic" police systems.

The most complex and appealing effort at a taxonomy of policing within and across borders is Ben Bowling's (2005). The basis of his argument is that the root or fundamental assumption must be that policing is grounded in the nation-state, and from that basis the taxonomy should be concerned with the reach beyond it. The overwhelming force, through financial aid, training, grants, and loans of personnel, of American-style policing, especially in regard to drug policing, has shaped and distorted policing throughout the cultural-political area of his focus, the eastern Caribbean, making various quasi-legitimate modes possible. Bowling (2005) usefully distinguishes five such modes: domestic (or national); international (by, between, and above national governments—police agencies operating outside their own countries); transnational (between and above governments—bilateral, trilateral, regional, and hemispheric); global (above all national governments—UN drug and crime forces); and private (beyond national governments, such as Securicor, Securitas, and so forth). This taxonomy has the virtue of seeing that these five types of policing interact and compete within and across countries and that *transnational policing* is too vague a term to specify what is now ongoing. Although the number of types of policing is debatable (see R. I. Mawby 2003), it is clear that the job of labeling and classifying types of policing is becoming more challenging. Typological distinctions are confounded by several recent politico-economic trends. These are discussed later in this chapter.

Context-Sensitive

A fourth type of definition and explanation is Bayley's (1975, 1985, 1992). Bayley uses what might be called a *context-sensitive definition* and restricts his interest primarily to Europe, although he occasionally uses examples from Japan and India. He sees policing as official sanctioning in the interests of promoting the public good. When police are paid and directed in some sense (are accountable) by the community that authorizes the policing, they become public in his definition. Bayley and Shearing's 1996 definition of policing echoes this position, but it is a contrast conception relevant only to distinguishing the shifting meaning of public and private policing, not the nature of policing itself. The public police of most interest are those associated with the nation-state with a territorial boundary. His most provocative argument is that public policing can exist outside the direct control of nation-states, as in the sheriffs and constables in medieval England who operated for the public good prior to establishment of the nation. Their enforcement may be based on religious rules, local loyalties, or the desires of landowners and the gentry, but it is still seen as "public" or at least publicly sanctioned. Furthermore, he argues that what is public and what is private are based on definition or context—for example, before Texas became a state, the Texas Rangers were a kind of semivoluntary posse, or private policing, but in 1901, they were designated as a state agency and were paid (modestly) by the State of Texas (Harris and Sadler 2007). Bayley also argues that nation-states do not of necessity create centralized public police but may have decentralized systems as well as competing police of other types (private, voluntary, temporary, and so on). He concludes as a working definition that police refers to people authorized by a group to regulate interpersonal relations within the group through the application of physical force (1985, 7–11). In later work (with Shearing) he conceives of policing as that which is sanctioned to create security (1996, 586).

Bayley adheres to (a presumed) police competence in the use of physical force as key and specifies the notion of domestic use to exclude "armies" (1985, 8) and "authorization" to marginalize organizations that use force outside legitimate authority. He focuses on "interpersonal relations" rather than on controlling groups with political interests and power and excludes the specific political interests, their own or others', that the police attend to. The question of what is a "group" and whether police regulate "interpersonal relations" as well as a great deal more is certainly an open one. A "group," such as an organized state, differs from a tribal band or group with a structured governance, and begs the question of the role of law, territory, and territorial authority. Like Bittner (1972, 1990), Bayley acknowledges that the threat of the use of force differs from the application of force but overlooks the fact that armies are used domestically in conditions of unrest and that policing takes place in revolutionary situations in which authorization is questioned and legitimacy at issue (Liang 1970, 1992; Wakeman 1995, 1996). Armies do police, and police can act as armies in times of war and rebellion (Westermann 2008). Furthermore, the term *authorization* is vague enough to include private as well as public policing, as his later work explicitly acknowledges (Bayley and Shearing 1996).

Liang (1992) moved the study of policing forward by placing the rise of modern policing in a European context and connecting the development of the state with the rise of modern policing. This work is limited because it is consciously and explicitly a study of European policing between 1819 and World War II. On the other hand, it lays out the analytical dimensions that are essential to any comparative work and touches on the value context of policing. These matters are largely assumed. Liang and Klockars each identify the features of modern policing that distinguish it from any application of coercive force to a population in respect to the collective well-being.

Bayley's work, the central example of context-sensitive explanatory ideas, explores well the limits of cross-national comparisons but does not explain why public police arise; he only states that they do and that they are not mutually exclusive with

other forms of policing. The most important limit to his 1985 definition is that it focuses on interpersonal relations, when clearly policing is about much more, including
defense of territory and boundaries and the morale and well-being of the group, and
not merely an aggregate of individuals interacting. Here, the brilliance of the Loader
and Mulcahy definition must be recognized. Policing is embedded in a culture of
beliefs, myths, presuppositions, assumptions, and unexamined axioms about "what
is right." These items must be explicated if policing as an activity or a practice is to be
revealed clearly. This definition also goes to the question of legitimacy—the public
police, above all else, must be trustworthy. To police using coercion implies restrictions and limitations that are not restricted to the law or other rules or norms.

Jones, Newburn, and Smith, (1996, 18–19) broaden the idea by including
many kinds of forms of activity undertaken by individuals or organizations that may
involve a conscious exercise of coercive power and where such is viewed as central
to their role (by the agent or attributed to the role by others). The broadest effort,
perhaps, has been that of Loader and Mulcahy (2003, 55), who want to include in
the idea of policing a "policing culture" all the attitudes and beliefs that surround
policing as a function. This permits them to see the police as a kind of symbol for
or representation of basic sentiments or feelings associated with a nation-state (my
paraphrase). I argued that the police were best defined tentatively (2003, 44) as
follows: the police in Anglo-American societies, consisting of many diverse agencies, are authoritatively coordinated, legitimate organizations that stand ready to
apply force up to and including fatal force in specified political territories to sustain
political ordering.

Analytic

A fifth type of definition is an *analytic definition* that relies minimally upon context
to situate its connotations. *The Encyclopedia of Police Science* (Bailey, 1995) and the
Encyclopedia of Women and Crime (Rafter, 2000), for example, contain no explicit
definition of *police*. A thoughtful definition by Shearing and Stenning (1983, 1439)
emphasizes preserving order between people in a community, noting that ideas
about this order may be widely shared or "imposed by a dominant group." Bordua's
entry (1968) in the *Encyclopedia of Social Science* is quite general. Maureen Cain's
thoughtful discussions (1973, 1979) refined police studies by adding the dimension
of political power as an element in policing. In her view, police maintain an order
that those in power deem is proper. Reiner uses a general taking-off point, defining
police as "as a specialized body of people given the primary formal responsibility for
legitimate force to safeguard security," and notes that they are an aspect of "modern state forms" (2000, 7), but he uses an undifferentiated amalgam of American,
Canadian, and English policing practices as examples. Wikipedia defines police as
"agents or agencies, usually of the executive, empowered to enforce the law and to
ensure public and social order through the legitimatized use of force." Again, we see
the false notion displayed that the police "ensure" public and social order and that
this is done through force.

All such general definitional statements are important, but these are examples of what Garfinkel (1967) calls the "etc. clause"—statements that assume the relevance of something unnamed that is the basis for their existence. Such definitions assume the presence of order. Terms such as *concerned with, providing order, maintenance of public order,* and even *enforcement of laws* are *shifters* that take on meaning in context and cannot be understood outside an understanding of situated, occasional police practices. The meaning of the terms arises as observations are assembled and cannot be assumed. The primary grounding of policing is of course their responsiveness and their producing aid, reciprocity, and succor in times of need. This is why closely observed ethnography must be wedded with structural analyses.

It is less than obvious, perhaps, as Reiner claims (2000, 47–80), that certain "ideals" governed the English Peel model of policing. It is unclear whether *ideals* refers to his preferences, historical evidence of intention of the legislators and the home secretary at the time (Mr. Peel), evidence of their actual workings, instances of a moral principle, or a sociological wish list. In any case, it has little value as a distinction, for it has no difference connoted or denoted. Reiner argues (my paraphrase) that democratic police should be:

- An efficient and effective bureaucratic organization
- Constrained by the rule of law and due process
- Adhering minimal use of force and proportionality of action to the violation
- Seeking political neutrality
- Adopting crime prevention as a mission and providing social service

Reiner argues that these are the bases for policing practice. These are most likely "ideals," or more accurately beliefs about how the police should have acted, might have acted, or could have acted. They are accounts about what parliamentarians, lawyers, and judges might have thought is what is to be expected. Consider some obvious limitations of this characterization. Police cannot be efficient in their work because there are no accepted standards by which their work can be precisely judged. What could "police efficiency" refer to? Low costs? The costs of policing are endlessly flexible, as they are "slack resources" held ready for emergencies. These costs are met as and when needed. Does it mean within a budget? Police budgets are notoriously vague and often in part secret. For example, the Garda Siochana as of 2007 had no clear budgeting (O'Toole 2007). One might ask efficiency in the use of resources to accomplish what ends or objectives? One could answer this as a tautology, namely, to do the good, sustain order, or the like. They are more likely to be expected to be effective—have an impact—than to be efficient. What could be said about the "rule of law" when discretion and deciding are the basic warrants of every officer (Sklansky 2007)? Violence and its variations are nowhere defined in law and are subject to basic local variations (Bittner 1972), so they can hardly be used as criteria. They are assumed. If one examines the budgets of police, there is absolutely no evidence that police anywhere in the Anglo-American world adopt crime prevention as a primary goal or purpose, let alone work at it. Arguably, the police do seek publicly to be seen as nonpolitical in spite of the obvious political character of their work. Police provide a variety of social services and stand ready to serve. It is difficult to provide any evidence of their preventing any crime anywhere. These ideals assume the mutually compatible institutional structures of a stable society. Such idealizations ignore the actual practice of people doing the job in an organizational context. They are misleading abstractions.

Because the influence of Egon Bittner has been profound and continuing, it is necessary to examine his views closely. His work has been misunderstood insofar as it is quoted and then combined with vague statements about law enforcement and order maintenance that are quite secondary to his foundational definition.

BITTNER'S DEFINITION

Egon Bittner published a resonating definition of policing in 1972.[8] His[9] analytical working definition of the police function and the police role (1972, 39) serves currently as the basis for most attempts to delineate policing. Although Bittner is sensitive to the nature of the police organization as a structure, his essays contain little data-based description or analysis of the internal workings of the police organization. He assumes that informal cliques, negotiation of the vertical and horizontal flow of information and authority and of command and control, and specialized groups of investigators exist. His is a view from the streets and a rather stereotypical rendering of policing and officers' knowledge that rarely meets the high standard he asserts obtains. This ethnographic base ironically produces a misleading and partial picture of "policing," because Bittner emphasizes the information basis of everyday patrol work, leaves the organization above the officer on the street as an undefined chaos, and does not articulate policing with the political economy of the city.

Bittner restricts the scope of his concern to public policing, that which is funded and supported by the state. Policing in the interests of foreign policy, corporate interests, or the government of the day is compromised, in part because such policing is driven by the interests of those who pay for it. This is true even if this is a government such as the United States sending police to other countries. Bittner's definition of what police do could be applied to private police, many federal and state agencies that regulate health and safety (not called "police"), groups active in self-help or revenge, and the actions of paramilitary groups (Bayley and Shearing 1996). Bittner's "police" could logically include agencies, such as private security companies, detectives, and reserve constables, regardless of their precise linkages to the state or the criminal law. The public police retain the broadest ambit to apply coercive force, whereas other agents have strict limits by place, persons, or violations. Neutrality is an aspect of the emergent professionalism of the police, and recent attempts at reforms such as community policing, problem-solving policing, and more focused crime control are, in Bittner's eyes (Brodeur 2007), moves to reduce the negative aspects of policing and to elevate the police's neutral and objective professionalism.

The phenomenological edge. Often cited, and more often misunderstood, Bittner's is a deeply analytical and phenomenological definition based on police practice—the situationally guided application of force. Bittner's efforts shaped the next several generations of researchers. His work is based on a kind of practical phenomenology, or the convergence of subject and object in the context of doing something. This point is elaborated below.

His notion that policing-as-practice is based in phenomenological sociology requires a brief interlude to lay out his premises. These are the grounding points of the Bittnerian view of policing. He would argue that the questions asked shape the resultant dialogue. The question of the social sciences is how do we know the world and its constitutive parts? It cannot be done fully with a resort to formal procedures, natural sciences, mathematics or philosophy alone. This means that abstract concepts must be defined and used contextually, as it is identified. If defined contextually and nonsituationally, they are misleading and misdirecting. Words are not alone the basis for order and ordering: what is done may not be expressed well in advance or later. Much proceeds on tacit knowledge. For example, Bittner notes that police may have difficulty articulating their use of force and its consequences. This is captured in paperwork only partially. Contingencies and deciding are done within a commonsense or taken-for-granted context. Life and policing involve intimately and continuously dealing with the unforeseen, but this fact in itself is not disruptive. Order is always present; order is assumed in context and revealed in the breach. Subject and object no longer exist independently; they are mutually codependent. Because most epistemologies, even pragmatism, begin with the existence of the biological and natural world, phenomenology as a frame of reference stands apart because of its radical assumption that understanding the constitutive process is essential to knowing. Thus, matters that are assumed to be central such as "crime," "disorder," and "arrest" are socially constructed. Knowing and doing are linked. Only by focusing on the concrete particulars, by grasping the world as presented and acted upon, responded to and confirmed over the course of interactions, is the world known.[10]

Bittner as a phenomenologist sees the police as employing the natural attitude: things are what they are. However, Bittner reverses the usual sociological pattern of initially positing values, beliefs, norms, or even a habitus and then inferring the effect of these on already-known patterns of behavior. Bittner begins with a *phenomenological conceit* that focuses on what is done and how it is understood. How do officers do what they do repeatedly, and what do they know about it? Although officers may not verbalize their knowledge of it, their practices mirror the natural attitude of the citizen who expects intervention when something goes wrong and should not be happening. They will "call the cops." This action in turn may require coercion of a most complex sort, and its use must in some sense be calibrated to the situational requirements. When police take on interventions they are driven by rather different practices—they act on their own assessment of what is needed. This is the "supply side" discussed in Bittner's classic articles on policing in a slum area ("skid row") and policing the mentally ill (both found in Bittner 1990), and as Brodeur has himself pointed out (2007), it is less visible and less easily monitored than demand-based policing. In effect, police work that does not require coercion is less than central to their sense of what constitutes "good police work." Thus, for example, community policing, problem solving, and the rest are "intellectual" exercises well removed from the job, as the police see it.[11] It is essential to understand that this definition of police and police work cannot be reduced to studies of "arrest," "force," and other noncontextual objects.

Theory. It might said that Bittner's work is a theory. "Theory" in modern social science implies a particular kind of variable-related system with certain a priori assumptions about measurement, prediction, correlation, and explanation. Bittner's characterization of policing is not of course a "theory" if one conceives of theory as an abstract set of variable-based propositions that are interrelated, testable, and empirically verifiable and can be rejected or falsified. But there is no such theory in social science and probably never will be given the essential reflexivity between action and meaning that is the basis of social science. Action has meaning as it is acted upon, responded to, and takes on a collective reality.

Let us ask: what would a theory of policing attempt to explain or represent? As societal differentiation has advanced, revenge and self-serving punishment have been reduced, and the state has arrogated the regulation of conduct. The relative role of the state and law has increased, and individual- and group-based social control has decreased. Police as a practice has been validated as an arm of the state, and as violence is less common, the police remain its most visible conveyors. The validated license to use force legitimately rests on the capacity to use force competently. This is an institutional characterization. Bittner says *it resembles the priest's administration of the sacrament—a central defining and unique capacity denied others.* In other publications ("Functions ..." in Bittner 1972 and "Florence Nightingale ..." in Bittner 1974), Bittner justifies his focus on competence, defines how it is to be applied generally, shows that law provides only a justification for action, and outlines the historic basis for the devolution of applied violence to the police alone. In some sense, this is an almost mystical or sacred power to intervene, a kind of secular magic, because, as Bittner observes, "under the circumstances," the police officer cannot be wrong (unless she or he acted with "malice or wanton frivolity") (1990, 255). Many organizations can apply force under specified conditions; the open-ended aspect of the police's use of force is distinctive.

Role versus organization. The police role has become equated with the purpose of the organization. This is a false and misleading equation. Bittner defines police as "a mechanism for the distribution of situational justified force in society" (ibid., 34). The police are required to stand ready to respond to all sorts of human problems when it is imagined that the application of force may be necessary (ibid., 44). He adds, "The role of the police is best understood as a mechanism for the distribution of non-negotiable coercive force employed in accordance with the dictates of an intuitive grasp of situational exigencies" (ibid., 46). Here he is speaking of the role of the police, not of the role of the police organization as a political force. The ambit of those in need of force includes people unable to care for themselves and those unwilling to accept the police definition of the situation, whatever that might be. This definition—its situational aspects, focus on violence, and reliance on the officer's "intuitive grasp" of the situation as the basis for intervention—combined with the absence of an explicit a priori legal dimension, is penetrating.

Policing as a practice, a set of routines, tasks, and jobs, must be distinguished from police as an organization with structural and functional features and as an occupation with its accoutrements. One approach is to distinguish "organization" from "role." The social role SR1 applies to expectations of officers on the job, while social role SR2, the societally defined role, applies to those of the organization in society. SR2 might better be termed the *police mandate,* that is, an ongoing negotiated bargain made tacitly between society and the police organization (Hughes 1958, chap. 6). SR1 is more precisely defined by Bittner as dealing with or intervening in situations that need regulation. One can finesse the dilemma by seeing "organization" itself as a useful fiction—a label people use for describing their ecologically constrained, common, repetitive actions that are authoritatively coordinated (Manning 2005, 40). Many organizations can apply force under specified conditions; the open-ended aspect of the police's use of it is distinctive. These situations are characterized by Bittner as those in which "something-that-ought-not-to-be-happening-and-about-which-someone-had-better-do-something-now" (1990, 249).

This elision of organization as resting on practices sets aside the bigger structural questions that many take as determinant of policing (seen as an organization), as argued by others: the law (Jefferson 1990), "legal" and "nonlegal" variables (Herbert 1998), social class (Black and Reiss 1969), gender (Miller 1996), and rules of various kinds (Herbert 1998).

Violence.   Bittner sees violence and its use as key to understanding policing, but he also argues that withholding force is as important as the use of it. The threat of violence, as well as its use, is essential to the operation and legitimacy of police. The mandate includes the exclusion of citizens in general from free use of violence toward each other. Bittner conclusively argues that the law does not define "excessive force" (1990, 34), and leaves it to local definition. Policing, he writes, is "above all making use of the capacity and authority to overpower resistance to an attempted solution in the native habitat of the problem" (1972, 35). In other words, it is the possible *resistance of citizens* and the right to overcome the citizens' initial formulation that drive intervening action, not the intrinsic features of the "native habitat" of the problem (how the citizen defines it). The actors' perceptions or consciousness, their definitions of the problem and its possible solutions, have no direct relevance to this praxis.

Bittner, citing Kelsen (1999), argues that police violence is not applied without authority; is legitimated ("authorized") and sanctioned by the state. This sanctioning is negotiated continuously in action and in public debate in a democracy. Law is one touchstone in the debate but does not entirely circumscribe the domain of discussion. Bittner is arguing not that the coercive norms of the state are the source of police legitimation but rather that the popular belief is that the state sanctions police violence as an extension of state legitimacy. The law is a kind of umbrella. Violence serves interests. In that sense, the police's interests as well as the state's are served, regardless of the intuitive bases for the situational application of coercive violence. Kelsen stands in the Weberian tradition: law is the means by which the state justifies its almost exhaustive power and authority, and it does so by violence. Bittner's nuanced argument is that it is by minimizing violence that police legitimacy is maintained. Bittner (2008) argues that the general or original authority to use force is not to be found in the law. The contemporaneous connection between the police use of force and legal grounds for justification is fairly recent (Bittner 1972). Deference to the law is a feature of police legitimacy as well as other sources of order such as class, age, race, and gender arrangements. Compliance with the shadow of class and status interests is reflected in the law's enforcement. Inevitably, the powerful interests that sustain the state provide a tacit "authorization" for policing. Police objectivity favors the interests of the elites even in a democratic society (Manning 1977, 40–41, 101–2). This results from the ways in which the police have maintained the direction of law (down) and the targets of their violence in modern states.

Bitter cites excessive violence, such as the civil disorders in the 1960s, as damaging the mandate (see also 1990, 89–233). This is the basis for his view (expressed in the interview) that the army, and by implication paramilitary or private police, should not be called in to quell domestic uprisings. Bittner also seems to reject the Schmitt argument (1986) that the defining feature of the state is its stance toward its enemies, or "the presence of its enemies." The importance of this later is that Schmitt, one of theorists of the basis of the Nazi state, rejects a legalistic basis for the state, arguing instead that it rules by exception. This is also characteristic of the police, since rules cannot determine that which they do or are expected to do or how they are meant to accomplish it. I suggest that Bittner's remark is a dramatic marker alerting us to the fact that even when legal grounds are referred to, they are symbolic and an ideological cover to sustain the trust the state and its powerful agents must maintain. Unlike Schmitt and Weber, whose student Schmitt once was, Bittner's premise is not that the state possesses a monopoly of force but that police have an almost open-ended and defeasible capacity to employ force and that citizens can exercise it only under precisely defined conditions.

The police are sanctioned to be violent, but citizens are restricted in this regard, except in self-defense. Citizens in modern states in turn rely on police to deal with fissures of ordering, even those involving intimates. Police often say that you never know what comes next. Whatever is done as a result of the notable is not predictable in the usual statistical sense. Distributions of time spent and tables of types of calls for service, arrests, or clearances cannot be the basis for predicting the nature of the situated response to an event coming to police attention. Any response or none could not be provided by law, police rules and regulations, or even the attitude of the observer. Thus, we observe the weakness and paucity of "policy" in police departments. The decision to intervene and how to intervene cannot be fully specified.

In the Brodeur interview (2007), Bittner articulates the counterintuitive aspects of the role of violence. The aim is not violence qua violence, although police both enjoy and frequently seek it in the modern context, but according to Bittner it is used to maximize incapacitation or to reduce the capacity of the citizen to create additional or more serious havoc, to flee, or to resist. Coercion, like the law, is a tool and a resource. It can generate new problems. The natural habitat of citizens is unacceptable; that is, their solutions, however creative, are unsuitable for the matter at hand. Evidence does suggest that class and gender do shape the "solutions" that result.

Under questioning, Bittner raises a potentially moot point: is police violence "value free" in modern states? By this it appears he means, is it open-ended and in police hands almost unrestricted in the interests of order? In this regard Bittner makes clear in the interview that the law and law enforcement are not the foundational bases for police actions. The potential for escalation and excess always lurks in policing; thus, the application of violence as a central competence is somewhat independent of the level and intensity of the coercive violence applied. That is to say, that the police apply force is but one aspect of the equation—they apply force with an acute awareness of its time-bound limitations. It is one thing to operate with force but another to apply it in a manner appropriate to the situation and citizens' expectations.

Furthermore, what the police seek out and shape, whether on patrol or in investigative work, is a projection of their views of the world about what needs fixing, not entirely in any case what the citizenry thinks, or even given what the formal rules of the organization, such as clearance rates and arrests, might reward. In an odd way, as discussed in the interview, because the police focus on the visible, what might be called "decent nineteenth-century crimes" such as burglary, robbery, and interpersonal violence, the supply and demand sides of policing are elided to some degree. Investigative work concerns many of the same people, places, and skills as does patrol work.

Bittner admits that the use of force potential is something of an oxymoron in a modern welfare state (1972, 39). Metaphorically, by the same token, the state will act toward itself (in the form of the citizens who constitute it) in a violent and punitive fashion, but more generally, the compliance of citizens and their unrecognized acceptance of force and violence directed at them must be noted. Symbolic violence, violence that "is wielded with tacit complicity between its victims and its agents, insofar as both remain unconscious of submitting to or wielding it" (Bourdieu, 1991, 17), is a reflexive aspect of postindustrial societies. "The function of sociology, as of every science, is to reveal that which is hidden" (ibid.). This search for revelation at least means probing the mechanisms by which the exercise of such symbolic violence is produced, the more overt and visible sort, and that which is protected or hidden. The operational solution of the police has been to focus on the marginal and weak, to seek to be accepted in their crudity of intervention on the grounds of necessity and time-framed expediency. The police, in short, are beneficiaries and guardians of symbolic violence. The police in every society are insulated in some fashion from those whom they police—by civil laws, traditions, legal conventions such as the common law, civilian review boards, and other modes of accountability. This is what Bittner elegantly terms "bureaucratically symbolized communication" (1972, 39). This is the connection between the state, the law, and the police. It is analogical. The police are armed and dangerous, and protection by the police is assumed, while protection from their actions, misdeeds, and mistakes is more problematic and perhaps less commented upon.

Overview. From these types of definitions and variations, as well as Bittner's gloss, one can infer several useful things in regard to a more refined definition of police and policing.[12] It is inadequate to simply describe policing in a given, unexplicated cultural-historical context as the first and second approaches to the definition do. The fifth type of definition, an analytical definition not based in a theoretical scheme, is also of limited utility. Analytical-taxonomic distinctions such as those made by Klockars are relevant to the types of policing extant in the Anglo-American world, but they are not in themselves an explanatory scheme. What these definitions lack is the ideological overlay that justifies the police as a neutral, collectively oriented, nonpolitical force abiding by and enforcing the law. The order that is maintained is not only a reality but a created and constructed reality to which people defer. Law is secondary to the practice because it is based on doing and acting, and the law is an account, a means to move a case, to rationalize deciding, and to call on other resources if necessary. Access of police to the criminal law and criminal sanctions is essential, not secondary, however. Each features in democratic policing, but some features are typically overemphasized to the exclusion of the contrary effects. For example, intense law enforcement is inconsistent with long-term peacekeeping efforts and concerns for promoting justice.

CONCLUSION

Democratic policing in some ways reflects and refracts the state and its interests, but these interests are balanced, on the one hand, between those of the police as agents and, on the other, those of citizens. Beginning with broad conceptions of the relationship between democratic society and the police found in the writings of key scholars, this chapter then assessed some definitions of policing. The search for a broad and theoretically informed definition of policing is somewhat disappointing in that none links the broader political and philosophical principles to the definitions offered. Five modes or approaches to definition were reviewed. The most featured and often misunderstood definition is Bittner's, which is deeply philosophical but limited. The ideological canopy, the protective umbrella of belief, makes probing the contradictions of any definition of policing difficult (see Raphael's Epilogue) and obscures how police practice is often inconsistent with claims. The following chapter discusses policing in the modern world.

CHAPTER TWO

Police in the
Sociopolitical World

The nature of the embeddedness of the police organization in democracies is elusive. Classic summaries of democratic theory and democracy have little or nothing to say about the role of policing in developing or sustaining democracy (Crick 2002, Dahl 1998). The stated-as-necessary conditions for modern democracy (Crick 2002, 93–95) do not explicitly consider policing. The most systematic considerations of the (necessary) "institutional characteristics of modern democracy" (ibid., summarizing and adding to Dahl's list at 107–8) do not include policing, although other "institutional structures" are listed (ibid., 95–96). The civilian control of the military and the police are included (Dahl 2000, 144), but this is not elaborated on, nor are police practices discussed. Although there is a huge literature on democratic governments and governance, the concept has not been widely explored in the context of policing, and conversely, scholarship in police studies, shown in the previous chapter, has paid uneven attention to the relationship between policing, police organization, and democracy.

Police and policing remain a context-based idea in democratic theory, and even serious scholars, reviewed above, remain rather abstract in their considerations. This suggests that the quest for a definitive and delineating concept of policing cannot be resolved merely by querying the current definitions, low-level empirical research, or institutional structures. The police reflect and refract the state, and their political role in the most general sense must be acknowledged. This is not clarified by definitions that rest on a single facet of their function, such as "law enforcement." The role of the police varies by social context—stable democracies are the forefront, but increasingly weak states with protodemocratic structures are experimenting with the social form of a democratic police. Even police organizations in states with a long

39

history of policing, such as the Republic of Ireland and Northern Ireland, are being transformed in democratic fashion. The question of the role of police as precipitating, sustaining, and escalating riots (Walker Commission 1968; Stark 1972), their corruption and veniality, is not viewed as a threat to democracy. These questions are usually dismissed as one of "rotten apples" (the barrel and the rest of the apples are healthy and edible), "rogue cops," or one-off instances of excess not indicative of past or future performance.[1] Thus, some effort must be devoted to defining the object "policing."

THE POLICE AND DEMOCRACY

The absence of a discussion of the role of police and police practices in a democracy is a surprising omission insofar as the police are the means by which other democratic procedures, official doctrines, and information flow are sustained. They play an important role in the political economy of a city. Police are the "face" of civil government and the primary contact point between citizens and the government. They are the personalization of state authority, whatever else they do,. Their practices impact directly on the lives of citizens daily. If the tenets bearing on the role of citizens—such as citizens must respect the rights of others in a democracy, "within a regulatory legal order" (Crick 2002, 13)—are to be realized in practice, it would appear necessary to have some means, even a force with violent capacities, to enforce that condition. Whatever the level of loyalty and compliance of citizens, there will be those unable, unwilling, or actively resistant to state authority. Persuasion and perhaps coercion are required (Feeley 1969). The sensitive political and moral questions such as how justice as fairness operates "on the ground" are left begging since the key operating institutional structure that mediates between peoples and their governments is not analyzed in respect to governance generally.

It is well known, however, that policing in a democracy is inevitably rooted in and embedded in the power of the people in a modest agreement to make elected officials accountable. Accountability was present in Nazi Germany neither in fact nor in law (Evans 2003; Chapman 1970). It was marginally present in Northern Ireland until post-1998 (Ellison and Smyth 2000). In modern bureaucracies where loyalty and accountability are diffuse (in Nazi Germany, Mao's China, and Stalin's Russia, the oath was to the leader, not to the state or to the people), holding individuals accountable is very difficult (Brodeur and Viau 1994; Brodeur 1997). Yet in order to delineate the denotations of "democracy" for "policing," one would need clear definitions of both as well as the logic that connects them. The concept of democracy has diverse referents, connotations, and denotations. It is consistently "debated both in application and in discussion. (It suggests government by the people directly or indirectly, as stated in the U.S. Constitution and elegantly rephrased in Lincoln's 1863 Gettysburg Address. Implicit in this definition is some conception of balance of powers among the segments of government and an echo of the ideals of eighteenth-century rationalism. It minimally requires consensus, notions of equality, freedom of choice, participation in deciding by the people, and consent of the governed. Having said this, as Newburn, Jones, and Smith (1996, 186) point out, the ideals should be balanced, and some criteria are needed to assess the ideal and its realization.

The connection between democratic policing and the state, the domain of social scientists, is not well researched.[2] Democracy as a form of governance stabilizes the structures of policing (Bayley 1969, 1992), and perhaps the policing can stabilize democratic ordering. Certainly, policing by paramilitary reserves and vigilantes, when combined with nondemocratic policing, can erode a democratic republic, as seen in the decline and fall of the Weimar Republic (Diehl 1977; Merkel 1975). Nondemocratic policing can prevent democratic policing from emerging (Weitzer 1990, 1996; Ellison and Smyth 2000; Mulcahy 2006) or dramatize inequalities (e.g., the Rodney King incident). On this point, Palmer's analysis of the policing of Ireland and England (1988) is ambiguous. He argues that the model of policing developed in Ireland was then transported back to England (see also Brogden 1989)[3] and was effective in England because the workingmen were more docile, the crowds more polite and the English, in short, were not Irish. Palmer argues that policing was one mode of governance and that as it grew in strength and scope, it served to develop government more generally in Ireland. This historical instance cries out for more systematic cross-cultural analysis of policing after conquest. This gap in knowledge certainly implies a needed comparative dimension to research. Bayley notes that since criminal justice as a field has not been comparative, and does not seek to be, it has failed to produce adequate theory. He argues that "any theory of criminal justice institutions, such as the police, must include more than one country." Furthermore, in a sanguine moment, Bayley sighs, "At the present time, we know hardly anything about the factors that shape the character of policing" (1996, 247).

A NOTE ON VIOLENCE

The role of violence and policing is a thread running through this text, because the structural concerns of police as an ordering and guiding force, and those of the state, are isomorphic, or, in theory, as Loader and Walker (2007) write, "homological." Violence by the state is justified by its rational legitimation. This associative move is slightly misleading, as the state *claims* a single modicum of order as a gloss over the very complex, varied, diverse conflicting and competing notions of order (Venkatesh 1997). Violence, of course, is contrasted to order rather than seeing it as a kind of ordering phenomenon itself. It is something that substitutes for something missing. Violence, as the use of physical force against others, is a means to accomplish an end without the consent of the other and to fill in for something that is absent.

As Lukes maintains, after an extensive and powerful critique, "neo-Durkheimian" rituals, including ritualized violence, reveal and reinforce the dominant and official models of structure and social change. That is, when routinely violence is displayed against criminals, suspects, hostages, or fleeing felons, it represents an order and an ordering that is otherwise assumed. Violent incidents "invoke loyalties"

(1977, 69) toward a particular version of social order and suppress other kinds of orders. The law and the police are actors in a political drama, modes of including and inviting compliance with the status quo; each traffic stop with acquiescence, each appearance in court, each surrender to a police siege indicates an ordering and the agreement that such is fair. By *ritualized,* he means here a mode of representing governmental power indirectly by deference and demeanor. As in the case of terrorism in general, unexpected violence confounds the conventional order and symbolizes alternative orders and ordering. The purpose is to symbolize other orders rather than to achieve an instrumental aim—for example, to overthrow a government. The long history of Irish violence directed against the English going back at least to the rural violence of the "Whiteboys" at the end of the eighteenth century suggests that it was both a hopeful marker of needed change in land tenure and taxation as well as instrumental violent actions.

The theme of violence and its association with the police was made in an early classic in the field of police studies, William Westley's "Violence and the Police" (1953, taken from his 1951 dissertation). Violence was rationalized as a necessary and quite legitimate tool in controlling those marginal to society, as the officer saw them. This analysis, insightful as it is, focused attention on the individual street officer rather than on violence as a fundamental and deeply significant aspect of state-sponsored ordering. Bittner's brilliant phenomenological work elevated the vision of social scientists and made the potential for violence the touchstone for sub-sequent police studies. His focus, however, is very precise: the police as purveyors of violence, not directly as agents of the state. He also notes that the violence of police since Victorian times has been seen as necessary but distasteful. Policing, even in the past forty years, is overtly less violent if one examines the number of officers shot, the number of citizens shot by the police, the generally declining homicide rate, and the movement toward "partnerships," "community policing," and surveillance and tracking rather than confrontation (see Brodeur 2007). As discussed below, however, the connection of the violence of the state, often in the form of state-produced ter-rorism, and toward the democratic state in particular, has not been well addressed by scholars in the field of police studies (see Gurr 1989).

The most profound recent thinking about the role of violence in democracies is found in John Keane's book *Violence and Democracy* (2004). Unfortunately, he addresses the role of policing only in passing, but the role of the core institutions—military, police, and courts—is central to his argument about the "civilizing" of violence. He rejects the arguments of previous masterful thinkers who have been accepted as having penetrated the essential nature of human violence (Sorel, Girard, and Benjamin, for example) by claiming that violence can be restrained—that it is contingent, publicly removable, and "erasable." The routines of modern life shape how strangers comport themselves in tolerance, and violence intrudes and destroys these standards. I would argue further that these routines are the bases of interper-sonal trust. Although democracies contain violence, they tend to blur its presence and deny its reality by metaphor, such as calling crime a disease, regarding policing as a dosage, and extending the clinical metaphor to dehumanize the people affected by such "treatments" (Sherman 2007). Violence is the hidden weapon resorted to in times of pragmatic urgency. Keane argues that "surplus violence" should be reduced, erased from democracies, although he does not set a standard against which "surplus" could be identified. Violence, Keane argues, has been "democratized" and broadened in its context of use (it no longer has exclusively ceremonial or sacrificial functions); it has been extended from a tool resident only in "core institutions" (military, courts, and the police) to other spaces, such as roads and households; is no longer seen as a function of "sin" or the original nature of human beings; and is restricted in its metaphoric use. Civil society, democracy, and reduced violence are linked: in effect, civility obtains when individuals cannot with impunity violate another's body, take personal or individual revenge, and refuse to delegate social control to the state. This argument maintains not that violence is fully controlled in democratic states but merely that it is focused and restrained. On the other hand, Keane, citing Z. Bauman, emphasizes that modern states have thoroughly modern rational, calculated violence at their control. The technique and capacity to terrorize the innocent and demoralize or destroy whole groups of human beings remain (Bauman 1994). The ways in which violence erodes the boundaries of states, defining both their presence and their absence, remains a powerful but denied note in the modern world.

Hannah Arendt's marvelous and pained analysis of the movement toward totalitarianism rests on the fundamental idea that absence, loneliness, and lack of connection give rise to desperate attempts to connect in totalitarian fashion. These social conditions, combined with an absence of legitimacy of democratic government, lead not to authority or power, which is the sustaining of legitimate authority, but to violence. Violence, Arendt writes, instrumental and short term, can only be justified by itself since it has no long-term rational ends. Its use always calls out tautological justifications: "Violence, being instrumental by nature, is rational to the extent that it is effective in reaching the end that must justify it. And since when we act, we never know with any certainty the eventual consequences of what we are doing, violence can remain rational only if it pursues short term goals. Violence does not promote causes, neither history nor revolution, neither progress nor reaction; but it can serve to dramatize grievances and bring them to public attention" (1970, 79).

I do not accept this generalization. Arendt was writing this variation on a theme in the context of the student riots at Berkeley and Columbia University in the seventies and arguing against the violence thesis of Fanon and others.[4] Hers was a textual violence directed to a modality of violence, pointing out that the consequences of violence may be reform, but finally it leads to a more violent world (ibid., 80). Her argument then was that violence brought about attention to grievances and to the need for change when it was short term and was justified in terms of the need for reform. The missing piece of this argument is found in her masterwork *Origins of Totalitarianism* (1985), in which she makes clear that state-based terror is based on just such intimidating coercive violence and the threat of violence. She further extends her argument by pointing out that it is state-based resources, and ever-increasing bureaucracy, that produce the capacity for extremes. The basis for totalitarianism is state-based terror: an ability to frighten the innocent and demoralize them into defeat and collapse. The ability to resist large and growing bureaucracies, in her view, was dwindling, and she saw the massification and alienation of populations in large states as self-destructive.

On the other hand, policing is the link between the civil society and the government of the day. When policing moves into monitoring the thoughts and feelings of people, their predispositions and proclivities, often attributed falsely in any case, the innocent are the targets of governmental terror—unannounced violence directed without warning to locales, categories, or groups for reasons other than their behavior. In this way, in my view, Arendt has connected the rationale for democratic police's eschewing antiterrorism: such activities beget government-sponsored terrorism.

A Preliminary Definition of Policing

Following is a working definition of *police* that highlights the police as an organization rather than policing as a function; assumes that the police are a bureaucratic organization; emphasizes the political nature of order and ordering, the new powers of surveillance and tracking that are balanced with coercion and violence; and notes that the police, because of their rather loose connection to the law, act by exception. That is, they act in the shadow of legitimacy and account or explain later if required. In this sense they act in exception outside or merely in the shadow of the law. The implication of this definition is that police practices follow from these features.

The police as an organization in Anglo-American societies, constituted of many diverse agencies, are authoritatively coordinated, legitimate organizations. They stand ready to apply force up to and including fatal force in politically defined territories. They seek to sustain politically defined order and ordering via tracking, surveillance, and arrest. As such, they require compliance to command from lower personnel and the citizens and the ability to proceed by exception.

Let us reprise the argument in which this definition is located. The police are an institution that arises as a result of the development of law, differentiation, and functional specialization in a society. It is an institution that cannot survive without the consistent support of other institutions that complement its aims and practices. They are purveyors of organized, rational (in Arendt's sense) coercion and the threat of coercion. The supporting institutions must complement the rationality, fairness, and processual commitment of policing, or else it creates and sustains its own standards beyond review and remedy. This is, of course, the basic argument of Weber in respect to the collaborative nature of rationality in modern societies (see also Merelman 1998). The specialized functions of policing that arise as nation-states emerge and develop rest on broader societal consensus concerning fairness and justice arising from the public trust. They are a product in some sense of a balance of powers among executive, legislative, and judicial branches as set out in the original documents of a nation's establishment. One tendency, seen in crisis periods, is for the executive branch to either co-opt the police, making them directly accountable (as they still are in the Republic of Ireland and have been since 1922), or suspend the habeas corpus that in effect places the police under their direction since protections granted by legislation and by the courts are bypassed

To rehearse the argument: Democratic policing is linked indirectly to a theory of democracy that imagines an administrative balance of powers (among executive control and legislative actions and court rulings) regarding policing functions as well as a degree of citizen involvement and freedom of expression (Dahl 1998; Jones, Newburn, and Smith 1996). As the division of labor increases, that is, social differentiation, it is no longer possible to base policing on known values, beliefs, or theories of citizenship alone. The police neither create order nor sustain it; they monitor it. The presumption that the state has a single and unified value system based on compliance, citizenship, and shared values cannot bear the test of close examination. This is perhaps less so now than before and certainly not true of the current weak states lacking regulatory and security capacity. Democratic policing must demonstrate in practice its fundamental restraint, fairness, and balanced interests (of both the state it represents and its own organizational-occupational interests). A police that represents one segment of a population, such as the Protestant-dominated (about 90–95 percent of its members were nominal Protestants) Royal Ulster Constabulary during the period from 1922–1998, cannot police democratically because it cannot be seen to be fair and solicit compliance on that basis (see *The Report of the Independent Commission on Policing for Northern Ireland* [Patten 1999], known as the Patten Report). This is where practices meet tacit notions about democracy. While current forms of policing in AADP nations maintain solid legitimation, if not trustworthiness, the origins of their legitimacy, by origination (the Peel model), by adaptation (the United States, Canada, New Zealand), and by conquest and drift (Australia and India perhaps), vary, and this foundational fact remains as a shadowing effect on current practices. In part, the origins are reflected in the degree of centralization of authority and the distribution of resources and slots throughout the nation—how many positions exist differs from how the positions are funded and how many persons occupy each named role (patrol, specialized units, administration, staff, and line). Degree of centralization and decentralization vary, as does the dispersal of officers. The role of private police varies, as does the strength of the ancillary policing, vigilantes, posses, part-time voluntary officers, and even bandits. These forms contrast with the full-time, uniformed, paid public police. The violence of police is considerable and not a full monopoly. The importance of state-sponsored violence is that it defines the range of legitimate violence, not its monopoly on the fully elastic nature of violence. Policing is a system of a collection of elements in all AADP societies. They are variously accountable to the people. They live in an organizational environment of competition and conflict, but like other public institutions, they cannot move or officially change the publics they serve, the range of products, or their broad mandate. Their flexibility lies to some degree in rhetorical flexibility: the capacity to recast their strategies and tactics in line with current conventional wisdom of "service delivery." They are seen as sacred, dangerous, mysterious, and distant and violent, profane, dirty workers in touch with the polluted, excluded, and marginal. For this reason, among others, they are not easily assessed in respect to performance, and in general avoid and eschew any such efforts to evaluate them and hold them accountable for practices other than on a case-by-case basis. The image of policing, or how in general the police are viewed, also varies in the AADP cultures (as used by Loader and Mulcahy 2003) in part because they reflect the expectations of the society of control and authority and its emergent "policing culture." In the United States, with great gaps in income, education, and access between majorities and minorities, the degree to which the image is positive varies by region, race, class, and education. The functions of the AADP police vary cross-culturally and historically, and there is always a tension between high policing (functions associated with national security) and low policing (routine domestic functions). Because they functionally vary from routine to emergency and the rules and regulations of policing have historically been used to punish rather than to guide the practice of policing, a tension remains between the paramilitary model of policing and day-to-day operating styles. These are in part reflected in segmentation and rank divisions.

Nine Dimensions of Democratic Policing

The roots of democratic policing are many and varied. Police functions, agencies or groups performing them, and those sponsoring and funding them vary cross-culturally and historically (Bayley 1985; Becker and Becker 1986; Marenin ed. 1996; Deflem 1998; Mawby 1990, 1999, 2003; Pino and Wiatrowski 2006; Dammer, Fairchild, and Albanese 2006; and Cerrah 2007). The study of this evolution in the context of the democratic state permits generalizing about policing as a democratic function. To some important degree, the organizational framework resources, structure, rewards, and interpersonal tactics sustain the practices.

Before further considering democratic policing, it is important to identify *social dimensions* along which AADP organizations can be arrayed. The AADP is an ensemble or rope of many strands with varying features and strengths. Each nation-state's set of police organizations has some unique features (not my concern here) and others that are shared. The salience of the features varies cross-nationally, and these matters are best studied in the classic works on these police forces. The discussion takes these dimensions of policing to be fundamental. It is guided by their (1) emergence as an organization with state-based police authority; (2) democratic and nondemocratic varieties; (3) collective orientation; (4) (perception as being committed) to fairness and sustaining trust; (5) construction as both sacred and profane; (6) varying degrees of centralization; (7) imagined functions and imagery; (8) location in a competitive field with other forms of regulation, with policing as the central node; and (9) mandate. These nine factors provide the basis for refining the definition.

1. The Emergence of State-Based Police Authority

While the emergence of the state and its relationship to citizens has been the salient concern of Marxist scholars, few have been students of the police as an organization.

Serious Marxist analysis of policing rather than the emergence of police (Harring 1983; Jefferson 1990; Chambliss 1994) exist, and critical analyses of the rise of the police (Storch et al.) are available. As the military role was reduced to control of national borders and repelling foreign enemies and the broad domains and extension of laws requiring capital punishment were reduced, the police acted as the symbolic face of state power, as the everyday reality of the state to the citizen (Sheptycki 2000; Liang 1992). These analyses see policing from a distance, as an institution standing between "the people" and "the government," or between the people and an exploitative coalition of the elites and the government.

Unfortunately, only Robinson and Scaglion (1987) have presented an adequate, testable theory of the emergence of the police. They draw on three sorts of knowledge: historical knowledge of the function and loyalties of the English police since their inception as citizen-members of local groups obligated to police; anthropological knowledge about the processes that led to the transition from tribal, kin-based societies to modern industrialized nation-states; and evolutionary cultural Marxist theory. They argue that policing as a modern form is linked to economic specialization and differential access to resources that occur in the transition from a kin-based to a class-based society (paraphrase from the abstract, p. 109, and Schwartz and Miller 1964). This part of the analysis is based on the transition of loyalty from kin to more generalized rules and orders (religion, law) as economic specialization occurs, a division of interests based on economic life chances that divides societies in new ways, and the resultant antagonisms and conflicts. States provide the basis for the emergence of public policing. The combination of defense of territory, a wish to mediate and reduce visible conflicts between resident groups, and surplus that accrues to the dominant groups and scale of societies leads to specialized public agencies. They argue further that a crucial factor in the transition from kin-based loyalties and conflict was shifting modes of conflict resolution where the government arises as a neutral third party with an interest in reducing internecine conflicts.

Shifting modes of conflict resolution rooted in the community (kin-based local groups) to specialized police agencies or functions was the attempt of dominant elites to control lower classes or those who opposed their interests. The Peel model, invented in 1829, is taken to be the epitome of democratic policing—focused on deterrence and prevention, reactive and responsive to public concerns, works, uniformed, visible, and order maintaining at best. They see the spread of this ideal as an ideological effort to produce consensus, advance the interests of the elites, and avoid conflict. Robinson and Scaglion conclude: "The police institution is created by the emergent dominant class as an instrument for the preservation of their control over restricted access to basic resources, over the political apparatus controlling this access, and over the labor force necessary to provide the surplus on which the dominant class lives" (1987, 109, 113–14). Yet the functioning of such an institution must in some sense be based on trust and citizen compliance.

Their full argument is complex and based in part on cross-cultural data from the human relations area files (HRAF) kept at Yale University and cannot be fully reproduced here. However, they make well the subtle point that the necessary infrastructure in modernity is control based on ties other than kinship, a more patently neutral force, but in fact it cannot be other than a force of government, or, as Black (1976) writes, government social control. This position, they show, has been systematically obscured by the ideology that has evolved since 1829 in Anglo-American societies. This ideology is one that equates the public with the police and vice versa, denies police interests (as an organization and occupation) and the interests of the state and its dominant classes, and focuses on benign reactive functions and crime prevention and order. These functions are to be mixed in liberal measure with evocations of justice, law, and service (Robinson and Scaglion 1987, 115–16). As will be discussed below, the positioning of the police as a neutral force is essential to modernity and to democratic policing, but this in itself does not mean that the police are mere dupes or hypocrites. As a result of the switch of police loyalty from the community to the state, their interests are suppressed and less visible, and they are in constant danger of criticism for failing to serve and protect.

2. Democratic and Nondemocratic Varieties

Democratic policing was diffused throughout the nineteenth century. This ideal type was discussed above in connection with typological approaches to policing and so needs to be summarized only briefly here. The democratic form was adopted voluntarily in the United States (Lane 1967; Richardson 1970, Miller 1977) and Canada (Forcese 1999; Dawson 1998), that is, North America more generally, with some modification given to local authority, the presence of minorities, and weapons carried. The Peel model was adopted more indirectly perhaps in Australia (Dupont 2002) and New Zealand. A case could also be made for variants such as the province of Quebec, the Republic of Ireland, and Scotland, which are highly influenced by continental or civil law, and India as a quasi-colonial and inherited democratic policing system (Bayley 1969). Israel, in many respects, because it carries out torture and uses antiterrorist tactics and terrorism itself, is marginally a democratic policing system. Although our interest here is common law–based democratic policing systems, democratic civil law–based systems such as those in France, the Netherlands, Italy, Japan, and Germany (Deflem 2004; Glaeser 2000) are "cousins" but contrast in their civil-law legal-juridical systems and the high degree of centralization of authority in the public police. Exploring the fundamental differences in patterning police practice based on continental systems, common-law systems, and Islamic law–based systems might be fruitful, and there are strategic sites for exploring the overlay and cross-pollination of such ideas in the former colonies of France, England, and Germany. Furthermore, studies of such complex law-culture loci in which patterns of law have been adopted by agreement or conquest, and overlaid on indigenous cultures, such as Turkey, Israel, and Japan, would illuminate the cultural-ethnic-religious patterning of overtly democratic policing systems.

Quasi- and nondemocratic systems are of interest here as contrast conceptions. There are three of note, the most important being the first subtype, "quasi-democratic systems." The police of the Republic of Ireland and Northern Ireland are in some sense making a transformation to democratic policing, although their origins in both cases were in antiterrorist, national security–focused high policing combined with everyday low or domestic policing. Weitzer, in an innovative set of studies (1990, 1996), has explored these quasi-democratic systems, calling them "divided society models of policing." They reflect a history of colonialism, imperialism, ethnic-religious divisions, and a corollary of focus on security and antiterrorism. According to Weitzer's list (paraphrased slightly), these systems have:

- A systematic bias in law enforcement, and members of the subordinate groups policed more aggressively and punitively than do the members of the dominant group
- Politicized policing, that is, a strong identification with the regime and vigorous police actions against the regime's political opponents
- A dominant group monopoly of top command positions and a disproportionate representation in the rank and file
- A dual responsibility of the police for internal security and for ordinary law enforcement
- Legal or extralegal powers, giving police great latitude in their control of the subordinate population
- An absence of effective mechanisms of accountability
- Polarized communal relations with the police, with the dominant group as a champion of the police and the subordinate group largely estranged from the police (1995, 5)

This sort of policing, in short, aims to defend the current administration or regime, and "the maintenance of a social order based on institutionalized inequality between dominant and subordinate groups" (ibid. 6). Notice that the seven points all revolve around an implicit democratic ideal. The first point refers to uneven and categorical enforcement tactics and argues against policing that is more proactive than reactive. The "politicized" nature of policing violates the restrained and civil expectations of policing and hints at the importance of legally guided restraint in enforcement. Although the mandate is based not in law but rather on legitimacy, peri-odic suspension of habeas corpus and military intervention also blur the line between war and policing and compromise the rights of citizens. Weitzer also underscores the importance of internal democracy, that is, fairness in hiring, firing, and promotion, seldom found in police departments. In his research, the matter of rank promotion and disproportionate hiring of minorities was shaped by religious preferences in these quasi-democratic societies, while in the United States and in the UK the issue is race and gender equality of opportunity. The tension between "security" or high policing and domestic policing has of course been dramatic periodically in Northern Ireland and in the Republic of Ireland since 1922. The question of modes and kinds of accountability remains vexing and unresolved in AADP countries in general. Its absence is dramatized in quasi rebellions or insurgencies in which behavior can be labeled as criminal, treasonous, political, or rebellious. Weitzer's final point about the polarization of the attitudes toward the police of the dominant and subordinate groups would appear to hold in AADP societies. The difference in Northern Ireland, unlike elsewhere, is that the opposition or support is double coded—an overlap of religion, ecology, and class status. It is therefore perhaps more explosive than the attitudes and experiences patterned by the overlap of class and color.

The tension between high and low policing is perhaps the most important problem of the police. Weitzer's focus on community policing and reform of policing means he presents the "public face" of such policing. He has collapsed the strategies of policing low-intensity conflicts and the tactics. The tactics include a less visible face of policing. This private face of such antiterrorist policing was seen in both the Republic of Ireland and in Northern Ireland. The private face would include the use in both societies of draconian laws to protect the order; suspension of habeas corpus, undercover and secret police units unaccountable to law or the legislature, and control of the police by the Ministry of Justice or the secretary of state for Northern Ireland absent strong civilian oversight of any kind until 1998. In the case of Northern Ireland I would add complicity with the military and the Secret Service of the British government in quelling violence, virtually imposing martial law in the North from 1969 to 1978; establishing special courts absent procedural protections (the "Diplock Courts"); the use of "enhanced interrogation techniques" and torture (Stalker 1988; Taylor 1980); criminalizing rebellion and insurrection and denying its political aspect (e.g., the establishment of special prisons for IRA members); consistent surveillance; producing misinformation and disinformation propaganda; using undercover and double agents and agent provocateurs; carrying out warrantless searches; and developing and using large secret databases of suspected criminals. These are features of quasi-democratic policing systems. As Weitzer correctly concludes (1996, 279–95), reform of such systems is impossible unless the configuration of power and policing and their connection to the legitimacy of the state are altered. It should be recalled that it is the total set of these features in powerful interdigitation that constitutes the ideal type. Particular features and tactics listed above in quasi-democratic societies are found in democratic societies from time to time; nondemocratic policing does occur in democratic societies.

The second are *radically nondemocratic systems,* those that do not strive for or represent themselves as democratic. These include, for example, policing in Germany, the Third Reich under Hitler from 1933 to 1945, the USSR under Stalin and subsequently and the states in the "communist bloc" from World War II until the early 1980s, China under Mao, and democratic states under occupation such as Vichy France, Belgium, Holland, Norway, Finland, and Denmark. Whatever the emergent properties of these policing systems since that time, they are not and never have been fully democratic.

The third subtype is *religiously based policing systems* based fundamentally on religious beliefs and principles and with weak or nonexistent secularized law. These are found in countries such as Iran, Iraq, Saudi Arabia, the United Arab Emirates, Kuwait, Jordan, and Syria.

3. Collective Orientation

The democratic police mandate is collective. That is, the obligations of the police in general are to the general will. They do not serve people but serve the interest of the state. The police do not have "customers": they do not respond to market forces of other productive organizations, they are not a business or an industry, and they apply their solutions to problems with the greatest flexibility on the ground. In an economist's terms, it is a good from which all benefit, and supply to any given segment benefits all. Thus, it is incompatible in theory with market-driven solutions.[5] The argument has been joined by social scientists who begin with the economist's problem—how to persuade or reward individuals to make "rational choices" when the goods offered are offered to all (they are nonexclusive) and where their key property is in fact symbolic—what economists call indivisible. The category of law that provides known public rewards or costs to comply with are often visible and violated by others, not only in personal affronts or crimes suffered but in observations of others' behavior. Feeley has called such items "public goods." This is the type of law that aims to achieve a general state of being for everyone and can be achieved only when a large proportion of the population contributes to the costs (1970, 513). What are, then, the benefits? Feeley asks. His argument is that it would be "rational" for each person to agree to be in a coercive system in order to ensure that others would likewise contribute their share of the costs (constrained behavior) to the collectively shared benefits (ibid., 514; my paraphrase). Coercion, or the threat of coercion, compels what might be called the good to contribute the costs by obeying the law. The function of coercion is to sustain the rational and compliant person. This position is somewhat analogous to the argument made here concerning the function of policing as a collective or public good.

A review of neoliberal views of policing as manifesting rational choice. Many of the standard critiques of rational choice theory are of course relevant here, such as the inability of individuals to assess their interests, to anticipate the consequences of their choices, to weigh the present decision and its outcomes against others, and to deny what is wanted and seek the wrong ends (Elster 1985). These sophisticated commentaries begin with the unit individual in a single instance of choice where the "facts" are in some sense presented to the decider. They are in many ways assumptions that must be at least tentatively accepted to take on the arguments on their possible merit. However, the Rawlsian argument assumes a level of individual trust based on the veil of ignorance and the fundamental proposition about equality. Nevertheless, the question arises concerning four questions of importance for the collective orientation of the police.

The first is in what sense are the police surrogates for the state and their behavior or actions seen as reflections of the "delivery" of collective goods. This would seem to be generally accepted and supported by social surveys that show high correlations between satisfaction with the police and general trust and acceptance of government worldwide. These surveys address the symbol of policing and their multivalent properties (they have many meanings that vary in context), their sacred aspect, and the pluralistic ignorance that attends their everyday actions—most people have no direct experience with police yet offer opinions readily about the extent to which they are violent, corrupt, trustworthy, and the like. In this sense, generalized global assertions about their accepted role in coercion and in producing compliance would be merely a specification of the general rule about the rationality of being coerced (in the general sense that Feeley uses it—being in a coercive system). As Bourdieu (1991) has argued extensively, citizens participate in their own coercion even against their own interests, what he calls "symbolic violence." The hierarchy of preferences is sharply drawn for most people not in the collective sphere but only once they are in the game. This occurs perhaps more from attachment to society via a differentiated division of labor than the exercising of individual choices about policing.

The second assumption of such rational choice policing is that the "constraint" of individuals who comply is equal such that it sustains equilibrium. This is clearly not the case, as the differentiation of lifestyles, preferences, opportunities for violation of the law, and resources to protect, defer, or alter sanctioning is all unequal. Given that the law works down to differentially sanction the lower classes (Black 1976), the costs are never equal, nor are they to the advantage of those most policed given the base of behaviors, places, and social structures. This would appear to be an odd place to begin concerning policing—questioning compliance when the matter to which compliance is required is not a question of compliance to the largest number of people. This does not address the question, furthermore, of the symbolic aspects of compliance and its differential costs.

The third question is about the degree to which policing is a public service. Policing is not an equally applied service, the benefit of which accrues to all. It dramatizes many inequalities as a result of the organizational structure, strategies, and tactics. This is discussed further in chapters 6–9.

- Police deployment is skewed inconsistently with actual workload and demand. That is, given the calls for service, the stops made, and the proactive policing carried out, the disadvantaged areas are by far underpoliced and the more affluent areas overpoliced (Kane 2005).
- The targets of proactive policing are focused on the lifestyle crimes of the poor. These lifestyles, dress, and public comportment in turn are criminalized as innovations occur in them. Consider the cycle of concern as "crack cocaine" became popular in the inner city and powdered cocaine remained a middle- and upper-class habit: arrests and sentencing (use of federal courts to prosecute and giving more severe sentences for crack than for other forms of cocaine use and distribution) were adjusted.
- Police policies concerning the patterns of policing reflect class bias in terms of services provided and those willingly or voluntarily provided (Wilson 1967; Skogan et al. 2000). Data on responsiveness per se based on time show equal treatment by class and neighborhood (Maxfield, Lewis, and Szoc 1980).

- Police differentially respond to calls from disadvantaged areas. They come less often to calls in disadvantaged areas and downgrade the calls they do answer (Moskos 2008).
- Police are not trusted to be responsive in targeted areas (Venkatesh 2008; Stotland 2001; Carr et al. 2007); they report consistently being treated roughly, rudely, or with great and systematic indifference; these citizens are cynical about the criminal justice system.
- Violent incidents, shootings, fatal car chases and crashes, and other events that endanger the innocent are clustered in these areas.
- Citizens in such areas do not report being treated civilly and politically, and observations of police-citizen encounters are consistent with this proposition (Mastrofski, McCluskey, and Reisig 2002).
- The principal kinds of encounters differ in areas of varying disadvantage such that service—taking crime reports for insurance; looking for lost dogs, cats, and children; and listening to concerns—are characteristic of areas other than the disadvantaged areas. In disadvantaged areas, while service is provided, a significant number of encounters that are well remembered are contentious, proactive, or police initiated (Venkatesh 2006, 2008).

This list suggests that the rewards for compliance do not equally accrue to all and that, ironically, those who are at the greatest risk in spite of their compliance are not rewarded with the service (benefits) or visibly able to see the quality of life being sustained. There is substantial reason to question whether compliance is rewarded in fact.

The fourth assumption is that local norms that might be the source of compliance and agreed-upon coercion are not dramatized, visible, shared, or readily marked by police behavior (Meares and Kahan 1998). Although "law and economics" lawyers such as Meares, Kahan, Ellickson, Lessig, and Sunstein accept the symbolic functions of law and its indirect functions, they locate order in legal norms and sanctions rather than practices and actions. Meares and Kahan argue at the conclusion of their important trendsetting paper that local communities are victimized by criminals more than by the police. They urge stronger and more effective enforcement (1998, 816–27). They do emphasize the points made above that differential law enforcement reduces compliance but argue that police can reflect local norms when they carry out juvenile curfews, gang-control statutes, crackdowns, "pulling levers strategies," and co-opting ministers to policing functions (816–30) and argue for "community empowerment" through law enforcement (830–31). Not the least of the oddities in their argument is that local norms are reflected in the police tactics they advocate be used more generally. As (2007) points out, this nominal adherence to local norms is a quasi-legalistic notion that does not rest on what these local norms are, whether the police represent them, or whether police effectiveness of the style developed in disadvantaged areas is consistent with local norms and strengthens local organizations and collective efficacy. Although there is evidence that disadvantaged areas are characterized by concerns about crime and citizens attend meetings in considerable number (more in percentage terms than nondisadvantaged areas), the evidence concerning the improvement in the quality of life in these areas, or collective efficacy, remains to be seen.

Policing is not easily located within organizational theories drawn from market-oriented notions. Public policing is unusual because it has general collective obligations rather than local ones; it cannot move location, alter its clientele to reduce competition, gather more resources by increasing "production" or profits, or even easily reduce the strain on its scarce resources (Thompson 2003; Downs 1967). Its degree of flexibility is limited except in escalations up in crisis: its resources must be slack yet held ready for uneven demand. The connection between the collective obligation and violence is complex, but the ultimate rationale for the state's use is its own survival, a vague and often tacit matter. Nevertheless, the threat of violence awaits and can be legitimately applied if citizens fail to comply. The use of legitimate violence and collective orientation is tightly linked because if the general principles are denied by citizens, especially some large minority of the citizens, violence can escalate. As Clark and Sykes (1974, 456–60) correctly argue, the balance of factors constrain AADP nations to negotiate, avoid, and finesse violent confrontations. The balance of equilibrating factors constrains police violence even when it is legitimate and generally accepted by the public. I suspect that this is in part because tolerance of minorities, to whom violence is often directed, provides some limits on militaristic operations that are based on eradication, demoralization, and absolute domination of citizens. These latter are features of the war on the poor and minorities identified by some scholars (Miller 1996; Tonry 1995).

4. (Perceived) Fairness and Trustworthiness

Democratic policing, as argued in the introductory material above, implies both a moral and a philosophic grounding that entails trust and fairness in their practices. There is some sense in which the police represent the *unstated sociality of society*—that sense of collective obligation that binds people to each other in mutual and tacit obligation and cannot be reduced to rationality, perception, coercion, authority, or threat. In other words, civil democratic society is based not on coercion, ignorance, and error but rather on some sense of mutual obligation that resists destruction and elimination (Rosseau 1999 [1762] 1920; J. Rawls 2000). In this sense, democratic policing is embedded in unexamined and tacit value assumptions (Jones, Newburn, and Smith 1996; Bayley and Shearing 1996). Ironically, as Bayley points out (1992, 548–51), the extent to which organizational and structural factors of policing shape the quality of the practices remains to be explored. There are doubtless interaction effects: the political unit or police district as well as citizen compliance affects the quality of policing.

It is expected that the police are "fair" in the sense that they provide opportunities for requesting their services to all citizens, are responsive, and enforce the laws in a fashion that is not vastly disproportionate to the levels of known and reported crime. This premise has several aspects. One aspect is that the punishment on the street fits the behavior at issue. It is also expected that the police are tolerant and respectful of uncivil citizens and do not take advantage of their power to invoke working rules leading to corruption (Manning and Redlinger 1977). It is also expected that the actions of the police do not further damage the life chances of the weakest members of society—the powerless, the mentally ill, the homeless, the disabled and diseased. Each of these premises may be violated from time to time and becomes the focus of media amplification and distortion. The violations that punctuate the everyday assumptions of the democratic policing are also elastic, flexible, and variable.

Policing is dependent on trust, its market circumscribed by collective obligations, and the absence of a standard measure of "success" or even routine acceptable levels of performance, and its technology verbal. It runs on trust: the in-advance assumption of the worthiness and credibility of the interactions and intentions of others. The police both embody this and represent it to and for others. Indeed, one irony of reforming policing by means of "managerialism" (setting goals, objectives, and measures of assessment and auditing outcomes as a basis for further resource allocation [see Newburn 2003]) is that the embodied, interactional craft-based idea of policing, grounded in public trust, may be eroded.[6]

As argued in introductory materials of this book, the underlying principle of democratic policing should be Rawls's "difference principle" combined with his assumptions about citizens and their general willingness to support such practices. Given the current range of inequalities in education, opportunity, income, and skills, any action by police should not further increase these inequalities. They have little if any chance, even working in concert, as claimed by community policing advocates, of decreasing extant inequalities and their correlates—arrest and victimization rates.

5. Sacred and Profane Attributes

Like the army, police are linked to matters sacred as well as matters profane (Durkheim 1961, 52–53). The attributes assigned to the police and policing are not concrete matters that could be derived from personal, embodied experience. They do not stand as a thing. These attributes could arise only from experience of emotions that are collective, mysterious, distant, and awesome, and in turn are stimulated by the appearances of the police. While the police are a totem, they do not as persons inspire awe. They do so only in costume. Let us consider this argument in more detail.

Recall that Durkheim identifies objects representing moral force, something residing outside the individual, as apparent, as standing for something else that cannot be seen, touched, felt, smelled, or otherwise reified or made objective. These are social facts. The externality and constraint of these strategies rely on their grounding in matters that are out of sight. This theme is stated clearly by Durkheim: "A man is only a man because he is civilized. So he could not escape the feeling that outside of him there are active causes from which he gets the characteristic attributes of his nature and which as benevolent powers, assist him, protect him, and assure him of a privileged fate. And of course he must attribute to these powers a dignity corresponding to the great value of good things he attributes to them" (1961, 243).

Durkheim follows with a "matter-of-fact" observation in a footnote to the above paragraph that brilliantly cuts to the essence of policing. "This is the other aspect of society which, being imperative, appears at the same time to be good and gracious. It dominates us and assists us. If we have defined the social fact by the first of these characteristics [its imperative nature] rather than the second, it is because it is more readily observable, for it is translated into outward and visible signs" (ibid.). He then refers to his "rules" in the preface to the second edition.

In other words, the argument of Durkheim with respect to the externality and constraint of the police is that while they stand ready as a representative of moral force and coercion and even as a source of damaging violence, they are converted in everyday terms into a "sacred" or wholly beneficial entity. As Anne Rawls noted (1996), Durkheim made it possible to see the line between the scared and profane as relative, found everywhere, rather than absolute. The police, in short, are a profane thing created and re-created as sacred.

Durkheim notes that society is constantly turning secular things into sacred ones (1961, 243). By this he means that such sentiment is conferred or attributed to them because of shared feelings that arise in and through interaction. The opposite could be and is true as well—sacred things become tarnished, demoted, distrusted, and tainted. How is this organized, violent, systematically intrusive force viewed as a sacred thing? *Police Work* ([1977] 1997 hereafter cited as PW) argues that policing is a sacred entity. Durkheim claims more than this: his point is that the attribution of sacredness to the police is a result of its being placed in opposition to the other, the profane. The sacred and the profane are two quite different moral consciences or "mental states" (1961, 242). The existence of the police organization rationally formed and standing in connection to the state raises the possibility that it will be viewed, at least at some points in time and by some groups, as profane (ibid., 243). How is it possible that an occupation, policing, one of the most secular of all occupations, has been defined in this century and the last as a kind of sacred occupation, and how has it maintained this status?

The police are immediate representatives of the state. The police are the face-to-face embodiment of the civil government, of body politic in everyday life (Silver 1967). The appearance of an officer, on the one hand, can communicate traditional values, patriotism, chauvinism, honor, duty, and the like or the repressive or suppressive aspects of governance. The social distance granted is a kind of everyday mystification. The success of this communicative package depends in part on how the implementation of the state and its intentions are viewed (PW, 20). Police act in the interests of the state and stand ready to enforce its interests in a variety of ways. The direct political nature of their work is made invisible for the most part because they are that part that stands for the whole, and this connection is conflated with beliefs in law, morality, and the neutral statement that they demonstrate the "best interest of the state in the well-being of its citizens." In some ways, based on belief, the actions of police are symbolically tautological—whatever is done is right and true and consistent with law. That is, the police have elevated "law" and the rule of law to centrality in modern life, have identified with these symbols and slogans, and have called upon this close association as justification for their occupational activities. They are a part of what Mark Cooney (1998, 2003) calls a "privatizing of violence" but that in truth could be called the "civilizing of violence." Thus, the everyday activities of police on the beat become an illustration of the action of higher powers. The broad ideological canopy that results from the conflation of law, morality, and public serves to suffuse policing with moral integrity in spite of any internal divisions, schisms, or conflicts based on union membership, segment, age, rank, ethnicity, or gender. Unity is strength, as slogans, flags, seals, and uniform patches display outwardly. On the other hand, the actual diversity of feelings and actions of police are concealed, just as their presence obscures the deep conflicts in modern society about fairness, justice, truth, and equal status under law. Police stand for stability and order when watching over ballot boxes, voting booths, and courts. They are again double coded in that their presence makes the occasion an important one, but the implicit disorder requires their presence as a preventive force. They are the means by which the political authorities sustain the status quo and the status quo ante. Officers perform less dramatic but still necessary duties. In Boston, officers stand watch over "dangerous" places—construction sites, repair work, traffic hazards, accidents, and sporting events in which many thousands are participating and watching, such as professional football, basketball, and baseball matches. Here, more banal aspects of their representational work emerge—they stand ready in proximity to danger, even in a most distant manner, because they protect those unwilling or unable to do so. These are liminal spaces, neither dangerous nor safe, and the police mark them in a willing way (they are paid well for this work). The police serve society in danger-ous occasions of all kinds—riots, rebellions, uprisings, and quasi-rebellious events such as surfaced in the late sixties and early seventies. This work is complemented by their role in natural disasters such as floods, hurricanes, tornadoes, earthquakes, and massive fires. Their presence signals danger and risk as well as management of the same. They stand as deterrent: the police represent the capacity to deter citizens from committing acts that threaten the order they are believed to symbolize.

The police in action have symbolic properties: the officer as an icon, or min-iature representation of that which he or she represents—a conflation of the moral authority of the state; the implicit association in this culture with Judeo-Christian religions and religious beliefs; and the law is seen as an instrument and a symbolic surrogate for democracy and other loosely associated values. These latter values can, of course, vary widely by city and town. That which is associated with the officer is a categorical matter, to some great degree independent of the age, gender, color, and visible features of the officer as well as the invisible matters such as gender preference, education, religion, martial status, and so forth. The officer, in person, links the state, law, and morality, even as the presence of an officer is personal and immediate. The actions and even the appearance of the police stimulate response. An officer generates feelings of fear, deference, compliance, and implicit violence. Officers easily conflate their personal authority with that which they represent. This has both symbolic and actual components insofar as the violence of police is seen on television and in person, films, and plays as well as on the nightly news.

Police, like other sacred objects and people, are set aside, marked and drama-tized by the society in which they work by (in the past) their size, bulk, uniform, and uniform appearance, that is, their arms and accouterments. They are both vis-ible and unique for the combination of features in their ensemble. Their uniforms are unique and quaint, often suggesting associations with past modes of dress and actions—cavalry-style riding boots and near-jodhpur trousers, flat wool Stetson hats, clip-on ties. The detachable ties, an invisible aspect of the uniform, suggest further precaution against the lurking danger of being garroted with one's own neckpiece. While others may wear badges and uniforms, they are not heavily armed; if unique in uniformed appearance, security forces often mimic the vehicles, colors, badges, and equipment of the public police. It is illegal to imitate a police officer, and it is a federal offense to kill a police officer. While members of other occupations—repair and maintenance people and those who service across organizations, for example, if in constant touch with others via cell phones, radios, and computer-based communica-tion channels—they are not associated with the same sentiments or feelings aroused by the officer of the law. The uniforms are replete with quasi-sacred symbols—the U.S. flag in small and large versions (more obvious in cars and uniforms of all kinds after 9/11), patches with slogans referring to the city and its origins, and cars with similar decorations and often bumper stickers, flags on car aerials, slogans, and ad-monitions referring to civic duty and "Call 911." They display the secular symbols of power (the weapons, ammunition, pepper spray, and handcuffs) and science (the radio, computers, large and powerful vehicles, and special weapons and tactics, with outfits resembling ninjas of the modern age).

The police carry out important functions associated with the state and political order and both generate sentiments designed so others are encouraged to rely and depend on them. The police rank and are ranked. This is in part because the police act as buffers against the dirty, the unclean, the violent, and the unwanted segments of the population. They maintain boundaries between good and evil symbolically and are in touch, vaguely polluted by their tasks. They do dirty work, in Hughes's terms (1958). This marginal status redounds in some ways to their benefit, as we shall see. While they hold a good standing with the general population, their prestige declines as contact increases and is lowest among minorities and other marginal populations (Hagan and Peterson 1998). This ranking and boundary-maintaining work reflect the ways in which the dominant majority and government maintain the ranking and status ranking of groups. Enforcing the law almost always sets one group's interests against another's. When failing to enforce, exercising what is given quasi-legal status by labeling it discretion, some interests are being made legitimate over others. The police thus underscore, dramatize, or suppress the interests of some groups, some lifestyles, some preferences, and some sexual habits over others, and serve to redistribute status within groups. The ranking of groups can be seen by the sanctioning rates of the police (Turk 1969; Beckett, Nyrop, and Pfingst 2006; Beckett et al. 2005). These sentiments are aroused in action, and in public occa-sions in which the police act as participants, watchers, and tacit bystanders, standing ready to act at the edge of crowds, in, before, and after parades. They are part of the symbolic package that is required at public parades, demonstrations, strikes, and natural hazards. These are semisacred occasions in which they both are part of and stand part from the events. Some police departments, such as the Boston and other eastern big-city departments, have special ceremonial performative groups such a Gaelic pipe bands, drum and bugle corps, and motorcycle groups that perform intricate displays and performances on their huge powerful and resonant chrome-plated machines. Fire and police officers are featured on semipatriotic occasions such as St. Patrick's Day, Memorial Day, and Fourth of July parades. The Royal Canadian Mounted Police (RCMP), for example, known worldwide for its ceremonial dress of scarlet tunics and brown Stetson hats, has a unit that performs a "musical ride," a very complex, dizzying weave of horses and men with guidons flying and martial music playing, throughout Canada to huge warm and receptive crowds. They have also been called "boys on ponies."

The police are in some ways "modern knights," insofar as they are honored as violent people, obligated to serve and protect others, well equipped in visible and unique paraphernalia, sworn to uphold well-established values, and oriented to the collective rather than to themselves or even their occupation. They are inward looking, seeking to sustain their honor and practices in the face of a hostile world. They are, in theory, like knights, obligated to look after the poor, the less fortunate, the compromised and weak, and they are to eschew personal glory. They are not to use their power and authority to exploit others less fortunate than they, and they are not to use their powers for personal gain. Honor in medieval society was a mixture of attribution and character, while modern police carry the status of honor as a result of an earned position. The ambivalence toward the police is based on this tension between an earned status and an attributed character.

Police organizations and police officers, among others, do policing. A theory of police connotes an organizational and sociolegal analysis, while an analysis of policing suggests a concern for the patterns of recognition, sanctioning, and processing that exist and are associated with police organizations. I call these practices. As Loader and Mulcahy argue very persuasively, a comprehensive study of policing would examine the degree of fit between policing as a practice and organization with the sociocultural milieu in which it is embedded. In a useful turn of phrase, they call this the study of policing cultures (2003, 39ff). As this suggests, it is virtually impossible to isolate an explanation of what police do from what they are meant to do—the moral and political context in which they operate and display through their actions.

It should be said further that because the moral consensus of modern society is problematic due to the division of labor, rapid communication, and global commerce, it is through the practices that we observe (e.g., their situational use of violence and coercion) that police become known to citizens. While it could be argued that police are dramaturgical figures, engaged in a massive theatrical attempt to sustain the illusion and allusion of order and ordering, it is perhaps more accurate to argue that the police engage in a form of magic (see Mauss 1990; and Durkheim 1961, 58–60). Policing as a kind of magic can be distinguished from religion by the fact that is not an inclusive church that is totally bound to the collective and the society; it stands apart due to the division of labor, specialized costumes, roles, equipment, routines, and beliefs. Yet policing draws on the collective, the emotive basis of display, marking, and deference. It evokes feelings, yet it also uses them for ends and purposes other than and apart from the emotional state of the collective. In that sense, then, it is a form of magic, or a practice that mimics or simulates religion but stands apart from it. Durkheim, overstating this, claims that there are no lasting bonds between the magician and the collective (1961, 58). In another facet of policing, they are healers, those restoring order after calamity—illness, death, loss—and engaged in ceremonial efforts to restore that which is lost as well as marking it. But in each of these facets they are distinctive, so this is not a fundamental characteristic but a variable. I should like to suggest, finally, that the police in their collective role are both victim and sacrificer, and that these interchangeable roles have to do with the mediation of the profane and scared aspects of modern society (Hubert and Mauss 1964, 102–3). The argument would be that the police stand in one sense as godlike, or have been endowed with sacred properties, and hence they must be sacrificed from time to time to maintain connection to the otherwise highly secular society. This means that the death of an officer represents many things, but in part the dead officer is seen both as victim and as sacrificer for the whole. The police sacrifice themselves as an aspect of the holy, even if they die in the line of duty, shot or killed in a crash or chase. On the other hand, when they kill, coerce, shoot, or main, they sacrifice a victim on behalf of the society. Violence and sacrifice go hand in hand. The police when violent are intermediaries. In this way, they mark, dramatize, sustain, and renew those features of society and confer on themselves and others "the things they hold dear . . . the whole strength of society" (Hubert and Mauss 1964, 102). This means that the drama of policing is an intermediary force that links the secular, the profane, with the sacred, but the connection is always reversible. While the police are the most visible extensions of the state and its authority, they appear only as tokens or symbols of some underlying forces, or emotions. In this sense they are ambivalent, dangerous, multivocal, multilevel symbols, but they are not the thing represented; they are cues to deeper connections. The face of policing also varies, as when they appear to be magicians, merely manipulating the feelings of others, rather than renewing and invigorating them, or when they are flawed sources of sacrifice, victim, sacrificed, or the sacrificer.

Even their animals, dogs and horses, are quasi sacred. Why have dogs and horses remained on the payrolls and in the budgets of police departments in North America and the UK? Why have the forces of rationalizing, efficiency, and zero-based budgeting not focused on these costly beasts? Perhaps one of most telling aspects of symbolizing (of trust as well as sacred status) by inarticulate means is the role and status of animals in the Anglo-American police world. The animals are liminal—quasi sacred, one might say, as they mediate between the public (the profane) and the police (the sacred). This quasi sacredness remains in spite of the other technological innovations in policing. A special, and indicative, kind of trust is extended to police animals, which in many ways are the "sacred" core of a quasi-sacred occupation. They have a historic role, in that they were useful in colonial administrations and associated with the cavalry units that were combined with domestic forces in India and Ireland in the early nineteenth century and were ridden by the precursors of modern police, the Bow Street runners.[7]

6. Varying Degrees of Centralization

Some democratic forces are centralized, and others are decentralized. Bayley (1975, 1994) outlined differences in image, rank structure, and the division of labor with respect to police powers and duties in Western European states. The degree of centralization of authority and distribution of officers varies (Bayley 1992). The internal arrangements of AADP nations vary, including such matters as their stated levels of rank hierarchy (Bayley 1985), the distribution of officers to these ranks, the deployment of personnel to the given spatial distribution, and the per capita concentration of officers per citizen. These are variables.

7. Various Imagery

The imagery of the police in the society varies—this can be easily seen by comparing the armed, violent, and active "law enforcement" imagery of the American police officer, the more constrained and likable British "bobby," and the national icon the Royal Canadian "Mountie." Even the diminutive names, such as "bobby" and "Mountie," suggesting closeness, intimacy, and a nonthreatening manner, is indicative of a national imagery. Contrast these names with calling an officer a "cop"—a thief taker, a taker, or a copper (Dictionary.com). These observations signal that a catalog of policing's duties, influences, or even structure is not adequate to isolating the singular defining features of democratic policing.

8. Competition with Other Groups and Organizations

While it is true that many organizations police democratically, the idea of democratic policing itself cannot be limited to the functions of state-obligated organizations (as Bayley and Shearing claim [1996, 355]). The public police, because of their sanctioning power and access to the criminal justice system (see also Clark and Sykes 1974, 456–61, on sources of the coercive power of the police), are the *central node* in a network of formal social control agencies with varying degrees of capital. They cannot relinquish this position because they are the only collectively obligated force. Furthermore, they alone have the authority, the information, the secrecy, and the continuity in command to maintain a legitimate position over time. They are the central node in a network of sanctioning organizations.

Policing as a practice, which involves sanctioning in the interest of order and can arise from a diverse variety of organizations, legal and illegal, must be distinguished from the public police. The relative importance of private forms of policing is both a theoretical and an empirical question: efforts to promote new forms of private relationships, problem solving, and networking, discussed in the following chapter, are, on the one hand, efforts at reducing the authority of the public police by emphasizing indigenous modes of problem solving, community integration, and conflict resolution and, on the other hand, efforts to broaden the scope of the study of policing and social control (Johnston and Shearing 2003, and Johnston 1996; Shearing in Wood and Dupont 2006).

While democratic policing can be carried out by privately funded organizations, the necessary distinctions between public and private police would appear to be two: the access to primary criminal norms-sanctions as resource-control assets and the capacity to enter a case into the criminal justice (legal) system. Although private police of many sorts can arrest or hold a person, as can any citizen, they can neither initiate charges nor transfer a case into the system without sponsorship or cooperation by the public police (Rigakos 2002). It has been powerfully argued by (1989) that the central feature of legitimate police practice is that the probability of resistance on the part of those *to whom the sanction is applied* is low. Empirically, three further aspects of public state-sponsored policing recommend themselves: the advantage of centralized and deployable resources of the state that cannot be matched by localized control systems, the mandate of the public police to generalized security rather than the needs, interests, and material well-being of those who can pay for policing and other forms of security, and the absence of access to formal means of sanctioning as noted above.

9. Mandate

Police legitimacy, or the basis of a mandate, is acceptance of the scope of the occupation's claim, not an absolute or unchanging matter. There are cycles of expanding and contracting powers and tasks. In some respects, policing has widened the net of functions in which it is engaged under the rubric of community policing even while its claims have become more stridently based on crime control. Serious internal conflict may implicate the military and militarization in domestic matters (Bayley 1975, 367; Horowitz 2000, 443–71).

Challenges to police legitimacy, and conversely conflict, seem related in most cases to ethnic conflict (Horowitz 2000, 443–71). In addition, even in relatively stable democracies, the percentage of visible ethnic minorities is correlated with ongoing conflict, violence, and crime. Only in democratic nations in which indigenous peoples of color have been massacred, died out, or were never present have very stable systems of policing remained decentralized.

Furthermore, the growth of miscellaneous forms of *formal* (legitimate, authoritatively, and bureaucratically structured) policing have proceeded apace— these include private policing, transnational private policing (such as the "corporate warriors" described in Singer 2003), and a variety of specialized federally employed police (e.g., British transport and nuclear police, special constables, reserve officers, and community support officers) (Johnston 1992, 2005; Bayley 1992, 523–27).

Clearly, the democratic police operate within constraints arising from the ecology of other organizations with which they compete, the economy, the polity, the cultural assumptions and practices of a people, the available technology, and the law (Clark and Sykes 1974, 466–72). Democratic police agencies have multiple levels of responsibility only partially specified by law (Morris and Geller 1992). These are in part a result of crises and special-event considerations (hurricanes, floods, demonstrations, national political conventions, major parades) and in part historically determined by political events (e.g., the division in local units such as constabularies; provincial police; county, township, and city divisions; and contractual arrangements for policing). Arrangements precipitated by homeland security issues in American counties and the RCMP in Canada and partially shaped by agreements of mutual aid (UK) or MOUs (memorandums of understanding) are ambiguous, negotiated, and fragile. Thus, the U.S. Army, the U.S. National Guard, the Gen d'armes, or the Caribinieri can be mobilized to do local policing in crisis situations. The recent history of Canadian rearrangements of provincial police (the creation of new areas such as the Hamilton Regional Police), the downsizing of British constabularies from some 125 in 1962 to the present 43, and the expansion and contraction of local police in the United States suggests that the shape of policing is altered by direct political decisions and laws. Some of the most radical shifts have been the result of the consolidation of city-county government in Portland–Multnomah County in Oregon, Charlotte-Mecklenburg in North Carolina, and Miami-Dade in Florida and the model of a public safety commissioner in Atlanta who heads both police and fire departments.

FUNCTIONS OR PRACTICES?

This brings us to democratic police practices. While the democratic police are legally guided, they are as a result neither *essentially* "law enforcement organizations" nor "security" organizations. Whereas the law is one source of police legitimacy, the connections made between police crime control and legal changes or the damage done to communities as a result have not been explored by commonsense "theories" of policing such as "fixing broken windows." Even democratic police can carry out nondemocratic practices that are grounded in misguided and wrong social science (these issues are discussed in subsequent chapters).

All nation-states have developed a domestic police of some sort. Domestic police agents are variously visibly responsible for national-security types of policing in which the active policing is linked to protection of national interests in addition to local interests. In effect, this broadens the mandate of "first responders" (as police and fire and emergency personnel have been labeled post-9/11). It shadows also the functions associated with high policing (see above and Brodeur 2003). The analogy that differentiates local democratic policing from intelligence-based high policing also obtains *within* the military with respect to its tasks and moral division of labor (Hersh 2004).

Nation-states have also developed security police for the protection of sacred persons, places, and buildings and to carry out high policing that connotes questions of national security (Brodeur 1983, 2003). All democratic systems carry out high policing, or policing directly rationalized as being in the interest of national security, and the significance and consequences of such policing vary over time. Since the amount of high policing done by domestic police is almost impossible to determine, it can only be said that it varies and increases in times of announced crisis, civil war, or internal or external threat. Democratic states vary in their concern for "high politics" and matters of "intelligence gathering" and use. Arguably, the German, Italian, French, and Japanese police have emphasized intelligence and monitoring of the civilian population more than other democratic states, and certainly more than the Anglo-American countries (Australia, Canada, New Zealand, and the United States). Their actions have included maintaining domination or the hegemony of the current government; strategies that avoid the appearance of compliance with the law; monitoring political dissent and terrorism; extensive use of undercover agents or agent provocateurs; preventive detention, raids, and surveillance; a preference for prevention or unknown interventions rather than known and named police "operations"; and anticipatory actions rather than responses to known events, crimes, or delicts. Importantly, democratic societies have sought, except in times of extreme crisis, to limit public police powers via law, civil traditions, and supervisory mechanisms such as commissions, special judicial inquiries, and civilian complaint processing systems. As Brodeur (2007) argues in some detail, there is an inevitable tension between high and low policing, as both are necessary.

CONCLUSION

This chapter has wrestled with the role of violence in modern policing, outlined some nine dimensions of policing, and distinguished high policing from routine domestic functions. This work provides a broad tapestry for the next chapter, which concerns the analytical framework of justice and policing based on the Rawlsian difference principle.

CHAPTER THREE

Policing According to the Difference Principle

The previous chapters examined some interconnections between conceptions of democracy, democratic policing, and definitions of police and policing. Much was omitted in these prior definitions. These omissions reflect the unquestioning natural attitude—taking for granted all that is outside the penumbra of the denotative. What is not said is what is tacitly expected of the police rather than the often repeated cliché that the police enforce the law, or fight crime, or protect and serve. Recall the abbreviated or skeleton version of the central argument of this book presented in the preface. This version was based on the two fundamental principles of justice with special emphasis on the difference principle. This states that any policy affecting extant inequalities should be to the benefit of the least advantaged (JF, 42–43). Since it is unlikely that the police can actually reduce inequality, and in fact have no obligation to do so, a political philosophy with policing in mind and based on the justice-as-fairness idea requires some modification. The preface argued that the justice as fairness principle in regard to policing should be refocused in a manner consistent with the Hippocratic oath: the police should strive to minimize harm. The working version of this abstraction in regard to policing means that any action, planned, stated, or enacted, should not increase inequalities. How can this grand working principle be grasped as a set of objectives or guidelines? The key points below reflect the arguments of Liang, Bayley, and Bittner in regard to democratic policing. General expectations of policing are questions of function: if the below principles or rules of thumb are observed, we might expect of (domestic) democratic policing that it functions as:

- Constrained in dealing with citizens and fair in procedure. These dealings should entail a degree of civility in interactions and in police practices. This excludes under virtually all conditions torture, mass detentions, "round-ups" based on political beliefs and not behaviors, and lengthy suspensions of habeas corpus for citizens.

- Largely reactive to citizens' complaints—reticent rather than sporadic—and not given to frequent secret proactive interventions, crackdowns, sweeps, and militaristic "operations."
- Equal in its application of coercion to populations defined spatially and temporally. The level of coercion is based on minimalist criteria, much like counterinsurgency tactics (Nagl 2007), rather than a mechanistic "use of force continuum."[1]
- Fair in hiring, internal evaluation, promotion and demotion, transfers, and disciplinary treatment of employees, officers, and civilians.
- Competitive in an environment that includes private police, vigilante groups, posses, and ad hoc policing under the guise of "self-help" and revenge. It may include the National Guard and the armed forces (army, navy, coast guard, and the air force). This implies formal and informal modes of cooperation rather than unified and unrelenting actions.
- Accountable and responsible for its actions individually and organizationally (Brodeur 1997).

Each of these points requires some elaboration and explanation.

"Constrained in dealing..." Liang has suggested a useful term—*legalistically guided,* rather than *law abiding* or *law enforcing,* as these later terms beg the question of what laws are not enforced and how often and the degree to which enforcing the law means occasionally breaking it. By extension, then, interrogations cannot involve either psychological or physical torture, and interactions should be minimalist and focused rather than pretext searches or stops.

"Largely reactive ..." The basis for this is the Rawlsian principle that argues that any policy should be stated in favor of the least-advantaged members of society (JF, 42–43). In fact, Rawls does not deal specifically with criminal matters; however, it follows that any application of sanction by the state is a kind of "policy," and systematic application of sanctions, even informal ones, in areas, to groups, should not be preferred. This restriction also includes the absence of secret, non-court-sanctioned surveillance, warrantless non-consent searches, no systematic named concern for antiterrorism, and no governmentally sponsored terrorism—tactics based on surprise, absent legal restrictions. This provision amplifies the procedurally fair principle insofar as antiterrorism and governmentally sponsored terrorism are categorically guided, targeting groups rather than the behavior of individuals.

"Equal in its application..." In effect, this means some proportionality and restraint in response regardless of the violence of citizens directed to officers. It also connotes

an aim that might be called, following Liang, "minimal damage to civility" or restraint in manners and morals in regard to others.

"Fair in hiring…" Police should be hired in line with fair competition of persons for the positions and, once hired, evaluated, transferred, promoted, or demoted by known and transparent processes that are in turn limited by appeal and provide for remedy. The resignation and firing of officers is generally well protected by civil service and or union contracts. The primary reason for urging such provisions is that if police are treat others fairly, they must be so regarded within the organization.

"Competitive in an environment …" Modern police work in the shadow of other regulatory or policing agencies broadly defined. Although it has long been assumed (since Weber) that the key defining feature of democratic policing is that they possess a monopoly of legitimate force, this is clearly not the case in modern societies. The modern democratic police compete with the above-named organizations for the policing mandate or, metaphorically, the "market share" of legitimate force, but the competition also obtains with semilegitimate groups such as lynch parties and self-help groups. Increasingly, this competition is blurred, as the armed forces are engaged domestically and abroad in "institution building," the police engage in more paramilitary activities, and private armies for hire are used domestically (e.g., Scahill 2007 on Blackwater in New Orleans). On the other hand, when the police or policing is secondary, such as the case of colonial police (India, pre–World War II, Northern Ireland prior to 1998, British police in Caribbean colonies, and French and German African colonies), police in the context of counterinsurgency activities (Shanghai in 1936–1939, Northern Ireland in 1969–1998, Malaysia, and Vietnam) or in totalitarian policing (Nazi Germany, the USSR under Stalin, China under Mao), or the police of the occupied nation in a period of conquest (Vichy France, Hungary, Poland, Romania, Czechoslovakia, and the rest of Eastern Europe under the Nazis) that operates without political constraints on citizens of the nation-state, the question of legitimacy is raised, and the competition slides into anarchy. The rules governing their proper operating seem to depend on the role of the individual rights (high in the case of policing under nonmartial law or suspended habeas corpus, low in regard to the military), the rules of engagement (periodic engagements and a passive-reactive stance otherwise for the police; constant conflict in the military case), the relevance of international and national conventions embedded in the law (high in the case of local law and little relevance in the case of international law [although this is changing with the growing powers of the European Court at Strasbourg], ambiguous with regard to conventions given the last years of armed conflict, especially in Iraq), the weapons permissible (limited in the case of police in domestic context and wide ranging up to and including nuclear weapons in the case of the military), and the definition of targets (civilians with individual liberties and protections for police, focus on combatants and the exclusion of noncombatants for the military). This last point, since the last years of World War II with the

firebombing of Birmingham and Coventry in the UK and Dresden, Düsseldorf, and Cologne in Germany and the nuclear bombing of Hiroshima and Nagasaki, is debatable. The present preference for local, regional wars rather than continent-wide or worldwide wars has made these distinctions between policing and war making, civilian and combatant participants, conventions about weapons use and torture, and the sanctioning force of international law subject to debate.

"Accountable and responsible..." Accountable means in this context that the police are required to explain, to account for, agency actions (Stenning 1995). The higher the rank of the person in the organization, the more they are accountable for the agency's actions. "Acting on my orders," on the other hand, the Eichmann defense, is not an acceptable standard (Brodeur 1997, 259–68). The organization is responsible, as are individuals, but the standard is higher for agencies and their top management. Since agencies of social control are based in part on secrets and secrecy, they cannot be forced to divulge matters deemed secret, and in parallel fashion, individual officers cannot be compelled to divulge agency secrets.

As a kind of overview comment, one might array policing systems in democratic or democratic societies as three ideal types: "democratic policing" as defined above, "quasi-democratic systems" such as that obtaining in Northern Ireland (Weitzer 1990, 1995), and nondemocratic systems such as that found in Nazi Germany (Manning 2009).

A DEFINITION OF POLICE AS AN ORGANIZATION

The police as an organization in Anglo-American societies, constituted of many diverse agencies, are authoritatively coordinated, legitimate organizations. They stand ready to apply force up to and including fatal force in politically defined territories. They seek to sustain politically defined order and ordering via tracking, surveillance, and arrest. As such, they require compliance to command from lower personnel and citizens and the ability to proceed by exception.

The modifications from a definition first offered in *Policing Contingencies* (2003, 41–42) are several (see also the epilogue). The police are embedded in a policing culture reflecting the values, beliefs, myths, and historical conventions. This, in turn, is a facet of the mandate or the ever-negotiated contract between the institution of policing and the public. Whatever the police do, as Bittner points out, is produced in a situation and explained or accounted for later. The rhetoric, I have argued, justifies in the political arena the idealization of policing, not its actual practices. The organization and the role may differ: the democratic police may not always police democratically, and police in nondemocratic states can police democratically. The belief that they do not violate unstated democratic principles is essential to their survival in a competitive organizational network of service providers (see Clark and Sykes 1974, 460–61, 466–72). Democratic policing, on the other hand, is an attempt to gear practices to the behaviors and actions of people in the interest of order. But it is not a single order that is to be produced by such police responses. It is the order suggested by that which touches off the ordering: calling the cops. By *authoritatively coordinated,* I refer to the fact that the agency is accountable, as are the officers. They can be fired. A second addition is the focus on compliance. The authority of the organization to sanction increases the probability of compliance with orders. The compliance of citizens to requests and commands is implicit in discussions of democratic policing, but often this is truncated into a Bittner-like point that police can or may use force, not that they very rarely do! A third addition to the earlier definition is marking the role of tracking and surveillance. This will continue to vex those who wish to control the police, as their capacity to do so has vastly increased in the past twenty-five years. Sanctioning powers, that is, the use of the criminal sanction and access to the criminal justice system, are an important feature that distinguishes the public from the private police. Private police on duty are often off-duty public police who can exercise the arrest sanction, so that the monopoly of control of the arrest sanction is less clear in use than might be expected, but the limiting factor is that private police cannot per se enter a case into the criminal justice system: they cannot apply the criminal-law sanction action to behavior. The implicit bargain or negotiated order between top command and lower participants is often overlooked in the capacity of police to act consistently. This does not depend on policing as a military rank–based structure. The importance of rule by exception is the key to the covert power of bureaucratic commanders—they can rule by exception in given cases to sustain top command power and authority. Police are ultimately dependent on citizens' compliance, and the organization relies on loyalty and willingness to act without question on order when required.

Some Additional Elaborations

The above working definition, like all definitions, contains key terms that could be subjected to a radical deconstruction or elaboration. This definition is intended to locate AADP policing as an ideal type that can be located in the dimensions laid out in the previous chapter. In this sense, policing is a system or configuration of elements that varies over time and place along the dimensions indicated. All of the stated points of this definition can be specified by some additional observations. These arguments are made by way of limiting the extension of the definition.

1. The police are a public entity and accountable. In fact, the police hold themselves accountable in their own terms and to themselves. The rhetoric of police management is misleading when the word *accountable* is used. This means in the police contest that managers can be moved around, embarrassed, or demoted if they fail to meet the expectations of the top command (Bratton and Knobler 1998). Evidence is consistent and convincing (Walker 2005) that police accountability in general is very weak to elected politicians, "the public" civilian review boards, or other modes of constraint. The most powerful constraints on police officers are their good sense, aging, and compliant citizens. Recent work by lawyers, political scientists, sociologists, and police administrators suggests that it is the good sense of the force and its leaders rather than law and legislation that produces and sustains democratic policing (Stenning in Beare and Murray 2007). On the other hand, the punitive aspects of law (federal civil rights restraining orders, affirmative action degrees, civil and criminal suits against individuals and departments) have reduced police authority considerably in the past twenty years.

2. Although police are the proximate face of the state shown to citizens, individual citizens cannot guide the organization. This guidance is ultimately political in the best sense of the word (Bayley 1992, 130–35; 995, 264–73) in an operational sense, not delegated (see Stenning in Beare and Murray 2007). The most powerful mode of ensuring compliance is a bureaucratic form in modern society. Voluntary, part-time, and semiorganized groups are not police in line with this definition. They may be norm enforcers, but they do not act on behalf of the collective interest and are not therefore police. In this sense, too, these groups cannot be seen as components in a network of police but are part of a network of social control. This distinction goes to the issue of "governance" of security. That remains a metaphor in which the primary and most powerful symbolic role remains and will remain with the public police. Furthermore, the public police must be the cynosure of the state's authority. They cannot abdicate or delegate their responsibilities or be anything other than the original source of authority (the common-law basis for policing of all citizens). In part, the centrality of the public police lies in their mandate within the moral division of labor. Recall that police legitimacy is the result of a negotiated acceptance of the scope of the occupation's claim by diverse publics, not an absolute or unchanging matter. It reflects local conditions, the local polity, and local elites' expectations of policing. Legal, cultural, and social forces combine to sustain legitimacy or to erode it. This legitimacy requires their attention to fairness and justice and to the protection of the less powerful. This obligation does not rest elsewhere.

3. The symbolic role of public police cannot be eschewed by them. Police actions symbolize trustworthiness and may increase trust via reassurance, but this is a positive externality of their actions. On the other hand, they can profoundly reduce the trust others have in them by actions that do not respect citizens and are part of wide and indiscriminate "operations," "sweeps," and "crackdowns" that take in all "known suspects" regardless of their current and observable or verifiable criminal activity and by arrests and stops based on color or national origin. Policing holds out violence and enacts symbolic violence, or actions that produce the complicity of people in their own destruction and reduced quality of life. By eroding social integration, police redistribute life chances not only immediately but in the course of subsequent "reintegration" (Rose and Clear 1998). As Loader and Walker have so eloquently stated, the symbolic burden of the police extends far beyond crime control, and in fact to be so limited restrains their powers and authority.

4. While violent and coercive, police violence is generally cautious, directed, and ready, but once in action can explode. Violence and the sacred are complementary not contradictory, and so the police are both violence and quasi sacred (1972). The violence is mannered and stylistic, not impulsive and random. The march of officers in full battle dress toward a crowd, the swarming officers to assist an "officer down," and the teams that appear at hostage situations are all organizational weapons, coordinated, guided, and ready, waiting. The term *standing ready* echoes Weber's terms that imply that the threat of violence by the police awaits and is there to be imposed if proffered solutions of the police are not embraced by the citizen. This is strategic power—the capacity to persuade in advance. The right to apply force and the capacity to do it should be distinguished as well as the questions of where, when, and how much. The questions of how and why the police are mobilized on behalf of the state, especially in massive public order uprisings, are still in debate (see chapters 10 and 11).

5. The specification of the relevant political territory in which a police legitimately polices is itself increasingly a problematic issue. In theory, it has been used since Weber's classic and parsimonious definition of the role of law in a state that rests on the notion that legitimate authority increases the subjective probability of accepting response (1947), and that with a monopoly of coercive force, compliance can be produced in the long run regardless of resistance. One can now define the active domain of a police force, but that domain can include anywhere a police can act with impunity. Power has trumped law outside the margins of national states. As Bowling (2005) correctly argues, the "relevant territory" for force is an elastic matter and not defined narrowly by the territorial limits of the nation-state. Police, even local—territorially bounded—police, now have international obligations as a result of local fears of terrorism, cheap global travel, rapid communications, and the U.S. creation of the Department of Homeland Security. Trends toward international, transnational, and meta-national policing; international agreements, task forces, ad hoc "policing actions," as in Kosovo, Bolivia, Colombia, and Haiti; and corporate warriors (Singer 2002) have blurred boundaries of policing and its links to land, or a defined territory (Sheptycki 2000). A further development is the increased use of the military in "domestic" or everyday policing as a form of foreign aid, an aspect of an internal revolutionary situation (as of 2009, consider the state of affairs in Iraq, Somalia, Colombia, and the Sudan), and troops acting as advisers, giving training to, assisting, and patrolling with local police (Kaplan 2005). Policing is done by extension through treaties, UN agreements, loose confederations such as the EEU, unilateral action, international task forces, and by fiat (e.g., U.S. extension of the twenty-mile limit, U.S. policing worldwide of terrorist weapons, and the occupation and policing of Iraq since March 2003). The growth of miscellaneous *formal* (legitimate, vocational, authoritatively, and bureaucratically structured) policing has proceeded apace. These include private policing, transnational private and public policing (such as the "corporate warriors" described in Singer 2002), and a variety of specialized public police organizations (e.g., British transport police, special constables and reserve officers, as well as municipal police [see Jones and Newburn 1996, 1998]).

The levels of obligation, federal, state, and local, and the mesh of laws in which such organizations operate suggest the value of a network or nodes-of-authority approach to policing (Johnston and Shearing 2003). Unfortunately, discussions based on typologies confound concrete nation-states and their police systems with ideal types composed of exaggerated, hypothetical abstractions designed to illicit contrasts and theoretical comparisons. It is perhaps a residual form that requires attention at this time, an *archetype*, or a form called democratic policing, rather than a specific subtype of policing organized (variously) around nation-states, political traditions, and legal or religious belief systems.

With these developments in mind, the current position is that the core of policing in AADP nations remains local in character, and decentralized authority is both preferred and sanctioned by law in Anglo-American societies. The case for this focus is the long-standing elision of the state with law and the structure of law that has produced tacit compliance in Western states and the view that the state protects individual liberties even as it stands as a threat to them; the centralized and deployable resources, capacity, skills, personnel, and education remain in the control of the nation-state.

While transnational and international policing patterns have been studied, the presumption is a basic model or paradigm of policing originating with the Peel model and the variations from it being taken as "data" or news. Diffusion of practices across borders (Deflem 2004), cooperation among states (Sheptycki 2002), imposition of quasi-policing practices as army based (Kaplan 2005), and regional imperialism (Bowling 2005) are all studies of public policing variations. The growth of these forms provides a variety of contrast conceptions. On the other hand, private armies, corporate warriors, and other mercenaries analyzed with great insight and detail by Peter Singer (2002) are not engaged in policing at all but are acting as armies in areas of international or internal conflict. They engage in torture and practice antiterrorism and terrorism and therefore are not democratic police.

6. Police manage order; they do not produce it. What can be said is that given visible variations in orderliness, the police act. In this sense they shape order and punctuate their role as so shaping it. It is a fallacy to attribute to them ordering per se, absent compliance, officer loyalty, citizens' obligations, and legitimacy. This is of course one reason terrorism strikes such fear in orderly societies—it demonstrates that virtually any concerted effort to produce violence is surely to succeed with fearful consequences. Clearly, the notion of providing order and ordering is a gloss on the basically contentious character of order itself. Policing, indeed, is a response to the need to create a sense of order that transcends the local neighborhood, blood kin–based community, and obligations that in the past have "trumped" those of citizenship. "Ordering" in short is a political matter. It is not defined in law; only its problematic or absent status is. As Bittner correctly points out, any action or group from which resistance might be imagined can be the target of policing. *Political ordering* has no fundamental or pure definition. When the police in cities such as New York, Newark, or Boston use crime-attack and crackdown tactics to differentially enforce order in small concentrated minority areas, they are ordering in respect to political values, but they may not be the values of the local community (Meares and Kahan 1996). When minor violations are used as a means to create an atmosphere of fear and risk for all citizens, regardless of their behavior, political interests are being invoked. This is the specious aspect of the broken-windows (BW) claim to define what is order and disorder and to act to coerce compliance with a notional idea derived from class-based interests (Harcourt 2001).

Perhaps the most sophisticated clarification of the Bittner position on order, central to this definition, is the work of Loader and Walker (2007, 106–15). They argue correctly that police supply direct coercion and violence in a direct physical fashion. This might be called instrumental violence, although the purpose of violence is always arguable, especially when it is applied situationally and justified later verbally and quasi legally. The justification function is an invisible aspect of state ordering—legitimation by naming.[2] They contrast this with what might be called expressive violence, or violence that rests on the compliance of those to whom it is directed. It is in effect violence that creates insecurity from whatever source. As noted above, this can be better seen as a matter of what is absent than what is present—anxiety, fear, or disease that attends a lack of connection, relatedness, and feelings of integration or attachment. Order is maintained by police in the breach in the sense that they apply coercion "as and when" they perceive it is needed to sustain a sense of order. This sense is perhaps a nostalgia, or a quest for the order once seen, rather than an abstract order. In this sense, the police are a conservative force (Loader and Walker 2007, 102ff). They are always looking backward in their efforts to front-load order. The interests of the state, whatever they might be materially or symbolically, are always in order, an echo of the past projected into the future. This is also why the police are neutral in favor of the state's interests in order and ordering. The question of whether states encourage a unitary order and sense of order is rooted in nineteenth-century thinking about community, projected cynically by modern states (Anderson 1983).

The police's claim for maintaining a single and rather counterfactual notion of order produces contradictions. The claim that law is universally and systematically applied cannot be sustained factually; the here and now and immediate aspect of "order" cannot therefore be tied to any particular order or ordering but rather are tied to its situated nature, and the equality of citizens before the law is of course a hypothetical. These consistent counterfactuals bring to the surface premises explored later:

- The necessity of dramatizing their work, especially through rhetoric, since the vast majority of people never encounter a police office in uniform and gather most of their imagery from television, is the centrality of the police to order and ordering.
- The trust in the police that they both sustain and cultivate is grounded in attachment to beliefs, local knowledge, and ignorance.

- The compliance of citizens to the police, consistent and overwhelming even in contested areas and neighborhoods of large cities, trumps the claims of the police to the fundamental necessity of their role and policing. Periods of police strikes in the last century in New Orleans, Montreal, and Boston were orderly.
- The elision with and confusion of law and order.
- The notion that individualism and the implicit social contract ensure equal treatment of all citizens.[3]
- The assumption that practices of policing must succeed in the here and now and over and over, whatever the philosophical grounding. All totalitarian states are governed to some degree by the rule of law and show high levels of compliance. In Nazi Germany, consistent support in elections was shown by the people of Germany for the party, the state, and, by implication, the police (Evans 2003).

7. The police are a political force, but they are not a neutral political force. While the police in Anglo-American societies have traditionally eschewed their political role as citizens and as an organization, the police as an organization are not a neutral, nonpolitical force. They reflect political interests in their choices; their allocation of resources and personnel to given areas and crimes; their concentration on gangs, persons, and ethnic groups; their hiring practices and their public statements; their lobbying for laws and regulations, their pressure on district attorneys; their use of the media to promote their policies and mollify criticism; their production of official crime statistics and arguments for their control of variations in them; and in their political activities as citizens. They are a powerful media presence in regard to any issue surrounding order, security, or crime. They occupy a niche in a competitive network of service agencies. The police have interests and ideological readings of events and often take self-serving actions. They can call for strikes and often are unionized in big cities. This enables systematic strikes, "working to rule," "blue flu" or "sick-outs," and sabotage at the lower levels of the organization. As Bayley points out, summarized above, in a penetrating introduction to his classic work *The Police in the Political Development of India* (1969, 16–30), the police can facilitate democratic political development in a variety of complex ways, but it is perhaps constraint or an unwillingness to alter the political process directly by differential threat to political groups, failing to support state policies, acting to benefit constituent political groups, and by the quality and kind of violence used. These are, unfortunately, policy or normative generalizations, not descriptions of practices. The book makes abundantly clear that the Indian police fail in respect to all of these ways.

8. Compliance with command and loyalty in the face of danger and risk are essential in an organization that is violent and faces uncertainty repeatedly. The process of ensuring loyalty and compliance with command has been seen in modern times, at least for the past forty years, as a matter of communicational surveillance, tracking, and command and control rather than a result of personal direct supervision and interactional nuance (Reiss and Bordua 1967). This notion of control and surveillance assumes that other norms are stripped of their relevance and power to influence behavior—by training, occupational socialization, punishment, and reward. The traditional concern of the chief, extending from at least 1829, has been occupational malfeasance, indolence, corruption, and violence more than the quality of police performance. Persuading officers to comply is a delicate matter in part because they are granted an a priori status of trustworthiness by citizens (this does vary by age, race, and class).

9. The police are engaged in dangerous work but are revered and respected more than others who do dangerous work because they do honorable work for us. Consider the comparative aspects of the job—danger, violence, uncertainty, and choice. The police chose the job and were then selected, trained, and acted voluntarily to accept the position and its vagaries—this defines it at least to some degree as an altruistic act. They take risks on behalf of others and manage risks for others. They direct violence toward others and also receive it. They are injured and die in the line of duty. Police take risks for others, manage other people's risks, and are seen to do this voluntarily and for minimal pay. Although they have overtime possibilities, their pay scale is flat, determined in most cases by unions, and highly limited at the top. The military and the members of the fire service also do dangerous work on behalf of the society and may be injured or die in the line of duty. Officers are volunteers. The military take risks for others and on behalf of the society, and thus their sacred status is parallel and shares perhaps historic origins. The military, however, currently is an ambiguous category, because in the past men have been drafted for service and have not chosen to confront risks or to be injured or die. The reservists serving in Iraq are also anomalous in that they chose not active wartime duty but "backup" and support, assumed to be in this country. The volunteer service that has been developed since the Vietnam War includes those who have chosen to serve but stands symbolically in an ambiguous place between a "professional service" and a fully draft-based, impressed armed force made up of those who have not chosen to serve. Members of the fire service act, it is seen, entirely in the interests of the collective, protecting lives and property and taking risks for and on behalf of others. They are called and serve; they do not set fires or intervene to fan the flames, as police can and often do. They act consistently otherwise in a preventive and reactive stance. They react to risks and take them on board. Other work—fishing, mining, lumbering, mostly primary extractive tasks—are also very dangerous. Their occupants are elective, although they are often hereditary in nature—as is policing—but they are not attributed altruistic or semisacred features because the risks are taken on behalf of their own self-interests and for their families, and their pay reflects both the risks and their successes. They are seen as courageous and honorable and deserving of respect, but do not garner sacred status. Consider, finally, professional athletes carrying out violent and dangerous work with both direct and indirect long-terms effects on health and well-being. They act on behalf of the society in many respects, as both serious amateurs and professionals. They take risks for others so that others may feel risks vicariously. They live "on the edge" for us in a positive sense. Their risk taking is self-satisfying and rewarded, and it is seen as a positive contribution to the amusement, distraction, leisure, and identity of crowds and masses of people. The violence directed toward athletes is in the interest of the game and to each other "by choice."

Thus, it would appear that policing is problematic and virtuous in part because of the uncertainty, negative risk, and implicit danger that are intrinsic to the work. These negative risks are endured in protection of others and at risk to themselves. The job is chosen in good faith, and officers serve the general will or collective well-being. This distinguishes policing from other dangerous, uncertain, and honored occupations.

10. The organizational environment of AADP nations is punctuated by concerns about loyalty and commitment. The organization is divided in its orientation to the external and internal publics, by management versus labor, by cliques and cabals, and, increasingly, by tensions amplified by gender and ethnic relations internally. These audiences or stakeholders shape the orientation of its top command, and thus implicitly the organization's strategies and tactics. The loyalty of the police is assumed but rarely tested. Having said that they carry out dangerous work and are committed in theory to the state or local government, to whom do the police owe their loyalty in a democratic society? Let us set aside other cases that do not fit the question because they do not involve societies with fully formed democratic policing according to the above definition. I include here formerly democratic societies policed under an occupation after conquest (countries under the Third Reich from 1939 to 1945). Policing in Vichy France from 1940 to 1944 is illustrative (2007; Marrus and Paxton 1995). The evidence of the very detailed historical analysis of Marrus and Paxton is that the heads of the police, whether ministers in the Ministry of the Interior or War, the prefecture of the Paris police, or the chief of the notorious special Jewish police operating semilegitimately under the Commissariat Général aux Questions Juives commission on Jewish affairs, were fully compliant with the wishes, explicit and implicit, of the German occupying forces. The Vichy system of policing mirrored that of the French state with mobile motorcycle police, gendarmerie, and local police. The Paris Prefecture, employing some 30,000 officers, remained in full force. The German Army, technically in charge of order, seemed to permit the SS and Gestapo (used as a general term for the three forms of policing in Germany that were a policing system based on loyalty to Hitler, the Nazi Party, and the Third Reich). With some 3,000 German army officers acting as police, some of them SS, (this figure, from Marrus and Paxton 1995, 242, for the summer of 1942, is unclear; it might include the military police as well as the other police organizations or not), These officers made arrests of Jews; carried out terrorist-like raids to arrest Jews for various offenses, such as not wearing the Jewish Star of David; loaded Jewish deportees onto trains; guarded and unloaded them at concentration and holding camps; enforced other laws that were not impinging on German interests, that is, ordinary crimes; guarded borders and denied movement of French citizens in and out of Vichy and to foreign countries; and were otherwise trustworthy. The turning point came perhaps in late 1942 when the "Final Solution" began to be enacted, preceded by large-scale deportation of French workers to be employed in the German war effort (see also Kitson 2008 on Vichy government agents' hunting Nazi spies within occupied France). While the French continued to police in collaborative fashion, their German supervisors in the SS began to have doubts about their usefulness after late 1942 (the invasion of North Africa and the collapse of the "nonoccupied" Vichy zone). I also include democratic societies with weak and transitional governments (the Weimar Republic from 1917 to 1933)[4] and societies under declared civil war or revolution (the United States from 1860 to 1865 Palestine currently [Lia 2006]). In all of the above cases, paramilitary forces, private police, the army, vigilante forces, and public police act, but the fundamental bases for legitimacy under these conditions are so tenuous as to make loyalty problematic.

Various notions describing the locus of loyalty such as "the law," "the job," slogans such as "We preserve and protect," well-displayed local icons, seals and symbols on the car, the viable and unique uniform, and the large, stark police buildings with jails attached all suggest clarity of purpose. In the British Empire, loyalty to the monarch is a stated, sworn obligation. The organization itself is a fragmented pastiche of personal loyalty; kinship, religious, and ethnic ties; cross-generational sponsorship; rank; and specialization. Although the metaphor of "family" is used (Van Maanen in Kappeler 2006), like all work, divisions based on ethnicity, gender, and rank pattern interactions, promotions, and internal politics—who gets what, when, and where.

A more perplexing matter is that of democratic police loyalty in times of crisis. Clearly, routine domestic policing differs from that arising in periods of acute internal division and crisis such as a civil war (Brodeur 1997; Reichel 1988); policing during an occupation (Marrus and Paxton 1995, 1992; Westermann 2005; Vinen 2006; Ousby 1998; Kitson 2005; Bayley 1991), during an ongoing external war echoed internally such as Shanghai after the Japanese conquest of large parts of China in 1936 (1956, 2002), rapid nationalist expansion (the Texas Republic in conflict with Spain and then Mexico [Webb 1965; Robinson 2000]), a revolutionary uprising of a colony (Horne 2006), and policing in the context of an international intervention (Kosovo, Bosnia, Korea). Domestic or "low" policing in times of defined extreme threat to national sovereignty whether in the context of a declared war or not might also be included.

The question unexamined is what modifications then result. Perhaps this is best addressed with reference to the loyalty of police officers in times of crisis and their obligations. The question of the loyalty of the police has not arisen sharply in Anglo-American societies since the American Civil War except at two points. The first was the civil rights crisis between 1956 and 1968 (roughly) in which the question of loyalty to local law and regulations, state law, and federal law came to the surface in regard to police duties with respect to voter registration, demonstrations, and school integration. The police, although violent and excessive in their actions, argued correctly that they were enforcing state laws. This position was supported by the governors and senators of Alabama, Mississippi, and Arkansas publicly in confrontations with the U.S. Department of Justice. The second point was the occasion of police strikes in Liverpool, Montreal, Boston, and New Orleans, to note only the most important examples. In each case, the matter was defined as a labor-management issue or something about the wages or the conditions of work, not the loyalty of the police to the city, the state, or the nation. All the strikes revealed the obvious fact that order obtains perhaps in spite of policing, and the unique contributions of the police, whose presence is briefly absent, cannot be determined (see Reynolds and Judge 1968; Bopp 1971; Russell 1975; and Brogden 1991).

The consequences of Hurricane Katrina in August 2005 and its aftermath (Brinkley 2006) revealed that thin blue line that appears when devastating crises unfold. It should be noted that communications were nonexistent in the first week after the hurricane, telephone lines were out or malfunctioned, cell phones did not work because the lines were overloaded and jammed (ibid., 360), and police cars were underwater, unavailable, or lacked gasoline (ibid., 2). The command structure was nonexistent because of the outage of communication faculties, the isolation of the headquarters from traffic, the absence of command officers in post, and the temporary police headquarters established at City Hall (ibid., 52, 108–9). Vice and narcotics units were moved to hotels (ibid., 116–17). Officers lost their cars, clothes, and homes (ibid., 207–8, 509). Two officers committed suicide in the early days of the flooding and its consequences (ibid., 510), somewhere between two and four hundred officers left, were AWOL, or were otherwise unaccounted for (it is difficult to know who was or was not on duty [ibid., 203]). Some were trapped in their homes (138–41). Some officers in NOPD vehicles were photographed in Houston (ibid., 202–3). The absent officers represented about 15 percent of the police department; although all were called to duty, regular shifts were not observed. Private police filled the streets (ibid., 342, 479; see also Scahill 2007). Police officers were reported looting, but because stores were open and there was little food or water for the police, the question of "looting" remained ambiguous (Brinkley 2006, 361–66, 500). By the end of the week, the "incompetent" chief of police was fired (ibid., 573–74). The National Guards from several states were called and were present (ibid., 413, 416–22). Police could not be deployed, supervised, or advised as a result of the communication breakdown. The police continued to act in situated unsupervised fashion, creating great chaos and discomfort at the Aquarium (ibid., 520) and the Convention Center (ibid., 599–602) as they tried to keep people inside living at that time in inhumane and barbarous conditions. Police were uncivil to citizens (ibid., 384–85). Everyday routines were impossible, and valiant individual efforts were most notable, according to Brinkley (2006, 2). Local coordination and external support were uneven and in conflict (ibid., chaps. 11 and 12). Police, National Guard, and the army were in conflict about priorities and procedures (ibid., 510). A newspaper article in 2007 stated that the original strength of seventeen hundred at the time of Katrina had been reduced by some 30 percent and that the force was now around fourteen hundred. Two years later, the city was still patrolled by state troopers and the National Guard.

The chaos in New York City post-9/11 did not approach this level of chaos, and the police generally received high marks—this is perhaps because although symbolically it was a great disaster and national tragedy, the chaos was limited in time and place, communications were quickly restored,, and police, fire and civilian contractors were quickly in role and working long hours (see 2002; and Langewiesche 2002). Their homes, families, cars, and lifestyles were not terminated, for mostly live at the edges of the city, far from Manhattan. Furthermore, the cause was a unifying external human force, not "nature." The deaths were invisible, unlike New Orleans, where bodies floated for days unattended and were soon bloated and stinking (2006, 376) and the chaos extended as far as the eye could see.

11. Police tracking and surveillance are increasing. The growth of the surveillance capacity of the police is doubtless their greatest advancement toward scientifically based respectability. Much of the scholarly writing on this matter is based on media reports (Staples 2000), ontological speculations (1996), somewhat thin ethnography based more on claims of capacity or potential than evidence of technology altering practices (Ericson and Haggerty 1997), or descriptive work (Sellen and Harper 2003), while most studies of technology in policing (summarized in Manning 2003, 2006) conclude that the present capacities are not well integrated within and across departments, databases are still to be converted to electronic and online capacities, traditional strategies and tactics for deploying these new technologies remain dominant, and new technologies such as in-car videos and microphones, closed-circuit television, forensic evidence, automated fingerprinting, and computer software for assembling and sharing information are making marginal impact. This is in part due to the tradition of the occasioned and situational nature of the work, as defined by officers on the ground, and the absence of incontrovertible evidence that such innovations produce clearances or arrests, save time or effort, or simplify the complexity of the deciding. Nevertheless, the capacity for tracking people's communication via cell phones and e-mails, in particular, associated with the warrantless-search potentialities granted by the Patriot Act and its abuse, is enormous and expands the capacity of federal police. Mapping in its various guises has been a favored tool of the police in authoritarian police states (Scott 1998; Marrus and Paxton 1995). Thus far, it has been used to identify addresses of gang members and their areas and to plot the location of crimes, disorder, and noise, especially gunshots and homicides, and has stimulated local police to emulate the mapping-based conferences begun in the NYPD in the early 1990s. This is discussed in chapters 6 and 7.

12. Police proceed by exception. The difficulty found in modern writings about the police is that they assume a stable, democratic, economically viable, and legally constrained nation-state with legitimate institutions and powers. The police are on the edge of this stability and historically have been permitted to act expeditiously in the event of threat. As an extension of the executive, the police are instrumentalities in crises. The interface between political crises, executive powers, and the democratic state has not been well explored, although political theorists, notably Carl Schmitt, have written about the importance of "exceptionalism" in the face of crises.

∞

In summary of these considerations surrounding a definition of democratic policing, the police organization as presently constituted in Anglo-American societies has evolved historically, and these patterns are reflected in the structure, function, and image of the police (Bayley 1979). The development of the role on the ground is a function of the emerging concern for managing risky situations that transcend in meaning the current kin-based events and relations. This means, as has been noted by Clark and Sykes (1974), the heavily loaded observational role of the constable or patrol officer, the wide range of choice in approaching situations, and the general support of tradition and the courts of the observational and intuitive skills of such officers. This choice of action is shaped inevitably by local traditions of politics and the economy as well as local police practices. Variations in the pattern of AADP sanctioning (Black 1980) are a function of the sanctions available as well as the targets seen as a source of uncertainty and incongruity. These are the shifting targets of police when they act proactively rather than reactively to citizens' complaints.

As nation-states develop, sources of conflicts move from local to national and transnational, and these require a neutrality in practice that may violate local norms and expectations for conflict resolution. As Robinson and Scaglion have most convincingly argued, the police in a democracy are double coded as both the source of violence and a protection against it. This is complicated by transcendental rules and norms propagated by the nation-state. Police are at the same time no longer obligated to kinsmen and their local norms and practices and obligated to other orders—feudal loyalty or state or legal loyalty (1987, 145–46). If we think of policing as encoding uncertainty, that is, responding to what it implies for order, then the job is to render the uncertainty in terms of continuous procedures of some kind. This, in turn, engenders trust in the police. In addition, as historical studies (Klockars 1985) suggest, continuity in the job as a full-time paid and responsible agent, associated with continuity of procedures, implies continuity in the office and the functions. These are in modern times associated strongly with the idea of a rational bureaucracy.

As has developed in the literature (Bayley 1985; Reichel 1988), the connection of public police with some form of accountability and direction in the interests of the "people" seems a tacit expectation of democratic police, but not of policing in general, or policing in fact. This question of accountability raises another one: how do the police sustain their role as a neutral arbitrator of conflicts? In other ways, the police are transducers or means of converting one sort of fact into another; they process facts into information. In some sense, they must display authority while being rooted in the everyday lives of citizens. They mediate and manage conflicts in terms inconsistent with the ways in which they are conceived (Bittner's point noted above).

CONCLUSION

This chapter has argued that a set of principles derived from Rawlsian liberalism and police scholars can guide the evaluation and judgment of police functioning. These principles include the following: the police are procedurally fair and constrained in dealing with citizens; are primarily reactive to citizen complaints and concerns; are equal in application of coercion to populations defined spatially and temporally; are fair in firing, hiring, and evaluation; are in an acknowledged competitive environment; and are accountable. Each of these was elaborated and further explained. A definition of policing was presented, and a series of qualifications and further specifications was laid out. Some twelve points provide a tessellation on the definition. Democratic policing is accountable, but largely in police terms; citizen demand cannot exclusively be the guiding rationale for policing; police play a symbolic role in society, whatever else they do; police are violent in a constrained and measure fashion; they are guardians of an increasingly blurred set of boundaries, nuances, and rules; they manage order but do not produce it. They are not a "neutral" political force; loyalty within the organization is always problematic, and compliance is a negotiated matter; policing is dangerous and honored for its production of collective goods; the loyalty of the force is assumed and rarely tested in democratic societies; police are being pushed toward surveillance, tracking, monitoring, and intelligence-lead activities in spite of their considered resistance; and police proceed by exception in times of crisis.

PART TWO

The Police As an Institution: Theory

CHAPTER FOUR

Studying Democratic Policing

The issues presented in previous chapters—justice and its relevance to police studies and policing, the degree of fit between "democracy" and policing in Western democracies, especially those in the Anglo-American tradition, and the features of democratic policing as an ideal type—lead us to the study of policing. The focus and background of police studies are the subject of this chapter. As the police were challenged to reform in the late sixties and early seventies, new efforts toward converting the occupation into a "profession" and developing research and development capacities arose.

The systematic study of the police by social scientists is a twentieth-century phenomenon, a fledgling in contrast with more established social science fields. The emergence of this field indicates a coalescence of pragmatism and public policy and to a lesser extent the internal dynamics of academic life and university politics. It has been shaped from the beginning by the practical occupational interests of the police. This coalescence perhaps best explains why the field of police studies, a viable and growing preoccupation, has very weak connections to the classic fields of moral and political philosophy, history, and, even more recently, political science. This chapter, then, moves from the big stage to the somewhat smaller stage of policing and the study of policing. It is a necessary leap.

Background

Two streams of thought and research coalesced in the past twenty-five years to form the field of police studies. This field holds a social space in criminology, in sociology as the parent discipline of criminology, and in criminal justice. The first stream, the administrative stream, is based on applied research and writing growing in part from public administration and in part from "police administration." In fact, it was a variant of public administration that took into account what was then considered the exceptional case—policing. The second stream is the scholarly research based on a handful of classic studies.

The first stream, as well described glowingly by Larry Hoover (2005), begins with the work of O. W. Wilson in public administration and reveals the changes in public administration and organizational studies that it reflected. Hoover might well have mentioned that the tradition of police reform had a long history beginning in the early twentieth century with the writings of Fosdick on European (1915) and American police systems (1920), Woods on American systems (1919), Bruce Smith on state police systems (1969), and Smith's classic, *Police Systems of the United States* ([1940] 1949). These writings focused on social reform from a legalistic and progressive government perspective, much as did the National Committee on Law Observation and Enforcement, or Wickersham Commission (1931). They were written by lawyers and had a direct political agenda—reform of big-city American policing (see also Reppetto 1978). The early concern, including Westley's dissertation at the University of Chicago, was trying to reduce police violence, corruption, and lack of accountability. This story is repeated regionally and in many large American cities (ibid.). As Hoover correctly notes, the early academic programs, at San Jose State University and Michigan State University (both programs were founded in 1935 by former police officers), were police administration programs aimed at internal reform and reflected an American version of social ameliorism. The idea was to construe policing as a public service, a challenging job, and a quasi-scientific enterprise.[1]

The second stream, that of scholarly research, was late in beginning. It was stimulated and brought to prominence by the events of the 1960s. In the 1960s, the two streams flowed together to create a slightly contaminated flood of ideas. The riots of the sixties stimulated interest in policing, and echoed concern for their violence, corruption and unaccountable nature. These events led to several national commissions. The first was the famous President's Crime Commission, leading to the report published as *The Challenge of Crime* (1968). This stimulated in turn a number of important studies on law, the police, courts, and corrections as well as science and technology. The second notable commission was the National Advisory Commission on Civilian Disorders (1968), which published the *Kerner Report*. This report predicted correctly the emergence of two Americas, black and white, and warned that policing should change or be part of the problem, not the solution. After the riotous behavior of police against attendees at the Democratic National Convention, the Walker Commission was created and condemned the police in detail (1968). Yet another commission formed at this time was the National Commission on the Causes and Prevention of Violence. Jerome Skolnick headed a task force for this commission, Violent Aspects of Protest and Confrontation, and its report was published in a popular paperback version as *The Politics of Protest* (1969). One of the more significant and early criticisms of policing as a cause as well as an effect of rioting was Rodney Stark's well-written and -documented book *Police Riots* (1972). Finally, an administratively oriented report was an attempt to set standards and goals within criminal justice. It was entitled *The National Commission on Standards and Goals* (1973), a rather flat document that intended to shape policing by urging standards and goals on agencies within the criminal justice system. This report featured a limp attempt to dramatize what was later called "managerialism" in Britain: setting goals, objectives, and benchmarks and measuring performance. It had little impact on the criminal justice practice and certainly not on policing. This approach, with zero-based budgeting and other auditing procedures, remains known but not practiced by leaders of modern American policing. Police budgets remain opaque and have never been systematically studied. The Law Enforcement Assistance Administration (LEAA), created as a result of the President's Crime Commission, was a research-policy unit within the Department of Justice devoted to stimulating research and policy in what came to be called "criminal justice." The famous metaphor of "the criminal justice system" was dramatized and used to organize a diagram–flow chart in the final report of the commission. This flow chart is now featured in every textbook on the police. This legitimation by naming was profound, as was the brilliant metaphoric rendering of this putative system as a dramatic, clear flow chart showing how justice works from the initial contacts through outcomes, branching off at various points in a logical, meaningful, and coherent fashion. This was to have lasting and important consequences. This naming and portraying, in turn, as noted below, led to the establishment of funded educational opportunities and university programs. The underlying agenda in the most regarded volume of the commission was to advance technology and efficiency; this set a paradigm for the next forty years. The notion of efficiency was tied in time to crime suppression and control rather than service, quality of policing, or enhanced administrative capacity. The pragmatic paradigm reflecting the preoccupations of the police, reviewed later in this chapter, was emerging.

Police studies arose in part by reactions to black-based rebellion in large cities, in part by changes in police perceptions of their role, and importantly by media amplification of their most visible and violent aspects. Police, especially as a result of their brutal, exacerbating work in mass confrontations, became seen at least in part as the cause of problems rather than as an uncritically accepted solution. As a cliché of that time went, "you are either a part of the problem or part of the solution."[2] The research that flowered in due course was a response to this moment of reflection, not to theoretical questions arrived at by a reasoned and sensible process. It was driven by notions of social engineering, not social science. The social science that did emerge was always seen as part of social amelioration.

In the early seventies, the questions on the study of policing as an academic matter were crystallized. Its present shape began to emerge. First, the academic study of the police was set in the context of the legally based criminal justice system. That is, departments, majors, and fixed operational budgets came to pass. This was legitimated by the founding of colleges and schools of criminal justice—for example, at Eastern and Northern Kentucky universities, Northeastern University, Michigan State University (renamed from the School of Police Administration), and the State University at Albany. These universities differed in focus and assumptions from the

University of California (Berkeley) School of Criminology established by Vollmer (and later exterminated as a political nuisance by Governor Ronald Reagan). While the colleges emerging in the 1970s sought and still aspire to policy influence via training and higher education of police and nonpolice, Vollmer's vision was to build a scientifically based police profession with strong academic credentials and a Ph.D.-granting program. This educational turn was amplified by the Law Enforcement Assistance Administration (LEAP), which paid for educational benefits and supported North American police union efforts to make the notion of "professionalism" a basis for pay rises (and not much else). The growth of an independent Ph.D.-granting discipline of criminal justice, differing from criminology and sociology in large part because of its policy-oriented coloration, is best indicated by the burgeoning number of jobs for people in criminal justice programs, schools, and colleges in the United States. This process continues, with nearly thirty criminal justice Ph.D. programs and countless undergraduate programs either under a social science departmental umbrella or as an academic major.

A second academic development was the appearance and acceptance of the metaphor now widely in unquestioned use: the idea that formal social control exercised by millions of people in some several thousand local organizations, each of which has different organizational goals and procedures (Reiss 1974), could be collapsed into a criminal justice *system.* It is unclear how "justice" became a conventional label and how the idea of a system was attached. In a sense it was an icon of the field.

As Hoover (2005) notes, perhaps a bit tongue in cheek, sociologists in the late sixties and early seventies "discovered the complexity of police work" (my paraphrase). The seventies were characterized by a series of important research publications that questioned the conventional wisdom about policing—including work in random patrol (negligible impact on perception or crime), detective work (police were ineffectual in deciding among priorities and investigated more than was needed), crime analysis (at that time descriptive record keeping), and a general interest in some confluence of streams of inquiry and practical issues (Manning 1979). The relationships between police command and their staffs, especially those in big cities, academics, the federal government, and foundations, became symbiotic.

One of the most significant developments was the funding of the Police Foundation by the Ford Foundation, hiring of the former commissioner of the NYPD Patrick Murphy to head it, and establishing a board including James Q. Wilson and a research staff headed by Joseph Lewis and later by George Kelling and his successor, Lawrence Sherman. The work of the Police Foundation, subsequently self-supporting as a result of government grants, impacted policy and elevated the idea that policing made some sort of difference. The paradigm of experimental operations-based research, set out originally by an operations researcher, Joseph Lewis, became the hallmark of the foundation. It set the stage for the now fashionable idea that only experimental research can produce valid scientific results (Sherman 2003). Early on, such studies were epitomized by the works of Sherman on hot spots, domestic violence, and various "crackdowns" (reviewed below in more detail).

The two streams are now virtually one. The subtext of this chapter is that the professionalizing movement in the field, bridging academe, educators, and progressive chiefs and their command staffs, with its scientific and quantitative pretense, has emerged as a narrowly defined field. It is focused on short-term results surrounding reducing official crime statistics (not standardized rates) rather than broader questions of justice, quality of life, and democratic policing practices. Ironically, Kelling's efforts in this regard, influenced by the writings of Jane Jacobs on city life, were in time seen as the rationale for more of the same—policing focused on direct arrest-based sanctioning of crime and disorder.

The aim was to find "what works," not why that might be the case (or not). While the solutions proposed were deeply sociological, that is, less militaristic policing (as it was then called) coupled with increases in civilian personnel, technology, and resources and personnel in all components of the justice system, structural reform was never discussed. Politicians and police developed a new set of unexamined pragmatic rationalizations that were driven by concerns about an unexplicated and undefined "crime problem," or the false notion that drug sales and possession caused crime, and that only through more sophisticated police tactics could the "war on crime" be won. The idea itself of a war was a misleading and crude metaphor, since "war" is fought by uniformed, viable troops against a named and visible enemy and aims to destroy the enemy, reduce the enemy's morale and will to fight, deprive him of space and material resources, and occupy his territory until he gives in. Police in theory cannot wage war against civilian populations as they are protected by law, not demonized, have privacy, are not a uniformed enemy, and cannot be defined categorically by neighborhood, age, race, or class. This limited version of policing, a variety of often announced new tactical modifications, remains the abiding conventional wisdom glossed in various rhetorical tropes and circumlocutions (see Weisburd and Braga 2006, 1–23). In fact, subsequent research has mimicked the concerns of police as practitioners rather than developing an independent, socially grounded theory of policing as a practice. While the American Society of Criminology is composed almost entirely of academics, the Academy of Criminal Justice Sciences (ACJS) is committed to a policy-oriented, ameliorative set of occupations and does relevant and practitioner-oriented research. Founded in 1963, it focuses on education, policy, and research relevant to practitioners and academics alike. Much like the earlier sociology of medicine, criminal justice and to a lesser degree criminology took the conceptual framework of the studied group as a map of relevant problematics. The field of police studies in particular reflects more the interests of the practitioners than the theories of the relevant social sciences. Even when the concern is the sociology of law, the research concerns police claims that they are engaged in "law enforcement." As discussed above, research is done *for* the police rather than *of* the police and concerns policing as a practice. It amplifies and mimics policing's concerns, but does not conceive of them in independent analytical terms. This rather narrow and even precious view of policing is complemented by the police view of the job. It does not question any fundamental assumption about policing mandate and strategy, but raises implicitly questions about tactics. It is in effect a regulatory triangle in which influential police chiefs and their staffs, complicit academics and funding sources, foundations and governmental agencies mutually reinforce their ideas about what works.

THE STUDY OF POLICING

The academic study of policing, an attempt to ground this activity in sociology, political science, and public administration in Anglo-American countries, is a recent development that can be traced through examining major publications frequently cited in the past fifty years. To review briefly the arguments of the previous three chapters, recall that the police are legitimate, bureaucratically articulated organizations that stand ready to use force to sustain political order (Manning 2003, 41–42) via various means. Consider also that Anglo-American policing is democratic policing, and this broader concept is also an essential piece of the policing puzzle. Democratic policing, which is valued in Anglo-American societies, eschews torture, terrorism, and counterterrorism; is guided by law; and seeks minimal damage to civility.[3] Democratic policing is embedded in tacit ethical and moral standards and shielded by the courts by tradition, and its procedures and practices are carefully examined only in the breach. It would appear on the basis of historical evidence that to be sustained, democratic police must be opposed by other competing forms of policing—vigilantes, voluntary associations, and high or political policing (Liang 1992, 2).[4] Although some forms of democratic policing are shaped by the continental–civil law model found in Mediterranean-based and Hispanic societies, most police research reported in English or French does not study democratic policing but rather examines policing in democratic societies (the work of Jean-Paul Brodeur is an exception to this generalization).[5] I focus here on research on the Anglo-American type of policing, a policing form developed by adaptation rather than conquest, and resulting from modifications of militia and police developed in Ireland and later modified by Home Secretary Robert Peel and the diffusion of the 1829 "Peel model" of policing to Canada, New Zealand, Australia, and the United States.[6] This is discussed in further detail in later chapters of this book.

Police studies, like policing itself, is based on interests, material, political, and cultural. The field has social and symbolic capital and vested interests. I seek to connect the social bases of interests and rewards to the patterning of knowledge production and its distribution in the field of police studies. This sociology of knowledge perspective draws attention to the interests and domain assumptions (matters taken for granted about the subject) of such research. I begin with a discussion of the grounding of research in the United States and the United Kingdom. I then discuss the research origins and key figures in studies of policing, the emergence of police scholarship, and some differences between the United Kingdom and the United States in funding, education, and training. These are matters shaped by sociocultural differences. I outline some tensions in research and teaching and public pressures for short-term funded research.[7] At the end of the chapter, I assert that a paradigm of policing research has now been refined and elaborated, and it conceives of the role of such research as illuminating successful modes of crime control at least implicitly to provide assistance in such matters.

THE ACADEMIC BASE

Consider first the most useful reviews of the literature in police studies. All but Peter Kraska's *Theorizing Policing* (2004) are organized topically rather than theoretically. The most recent are those of Loader and Sparks (2002), Bowling and Foster (2002), and two chapters and section introductions by Tim Newburn (2003). Other relevant reviews are (Cain 1979; Bayley 1975, 1985, 1992, 1994; Reiner 1992, 2000, 2003; Smith, Small, and Gray 1983; and the collection edited by Tonry and Morris 1992). Three rather important overviews exist (Bayley and Shearing 1996; Johnston and Shearing 2003; Loader and Mulcahy 2003). Several useful edited collections have appeared (Calker and Hough 1979; Punch 1983; Leishman, Loveday, and Savage 2000; Weatheritt 1986; Brodeur 1997; Waring and Weisburd 2001). Several publications, including the *Oxford Handbook of Criminology* ([2003] 2007), now in its fourth edition, a parsimonious rendition of crime and social control, Newburn's edited *Handbook of Policing* (2003), and his work with Williamson and Wright, *Handbook of Criminal Investigation* (2007), are essential reading. The work on comparative policing, reviewed in the previous chapter, tends to be atheoretical. An exception that captures the impact of high modernity on policing and crime is Katja Franko Aas's penetrating analysis (2007).

Second, let us consider scholars who have shaped research on policing and are the foundational sources for police studies. I focus but not exclusively on books rather than articles on the grounds that books change paradigms, whereas articles, though heavily cited, do not. To briefly mention articles of influence, I would include Bordua and Reiss (1966), Cumming, Cumming, and Edell (1965), Bittner (1967), Westley (1953, 1955), and Black (1970). These all sketched out the ways in which facts are processed into useful information within the police organization. The main figures are few, and the influence of single books in fact is considerable—for example, William Westley's *Violence and the Police* ([1950] 1977); Michael Banton's *Policeman in the Community* (1964); Skolnick's *Justice without Trial* (1966); Preiss[8] and Ehrlich's study of the Michigan State Police, *An Examination of Role Theory* (1966); Arthur Niederhoffer's *Behind the Shield: The Police in an Urban Society* (1967); David Bordua's edited collection, *The Police* (1967), several chapters of which, those written by Silver, McNamara, Reiss and Bordua, and Wilson, are foundational; James Q. Wilson's *Varieties of Police Behavior* (1968); Maureen Cain's *Society and the Policeman's Role* (1973); Bittner's *Functions of the Police* (1972); and Reiss's work *The Police and the Public* (1971). An important book on the racial context of policing in Birmingham (Rex and Moore 1967) was all but ignored until later issues arose as a result of the Brixton riots. John Brown, a classicist by training based at the Cranfield Institute, was influential in the period between the publications of the early works and the development of an academic infrastructure and talent at the London School of Economics (LSE) (Terry Morris and students, Jock Young, Paul Rock, and Stan Cohen, and later Rock's many students, such as Simon Holdaway and Nigel Fielding). Also influential, albeit later, are the books of Manning (1977 [1997]), Punch (1979),[9] Brown (1969), Smith, Small, and Gray (1983), Reiner (1978, 1991), Sherman (1990, 1992), Waddington (1991, 1999), Fielding (1988, 1995), and Holdaway (1979, 1983, 1996). All but Wilson (political science) and Banton (anthropology) were trained as sociologists. Two books of great promise went unnoticed—Sykes and Brent's systematic observational study of police public interaction (1983) and Klockars's truncated sketch of a theory of policing, *The Idea of Police* (1985). Two other books that influenced early work are now rarely cited: Peter Laurie's sensitive and insightful ethnography of the London Metropolitan Police (1970) and Wilson and Martin's study of police manpower (1969). Some senior authors and researchers (Reiner, Manning, Bayley, Newburn) have published research as well as review articles and chapters.[10] Important contributions to the study of Anglo-American policing[11] have been made by Commonwealth-based scholars Margaret Beare, Janet Chan (1998, 2003), Richard Ericson (1977, 1981, with Haggerty 1997), Chris Murphy (1998), Jean-Paul Brodeur (2000), Clifford Shearing (with Johnston 2003), and Philip Stenning (1995).[12]

Third, consider that these key figures in police research form something of a network of relations. Through these networks flow rewards and sanctions-invitations to write, to visit, to present, to serve on Ph.D. committees in several countries, and to be feted when appropriate. Gossip, competition, and envy make dynamic the almost invisible rankings within the network. Most of the "senior" figures in the policing drama have known each other since the 1970s; attended many police-oriented conferences in the United States, United Kingdom, and Canada and on the continent; and appeared in, reviewed, and praised through publishers' blurbs each others' books. Most have held many grants from a few sources, such as the National Institute of Mental Health (NIMH), (infrequently) the National Science Foundation (NSF),[13] the National Institute of Justice (NIJ), and its predecessors in the United States, the Solicitor General's Office in Canada and the Home Offices (Scottish office and the London office) in the UK. There has been a "circulation of the elites," or movement of personnel between the United States and the UK, the Home Office and academe, the U.S. Department of Justice and the Office of Community Oriented Policing Services (or the "COPS office"), private foundations and universities. For example, the Home Office has spawned a notable number of professors in the United States and UK, including Mike Hough, Ken Pease, Ronald Clarke, Nick Tilley, Tim Hope, Tim Newburn, and others, and the Police Foundation has rotated personnel across the Atlantic from time to time. The key figures have lived, researched, and taught on both sides of the Atlantic for some brief time on fellowships of various kinds, private arrangements, grants, visiting lectureships, and professorships. Many scholars worked (researched, studied, wrote) and lived for a considerable period of time in a country other than that of their birth or citizenship—Frances Heidensohn, John Van Maanen, myself, Clive Norris, Nigel Fielding, Michael Banton, David Bayley,

Lawrence Sherman, Margaret Beare, Janet Chan, Philip Stenning, Clifford Shearing, Richard Ericson, Betsy Stanko (a sociologist now serving as a strategic planning and research in the London Metropolitan Police), Jean-Paul Brodeur, and others—as did police officers or professors, who took brief fellowships in the UK and in the United States. Some links have been formally established (e.g., between Bramshill and the John Jay College), and others are informal. Other universities that played and continue to play a key role in these exchanges are Michigan State, MIT, State University of New York at Albany, Goldsmith's and LSE (both colleges within the University of London), Manchester University, Oxford (both the Socio-Legal Centre and the Centre for Criminology), Cambridge, and the University of Surrey.

Fourth, there is an institutional base for research and teaching in police studies. These were initially in very large and prestigious universities in both countries. A handful of universities, at least until the eighties, were fundamental in nurturing the growth of police studies. These included at Cambridge the Institute of Criminology, at Oxford the Centre for Criminology and the Wolfson Centre for Socio-Legal Studies, and elsewhere in the UK, the Institute at Sheffield, and the LSE's Mannheim Centre. In North America, the University of Toronto Centre and perhaps, stretching it a bit, Michigan State University,[14] Harvard University, and the University at Albany in the United States were early centers of research and teaching. The Police Foundation and Police Executive Research Forum (PERF) have sponsored and encouraged important landmark research as well as employed many Ph.D.'s as directors of research, as consultants, and as contractors on grants.

Fifth, although many trends and interests such as community policing have been transatlantic until recently, the study of policing in the United States has maintained a pragmatic concern with police effectiveness in crime control in the short term. Matters of accountability, justice and fairness, quality of service, broader questions of trust in the police, and the extent of their collective-good orientation have been neglected.

Sixth, funding perhaps stimulated at first by the LEAA and renewed under COPS has been very sensitive to racial conflicts and media-amplified crises of confidence. In both the UK and the United States, police studies have been funded, supported, and shaped by central government policies, crises- and crisis-oriented documents by commissions and judges (the *Kerner Report,* the *McCone Report,* the *Scarman Report,* the *MacPherson Report,* and so on).[15] On the other hand, much of the early work was not funded directly but was the result of solo scholars such as Van Maanen, Punch, Manning, Holdaway, and Chatterton and other students carrying out Ph.D. research.

Finally, there has been almost no systematic attempt to refine a theory of policing per se. This is consistent with the increasingly pragmatic, empirical, and narrowly focused research ensemble that has emerged—a symbiotic relationship between research foundations and research institutes in large universities such as Michigan State, Northeastern University, the University of Maryland, and the University at Albany. Attempts to examine policing see it as analogical work or metaphoric exercises—seeing something in terms of something else. Policing is a kind of totem, or icon, a symbol of the state; it cannot be equivalent solely to the state or other forces. Its image differs from country to country.[16] The power and authority of the police is thus not of their own origin; they are custodians at best and draw on the font of moral credibility for which they are mere surrogates. Police, as noted above, function actively in a political order for which they nominally stand. Police generate feelings and sentiments, memories and entanglements of the mind. They are an object set in a cultural context whose power and authority are grounded in compliance and complicity. They are sheltered by law.

SOME ANOMALIES IN THE PATTERN OF RESEARCH

A useful distinction is that between sociology *of* the police and sociology *for* the police (M. Banton, personal communication, 1971). The first, being a sociology of the police, explores the relevance of theories and concepts as they apply to the organization, occupation, and its impacts, an enterprise that is analytically driven and data based. It has been very powerfully shaped by a handful of scholars and political events. The second, a sociology for the police to overdraw the contrast, is devoted to ameliorative aims—to elevate the status, management, and level of performance of the police while reducing negative matters (corruption, violence, veniality, and malfeasance). Commitment to research for the police may require differential revelation of facts and findings, suppression of contradictions and impediments, and a willingness to please the "police audience" rather more than an academic or scholarly audience. On the other hand, academics with very strong political values may do the same in the interest of their rather more pessimistic and negative views (e.g., Jefferson 1990). It might also be said that the policy-oriented work of Kelling and Coles (1998) and Wilson and Kelling (1982) has rarely been criticized in the depth it deserves by scholars not only for uneven and rather dubious scholarship but also for value commitments that shape the pronouncements that appear to be but are not data based. Their clear commitment is to "policy," the police, and policing.[17]

EXPLORATIONS IN ANGLO-AMERICAN POLICE RESEARCH

There is great difficulty in drawing inferences and in establishing the scope of generalizations resulting from some well-known research. Consider, on the one hand, the data-thin basis for generalizations across Anglo-American policing studies (Bayley's use of calls for service as a measure of public demand [1985]) and, on the other, ethnographic case studies that treat the two countries as implicitly comparable (Manning 1977, 1988; Forst and Manning 1999). These issues will continue to be salient as the slogan of "democratic policing" is taken as a model by the United States in its foreign policy.[18]

Consider, in the context of generalization and inference, the issue of the origins, role, and consequences of the police "occupational culture" (OC) or "subculture" (compare Reiner 2000 and Reiner 1992, 465n16; Holdaway 1979; and Manning 1977, 1988, 1992; and these to Waddington 1999). American police studies, as shown in texts in criminal justice and policing, utilize a narrow, misleading, stereotypic rendition of the OC-based ideas and data gathered some thirty years ago and derived from the views and observations of white male police officers working in crime-ridden areas in the very largest American cities. This is a misleading gloss. While Skolnick (1966) outlined in a few pages the idea of an occupational culture and a police personality, in part following Westley (1970), it has now become an unquestioned leitmotif of textbook treatments. Other writers use the OC as a determinant or independent variable and see behavior (violence, illegalities, corruption) as the dependent variable. Some see behavior as a dependent variable arising from a very complex set of situational determinants as well as "pressures" arising within and outside of the organization (Mastrofski, Reisig, and McCluskey 2002; Alpert and Dunham 2004). Shearing and Ericson (1991) see the idea as a configuration or set of ideas and values that were something of a resource on which to draw and by which to connect the odd, fragmented "raw" experiences, episodes, interventions, and encounters between the police and the public. For Shearing and Ericson, the OC is not a thing but something of a "toolbox." A working hypothesis might be that the occupational culture of police is a way of accounting for behavior, and not simply a portmanteau concept that explains everything and nothing (Crank 2003). Most studies of the OC ignore and do not measure the organizational context of the behavior (for an exception, see the Mastrofski paper cited above as well as Jermeir et al. 1991; and Terrill, Paoline, and Manning 2003). OC studies neither distinguish the police organization, composed of almost one-quarter "civilians," including lawyers, forensic scientists, clerks, operators, and repair staff, from the police occupation nor the occupation's tasks and practices from its verbalizations and accounts. While no study, save John Clark's early work on the police role (1965), has measured any of these "variables" cross-culturally, the concept of an occupational culture continues to be a major theme in writings in English on the police and policing. It is a "variable" accounting for everything from friendships to levels of violence on the job.

A parallel idea that has not been explored well is the ethnocentrism of American and, to a lesser degree, British police studies. American police studies are apparently supranational and are characterized by statements like "police do ..." and "policing is ... ," (see the epilogue), but these refer only to urban American policing. The work is in fact ethnocentric, narrow, and parochial. This has consequences beyond academic discourse. Specifically, the growth and exporting of American policing under various empty buzz words such as *democratic policing, community policing,* or simply *policing* ignore the essentially cultural, political, historical, and economic traditions and constraints of the "host" nation.[19] They also suppress the colonial or imperialistic aspect of this cultural diffusion sometimes by force and violence. These patterns of policing and new and emergent types of policing have not been studied in depth, while many thin essays suggest their importance.

As soon as policing studies became somewhat international, issues of typologies, ideal types, and differences within and between ethnic organizations, nation-states, cultures, and "civilizations" in Huntington's terms (1996) become salient and perhaps troublesome. Consider, for example, one of the more misleading commonsense distinctions—that between public and private policing. The distinctions between the ideal types "private" and "public" police (Johnston 1992; Rigakos 2002; Forst and Manning 1999; Jones and Newburn 1998; Johnston and Shearing 2003) seem unclear. Absent close ethnographies, we must speculate about their numbers, costs, consequences, violence, and functions. In general, states in the civil law tradition have more elaborate, state-based forces such as the Gendarmes and Caribineri, and few private police forces or agencies (Bayley 1975). Common-law states have large public and private forces (per capita). As questions of national security are being addressed, the role of the "private" police in public security and political ordering may require closer examination. The most desperate need is close-at-hand comparative studies of actual policing practices.

TENSIONS IN POLICE RESEARCH ARISING FROM FUNDING AND POLITICS

There is an ongoing tension in the policing world in both countries between what might be called theorizing and organizing proposition-generating research such as Westley, Banton, Cain, and Wilson (noted above) and short-term evaluative and funded empirical studies (read any professional journal in criminology for an example of the latter). As noted by Reiner seventeen years ago (1992), police studies have been characterized for some time as studies of policing rather than studies of policing as instances of broader socioeconomic and political trends, as a part of the political economy of control, as an aspect of the production of further inequalities and contradictions in the democratic state, and as a type of organization. Reiner's reviews (ibid., 2000) are organized by headings such as "Efficiency," "Training," "Crime Control," "The Role of Legal Controls," and so on. Both British (Reiner's summary) and American (my conclusion) research is driven by low-level policy-shaped questions, not theoretical ones.

There is also a tension in the UK, albeit centered at Bramshill Police College (Hants), between crime control and analysis and police management and leadership concerns more generally. The National Crime Analysis Center, a bunker built deep into the chalk ground of Bramshill with direct crime-control aims, sits across from the seventeenth-century mansion in which "police training" takes place covering topics such as management, policy analysis, leadership, and the like.

This tension has not emerged in the United States. There is no single national police academy for training in the United States, though there are some regional training academies sponsored and funded by COPS, and a division between Ph.D.-granting and higher-degree-granting universities and others who teach "criminal justice" in state colleges, liberal arts universities, and junior colleges. There are now distant learning programs in criminal justice (e.g., University of Phoenix and Athabasca College in Canada) and one connected with the European Union. This division is very crudely revealed in the membership and concerns of those in the ASC, British Society of Criminology, and the Academy of Criminal Justice Sciences (CJS) (based largely in the United States). In the UK, the Universities of Plymouth, Leicester, and Exeter now have thriving programs in police and criminal justice studies, and it is possible to study policing via Cambridge and these universities through Bramshill. In my judgment, the evolving strategy of police studies in these two countries has been from a sort of practical-applied set of local and regional training academies (associated with police constabularies or departments regionally or directly) to university locations. This in turn has provided the academic base for Ph.D. programs in criminal justice and the birth of undergraduate programs in criminal justice in the United States.

Academic studies in both countries are stratified, with a few leading places supplying faculty, Ph.D.'s, and lawyers for the second-level places that produce some Ph.D.'s and research and a third level of quasi-emergent "professionally oriented" universities and colleges. This is close to what C. Wright Mills called the producers, the wholesalers, and the retailers of knowledge (2000). The producers tend to have fixed syllabi, clear specialties, directed studies and tutorials leading to research, and an awareness of the connections of the field to the broader social science developments (including theory). The dominant method, when of concern as it is in the United States, is rampant empiricism based on observations, interviews, questionnaires, or official records. Very little ethnography is now done, although the penetrating work of Steve Herbert (1998, 2006), Tim Newburn and associates, and Loader and Mulcahy remain as signposts, but citations tend to be of known studies of Van Maanen (1988), Fielding (1988, 1995), Westley (1970), Rubinstein (1973), Skolnick (1966), and Manning (1977) in the past generation (also see previous citations). This is odd, given that the aim of social science is to connect practices with theory in the context of police organizations.

The FBI academy is neither an academic unit nor a national training establishment.

Pressure for valid and detailed federal statistical bases, used to justify policing, is still emergent. Although a national incident-based system of crime reporting has been mandated, it is not in general use in the United States. A household victim survey now complements police reporting systems, but it does not command public and media attention. The much criticized uniform crime report (UCR), though dealing with only *reported crime* and not crime that has been validated or "founded" by police investigation, continues to be seen as the most valid measure of crime by the media and the general public.

THE ABSENCE OF THEORY

Theories of policing must in a sense be metaphorical or about *something* rather than referential or about a person, role, or even an organization. Social theory is a way of thinking about one thing in terms of another (Burke 1965; Pepper 1972). It cannot be reduced to "variables," "hypotheses," and tests because theorizing precedes the process of arguments concerning its truth value. But the workings of language can be further specified. To say that some theories of policing are *metaphoric* in the sense that they use a broad scheme to generalize about policing, including sociocultural theories such as those of Bittner, Loader and Mulcahy, Manning, Shearing and Ericson, Young, and Holdaway means that the aim is to characterize policing as a collective organic and integrated whole. These writers, more than any other, are influenced by Durkheim and eschew the currently fashionable theories in criminology that are reductionistic, pragmatic, and focused on individual careers and patterns of offending. In contrast to these metaphoric ideas, consider those that are based on *synecdoche*. These works, by Skolnick, Scheingold, M. Brown, and Lipsky, illustrate policing by focusing on a part of a whole, its administrative format, its dominant or modal personality, or its role in local politics, and use this focus to generalize about policing as a whole. They elevate this part to centrality in their theorizing. In these approaches, each of the elements of policing—structure, function, administration, ideology, strategies, and tactics—are equally important, almost essential, parts of the police organization. They cohere as a whole made of constituent parts. Still other theorists—cultural Marxists such as Hall et al., Jefferson and Grimshaw, and Chambliss and Bourdieu–influenced Janet Chan (2003)—employ *grand theory* using police and policing as an example. Finally, some theories are *metonymical* in that they adopt a partial list of features, one at a time, rather than as a part of a whole, synecdoche-like, and select some as indicating the most important part of policing. The most important empirical works, cited above, and the ones that I would most emphasize (those written by Albert J. Reiss Jr. and Steve Mastrofski and coauthors, as well as Clark and Sykes 1974; Banton 1964; Rubinstein 1973; Cain 1973; and Chan 1996), are metonymical. Policing in this sense is not a whole but is represented through a partial display of a part, such as interactions between police and citizens, the uniformed officer's role, and the sensibilities of the patrol officer. All such theories assume the fundament of sentiments that make formal ordering a possibility. (I am not sure if asked to name a "theorist" of policing that those in the field could or would name one.) The shape of funding and research has meant that such theorizing is done ad hoc rather than as a direct function of the research carried out. This is true throughout the Anglo-American world.[20] On the other hand, it is clear that many of the questions raised by early writers concerning police use of violence, the impact of the organizational structure on policing, the powerful effects of the occupational culture, and the centrality of patterns of citizen-police interaction in sustaining trust have continued to be viable and important topics for research for forty-plus years.

Although there are some theoretically informed works in police studies (Bittner 1972; Chan 1996, 2003; Manning 1977, 1988, 2003; Reiss 1992; and Black 1980), in general, theorizing policing has required a transformation of concepts and inferences from bodies of extant theory such as Marxian (Hall et al. 1978; Jefferson and Grimshaw 1984), dramaturgical (Manning 1977, 1988), symbolic interactionist (Fielding, Punch, and Holdaway, cited above), behavioral-interactionist (Sykes and

Brent), and organizational-institutional analysis (Reiss and Bordua 1967) to policing research. The work of Loader and Mulcahy (2003) and Loader and Walker (2007), reviewed above, is the only self-conscious effort at theorizing policing in the context of a culture in the sense of the police culture, specifically and particularly English policing culture, "a concept (not to be confused with the more familiar and limited, 'police culture') we use to refer to the amalgam of institutions, practices and policies, myths, memories, meanings, and values that, at any given time, constitute the idea of policing within English society" (Loader and Mulcahy 2003, 55). This bow in the direction of aesthetics is a broad and imaginative effort to locate policing within the structures of feeling in a society (a term they adopt from the English cultural essayist Raymond Williams [1964])" thought as something felt and feelings as thought (Williams 1977, 132). This is a Durkheimian twist on policing as located in a cultural and sentimental context, an effort to elevate the discourse about policing and how it is neither felt day-to-day nor imagined by those in the field of police studies or police practitioners. Loader and Walker take an even more precarious leap in their most recent book, arguing that policing is now a part of state-entrusted "thick security." This broad idea combines several elements in a powerful entourage: the attachment of citizens to their society and culture as an entity; the ways in which this is a part of the attachment of citizens to each other, or social integration generally; the trust that underlies both of these—trust in the institutions of the state as well as trust in other citizens (an echo of Durkheim, Kant, and Rawls, an impressive threesome); and, finally, the mutuality of the state's obligations and entailments with citizen expectations (Loader and Walker 2007, 5). They state unequivocally that the state is essential to the realization of this "thick security" as a public good because the state should and must encourage the affective bonding, attachment, and trust, the abstract solidarity on which political communities depend (ibid.; my paraphrase). This level of discourse, combining jurisprudential ideas, the sociology of Durkheim, and penetrating insights into the functions of police practice (ibid., especially 105–15), is a challenging effort to place policing in grand theory. As argued in the first chapter of this book, this is a rare effort to connect policing as an organization and as a set of practices to theorizing about democracy and policing. On the other hand, their book and its thesis are to some degree removed from the actual day-to-day aspects of policing that have most attracted research and funding in the past thirty to forty years in Anglo-American societies. To this we now turn.

Previous periodic calls for empirically based theorizing (Reiss 1992; Cain 1979; Bayley 1992, 1994; Reiner's 1992 chapter noted above) have not been taken up. The most provocative of recent attempts is Janet Chan's (2003) uneasy fitting of Bourdieu's ideas to police socialization. The work in police studies, to be blunt, is empirical, and focused on immediate and policy-driven issues such as "excessive" violence, abuse of authority, citizen satisfactions with interaction, and the programmatic contingencies in community policing. Some questions have not been addressed, such as the issue of long-term deployment (Lum, personal communication, July 6, 2004), the negative consequences of crime-focused policing on trust and community support of policing, the role of budgets and "managerialism" on morale and goal attainment, the high politics of policing, and the politics of police organizations themselves. In many respects, policing studies is too much about the police and too little about the context or culture of policing, including its legitimacy, grounding in democratic values, restraint, and tolerance of differences. Policing, like medicine, should be judged by the extent to which it does the least damage to civility. The vast and impressive body of such work done by a few outstanding scholars such as Lawrence Sherman, Stephen Mastrofski, David Weisburd, and Wesley Skogan, the policy-oriented work of the staff of the Kennedy School, and the work of research groups such as the Institute of Law and Justice, Urban Institute, London Institute for Policy Studies, PERF, and the Police Foundation continue to shape the empirical published research in criminology and in police studies. This short-term research horizon complements the orientation of top management of police organizations to "today," to the current or next possible crisis, and their abiding, awesome fear of a major scandal or failure.

In spite of the emergence of police studies as an academic field, there is concern about ethics, or reflection on the values and aims of the practice of policing.[21] The pragmatic roots of the work are the source of its effects, but it is little given to reflection. Given this history and research base, some shifting and shading have occurred that have become a scientifically grounded "sociology for the police." I should like to explore, finally, a paradigm that has emerged that obscures the question of political and moral philosophy, the touchstones of social science.

THE PRESENT POLICE PARADIGM

In the late 1960s a very influential book was published featuring the notion of a paradigm (Kuhn 1970). The argument was that an innovative piece of research broke through the previous paradigm that set the boundaries of appropriate scientific research, and this landmark research was in time extended to produce a new paradigm or set of assumptions about how to proceed scientifically. The elaborations and findings relevant to scientific advancement were set within such a paradigm or mode of proceeding. In many respects, it was argued, this was tacit or assumed rather than explicit and empirical in nature. However, the aim of this book is to assess policing by independent criteria, not those of the occupation itself, or even those of the researchers.

The argument that policing in a democratic society should observe the difference rule points us toward the body of relevant research in criminology, criminal justice, sociology, and the other social sciences.

Policing, especially in the past twenty-five years, has been studied largely from the perspective of the police, using data gathered by and for the police and in sympathy with the public view that the police can and do control crime. Although there are exceptions, including studies of corruption and deviance and attitude studies critical of police, the "top-down," management-oriented[22] "sociology for the police" has repeatedly dramatized the singular notion that the police, and the police almost alone, control officially recorded crime. To this is added the grandiosity of chiefs' claiming their role and notions of leadership in the police world (Bordua and Reiss 1966). The fluctuations in the crime rate as officially measured are then studied with conventional variables that are attributes of the organization and secondarily that of (primarily) disadvantaged areas. Their impact on crime has lately been more systematically studied, and this cannot be eschewed as a source of public trust. By the same token, other consequences of policing or lack thereof, whether positive or negative, therefore are minimized, not studied, or simply never mentioned in the literature. On the whole, as noted in the preface to this book, since the mid-1990s, the police have been given respect and status for serving as putative "first responders," cogs in the homeland security wheel, crime fighters, and smart managers. This rhetoric, in turn, has been adopted by the media as the explanation for the crime drop in the late 1990s. Media, police, and researchers have not figured how or why officially recorded crime has been dropping slowly for the past fifteen years.

As argued above, the focus on the myth and ritual of crime suppression rather than justice in regulation of society's failures has been the cornerstone of the police mandate since the late 1920s. This has been accompanied by blindness to other associated strengths and weaknesses that can be identified through political philosophy or sociology.

The research literature on policing, while punctuated by the concerns and failures of "community policing" over the past twenty-five years, remains focused tightly on crime, criminal offenders, and offenses. The texts are more broadly based in their characterizations of policing. Consider what might be called the "high spots" of policing studies in the past twenty-five years. As the incarceration frenzy, now in its twenty-fifth year, accelerated, so did police studies of crime and attempts at direct crime suppression increase and the arguments supporting them (see, for example, 1990, 1992, 2005; and, for an opposing view, Thacher 2001). Paramilitary policing, almost unnoticed, became a sought-after standard, with police appearing in glorified-ninja attire, heavily armored and armed, in specialized units in virtually all American departments, small, large, or monolithic (Kraska and Cubellis 1997; Kraska and Kappeler 1997; Kraska 2001).[23] Experimental method was touted above all else as the solution not only to social science theory and method but to the control of crime, while vague prediction studies were to be the best basis for state coercion (Sherman 2007).

On the other hand, some exceptions to the glorification of policing and the consequences of the arrest and jail frenzy appeared in major monographs by serious scholars (Donziger 1996; Tonry 1995; Rose and Clear 1998; Clear et al. 2003; Garland 2001; Harcourt 2001; Simon 2007; Western 2007; Uggen and Manza 2006), but these sophisticated, data-based analyses were more than offset, as argued above, by well-received encomiums from the police themselves (Maple 1999; Bratton and Knobler 1998; Bratton and Kelling 2006); about the police by their advisers (e.g., Braga; and Kelling and Coles); and those devoted to the Wilson-Kelling "broken windows" of policing viewed as a "dosage" to wipe out a metaphoric disease (see Sherman 2005, 2007; compare Thacher 2003).

The question of what other good is done by the police is bypassed. Police studies, on the whole, are based on official data, view the problem narrowly from the top down and from the conventional crime-control police perspective, and see the issue of concern as solely one of reducing what is taken to be crime. This allows them to freely speculate, data free, about or ignore the sources of order and ordering, and avoid raising fundamental questions about the impact and consequences of policing on any ongoing social order. Reduced crime based on a single indicator, crimes known to the police and recorded, apparently speaks for itself. This is perhaps a generalization that needs closer examination.

One way to examine the paradigm of a field is to examine the key journals that set the current questions of interest and the current fashionable methodologies, statistical models, and fashionable icons of the field. Consider the field of police studies as it is presented in the key journals of the field—*Criminology, Justice Quarterly, Police Quarterly,* and some of the secondary journals (e.g., *Policing, Police and Society,* and *Police Management and Strategies*). It is here that we find the assumptions that drive the field as a subjective and objective set of forces. The field, as Bourdieu writes, contains several kinds of capital: symbolic, material, and cultural. Journals, however, represent notional symbolic capital or the capital that accrues from legitimate knowledge. The research found in these journals is based on the following assumptions and practices that give life to notions of crime, disorder, civility, law enforcement, and justice. This perspective is up close and focused, laserlike, on crime without the luxury of standing back, reflecting, or cogitating basic assumptions that drive the work. From these assumptions emerge "truths." The work proceeds as follows.

Police have a clear picture of the constraints under which they operate. Researchers share these commonsense grounds of action. There is a powerful set of objective *structural conditions* that are measured by proxy (e.g., percent unemployed; percent with a given educational level, modal income, and percent African American). These conditions are assumed to act to constrain and guide social action. They are stable background conditions subject only to an "etc. clause"—they continue to act as they have in the past. The reality of them is largely unquestioned. These structural conditions are reinforced by beliefs, values, and norms shared by all. Measurable, objective, standardized norms and values are general and held in various degrees of intensity—for example, "success" and "work," defined within conventional occupational pursuits, "quality of life" and "disorder," as seen within a middle-class perspective, and so forth. Disorder is obvious when seen. Failing to meet these assumptive "standards" leads to "strain" and "anomie" and, more often than not, to crime. On the other hand, the existence of the worthies, those who respect and value policing, is a necessary fiction. These "worthies" provide support for police actions and back them up in times of crisis. The police, by extension, act as reflections of such general values, beliefs, and recipe notions about society and its workings. They reflect society's best. They are mourned in death and elevated dramaturgically in life.

The institutions, education, religion, the economy, the law, and the "criminal justice system" guide individual choices that tend to be seen as "rational." Crime is a choice made rationally after consideration, weighing of options, taking into account the long-term consequence of being caught, and so on. Crimes and criminals are seen as independent units not entangled with other crimes as a process (co-offending) but displayed as cumulative, analytically comparable events rather than the outcome of a series of organizationally determined decisions (Meehan 1992, 1993). The primary fallacy, of course, is mistaking organizational records for the things to which they refer. This is the classic confusion of sign and referent.

Crime, like violence, is seen as irrational for the most part, and thus its rationality has to be explained as a special case. Since crime is seen as a failure to meet conventional normative standards, it is also multivalent, symbolizing, and indicative of deeper flaws. Moral standards in turn are conflated with law, religion, and conventional lifestyles. Absolutist notions such as these obscure complexity, and the job in the end becomes one of control and short-term decision frames.

From the perspective of most police researchers, ethnographic work, while useful and valuable, never alters and could never alter findings based on large-scale statistically based surveys. It is thus marginal and marginalized. Many inferences about lifestyle, causes of violence, and cultural patterns are made with impunity without closely observed data interviews or statements of key informants (e.g., Kane 2006; Nunn et al. 2006; Weitzer and Kubrin 2003; and Braga et al. 1999, 562–63). On the other hand, Anderson's *Streetwise* is repeatedly cited as an accurate picture of "street life" crime and African American lifestyles. Middle-class African American life, strong kinship patterns (Stack 1974), and cultural differences making crime an extension of racism are not considered in detail. Police value stories and narratives, little snippets of life, and have an ethnographic sense of their work when not speaking in generalities about "the job."

Researchers, like the police themselves, feel that policing, even given a range of practices, proactive and reactive enforcement, has known, understandable, predictable, and invariably positive results. In the classic studies of the impacts of policing carried out by major scholars such as Weisburd and associates; Skogan, Sherman, and students; and Braga, not a single instance of negative consequences of policing operations are noted (other than a decline or attrition of the measured effects of policing). Failures are seen only as error variance in statistical tables. Even negative, unanticipated feedback loops that result from police actions (e.g., sweeps, raids, crackdowns, "operations," and other announced programs) are either omitted or not presented in published research. On the other hand, when these are suggested, they are based on logical analyses (Rose and Clear 1998). The absence of empirical work indicates an absence of the phenomena.

Analyses of rises or falls in chosen indicators of activity (e.g., calls for service, officially recorded crime statistics (ORCS), complaints about police actions, and so on) omit consideration of the impacts of third parties on the conflict resolution that has preceded the event or incident (cf. Carr, Napolitano, and Keating 2007; Warner 2007). In other words, the actions reflected in the calls, for example, are direct indications not of behavior but of the negotiations between parties prior to the call. This becomes telling when questions about collective efficacy are asked—"Would you call the police if . . . ," absent the context of who is the victim, who is the offender, and what relationship the person asked has to these others in that event. Of course, immediate rises and abrupt changes in crime rates become objects of analysis (e.g., Rosenfeld, Fornango, and Rengifo 2007) with no mention of the reflexive consequences of policing in the model, or brief mentions of the fact that civil liberties and the quality of life may be affected by arrests that focus on disadvantaged areas (e.g., ibid., 378). Calls for service are used uncritically as a proxy for "service," "crime," "disorder," and "drugs"—using or dealing, wholesale to retail, regardless of the drug of interest, its market or usage patterns and consequences (other than marijuana, which has practically been decriminalized) (see Weisburd et al. 2004; Weisburd and Green 1995; Weisburd and Mazerolle 2000; Warner 2007; Nunn et al. 2006). This overlooks the context of the call (how it is defined by callers, operators, dispatchers, and officers); the meaning of the incident called about and what is done about it; the totally ambiguous relationships between the symbol (a call about drugs) and the referent (dealing, using, what drugs?); a conflation of "crime" with a call that contains talk that can be coded in some fashion consistent with the available categories (e.g., Nunn et al. 2006); and the ambiguous nature of a call about "drugs" or noncriminal matters ("disorder," "litter") when the crime(s) involved cannot be pursued on the basis of citizens' claims. Other obvious flaws with reference to "controlled" experiments (e.g., Braga et al. 1999; Braga and Bond 2008) using calls for service from the police (CFS) as a dependent variable are well known: calls and places about which the call are made are distinctive and cannot be disentangled even with caller ID (this only states the number and its location, not that of the incident); the endless errors in addresses and the location of a incident, given that any address on one side of the street is grouped with all the others on the side of a given block; calls from public places such as parks, stadia, and auditoriums, places with large areal volume, made to dispatchers, operators, officers, and citizens; and the inexact position of cell phone calls and callers. The ecological fallacy haunts all this published research. Calls to the police in any area are a misleading, crude index of activity (see Manning 1998, especially 243–66). Why is reducing calls of value in any case? Isn't increased calling encouraged? Isn't "Call 911" painted on the side of every police vehicle?

Places, ecological areas, parks, squares, or blocks, even named and known, are treated as uniformly objective matters rather than socially constructed, named, and objectified by residents or other citizens (Herbert 2006; Taylor 2000; Hunter 1974). This is a more focused critique of the long-standing and obvious point that *community* is a placeholder, a buzzword that indicates police are aware of the social areas in which they police. On the other hand, police do not find the idea useful in practice (Herbert 2006), nor do they consider societal and cultural matters things they can modify. Only one city, San Diego, has redefined its policing districts to reflect cultural political and ethnic diversity rather than traditional measures of workload, size of the population served, or crime.

Areas, places, and known localities that have been recently known as areas of violence or crime are seen as "hot spots." These are consistently areas in which police and citizens agree. Here, statistical models and commonsense attributions are in agreement, but notions like "police district," "precinct," "division," and "beat" have little or no meaning to citizens living in these areas. This is exacerbated by 911 call systems that mean that the local police station is not called or visited about local matters. Matters of meaning and experience are collapsed into questions of collinearity, displacement, diffusion, or embeddedness.

Research on social processes and structures can be understood by cross-sectional data and panel studies; longitudinal studies are rare. The processes that are of interest are inferred. Cultural and social processes in general are inferred from the analysis of large data sets rather than from close observations. Those studies that do are not very revealing of the interactions between citizens and the police (an exception to this is the work of Venkatesh 2002, 2006, 2008).

Police are treated as "cultural dopes" acting as puppets, reflecting the values and roles attributed to them by the researcher. The rewards and supervision and punishments within the police department that might shape, affect, reduce, or increase the ORCS are rarely discussed (see Moskos 2008 for exceptions)—for example, the influence of the absence or presence of overtime, how it is allocated by the department and the city and with reference to what, and periodic changes in management and supervision.

Whatever appears disorderly is disorderly. Deep, patterned, and consistent exchange relationships among people living in disadvantaged areas—exchanges between ministers, shopkeepers, homeless people, "criminals," and other residents of the area—are rarely seen as the essential infrastructure of life in these areas. Some of these essential exchanges produce the incidents called "crime." Conversely, if crime is taken as the only indication of order and ordering, the remainder of the orderly processes is omitted from consideration. As both Anderson and Venkatesh demonstrate, many of the processes that produce order can be called criminal but are not because of tacit agreements between police, shopkeepers, and tavern owners. These processes are not captured in conventional criminology.

This is a cross-sectional picture that will be elaborated in chapters 8, 9 and 10. Police research in criminal justice and criminology is crime focused and pragmatic, a reflected version of policing's problems without an understanding of how police practices produce the studied object of concern: crime, disorder, violence, drugs, or the number and types of calls for service. The focus on this research sustains a blindness to the social consequences of policing, especially those subtle matters of civility, restraint, and justice that embed "crime" but do not vary with its presence or absence. Ironically, the glorification of crime control efforts seemed to be ratcheted up regardless of the outcomes revealed in the vast costs, damages, and underlying long-term disenfranchisement of African Americans. The stark facts are embedded in quite different public policy concerns, each championed by quite different scholars and policy makers.

This series of points captures, on the one hand, the actions of researchers and is a reflection of the deep assumptions made by the police in action. We might call it a mode of action, or *métier*. This métier omits consideration of the wide range of effects of policing on those policed, the feedback loops that are sustained by these practices, and the effects of such policing on trust and police legitimacy. It envisions only the need to control, deter, and punish the visible and known contestants. While the valued outputs are called crime statistics, these are merely dramaturgical high points in an ongoing drama of control.

The question that then arises is: given the prior definition of democratic policing as a form and style that avoids further damage to civility and increasing inequalities, among other general points, does a given observed pattern of policing and responses to it reflect democratic policing? If not, why not? This question requires an examination of policing's assumptions and their tools, what is known about the effects of policing in local areas of cities, and the ways in which social integration is shaped. The police métier as given is an idea shared and largely unquestioned by the researchers.

COMMENT

Returning to the sociology of knowledge perspective, one might ask: how did it happen that a field generated by creative individual scholars working with little or no funding is now radically dependent on funding, features trivial research often supported by "soft money," and is embarrassingly eager to study any currently fashionable question without theorizing it? The preferred genre for students in police studies is the brief empirical study. Graduate students are subject to pressure to publish early and often and to limit their first publications to several (at least one or two a year) unrelated empirically based reports. This research in turn is produced by a few centers, and the conceptual work that is cited briefly in the opening paragraph of the paper is drawn from the original research of a few known scholars. Police studies draws on many disciplines, including the emergent field of criminal justice itself—anthropology, social psychology, political science, some economics, and policy science and secondarily from statistics. Police studies as a field, while tightly linked to funding from the Justice Department, is also vulnerable to trends, changes in administration, and political trends in crime concerns (e.g., shifting focus on youth homicide, neighborhood safety, drugs, or gangs). These trends in funding undercut replication or at least repeating and testing the findings of previous key studies, hinge work on a few key works written some thirty to forty years ago (e.g., Banton, Westley, Skolnick, and Wilson). Some three generations (a twenty-year cohort)—it is almost sixty years since Westley's work was begun in Gary, Indiana, and my fieldwork was done more than thirty-seven years ago—have now pursued police research in earnest. There are continued differences in the research done and in the funding sources in the United States and the UK. While there has been considerable research and some that is cumulative, there is no theory of policing or of police. The circulation of personnel and joint programs appear possible in the future in police studies, but the driving force in both the United States and the UK is policy-based, short-term crisis funding that stimulates brief and limited research reports. In this flurry, much of it mirror work, reflecting the interests of the government of the day, challenges thrown up by transnational and corporate policing for pay, restorative justice, and the fragmentation of ideas of justice under the smashing forces of the market.

It would appear that emergent issues in theorizing are a result of broadening the ambit of concern and refining new paradigms such as "security governance" (Johnston and Shearing 2003), "police studies" (including public and private and examining the blurred boundaries), "governmentality" (Garland 2001), "governing through crime" (Simon 2007), "thick security" (Loader and Walker 2007), and policing the risk society (Ericson and Haggerty 1997). Such reworking and a widening concern for analysis of networks of social control in which police play a partial role, and policing in general rather than the public police, are now foci (Cooley 2005). Concern with justice seems restricted to the "critical criminologists," some of whom call themselves Marxists, and a few philosophers. Nevertheless, the underlying subtext of many of the key works in criminal justice—here I consider the works of W. J. Wilson (1987), Robert Sampson and colleagues (1997), and David Garland (2001)—concerns the consequences of a growing government-backed and -supported massive inequality in capitalist society and its ultimately eroding effects on the democratic ethos. This concern has not been translated well or brought out as an issue in the empirical studies published in the key journals.

On a more pragmatic level, one can say that the claims for respect and status have been validated in the past ten years more than the previous eighty or ninety years since the writings of the police reformers. The field of police studies has captured public attention prior to the Iraq War by insupportable claims that the police have reduced crime, notoriously in New York City. This claim is based on ORCS and implies "effectiveness" and even efficiency in crime control. This begs the question of what effectiveness would be in a democracy, given the balance between civil liberties and security or crime control (this is discussed in more depth in chapters 6 and 7). It also leaves unasked the question raised in the introduction of this book: what are the police good for? This "good" is certainly under no circumstances restricted to reducing officially recorded crime if it also reduces the quality of life, responsiveness, the wide range of services that the police provide, and increasing inequalities. This balance should be recognized, rather than a narrow and misguided concern with crime reduction alone. Because the research enterprise has increasingly propounded the notion that crime control is the essence of policing and that policing should be more efficient (with no criteria provided by which to judge this) and seized on the idea that policing is not just based on several sciences or disciplines but is itself a science (Hoover 2005, 15–21), driven best by randomized experimental projects, it has narrowed the vision of the police studies field to that which can be measured and manipulated rather than any political, moral, or value-based explicitly democratic position.[24] One of the most common fallacies in much recent empirical work and proscriptive essays is focusing on "what works" and "what can the police do?" rather than asking about and measuring the moral, political, and social consequences of any police action (Rose and Clear 1998; Moore 2003, 491).

CHAPTER FIVE

Structural Features of American Policing

To some important degree, the scholarship outlined in the previous chapter has shaped policing, and the ideas about policing. The pattern of American policing is decentralized, diverse, locally funded, and locally shaped. While the United States follows the Anglo-American pattern of democratic policing, it also manifests some distinctive features. The United States is more flexible than Western Europe in developing and facilitating a wide range of federal specialized agencies, state, county, townships, and local police agencies. It is locally funded, locally driven, and locally oriented. This is in part a residue of the colonial heritage—a disdain for the centralized monarchical system in which all the power was held, in theory, by the monarch. American policing is localized policing, and it reflects long years of frontier status, large assimilating minorities and immigrants, a palpable emphasis on violence and individualism, and deep suspicion of government. Its Puritanism remains very close to the surface. The United States does not discourage private enclaves, insular communities, and those who can pay for additional protection. It facilitates and encourages private policing. It is, however, less flexible than Western European nations in nurturing variations in municipal policing, such as community support officers (CSOs), part of the police "family" found in the UK and the Netherlands. On the other hand, it has fostered large numbers of business improvement districts (Greene 2007). These small areas, often bounded by near-slum or declining areas, are privately policed in order to encourage commerce. These observations perhaps reflect the assertion that in Western Europe the viability and survival of the state supersede the value of the capitalistic economy, and in the United States the opposite is true. This pattern perhaps accounts for the sustained growth in private security organizations and specialized federal agencies that are a product of the interpretation of the commerce clause in the U.S. Constitution and related legislation.

AMERICAN POLICE AND POLICING

American police organizations in their formality resemble police organizations in all industrialized nations. That is, they are bureaucratically structured, are punishment oriented to sustain discipline, serve the state and its interests as well as their own, and are violent and "bottom heavy." Given this frame, an analytical definition of police remains elusive, in spite of abundant published research. While police can be divided by level of obligation (federal, state, municipal, private, or corporate), there have been recent efforts to create a more coordinated policing system combining first responders (fire, emergency services and hospital personnel, and police), simulations of massive emergency situations (a disaster followed by a second or massive failures of first responses), and the National Guard (state-based militias).

As discussed in previous chapters in some detail, American policing is a subtype of what might be called the "Peel model" of policing as refined by Sir Robert Peel from his experience as home secretary and secretary for Northern Ireland. It was in effect transported forward and backward over the course of the late eighteenth and early nineteenth centuries (Brogden 1987). Peel also drew on the pattern of policing developed in India by Napier—a visible, often native-based police force on the ground and a small well-armed group of men housed in barracks, out of sight and ready to respond with varying levels of violence in the context of riots and rebellion. This also was the nexus of recruiting ethnic soldiers (e.g., Gurkhas, Moroccans, and Algerians) to police ethnic groups other than their own on behalf of the colonial or central state. The Gendarmes and militias (also earlier versions of this mode of militaristic policing [Enloe 1980a, 1980b; Palmer 1988; Emsley 1996]) were seen as "backup" to the (usually) unarmed urban patrols. The urban version of this model can be characterized as featuring uniformed police patrolling as reactive, disbursed, discretionary agents operating within a bureaucratic framework and seeking to prevent crime by visible presence (Klockars 1985, 45ff; Rawlings 2004, 118). This at least is the conventional wisdom about the origins of policing. As Brodeur (forthcoming) has pointed out repeatedly, policing has always contained an element of and obligation to carry out high policing—secretive, quasi-legal, unaccountable, and devoted to issues of national security. Variations on this are agents who work in designated places with limited powers, and specialized federal agencies who work either on a proactive intelligence-based model, a regulatory model (not employing criminal sanctions), or a case-based reactive model. These are discussed below.

FEATURES OF THE AMERICAN POLICING SYSTEM

Police expectations of themselves, combined with and in some tension with public expectations, if validated, yield a mandate (Hughes 1958). The mandate excludes others from the tasks assigned; provides the basis for a neutral "professional" attitude toward the work, especially its typical mistakes; nurtures a special etiquette of dealing with those nominally served, that is, citizens, clients, or customers; and expands and contracts over time. The mandate is a dynamic matter and is affected by the political field or local competitions among agencies and organizations and the larger sociopolitical ambiance or the surroundings. Clearly, since 9/11, the police have seen their powers and prestige grow and the courts far more willing to grant them license in their legalistic affairs.

Consider these features of American policing as an ideal type (see Manning 2003, 43–52). The public preference for a decentralized system is indicated by the large number of local agencies and the disproportionate number of local and state agents when compared to the number of federal agents (Bayley 1994). This is a not a system; local police are virtually autonomous and respond to local regulations, laws, and preferences and have little to do on a routine basis with federal agents and agencies. The largely independent federal agencies that enforce federal laws are relatively small given the size and wealth of the nation. The number of federal agencies and agents with arrest powers was ratcheted up only in the last part of the twentieth century (Richman 2000).

American police defy any easy or simple description. They are by design and preference the product of an antiauthoritarian, quasi-revolutionary country. It is possible to make some generalizations, especially about local police, consistent with this characterization of American policing.[1] With the exception of federal specialized policing, policing in the United States is as follows: it is constituted by organizations of diverse, uneven size, with uneven training and local standards for it; it is located in the executive branch of government; it is locally accountable; it is grounded in the politics of the city, state, and region; it responds to (and uses) overlapping, contradictory, and abundant legal standards; it is bottom heavy and demand oriented (responding to phone calls via 911); it is reactive by impulse and practice; it is staffed by officers who are heavily armed and dangerous; it is dependent on citizens for information and compliance; and it is shaped by information technologies. Most important, American police organizations are quite small on average, and while the modal or the most common size varies by state (Reiss 1992, 61), the majority of American police officers work in organizations of less than thirty officers.

One of the most striking things about American policing is that the numbers of officers, the numbers of agencies, and the division between part-time and full-time employees are still being debated (Bayley 1994; Maguire et al. 1998). This is because definitions of part-time, reserve, full-time, and sworn officers are inconsistent, as is the number of agencies sampled (Maguire et al. 1998). In addition, policing functions are elastic. For example, some lists of police agencies omit agricultural inspectors, OHSEA and EPA inspectors, but include investigative officers within the armed forces; others define police as those who carry a gun and can enforce the law (Morris and Geller 1992).

The problem of estimating the number of police officers and agencies begins with the failure of the government to monitor their numbers. There is a difference of 90,000 officers between the U.S. Census and LEMAS (a mailed survey sample of police agencies) estimates. The census counts 560,799 officers, and LEMAS shows 649,037. In 1997, according to LEMAS, there were some 18,769 local, 49 state, and an unknown number of federal agencies that "police." LEMAS shows some 90,000 federal employees carrying out some law enforcement function. It defines a police agency as any agency employing more than one full-time officer. LEMAS said in 1997 that there were more than 650,000 full-time public police officers, some 8.2 percent (53,300) of which are federal employees, and another 250,000 part-time officers (Reaves and Goldberg 1998). This would mean a total of some 800,000. Civilians constitute 27 percent of police employees and have increased by 161 percent as a ratio to the population. Maguire and colleagues compare LEMAS, the census, and a sample drawn by the COPS agency and present a more systematic critique of the samples and biases of each and tabulated the several estimates. Maguire et al. add omitted data (1998, 109–10) and conclude that there are in total 21,143 agencies in the United States: 14,628 local, 49 state, 3,156 sheriff-headed, and 3,280 special agencies. They conclude that "there may be as many as" 681,012 "sworn" officers as a result of combing the estimates: 383,873 in local agencies; 53,336 in state agencies, 137,985 in sheriff-headed agencies, and 58,689 in special agencies. The local agencies vary in size from a handful in departments serving small towns and villages to the more than 38,000 officers in the NYPD. Two county forces, Cook County and Los Angeles County, range from 3,000 to 5,000.

The salary structure (level and variation in pay by rank) varies in relation to the size of the organization. In 2000 the salary of an officer in the smallest force (less than 2,500) ranged from $20,900 to $22,900, while officers in the largest ranged from $35,900 to $51,300, and a similar pattern characterizes sheriff departments (Reeces and Hickman 2003). Federal pay mimics the pay in the largest departments and includes better benefits and retirement packages. In all three cases, the difference between the top ranks and the lowest is remarkably small.

In part to protect police operations from overt political commands, public policing historically stands in the executive branch of government. Policing powers, de facto, are quite widespread and shared among individual citizens, private investigators, citizen self-help groups, private policing agencies, and, occasionally, the military (National Guard, reserves, and regular forces). Territorial limits or jurisdictional boundaries, once binding in Anglo-American policing, now are largely irrelevant at the federal level, since American law is extended and applied within foreign nations with startling impunity and global and task force–based transnational policing is growing.

The American police exist in a network of telecommunication links. Information technologies are now shaping policing in many perhaps unanticipated ways (see the summary in Manning 2003). IT capacity is rather closely correlated with the size and location of the agency, as is its own accessibility to the media via media information offices (R. I. Mawby 2003). The practice of policing is affected only marginally by use of the Internet, the paperless office, the fully automated police car, crime mapping and crime analysis, and the 800-MHz radio capacity. The future influence of Compstat, crime mapping and crime analysis, while promising, is yet unproven (see chapter 6 and Manning 2008).

American police are demand led in the sense that since the 1920s they have presented themselves as ready and available. They encourage demand by advertising—"Call 911" is emblazoned on the side of nearly every vehicle. While they screen calls and reduce the demand by 50 percent through careful formatting and queuing of calls, they emphasize for political purposes that they are available and visible. They are in fact bottom heavy and reactive and mount periodic tactical crackdowns (Sherman 1992). Police allocate some 63+ percent of their sworn personnel "on the ground" in shifts of five days at eight hours at day or ten hours for four days: 8/5 or 10/4 (with other days off) through the year. This allocation of personnel means, given holidays, overtime, and comp time, as well as disability and sickness, that roughly four to five times the number of officers on duty on a given shift are required to sustain fully staffed shifts over a twenty-four-hour period. The police react to calls for service, investigate further some of those that are crime related, and manifest minimal formal specialization. Some 5–8 percent are in detective work and other specialized units. The police are divided into line and staff, with patrol as the "line" and "staff" meaning administration, internal affairs, detectives, and the service division. The top command and support are a very small part of the personnel, around 12 percent. Most officers prefer to remain on patrol, and city budgets constrain the available slots.

The public police carry arms, some of which are visible. Policing combines a visible and distinctive uniform with an astounding array of tools, including high-powered semiautomatic weapons and burgeoning IT (Manning 1997, 102–6). Police hold unique powers, even though fatal force is not restricted to the police in law or by practice, and stand ready to intervene variously in an infinite, open-ended range of social situations. Their failure to uniformly apply violence in moderation, although it is clearly the general case, is often a public issue and the basis for a media spectacle when the rare public and known shooting occurs.

The public police both seek and avoid violence, both symbolic and "real." They differentially distribute violence to groups within the state, eschew its role in their work, and conceal and deny its emotional satisfactions and attractions. There are patterned police tactics for managing citizen encounters (Bayley and Bittner 1986; Bayley and Garofalo 1989; Mastrofski, Reisig, and McCluskey 2002). These patterns suggest conditions under which events may escalate, or require force, although official reports suggest that violent episodes constitute less than 5 percent of police encounters (Alpert and Dunham 2004). The use of violence, ultimately sanctioned by the state, varies empirically rather than being, as Bittner (1972) claims, an "essential feature of the role."

The American public police seek demand, that is, they believe their legitimacy and political power rest on their being available 24 hours a day, 365 days a year. Their slogan, in slang terms, is "You call, we haul." They encourage calls, then screen and selectively respond, and even then are occasionally overloaded. The level of service is affected by technology, by roles and tasks of the participants in the police communications systems (PCS), and by the ecology and interpretive practices of patrol officers. The publicly stated aim is to increase demand and provide service, but these are in some tension from time to time. They do plan some demand, such as for parades and demonstrations, and have elaborate plans for major disasters; initiate stops and investigations; control demand for investigative services by controlling personnel and overtime; but are primarily responsive to called-in demand. Called-in demand is shaped. Police do this by screening, prioritizing, and assigning calls to loose and rather arbitrary categories; receiving calls from cell phones[2] and land lines (911, 311, and seven-digit numbers); reclassifying them formally and informally; shifting levels of personnel to respond to them; and altering their information technology to reallocate calls to automatic answering systems.[3] They are periodically unable to handle demand, thus indirectly showing their differential availability and therefore sustaining their importance and power. Police develop and state organizational operational strategies, systematic allocation and mobilization of resources (personnel, equipment, time), and presentational strategies and tactics. These may not match because what is claimed in a presentational or rhetorical strategy—for example, that community policing is the policy of the force—may not be revealed in the deployment of officers and their actual day-to-day duties and routines. They periodically deal with overloads in demand by informal means rather than by policy, phone menus, workable differential response systems that attempt to set priorities, or using designated units for calls requiring nonemergency responses.

TRENDS IN EMPLOYMENT OF AMERICAN POLICE

America has four broad types of police: local; state (forty-nine states have them; Hawaii does not); federal, including specialized sworn officers and investigators; and private police. Large university police departments have of late been required to submit their crime figures to the Department of Justice, but their size and the number of university departments are still debated. In addition, there are a number of shadow functionaries who police, including reserve or auxiliaries and ad hoc volunteers with quasi-legal status such as senior citizens who patrol schools looking for truants or people parking in spots for disabled people (both done in Lansing, Michigan).

Let us look at the growth in public police. Unlike other industrialized nations, the United States has continued to hire more police even during periods of economic downturn (the 1980s in particular) and crime declines (the decade of the 1990s). The number of counted public police agents has increased in the past forty years. Public police have increased in number and per capita (Walker and Katz 2002, 90). This growth is in part stimulated by direct block grant–type funding from COPS and in recent years, since 2002, Homeland Security funds.[4] The size of the police organization in America varies widely (ibid., 64). As the range in size would suggest, the ratio of police per 1,000 people also varies from the national average of 1.5 per 1,000. This ratio is radically skewed by the vast numbers of small agencies. The most densely policed city is Washington, D.C., with 6.7 per 1,000, while at the other end of large cities, San Diego is policed with 1.7 per 1,000. Expenditures at all levels for "security" in the form of public police likewise have increased both absolutely and per capita.

As noted above, and emphasized by Maguire's study (2003, 3), the variety of functions due to the size of police organizations is astonishing: he notes that ranks vary from four or five to twelve; some have centralized headquarters, while many others have precinct houses; generalization in tasks ranges widely (specialized units are a function of size, though not entirely, as even small departments have special units such as water police, SWAT teams, and traffic units); some give supervisors great leeway, and others are very strict and controlling; some have highly informal and unwritten policies, while others have written policies covering "almost every imaginable contingency" (ibid.); some invest great resources on the street, and others do not; and, finally, they are variously staffed by civilians (or nonsworn officers). Patrol functions and modes vary widely, too, with some using motorcycles, horses, bicycles, and walking officers and others confined almost entirely to motorized units (Reaves and Goldberg 1997).

The percentage of civilian police has increased from 11 percent in 1960 to 18.4 percent in 1980 to the 1997 figure of 28.6 percent. In general, they are employed in larger departments with greater specialization of function. Because of specialization, differentiation of size, and costs of retirements, salaries, and union contracts that protect officers, the number and percentage of civilians will continue to rise, regardless of variation in growth in sworn officers.

The consequence of these political preferences for weak, local, nonfederal, small police forces is clear—77 percent of American public police are employed by localities (Reiss 1992). It should be emphasized that in contrast to other Anglo-American forms of policing, the American small local force is rarely consolidated (as has happened in England in particular over the past thirty years), and a close examination of any large city will show a patchwork of amazing overlap and competition (Walker and Katz 2002, 73).[5]

Consider a final point about the division of labor in policing. Recall that the figures for total number of local public police are not agreed upon and range from 660,000 to 800,000 depending on the source. Estimates for the number of private police range from 1.5 to 2 million employees. This means that the ratio between public and private is approximately 2:4 in favor of privately employed agents. If one adds state, sheriff, and federal agencies, it does not alter the ratio very much. If it is further assumed that these agents work primarily in large cities and near suburbs, serving businesses, corporations, or middle- or upper-class housing estates or homes, it is clear that the concentration of security officers is heavily skewed toward the suburbs and small cities and inversely related to the prevalence and incidence of crime.

ORGANIZATION AND ACCOUNTABILITY OF AMERICAN PUBLIC POLICING

Histories of American policing, found in several fine overviews (Miller 1977; Monkkonen 1981, 1992; Reppetto 1978; Reiss 1992), disproportionately focus on large departments (Boston, New York, Los Angeles, Chicago, and Philadelphia). The most comprehensive studies are of specific cities such as Lane's fine work on Boston (1967). This focus obscures the dominance in American life and memory of hesitant, fragmented, locally grounded, and accountable small police organizations, with limited official legal powers, combined with the growth of wide-ranging activities unimpeded by federal control, regulation, or intervention. It follows that accountability is a contextually defined matter that defies generalization.

Police organizations are patently and obstinately resistant to reshaping and changes in structure and function (Maguire 2003). Some of the influences resisted are "internal," resulting from changes in demography and ecology, while others are the result of external sociopolitical trends. Local political issues shape the size, functions, and budgets of American departments more than general principles such as efficiency, low costs, or effectiveness (Reppetto 1979; Reiss 1992). By local political issues I mean those that become axial media events like the Rodney King beating, the sodomizing of Abner Louima, or the verdict of innocence in the O. J. Simpson trial. These alter perceptions of risk and shape political campaigns based on law-and-order politics. No research has shown clear and consistent long-term correlations between crime, budgets, and policing patterns, nor the impact of the environment on such matters as police size and organization (Maguire 2003). Additional officers do suppress official figures for short periods of time (Harcourt 2001), although it is not entirely clear why or how this takes place.

From the beginning of the nineteenth-century Peel innovation, the concern of politicians and police top command has been to control corruption and veniality among patrol officers. This issue appears now as a concern with training, supervision, and control and a lesser concern with loyalty. Corruption scandals, as Sherman demonstrated some time ago (1978), are cyclical and present themselves on a regular basis. This is in part because in a punishment-centered bureaucracy (Gouldner 1954, 207–28), officers are constantly inventing ways to do the work that blur the formal and the informal (Manning and Redlinger 1977). The kinds of distinction that characterize the differences between what is said by officers and what is done, their practices, remain unexplored.

Advocates of training (Haberfeld 2006) assert its efficacy, yet the brevity of American police training, its nonstandardized nature, its focus on physical skills and rote memory of legal procedures (recipe knowledge to keep you out of trouble), and its almost total absence beyond the police training academy mean that training as now constituted is not a solution to corruption or the development of management skills. This is becoming more apparent as business-speak, that is, policing as a business (referring to efficiency and "service delivery," "customer satisfaction," and police chiefs as managers with sophisticated management skills), clouds the reality of everyday policing.

A parallel "silver bullet" solution to scandal and cleanup cycles along with training is better communication-as-supervision. As Reiss and Bordua (1967) and Bordua and Reiss (1965, 1967) noted presciently some forty years ago, information technology systems, or more generally the PCS that funnel demand in and out of the organization, have increasingly become the mode of supervision, control, and accountability for American forces. With the increased mobility of the population and the dispersal of populations out of large, dense cities into suburbs, pressure was placed on policing to serve via the rule "You call, we roll." The vast network of efficient telephones increased demand, and the police emphasized "responsiveness" as a theme in presentation of their mandate. This demand-driven theme, in due course, increased social distance and the quality of local control of policing. This punctuated the demise of the local political machine in all save a few American cities (perhaps Boston, Miami-Dade, Chicago, and Philadelphia), and of police union strength and control of conditions of work (strongest also in these cities). The ethnic composition of policing has always been a striking feature of American policing as WASPs declined in power in big cities, the Italians and Irish became the stereotypic police officers, and the patronage and a succession based on ethnicity became powerful from 1890 on, in effect excluding women and people of color successfully until affirmative action penetrated local police and firing and hiring procedures in the seventies.

The question of the locus of loyalty of police in the United States remains unexamined. Bordua noted (1968) that the concern of the English was to isolate the officer from the influences of politics, temptation, and the banal politics of self-interest. This appears to be largely successful at present insofar as officers identify with peers within their organization, and with "the job," rather than with the organization as a whole.[6]

Three trends have affected local police accountability. As Walker (2005) has shown, public modes of regulating police by citizens (complaints, citizen review boards, advisory boards, and externally staffed and funded agencies), or in general some efforts at "civilian oversight" have a brief, unsavory, and weak history in the United States. No national effort has been made to alter this except through ad hoc court orders. A second influence has been court orders dealing with fabricated official statistics, failures in hiring in line with affirmative action rules, racial profiling, jail conditions and services, and individual and collective-organizational liability in civil suits. The third influence is rather indirect and tenuous. This is the "managerialism" evidenced in policing by objectives, mission statements, value commitments, and public pledges. This is often combined with the rhetoric of community policing, problem solving, joint partnerships, and the "coproduction of order."

As Bittner (1972) and Klockars (1985) have pointed out, the courts in their wisdom have left the definition of violence, brutality, excessive force, and coercion to local standards, much like those that govern physicians' and lawyers' liabilities and the remedies offered by the civil courts. Thus, while the law is a dramatic point of justice, its standards in this and other matters are flexible, local, and subject to the politics of the day (Lawrence 2000). If the problem of policing, as Reiss (1992) argues, is maintaining a balance between the internal equilibrium and the external challenging environment, then policing is likely to be less constrained in the future by massive political machines, central city bureaucracies, and even state governments. The growth in per capita policing is in midsize towns, suburban departments, and rural areas with typically weak governments, low taxation, and low services in general. With the exception of a few large cities such as Washington, D.C., and

New York City, policing in large cities shows low growth in the number of police per capita.

American policing, less than European nations, has been influenced by transnational policing, ad hoc task forces, and formal cooperative arrangements. Ironically, the courts and the American executive branch have been viciously imperialistic in extending American policing into international waters, denying the Geneva Convention, snatching and kidnapping foreign citizen-suspects without warrants, and mounting searches and seizures on the high seas, sometimes in pursuit of suspected drug dealers. All of this stands in violation of international law and semilegal conventions governing international relations that restrain policing across borders (Nadelmann 1993; Deflem 2002; Sheptycki 2000).

The idea of policing reform linked with accountability has had no viability in the United States. The notion that some forces, internal or external to the police, are manifest in visible change is dubious at best. For example, recent trends do point to a reduction in functions provided, or "load shedding" (Button 2002, 35–40), contracting out functions, adapting businesslike managerial techniques, and a tendency to charge for services rendered. These include charges for false alarms answered, charges for arrests and costs at accidents, fees for licenses and for processing insurance claims, and increased use of civilian employees to increase traffic revenue. These costs amount to a reduction of the general collective will as expressed in and through policing (Bayley and Shearing 1996).

COMMERCIAL SECURITY

Private security prior to the late 1980s served as an unexplicated contrast conception to illuminate what public policing, or policing, was or was not. Once interest emerged in private policing, and it has been growing in the past ten or more years, the weak conceptual basis for empirical analysis became more apparent.

The number of private police is difficult to estimate (Nalla and Newman 1990; Johnston 1992). The estimates range from 1.5 to 2 million in some 60,000 firms. The number of both agents and agencies has grown since 1970 (Kakalik and Wildhorn 1971; Cunningham and Taylor 1985). Given the flexibility in these estimates and the heavily ideological character of the arguments (primarily negative with some exceptions [e.g., Forst 2000]), one should be cautious in advancing explanations for future growth. This is in part because computers and information systems have been substituted for some officers and "de-skilling" and "civilianization" have occurred, shifting some security-type jobs to nonuniformed clerks.[7] However, even among Anglo-American democratic states, the comparisons between private and public police numbers seen in terms of ratios are suggestive of other factors at work. Button (2002, 98) reports from several sources that the ratio of private to public (excluding non-home-office officers) officers is 1.4 in the UK, 2.6 in favor of private officers in the United States, 2.0 in Canada, and 1.5 in Australia.

However, sophisticated observers such as Nalla and Newman (1990) point out that the problem of estimating the numbers of private security employees has at least three aspects: defining a security organization, an officer, and security-related functions (carrying out what duties—desk work, patrolling, watching doors, cutting keys, answering alarms, scrutinizing videos). How do these functions reduce or prevent risk or loss? What range of functions does "security" cover—contract security, corporate police, and policing jails and courts as transport officers? Are locksmiths security experts? In what sense do they provide security? In addition, because the number of employed in these functions rests on the definitions of human resources divisions rather than an analytical definition, it is difficult to get accurate data from private corporations.

The first major study of personnel and trends in private police was published in the United States in 1971 (Wildhorn and Kakalik 1971; Kakalik and Wildhorn 1971, 1977), followed by the overview found in the Hallcrest Report on the potential growth in private security (Cunningham and Taylor 1985). Johnston's work (1992, 2002) advanced an analytical approach that builds on earlier work on the history of private security in the United States. The growth of private policing in the United States was stimulated by at least three trends. First was the growth of unions and unionization that led to large strikes and demonstrations in the late nineteenth and early twentieth centuries. These were led by miners in the West and the central states (Pennsylvania, West Virginia, Ohio, and Kentucky) and stimulated not only the use of agent provocateurs, private forces to break the strikes, but the establishment of state police forces. The second trend was the growth of the frontier and the need to protect the transport money, gold, and valuables long distances to the Far West. This gave rise to Wells Fargo and other protection agencies similar to those that transport money to and from banks. The third trend was the growth of threats to the wealthy and investigative needs unsatisfied by public police, especially when a crime was anticipated rather than having already been committed. This led to the establishment and growth of Pinkerton, the most famous of the early investigative agencies.

Shearing (1992) argues that massive semiprivate space has stimulated the great growth in private policing. This semiprivate space includes shopping malls, sporting arenas, and the like. There are clearly other factors in the apparent growth of private policing discussed, if not empirically documented (Button 2002, 98–99). These include the rise in crime and fear of crime (sometimes associated with the growth of the rhetoric of risk rather than the facts of risk itself [Ericson, Doyle, and Barry 2002]); the risk of terrorism since September 11, 2001; expanded demand for protection and police services, perhaps related to community policing and efforts to reduce social distance by public policing; and the growth of the insurance industry and its capacity to demand security and protection of assets. These are facets of the more general argument concerning the "shrinking state" under the influence of neoconservative thinking (Garland 2000) and the growth of privatization of previously public functions (running prisons, guarding courts, transporting prisoners).

The Hallcrest Report set out some of the basic parameters of assessing private security. The report divides the security service and manufacturing sector into armored car (cash-conveyance) companies, alarm companies, contract guards, private investigators, consultants and engineers, locksmiths, and manufacturers and distributors of security equipment (Cunningham and Taylor 1985, 192). It shows tables for 1980, 1990, and projections for 2000. Some general trends are discernible above the actual numbers: the percentage of the sector that is security or contract guards has declined, although they are about 50 percent of the sector; alarm companies have the most robust growth; and there is very little category-specific growth (the report estimates a 4 percent growth from 1990 to 2000). These figures are subject to debate. For example, the Bureau of Labor Statistics counts only 39,000 private investigators in 2000 (Dempsey and Forst 2005, 55), while the Hallcrest Report claims there were 45,000 in 1980 and that the total would continue to rise to an estimated 90,000 by 2000.

Some sociological generalizations might be made concerning the balance between private and public policing in the United States and the organizational pattern of police organizations. The United States has the largest number of private security officers and companies, both in real terms and per capita. There is very little perceived competition, tension, or concern about the growth or size of private policing organizations in the United States. This is in part because of the wealth of the country. The tendency to hire more police when crime rises means that there is no loss of public policing jobs even during budget crises. The number of public police is close to comparable per capita across the several Anglo-American societies. Their operations are noncontroversial and of little concern to the public. They are legitimate, but relatively unregulated. The federal government is a contractor for the largest number of private security officers through the auspices of the Federal Protective Service and the Transportation Security Administration. Their functions (cash conveyance, locksmithing, selling security products, patrolling parking lots and malls, and monitoring screens) vary so widely as to suggest they are not a precise category but a residual category based on the organizational premise that "policing" is public policing. Corporate security organizations, designed to protect assets and reduce "shrinkage," are being replaced by contract security and outsourcing of skilled functions such as investigation, and the work of "security" is more likely to be in some relationship to monitoring quasi-public property and places. The most radical decline is in the number of in-house corporate security operations that serve the interests of the chief executive officer, board of trustees, and management in general. While they began as a kind of easily mobilized force to destroy the union movement in the 1930s, they are now being "downsized."

This change in the composition and mode of employment in workers in private security is the result of several interrelated factors. Such private security forces are vulnerable, as they no longer can sustain roles as personal chauffeurs and body guards for top management. Management is less stable and likely to be a shifting, unstable coalition. Private security officers in corporations have lost out in the struggle to define and control "loss prevention" and risk management. New functions in this arena are carried out in the human resources and risk management sections of corporations. Audio and visual surveillance systems now substitute for personnel. Advanced computer records are kept by human resources and insurance or risk management divisions within companies, not in the files of the security office. The rise of a specialized chief information officer and office has centralized corporate information-gathering functions. As in public policing, the division of labor is leading to outsourcing of specialized tasks and a shifting of other tasks into more specialized organizational roles.

Regulation of security in the United States is loose, even haphazard. Most states require modest licensing for work in private security, and only recently have national organizations such as American Society of Industrial Security (ASIS) arisen to monitor and regulate standards and to provide seminars, certification, and continuing education.

MUNICIPAL POLICING

The United States, unlike continental systems, has not encouraged semilegitimate private-city organizations, in part because the pervasive use of private guards and contracts with private security organizations leaves no ecological niche for such organizations. In addition, the pressure felt nationally in the UK and the Netherlands to integrate social services, including police, into planning to control disorders such as noise, rubbish, crowds of drunks, and maintenance functions in central cities has not had any appeal in the United States. Such civilian quasi-legal groups, seen in the UK and in the Netherlands, are not present in the United States (see Johnston 2002, which suggests that these officers with quasi-legitimate status are at a loss to define their duties, obligations, and roles). Some police departments have encouraged police academies to co-opt citizens, citizen advisory groups, and volunteers, such as the San Diego RSVP retiree groups that provide clerical functions in the department, but no formal groups with a national presence and sponsorship exist. There have been a few innovations in nonsworn forms of policing, such as private nonsworn police regulating order in urban business areas. These are found in Washington, D.C., Philadelphia, Pennsylvania, and New York City, for example.

Local policing-regulatory groups such as park services, sewer and water, rubbish collection, code enforcement, health and sanitation, and the like are not integrated with policing, nor are there any formal or informal ties except in Chicago. (In Chicago the Mayor's Office coordinates response to complaints about city services, streets, lighting, parks, and so forth that are forwarded from police districts.) Some cities, such as Philadelphia and Washington, D.C., have urban development areas (e.g., Northwest Seventh Avenue near China Town and the MCI Center) that are patrolled by semiuniformed agents who give advice, tidy the area, communicate via cell phones, and liaise with public police in the area. Large cities also have overlapping jurisdictions that arise from university and park police who patrol in and around the university areas but are not restricted to them.

OTHER POLICING BODIES

The 1997 LEMAS survey (Reaves and Goldberg 1997) indicated that there were 53,300 federal officers at that time. Maguire et al. (1998) argued based on several samples that there were some 30 federal law enforcement agencies that employed some 47,129 agents. This is probably the most accurate survey, but clearly the definition of *agency* is elastic. Geller and Morris (1992) stated that there are 50 federal agencies that carry guns and make arrests. This is a partial list of federal agents and their policing functions. Geller and Morris (1992, 231, abstract) wrote concerning federal agencies and their integration seventeen years ago, "There remains a vast ambit of overlapping federal and nonfederal criminal jurisdiction guided primarily by political fashions." It would appear that there are 43 agencies with broad obligations. The variable definition of federal agency and their duties makes counting agents and agencies difficult (Richman 2000).

While there are various estimates of the number of federal agents and agencies, there is some consensus about the most visible, the largest, and the most prestigious agencies among them: the CIA, FBI, DEA, Treasury Department, and the Department of Defense, as well as agents affiliated with Department of Homeland Security. After September 11, 2001, and the establishment in 2002 of the Department of Homeland Security, the blurred boundaries between policing, high policing, intelligence, and security functions emerged (Kean and Hamilton 2004; Odom 2004). In part because the intelligence functions of the CIA in particular are hidden in both budget and numbers and in part because the line between intelligence, policing, and military action was systematically distorted by the George W. Bush administration, the numbers are misleading.

The dense thicket of specialized federal agencies in the United States is a map of unknown territory. We lack descriptive overviews and analyses. Even the most expert of observers, such as Howard Odom, former director of National Security Agency (NSA), is slightly bewildered at the division of labor within and across agencies, even within the subset of federal police agencies, the "intelligence community" (Odom 2004; Kean and Hamilton 2004).[8]

The work on federal enforcement and specialized federal agencies is thin, most of it done by extraordinary journalists (Powers 2004; Kessler 1994, 2002, 2003; Bamford 1983, 2002, 2004; Epstein 1990) focused on a few major agencies such as the NSA, CIA, FBI, and DEA. The finest analytical works are now dated (Kaufman 1960; Moore 1977; Epstein 1977). The materials on specialized smaller agencies are virtually nonexistent apart from encyclopedias and listings of federal agencies (see Sullivan et al. 2005). Other forms of federal policing involve regulations and using civil sanctions with occasional recourse to the criminal sanction.

Specialized federal agencies are divided in the origin of their authority. The executive branch has thirty-eight policing agencies under its control, and within the executive branch, State has one policing agency, Agriculture two, Treasury eleven, and Justice seven. The other policing agencies are distributed between Interior (five), Defense (nine), Commerce (one), and Transportation (two). The legislative branch has three police agencies, while the judicial branch has one. There are two independent specialized federal policing agencies—the TVA (Tennessee Valley Authority, which is a semiprivate public development agency) police (and fire department) and the Amtrak (public rail system) police.

A Taxonomy of Specialized (Federal) Agencies

A full discussion of federal agencies in the United States requires a more differentiated taxonomy. Law enforcement, as the recent interest in plural policing and governance of security has brought to mind, is not restricted to those who carry guns and can make arrests. Governmental social control takes many forms, and the term *law enforcement* is a rhetorical device associated with the rise of "professional policing." The term divides and conquers by depriving status to those lacking guns and the criminal sanction, but does not change the powers that the other agencies have to apply coercive authoritative control. It also obscures the inspection function and the meta-inspection function, even though some inspection agencies listed by Geller and Morris (1992) are gun carrying. Since 9/11, reorganization has occurred by amalgamating several agencies into a national Homeland Security office. This has not altered their traditional functions; it has dramatized those that represent protection against various forms of invasive foreign-based terrorism. Consider some of these complexities.

The sanctions used are various. Not all federal agencies that enforce "the law" use the criminal sanction, or they use it extremely rarely. Some are principally criminal sanction based, some are more regulatory in nature in which the civil law works most frequently, others are inspective in nature, and still others are meta-inspective (these are agencies that inspect the inspectors). If we consider law governmental social control, then law enforcement must finally include those agencies that sustain the government's notion of safety and security, such as Environmental Protection Agency, Department of Energy, and the Atomic Energy Commission, agencies that monitor what has been established as safety with respect to the risks of industrialized life. Here, I make reference to establishing standards for drugs, air pollution, nuclear radiation, water pollution, and foods, standards that are in fact arbitrary and changeable but unchallengeable in courts, as they are based on the absolute premise of national survival rather than empirical evidence.

When criminal law is used primarily, distinctions between and among agencies are not easily established or "amenable to any categorical distinction" (Richman 2000, 82). As Richman (2000) argues, trends in legislation make even this distinction slippery:

- While the U.S. Constitution does not grant the federal government general police powers, legislative moves, especially in the twentieth century, granted increasing power to federal agencies by use of the commerce clause, civil liberties, and legislation broadening mandates (83–91).

- Growth occurs through the passage of substantive law, "budget creep," and ad hoc laws responding to specific worries (kidnapping, drinking, drugs) rather than through mandate expansion of given agencies (81).
- Boundaries are not set by law or narrow jurisdiction but by negotiation between federal, state, and local agencies (91–96).
- Legislatures pass laws that are open-ended in part to permit agencies to explore, expand, or contract their responsibilities (ibid.).
- Tacit agreements, rather than written memos of understanding or statutes, guide the division of enforcement labor. These, in turn, are known through breaches or violations of what is taken for granted about what is a "federal" case and what is a "local" case (95). As is commonly noted, these exceptions are negotiated on a case-by-case basis. Exceptions tend to favor the more powerful, that is, federal agency.
- Limits on federal enforcement are due not to the absence of reach, jurisdiction, or resistance but to the small numbers of agents, resources that they lack for local enforcement (information and informants and inadequate local knowledge), and the political autonomy of U.S. federal attorneys. These form a network extending from the Department of Justice and headed by the U.S. attorney general (101).

Agencies, to defend their niche and perhaps to expand it, specialize. The most specialized federal agencies have a specific territorial and organizational remit to police a place, or places, with defined features. These range from policing zoos and art galleries to the Pentagon and the FBI (the FBI has it own a police force that polices FBI properties and personnel) to international transborder policing. Civil regulatory agencies that do not employ the criminal law routinely tend to have broad rather than specialized mandates. Inspection services, such as the Office of the Inspector General and the twenty-three agencies that have inspector generals within their boundaries, and meta-inspection agencies (those that inspect the inspectors, such as the IRS's inspection agency) have a monitoring function. They monitor the monitors who monitor agency actions. Some of these agencies are themselves monitorial in function. This represents bureaucratic attempts to ensure trust by adding layers of bureaus. The broadest obligations of agencies are those that include high policing and homeland security functions.

Clearly, not all agencies are equal. They vary in their political visibility, power, and salience. This is in part due to the broad range of laws they are authorized to employ, and these in turn give them power. These agencies can be separated by the sanctions used, with the most visible and dramatic agencies being the criminal sanction and secret agencies that are devoted to national security and to criminal matters involving the national welfare—FBI, CIA, NSA, Treasury, and others. Those with more mundane mandates use regulatory sanctions in part to sustain the environment and industries of merit rather than to eradicate a market in illegal transactions (goods, services, people). There are specialized agencies that work as inspectors,

Occupational Safety and Health Administration (OSHA), the U.S. Postal Inspector, and the Federal Aviation Administration. Finally, there are meta-inspective services that audit the inspectors and auditors, such as IRS auditors and the Offices of the Solicitor General and the Inspector General (see Geller and Morris 1992, table 1, appendix, especially the note).

Without doubt, a broad taxonomy hides the fact that some of the agencies said to have "internal obligations," such as the FBI and military investigative services, are in fact international and worldwide. They can be sent to investigate or are stationed abroad (there are some forty-three "legates" housing FBI agents in foreign countries). As the *Report of the 911 Commission* (Kean and Hamilton 2004) shows, boundary disputes between the CIA and FBI continue in and outside this country because the questions of national security can be defined variously, include criminal actors and acts within this country or abroad or both, and may involve both U.S. crimes and matters that are not yet criminal but are conspiracies. Ironies remain, such as the fact that the CIA cannot investigate itself and must call on the FBI when it suspects "moles" or spies within.

Any listing or taxonomy of agency functions can capture only a moment in time. Agencies are reorganized periodically, and their duties shifted in accordance with current political concerns. The reorganization that created the Department of Homeland Security is a good example of the impact of politics on agency function and accountability. The Bureau of Land Management and Forest Service officers, for example, are required to seek to eradicate marijuana growing in federal parks and lands, the Treasury Department (Secret Service) has had inherited duties relating to computer fraud since 1984, the Department of Interior land management and resource police have responsibility for wild burros and horses, while the TVA police have responsibilities for police and fire services in the lands regulated by the TVA. Although each agency has a mandate and a name, the categories of policing duties within a given branch can be wildly diverse. For example, the Department of Defense has world security obligations to oversee buildings and lands on U.S. bases; within the Treasury the duties range from protecting elected officials to patrolling the U.S. Mint.

The level at which the agencies police or regulate varies enormously. At one level, the military police and shore patrol, for example, patrol bases and shoreline around the bases, while at the other extreme, the IRS inspector inspects the IRS inspectorate (it is an inspectorate of an inspectorate, which in turn regulates the IRS as a regulatory body). There are twenty-five inspector generals in the federal government, and two of these are law enforcement bodies whose agents carry guns. Very large units police fraud, embezzlement, and white-collar crimes that are largely invisible and not traditional nineteenth-century visible crimes.

If one divides the federal agencies by the sanctions used, one can see that some agencies use traditional criminal sanctions and that the cases are entered into the criminal justice system. Other agencies are regulatory and rely on civil sanctions. Some agencies are primarily inspective or regulatory and supervise or audit other federal agencies. There are, finally, those that are meta-inspective, that is, they inspect the inspectors. At the bottom, symbolically, are agencies that police the status quo ante.[9] These are ambiguous agencies that seek to sustain the truth as government defines it. They monitor the nature of the viability of life, the water, the air, or the sky and sea, as the government of the day defines it. This includes setting the level of danger a citizen can expect from water, air, emissions, and nuclear radiation and preserving the survival of the country. One can label models of regulation as the criminal coercive model, the compliance negotiation model, and the cooperative model.

The investigative function is performed by some, while others are committed more to patrol and order maintenance, or at the other end world security and high politics. As noted above, some agencies are quite specialized in their ecological obligations, the most extreme examples being the National Gallery, Supreme Court, U.S. Mint, and Library of Congress police. Some are truly federal, such as the FBI and fisheries and park police, for example.

The legislative, judicial, and special establishment police are concerned primarily with order and ordering and protecting property, visitors, and personnel in specific ecologically defined sites. This ecological basis for authority stands in contrast to the broader mandate of the agencies within the executive branch of the federal government. Here, a rather specific listing of distinctions is required. Federal agencies accountable to the executive branch vary in their:

- Analytical focus—intelligence, reaction to crime, or patrol and ordering
- Level of attention—here and now, inspective, or meta-inspective
- Sanctioning range and which sanctions they typically apply
- Foci: criminal, civil, or broader ordering and status quo maintenance
- Tactics and enforcement practices
- Obligation for national security
- Territorial limitations and concern for legal procedures, the integrity of boundaries and borders, secrecy, and visibility
- Mandate, whether data integrity, fraud, or contracts versus people or material property
- Political orientation, whether national or international or both
- Degree of statutory obligation for carrying out high policing or national security and control of prisoners versus people on probation or citizens at large

Note also that the functions of the agencies within the executive branch are much broader than other branches and that they reflect the expansion of federal powers through the commerce clause and the need for inspection functions given the huge number of agencies and agents. The functions within policing agencies in the executive branch can be high, as in Department of Defense oversight of security, or low, as in patrol of buildings and grounds. This variation is not found in agencies in the judicial, legislative, or special establishments because they are quite restrictive in locale and obligation.

EXTENT OF INTEGRATION OF POLICING FORMS

While Geller and Morris note that both incentives and disincentives exist for communication, cooperation, and coordination among federal and local agencies, their analysis is rather pessimistic. They conclude that continued progress in integration is hampered by "powerful mythology" and "political realities" and note the continued independence among the "14,000 local and at least 50 federal police agencies" (1992, 231, abstract). It might be noted further that the division between criminal sanction–based policing, civil regulation, and inspection cleaves the large set of enforcement agencies and that unlike processes within the "criminal justice system" (Reiss 1974), the code of legal language by which cases move in and out of consideration does not integrate the larger network of rule-enforcement agencies.

Relations among local, state, and municipal agencies, as well as with the federal agencies, are weakened by the overlapping laws, regulations, and rules that govern response as well as differing investigative procedures. Specialized agencies are in theory restricted to territories, places, locales, symbols, or others for which they are held responsible. However, the mobility of criminals, the negotiated nature of the investigation (e.g., which organization should investigate crimes within reservations, Indian casinos, or Indian territories), and the notional place of the crime—where it is said to be when there is a doubt of its actual location—create ambiguities. While jurisdiction may be clear in law, it is negotiated in practice; for example, for crimes within Indian territory, jurisdiction is negotiated among the Bureau of Indian Affairs, county police, Indian tribal police, the FBI, military investigative agencies, or some combination thereof.

The globalization of criminal opportunities further makes easy territorially based distinctions less viable now than even ten years ago. Agencies are bound together in large part by three things: *routines* that organize their tasks, such as case making, investigation, and closure; the oral culture and place-based ecologically situated *density of interaction*; and traditions and historically drawn *boundaries* around the scope of their responsibilities and practices. The internal conflict between levels of officers, especially between command and the lower participants, is suppressed by the tacit system of *shared misunderstandings*—the idea that their shared experiences as uniformed patrol officers, beliefs in "good police work," and the threat of the public reprisal for their actions bind them together (Manning 1977, 145).

Agencies that enforce the law are based on the premise that their work must be secret, stealthy, of low visibility, and clandestine until action is taken. They prize secrecy, territorial dominance, and boundary maintenance. They prize backstage teamwork within a given agency. They elevate their own traditions and practices over other organizations' and cling to the notion that secrecy and secrets are to be guarded with a bodyguard of lies if necessary.

Domestic specialized federal policing is predicated on the idea of the *case* as the center of action choices. If a case is not extracted from the natural events "on the ground," what is seen to be taking place, or further along if the investigator decides no crime has been committed (the record of crime is "unfounded"), no case exists.

In the investigative world and the world of internal affairs, cases can be constructed a priori, but in general the aim of these agencies is to bring criminals to justice. This aligns investigators more with the high police and federal police whose obligations are to ensure domestic security (agencies primarily in Justice, Treasury, Homeland Security, and the Department of Defense). On the other hand, since cases and information are considered by investigators to be one-time matters to be worked without broader connections, such as connecting a series of burglaries, thefts, or deaths and a matter of personal "property," and these beliefs are reinforced by the routines and practices of "working a case," constraints mitigate against shared cases, data, informants, clues, or even hunches.

These matters make the development of cooperation erstwhile, fragmented, personalized, local, incident driven, and historically shaped. By *erstwhile* I mean that formal modes of communicating are not consistent and well formulated and formalized. By *fragmented* I mean that the overlapping of jurisdictions, the different relevant laws, and the hierarchy of local, state, and federal violations ensure that what binds one agency to another are partially complete networks rather than systems (bounded, closed, and organized by a code and channels of communication). These patterns or habits of communication begin locally and end locally in that enforcement usually requires some contact or liaison with local agencies. The tendency for cases originating in a locale to stay in the originating organization is a hypothesis that one could test. Cooperative networks, when they do arise, come as a result of a major disastrous spectacle—incidents such as the Washington, D.C., sniper who terrorized that area for three weeks in October 2002, coordinated by the Montgomery County Police; the 9/11 terrorist attacks; the Murrah Building bombing and subsequent federal investigations; or as a result of a task force formed for a stated short-term purpose such as suppressing gangs, reducing youth homicide, or enforcing drug laws. By *historically shaped* I intend that if the relationships have been friendly in the past, they will be continue to be so if personal relationships have been formed between the agencies. By *personal* I mean one officer who knows another and trusts him or her enough to divulge problems, errors, or needed assistance.

Case studies, it would appear, suggest that the hierarchy of authority in a locale or event is established by tacit admission rather than legal authority (see chapters 11 and 12). In longer-term planning around major national security events (as they are now designated in the United States), working arrangements require local politics and economic agreements to form the network and planning. Once in place, the dominant organization assumes its pride of place to determine where and when it will serve in the enforcement role. The arrangements for the division of labor between agencies are set out with a hierarchy of resort based on firepower and resources available to a given organization (the distribution of additional firepower and resources, "federal assets," is under the control of the federal agencies), and if an incident occurs, the federal agency most central to the matter, usually either the Secret Service or the FBI, takes operational command. In this dance, evidence suggests, private security is generally omitted from planning and liaison. The most famous instance of coordinated public-private police planning is the Christmas celebration at Rockefeller Center every year.

In summary, coordination of levels of enforcement cannot be easily understood by categorical listings of powers, jurisdictions, or sanctions. Most of the work that has alerted scholars to the study of policing generally has been taxonomic, or has pointed out from a sociolegal perspective that sanctions, even the criminal sanction and carrying a gun, do not delimit the interventions that can be undertaken or are undertaken. For this reason, among many others, the term *discretion* is misleading. The decision to intervene, investigate, open a case, or make a stop does not require a legal basis; deciding among options in arrest and charges and the system to which the case is to be submitted is patterned by law and is glossed with the term *discretion*. As Richman (2000, 101), for example, argues effectively, U.S. attorneys are gatekeepers to the federal system and in practice determine what a "federal" case is. These agreements are difficult to uncover in official discourse, and too few studies have examined it closely. These ambiguities are made more complicated by the pressure of federal agencies to encourage the application of federal rather than state or local standards in many areas (e.g., federal sentencing guidelines, the informal symbolic power of federal agencies to which local agencies tend to defer, especially in times of crisis, and past practices and personal relationships that shape cooperation).

Conclusion

American policing is local policing, complemented by county, township, and federal agents and agencies. They supply sanctions, largely reactively, to a wide variety of rule breakings, including law breaking. Private policing is a major figure in policing, but is not viewed as competition or an enemy. There is little pressure for innovation in respect to building a network of security expanding policing to include CSOs or the equivalent and no questioning of the worth of policing in its modern guises—community oriented yet crime focused. The decline in official crime figures has shored up the policing mandate and given new credence to the American police ideology that states that the police stand between the citizen and chaos. More detailed understanding of police operations is found in the following chapters.

CHAPTER SIX

Theorizing Policing

Recent Efforts

The unfortunately unasked question with which to begin a review of theorizing and reform is: "What is policing for?" Or more radically, "What is policing good for?" The questions frame important research matters more than the answers that might be produced. This emphasis parallels the medical maxim that one should first do no harm.

All policing is a socially constituted and embedded practice, constrained by the social conditions of the work, high and low politics of the organization and the society, as well as the tacit consent and abundant compliance of the policed. Policing as an institution and practice plays an acknowledged role in arguments about the bases of democracy advanced by political scientists. Policing is rarely discussed in the context of democratic theory by social scientists. Historic arguments about democracy have omitted a discussion of policing or assumed (as in the Rawlsian argument) that for all practical purposes a system of laws is a representation that is fair and sensible, somehow collectively supported and enforced by the police. Nevertheless, a democracy requires a policing reflecting its principles. Implicitly at least, viewing policing as a hinge between social order, ordering, and the broader commitment of citizens to society means that policing must play a role in current theories of democracy. Perhaps because other institutions are said to be conducive to order, while policing deals with failures, policing has not been given pride of place in the construction of features necessary for sustaining democracy. Policing emerged from conflict and dealt with those viewed as dangerous, marginal, and threatening; the more civilized modern police reflect the pressures of modernity and its requirements for trust and equal treatment. The study of policing outlined in the previous chapters suggests that it has become increasing pragmatic in nature and positivistic, eschewing theory and ethnographic work. The narrow and parochial focus of American police research reifies the crime-fighting focus and neglects broader questions of order and equality. The following chapter will review the meager results of efforts to reform policing in the past twenty-five years, and chapters 8, 9, and 10 assess current police practice.

While American policing operated in a conflicted society from the beginning, in many respects creating and marking boundaries between the classes and recent and current immigrants, three fundamental issues have plagued serious discussions of the role of the police in the context of the democratic politics of American society. Each issue is obscured by the ideological commitment to equality paired with the denial of inequality, even as it grows. The first is the belief in the "rule of law," and the second is the dismissal of prejudice and structural barriers to equality (Wilson and Taub 2006). These beliefs provide an equality umbrella under which sits the coveted violence in this frontier country, an essential means of coercing those who are unwilling or unable to comply, and the threat of the state to its citizens. This paradox was pointed out by Loader and Walker (2007)—the state has the power and authority to protect citizens' security but also can crush citizens, destroy their freedom, and undermine their sense of liberty and selfhood. Third is the narrow focus of police studies on matters of effectiveness and efficiency. While these concepts are left undefined and have little utility in organizations that serve the public, they serve to obscure broader questions of equity and proportionality in police work and its consequences. These beliefs obscure the need for a theoretical basis for assessing democratic policing.

As argued in the early chapters, police studies should examine the extent to which policing meets the difference principle and associated features. This chapter will review the lack of theoretical guidance in policing, seeing it as research dependent and building on the taken-for-granted problems of the police as an occupation and organization. The result of emulating police occupational problems in research means there is no theoretically grounded investigative agenda. Even a national commission took up commonsense questions and in the end provided no answers (National Research Council 2004). Words like *justice, efficiency,* and *the rule of law* were used as buzzwords without precise definition. If the question of the value and purpose of the police is to be addressed, the terms of reference cannot be left to echo the occupational ideology and reflect politics as usual and reduced to small studies of the latest attempt to control officially recorded crime.

THEORIZING POLICING

There is no theory of policing, nor even a systematic failed attempt. Efforts to "theorize" policing have not been successful in part because of the amalgamation of disciplines that study policing, in part due to the newness of the area of police studies and in part because the field mimics the concerns of the practitioners rather than other theoretically grounded fields such as sociology, economics, and psychology.

Theorizing police as an organization and policing as an activity or a practice, although considerable organizational research is available, as noted in chapter 2, remains an open-ended, unfinished task. Absent a theory of policing, reform will always be a contorted and distorted set of feeble and often self-serving attempts at guided change. Because the reform efforts assume that the present paradigm and structure are adequate, all the suggested reforms are based not on principles but on a reflexive gaze back at what police now do. It is particularly unfortunate that the aim of reform has consistently been to make policing "better" (an undefined term), more efficient perhaps, rather than more modestly to constrain it not to do worse or to damage further the web of collective life. This reformist urge has been confounded and thoroughly muddled by the insupportable claim that only quasi-experimental research is "scientific" and valid and the means by which a utopia of scientific policing will be achieved (Sherman 2005). This is a caricature of science and its range of approaches, a crude dismissal of the many ways policies can be assessed, a narrow view of what indeed is a problem, and a confounding of metric and measurement for analysis, causal or otherwise. No method establishes truth.

The vast proportion of published research done under the guise of police studies and perhaps criminal justice as a whole, funded or not, is conservative. Much published police research focuses on citizen-patrol interactions and crime-control features of policing, to the exclusion of political and organizational concepts such as compliance, leadership, legitimization, and the sociopolitical rhetoric and imagery that police employ. The role of the police is the larger network of politics and power, and the impact of policing on local politics is left unexamined in the criminal justice literature.

No published research questions the fundamental mandate that the police are to control crime, protect deserving persons and their property, and can and should do this. As Moore, Kelling, and Trojanowicz once wrote (1998), "No one questions that the police's primary role is to control crime." No one has asked what the limits of policing are, given moral and political principles. No police researcher has asked what have been the direct and indirect repercussions of an approach focused on a criminal-sanction crime-control disorder. These questions have been raised by other nonpolice researchers (David Garland, Michael Tonry, Jonathan Simon, and Jerome Miller). Only Clifford Shearing and Ian Loader have questioned the idea that policing should be and is the fundamental source of "order." This is true even when significance is given to "community co-production" and community priorities. Few studies derive propositions from theory or use systematic criminology to explore police strategies and tactics. The research of concern has been police oriented, inward and relatively unreflective, rather than outward toward integration of public services, fairness and justice in policing, and value-added approaches to policing (Moore 1995). The most commonly cited works about policing (e.g., Wilson and Kelling 1982; Trojanowicz and Bucqueroux 1990; Skogan 1991; and the writings of Sherman and Weisburd) are relatively recent and methodologically refined, while the often cited empirical-ethnographic works, those of Westley, Skolnick, Wilson, Rubinstein, and Manning, were published some forty years ago.

Leadership is assumed to emanate powerfully from the top, from chiefs and their acolytes, and to be charismatic and personalistic (Haberfeld 2004; for a counterview, see Mastrofski 2006). The political system in which such interactions are cast is left unexplicated. Policing is seen as a nonpolitical function carried out by a neutral organization; it is a mere public servant, as the police reformers have often told us.

Scholars in the police world have seldom looked to the very large and systematic literature on organizations to shape and refine their research agendas (for a recent exception, see Willis, Mastrofski, and Weisburd 2007), and have in quite an odd and indefensible fashion seen the police organization as quasi unique. Police organization is rarely seen as a type of organization, nor is the literature cited appropriately (see, for exceptions, Crank and Langworthy 1992; Greene 2000; and Klinger 1997). There has been little or no concern with the larger field of organizational studies, comparative and historical studies, the political economics of public agencies, or any effort to see policing as one of a comparable sort of public service agency. The role of police as a semisacred representation rather than as an instrumentality is rarely explored, and the research focuses on measurable and rather manageable problems of policing, as seen by the police as experts in their own craft. The managerialism and performance focus remain entirely on the individual officer rather than the organization and its management in the United States.

In spite of this concatenation of preferences and research directions, there has been an interactive relationship between the police, police academics, and policing. The isolation of the study of the police organization intellectually is paralleled by placing it in an empty sociopolitical context absent all but a few measured and measurable features such as ethnicity or crime rates. The dynamic, historical, structural, and ideological context of cities is left unexplored but carefully and precisely measured (e.g., Levitt 1998, 2004 for a creative analysis). The police have fostered the belief that they are the experts in crime, there to coerce, punish, lead, and symbolize formal social control at its best. They have been until recent years profoundly and deeply anti-intellectual and still are from time to time (Bratton and Kelling 2006). Yet social research shows that the social nature of crime and disorder can be explicated and understood and that the role of the police in maintaining order is slight in comparison to other factors.

Understanding this relationship between the assumptions of the police leadership cadre and police researchers is critical to understanding the refracted nature of criminal justice research. What might be called a "reflexive paradigm" has developed, and it resembles the natural history of development suggested by Abbott (2005). It also resembles the argument made about the merging of the two streams of sociology for the police and sociology of the police in chapter 4. The first step is the development of an intellectual network of people who stand apart from the current field itself (ibid.) yet are engaged with its practitioners. Some may have been employed as, for example, police officers, military police, or in private security. They are sometimes sons or daughters of police officers. These groups, key leaders, then write about the field within the confines partially of their own discipline. However, they bring to the analysis the inherited problems, worries, and solutions sanctioned within the field. These include key assumptions about behavior and the tasks of the occupations; their mini-ideologies concerning causation, treatment, and preferred outcomes; and their views of proper practices, or "good [police] work." A second step occurs when research elaborates and refines this commonsense view—for example, that police create order; that arrests, jails, and prison are "deterrence" teaching lessons, frightening and warding off evil acts; that social scientists are abstract and out of touch with the real world and propose tactics that are naive or believe that crime is caused by social inequalities, injustice, poverty, and unemployment; that response time and more officers are critical in controlling crime; and that only the police can understand the real work. In time, a third step is taken: these ideological positions become the basis for research agendas, both at the university and federal Department of Justice support level. Because the belief system is tautological, that is, the police control crime, if crime drops, they must have produced this effect (and their created and constructed figures—calls for service, officially recorded crime, and even clearances—demonstrate the truth of the tautology). This third step is in some ways retrograde because the intellectualized version replaces the actual practices and commonsense knowledge of officers with abstract and theorized versions that do not reflect this grounding. I suggest a fourth step in the reflexive paradigm advanced by Abbott. The leaders of large police departments are a constituency of the federal government's funding agencies, especially those in the Department of Justice (Community Oriented Policing Services Agency, Office of Juvenile Delinquency Prevention Programs, NIJ). They serve on review panels and on the board of influential foundations in the police world: the Police Foundation, the Police Executive Research Forum, the Manhattan Institute, and others. They produce the material and cultural capital that legitimate the research enterprise and vice versa. Academics serve as consultants, editors, reviewers for journals, publishers, and funding agencies, and they circulate in and out of private research institutes (the Urban Institute and so on), government, and academic life. They also shape publications, as they serve on editorial boards, review papers, and advise on tenure decisions for junior colleagues. The academic research legitimates the concerns of the top command and the wish of the research agencies to maintain credibility with both the academic and the practitioner world. Thus, the field of police studies combines symbolic, cultural, and material capital in a powerful fashion.

These steps when combined with well-funded research produce the virtual police organization (VPO), an organization based on assumptions, reified by research findings that reflect these assumptions, and data that are designed from the beginning to amplify the original claims of the organization (see Manning 1977, chaps. 4 and 5). The facts stand little chance in this reflexive and redundant network of spurious reasoning and elaborate rhetoric. This VPO stands in contrast to the actual, concretely observed practices of police. This might be called the POPO, the actual or practice-oriented police organization. The loops that sustain policing practice in spite of years of research showing various assumptions and practices that are counterproductive are powerful. Theories, known evidence, and long-standing

understanding of cities and their dynamics have little purchase in the police imagination. The most powerful concept to have emerged in urban sociology since the 1920s,
the idea of collective efficacy, has escaped police notice, and there are no studies of
the impact of policing in CE.[1] They appear to be less interested in what are present,
strong informal controls, than what is absent, forces associated with crime that they
can appear to control via arrests. The reason that theories and abstractions have
little place in policing as a day-to-day matter is quite clear: it is a political agency
with concerns about its power, authority, place in the ecology of city agencies, and
legitimation. What passes for "theory" is in fact a pale imitation of conventional
police ideology: broken windows and its constitutive mode of policing.

BROKEN WINDOWS AND THE "CLIMATE OF OPINION"

The most salient idea shaping policing in the past twenty years, essays by Wilson and
Kelling, is not a theory.[2] Whatever the intention of Wilson and Kelling in proposing
the idea that police should deal with disorder and quality-of-life issues, the idea has
become an easy justification and institutional account for arrest-oriented actions.
Inevitably, then, it thus increases inequalities and punishment in the form of arrests
and stops. I want to set out the context in which it found a welcome reception prior
to characterizing the essay, reactions to it, and the major criticisms that have been
leveled at it as a result of research.

While policing is a very conservative, stable, and ossified organizational form,
it is subject to trends, fads, fashions, and ripples of opinion that sweep through the
elites of the occupation and the opinion leaders and trickle down to chiefs in midsize cities. One such trendy idea, the broken windows or "incivilities" thesis (Taylor
2000), is vague in conception and appealing precisely for its vacuity. It has moved
from a scattered set of observations, slickly packaged and full of the turns of phrase
associated with advertising and sales promotions, to semantic mastery, as a "theory."
It is a subtle, well-written text with an open-ended possibility for interpretation and
rationalizing. It established in the period of a few years what historian Carl Becker
(1969) called a "climate of opinion" within which the police found themselves com-
fortable and indeed popular. Like all other mini-ideologies, it defended the status quo
ante while revering an imagined past of order and orderliness. It evokes nostalgia,
even drawing on the image of the benign and never-extant present "street cop" who
in his personalized authority rules his corner without appeal.

The power of this vague collection of inferences and assertions is that, on
the one hand, it argues for a reshaped police sensitivity that encompasses citizens'
concerns about the increasing distance, invisibility, and inaccessibility of the police,
the lack of connection and identification with the police and the police with the
public, and, on the other hand, it emphasizes the deeper commitment to a sanctioning deterrence: an arrest-based crime-control focus. The contradictions embodied in
this little essay have not been well scrutinized because the two faces are ideologically
connected to the commonsense assumptions of police. If disorder obtains, they would

argue, arrests are the last resort and a message that communicates unequivocally. To assess the impact of these ideas, what is written as well as what is done in the name of "broken-windows policing" must be examined.

The impact of the BW thesis came slowly, via promotion of the mass media, the Manhattan Institute, and popular essays, and resonated with other surface indications of moral and political change in America. There are less obvious matters of the changes in demographic compositions of cities, their increasing Hispanic and immigrant populations, and the increasing ghettoization and marginalization of African Americans. Although a variety of political changes have taken place and are discussed by several acute observers, such as Jonathan Simon, Stan Cohen, Jeffery Fagan, David Garland, Bernard Harcourt, and Wesley Skogan, the observers underscore changes in the climate of opinion on key matters of social control: the enormous increase in the use of regulations and misdemeanor laws to punish and control minorities; the massive increase in incarceration, both in jails and on probation under surveillance of the criminal justice system, including electronic devices; the sanctioned use of law enforcement and arrest as a proxy for order; and the decline in informal social controls due to mobility, cheap and rapid transportation and communication, and the rise of science and factual knowledge as a basis for risks. In short, these are indicators of modernity (see also Garland 2001). Why concern about such changes, which undercut trust in institutions, should be converted into a wide-ranging support for arrest and incarceration is unclear. Nevertheless, at this point, the BW thesis has captured public policy.

Recall that the professionalization movement, begun with Vollmer, as noted in chapter 4, aimed to root policing in science and crime control through "law enforcement" and modern technology; it embodied the technological conceit—that more and faster of the same would soundly ground the mandate of modern policing. This claimed scientific basis faded in time and was replaced with the modernist idea of technology, mobility, two-way communication, better record keeping, and the like, all of which as means, not ends, would reform policing, almost on their own. This was coupled with the hopeful idea that better education of police would also serve to enhance the quality of policing (Sherman 1976). The assertion that police could control and eradicate crime in the 1980s proved visibly empty and perhaps fatuous as serious crime rose, new drugs, mainly crack cocaine, swept through cities, and the economy foundered. The homicide rate rose, especially in large cities. In fact, the BW thesis stimulated a backward-looking defense of arrests and punishment while ignoring scientific and technological advances, sociological knowledge, and the reforms advocated at great length and expense by the President's Crime Commission report of 1967. Reactionary thinking based on the free market, low wages, and a flexible labor pool dominated public policy.[3]

The essay did not argue exclusively for arrests and misdemeanor-based policing as a source of order. It focused on what takes place if order is not maintained. It also argued that the police and the community had obligations to sustain order. But this summary is premature. Let us begin with the early and important ideas of one of the earliest social scientist observers of policing in this country, Harvard

political scientist James Q. Wilson. He had noted the significant problem of policing social order in *Varieties of Police Behavior* (1968). While law enforcement can
be rationalized using the law as an umbrella and easily defended in courts and in
the arena of public opinion, disorder varied in its nature and consequence, and the
public was typically divided about its merits or demerits. Wilson in 1968 did not
advance any suggestions about how it ought to be managed, but argued at length
that how misdemeanor arrests and traffic enforcement were encouraged or not, on
the one hand, and whether arrests for robberies and burglaries were rewarded, on
the other, were indicia of the political culture of a city. His concern was the extent to
which the political culture of a city shaped its policing. He did not mention citizens'
concerns, priorities, or attitudes toward policing or the police. His concern at this
point was the dilemmas of police administration.

After serving as an adviser to the then attorney general of the United States and
a former colleague at the University of Chicago, Edmund Levi, Wilson published
a set of ruminations on crime. Later essays, most notably "Broken Windows," with
Kelling (1982), were modeled on a polemic written in his *Thinking about Crime*
(1975 [1985], 75–89). It set an assertive tone and approach to what might be called
policy in policing. Wilson, who was influenced in this thinking by conservative
political scientist at the University of Chicago Edward Banfield (1958), began
with an unstated concern and even distaste for disorder. His view, like Banfield's,
was that decline and demoralization lurk in any community. His essays display a
microcosm of the conservative view of history in general—one witnesses a constant
decline in standards, morality, and order, and what thin veneer of order remains
is always threatened by the masses, the disreputable, the disorderly, the unwashed
and unwanted. Those in more privileged positions in the social order are there as
a result of merit and should be protected and valued. This message was clear. The
question in several of his essays in this collection was: what shall the police do, given
the uneven distribution of disorder and crime? How can they act to produce what
communities are said to crave: order?

His interwoven concern for public policy in respect to policing, crime control as
a focal police concern and something by which they could be judged, and organizational analysis all served Wilson well. They were becoming hot public issues as crime
and concern about "drug use" escalated.[4] Wilson wrote, supported by some passing
and incomplete academic references, that since crime was not randomly distributed
in cities, the police could either attempt to distribute it evenly or concentrate their
efforts in areas that might yield to change or become less characterized by crime.
This was a powerful insight based on public administration and organizational
analysis. It had not been explored previously in regard to policing. The assumption
was: police work equally in all areas, detect and control crime, and are democratic
in that they serve all citizens all the time. He argued that it would make no sense to
spread "crime," by which he refers not to white-collar crime, embezzlement, and other
crimes involving the violation of trust, but to known, visible street crime located in
marginal and disadvantaged areas. As a result, the obvious policy was to concentrate
police efforts in a few areas where crime could be controlled. Wilson's view is that

policy requires one to make focused resources available and do something rather than to accept the inevitable growth in crime.

In a revised version of the essays, he argued that more focused crime-attack modalities were superior to random patrol (1985, 74). This is an obvious point now, but was original at this time. Random patrol, however, remains the mode in all police departments. Wilson did not discount the social causation of crime but considered causes irrelevant to policy making. The point is not what causes it but what can be done to reduce it in the short run. There is a strong theme running through the section on police in his essays that order is to be honored above individual rights and that individualism will in time damage the social fabric. Implicit in this is the notion that procedural justice must at times give way to pragmatic order-maintaining practices—the "Officer Kelly" approach to justice (see below).

The BW thesis and policing came into common police parlance as a result of the Wilson and Kelling essay published in 1982 in *Atlantic* magazine. It elaborated much the same thesis as Wilson's earlier essays and was titled "The Police and Neighborhood Safety: Broken Windows." In due course it became a locus classicus, arguably one of the most frequently cited and reprinted articles in police studies, even though it included modest and general references, had no scholarly theoretical rationale, and appeared in a nonrefereed literary magazine published in Boston. It manifests a confident and breezy style, contains an argument seasoned with a story or two, and makes a bow in the direction of scholarship. It is a moralistic tract, a polemic peppered with degrading terms for those seen as disorderly or disreputable. It is rich with opprobrium, heavy with moralistic labels, but unfortunately extremely light on fact. It draws loosely and analogically on experimental social psychology and provides anecdotes. It tells little "as if" anecdotal stories such as one about Officer Kelly in Newark who is applauded for his personalistic, local, and arbitrary rules for controlling disorder (p. 35 in the *Atlantic* article but moved several pages to the rear in the revised 1985 Wilson essay). The BW thesis is a programmatic, persuasive conservative statement that has been used to buttress a range of police activities.

The picture painted is one of fragile orders. It has a Hobbesian or Vicoesque flavor that sees the evil of men only briefly constrained by authority. Local orders are in conflict and endure always some sort of struggle: disorder is everywhere, but the balance between the reputable and disreputable varies and affects the probability of further disorder. In areas with a balance in favor of the reputable, police are needed minimally, if at all (1982, 86). Neighborhoods should be encouraged in their crime-control efforts (1975, 123), and Wilson urged stops, searches, and actions based on a sense of order rather than legal standards (1982, 89). This idea the NYPD carried out with a vengeance for more than seventeen years (Fagan forthcoming). Police, Wilson and Kelling argued, should work to strengthen informal social control (1982, 83), or else a neighborhood might reach a tipping point (ibid., 88) and decline in such a way that, failing to do anything, "a hundred drunks or a score of vagrants … may destroy an entire community" (ibid., 84). This idea of totalistic decline and destruction, offered from the distant banks of the Charles, is ominous. It echoes the view of the officer on the ground who sees only decline and human ignorance and error in his daily rounds. While police use shrewd pragmatism when on the job, their ideology or underlying justification for their work is crystallized in the BW essay.

The essay relies on stereotypes to orchestrate, amplify, and direct its repugnance. Places such as shopping malls and quiet suburbs attract and have only two types of people: "respectable" and "unrespectable" (ibid., 86). If challenged by the rowdy teenager or the ill-smelling person and controls fail, the neighborhood can become an "inhospitable and frightening jungle" (ibid., 79). The police can stimulate informal controls if these controls and sanctions are failing and can thus can act to sustain order—"Serious street crime flourishes in areas in which disorderly behavior goes unchecked" (ibid., 82). The job of the police, in short, is to sustain and maintain order, using various means (legal and illegal). An officer who was asked how the police rousted gangs from a housing estate is quoted with approval when he says, "We kick ass" (ibid., 85). If initial efforts fail, others must be devised (ibid., 89). Consistently, Wilson argues that actions guided by law and procedural protections are weak in the face of such disorder. The implication, carefully hedged, is that there is a need for ordering and coercing at the edges of the law (ibid.). Wilson makes clear he knows about the objections that will be and have been made about such defining, enforcing, sanctioning, and coercing on the basis of some undefined, intuitive sense of desirable order.[5] If these informal controls arising within the neighborhood and punctuated or created by the police do not operate, criminals may move in and take advantage. Then the area will suffer a "criminal invasion" (ibid., 79). While the mythical Officer Kelly and others are elevated as judges, the argument is made without reference to whose order, by whom, or what; rather, "orderliness" is advocated and to be encouraged by both formal and informal means (ibid., 89). When Wilson writes, "None of this is easily reconciled with any concept of due process or fair treatment" (ibid., 85), his candor resonates.

Kelling, in a later series of observations made in the same vein (1986), asserted that while disorder was relative and difficult to define, the authority for "aggressive order maintenance" came from communities. Community, of course, referred to the people who agree with the observer and was not defined or restricted. The communal source of this was simply asserted absent any data. This rhetorical point was seen as a basis for police definitions of order and disorder as they were in effect the symbolic leaders in such matters and unchallenged in their deep knowledge of city life.

The point was well taken in the sense that police have always fancied themselves as "doing order" and producing order in spite of the severe limits on this ability in fact (Walker 1984; Harcourt 2001). Similar arguments for self-assertive order maintenance were made by Klockars (1985) and Sykes (1986); they asserted the essential aspects of the police role and its intimate connection to violence, coercion, and order. These observers pointed out the theoretical limits of the legalistic practice of policing. None of this was news to police, from the top command on down. The notion that the police have been "handcuffed" by the law had been the core of gossip in policing since the late seventies and was reinforced by the Miranda decision, among others. Although these essays were not protocols for research projects, they had great appeal because they held out hope for policing in a period of intense criticism. The essays made an argument for pragmatic intervention; such interventions require little concern for the causes of crime or even its immediate manifestations. Crime should be controlled where it can be controlled, and this is for the police to decide.

In a latter reflective essay Kelling and Sousa remind people of the many comments that were misconstrued (2006, 79). They suggest a tension between individual rights and neighborhood order and ordering, but the thrust of the essay is that these are secondary matters. There is certainly validity in their points—the *Atlantic* essay was not intended as a programmatic statement for immediate implementation, and clearly many of the subtleties have been totally lost in police execution. The focus on order over individual rights, however, is the basic theme of the first few chapters of *Fixing Broken Windows* (Kelling and Coles 1997). Kelling and Sousa also advance a series of ad hoc points that might have been the logical basis for the strident assertions found in the original essay.

Simply put, the BW thesis is that informal social controls in neighborhoods are weakened insofar as it is perceived that disorder abounds; that others, one's neighbors, are not concerned about such decline; and that these matters of trust, actions, and attitude are symbolized by "broken windows" or other matters uncared for. The driving force is the disorder, physical or social. Neighborhood decline is accompanied by small crimes and disorderly behavior, and this in turn inevitably brings further more serious delicts. It is apparently a one-way spiral absent direct intervention of some sort. How neighborhoods might recover is left an open question. The weakened internal social controls mean that criminals from outside the area perceive an opportunity to take advantage of people in the area by committing crimes. It is argued by Wilson and Kelling that the police can strengthen informal controls by acting to sustain order, legally and informally. These actions may involve means that border on illegality. Ordering is the police job.

The subtext, elevated to the front stage in Kelling and Coles's *Fixing Broken Windows,* is that liberal politicians, judges, and policy makers have stripped the police of the needed powers to control the streets (see ibid., 7, chap. 1). Not a scholarly monograph, *Fixing Broken Windows* is a mass-audience "trade" book with a foreword by James Q. Wilson. Their claim is that the sources of disorder are broad and results from the limitations in law constraining police made by liberal courts, especially Supreme Court rulings. Individual rights trumped order, much to their dismay. They applaud Bratton and the NYPD and claim that it alone produced the crime drop in New York City. The Kelling and Coles book is focused, on the one hand, on improved management of policing to ensure crime effectiveness and, on the other, on the need to develop flexible laws and regulations in large cities to enable the police to keep order. Those at issue and in need of control are a wide range of deviants—jaywalkers, squeegee men, panhandlers or beggars, and the homeless.

Interest in the ideas had escalated after the media accepted uncritically the post hoc, ergo propter hoc arguments made, especially by Kelling and Coles and Bratton. The argument featured in both of Wilson's essays, his essay with Kelling, and the work of Kelling and Coles is perhaps about trust and perceptions of neighborhood order and the lack of care and concern indicated by broken windows, abandoned cars, litter, and visible "street people." They do not say how very precisely and through what social mechanisms such a process eventuates, but they suggest the police can truncate or stop it in some areas. They do not comment on what happens then or why (see Kelling and Sousa 2006).

It would appear that the argument is that insofar as disorderly signs are present, people feel uneasy and may withdraw efforts and affect and feel the neighborhood is in decline. These attitudes and perceptions, in turn, make the environment in some sense more conducive to crime and misdeeds. The rise in disorder and minor crimes is the basis, they argue, for further withdrawal of informal controls and thus may reduce crime-control efforts and informal controls essential to neighborhood safety. Conversely, if police, formally and informally, enforce norms of order, more serious crime will not thrive. Crime reduction and crime prevention flow from the same sources—marking norms by the police, perhaps in cooperation with neighborhood patrols, private security, and the like (Wilson 1985, 86–89). The basic idea is that some fundament of order must be maintained, or the edges become more and more blurred such that effective social controls are eroded—the distinctions between disorderly behavior, minor crimes, and common felonies (auto theft burglaries and robbery) become moot in this model of "neighborhood safety," as are distinctions between order maintenance and law enforcement. Whether the police are controlling or reacting to minor delicts or more serious ones becomes unimportant because they are all indicators of a disorderly future that could be much worse. It is a caveat, "It could be worse if action is not taken," that echoes the standard police ideology (articulated best by Bittner 1972) concerning the need to intervene when they have done so. It is possible that through the accumulation of misdemeanor arrests, those frequently stopped are likely to be arrested for a felony offense and their incarceration reduces officially reported crime. This has not been provided: the studies are correlational studies of the relationships between the rate of arrests for misdemeanors and subsequent reported felony arrests.

These ideas, as interpreted—called "broken windows policing"—have been widely used to rationalize sweeping the homeless away to unknown destinations, arresting people for drinking beer on their front steps, jailing "squeegee" men, and arresting people for gathering on street corners ("gang behavior") (see Kelling and Coles 1996).[6] The BW essay and its companion piece (Wilson and Kelling 1989) is a proximate stimulus and academic support, if any is needed, for police to focus on the minor offenses of the dispossessed and the poor and to target their lifestyles in the name of order. While neither Bratton nor Kelling, in writing, speeches, or advice to cities, including London and Caracas, have called for "zero tolerance," and it is not clear who coined the phrase, the idea of combating disorder actively and systematically was easily translated by police officers, in their enthusiasm, into flurries of arrests, targeting visible and somewhat annoying delicts such as squeegee men and those begging, loitering, and smoking marijuana in public. This "translation" was perhaps amplified by two other factors. The first was that the police officers hired in the 1990s were young, and young officers tend to be more violent and to make more arrests than more experienced officers. The second factor was the policy that meant that additional new officers would be disproportionately deployed into disadvantaged areas of the city and urged to make arrests and stops. This produced a massive wave of misdemeanor arrests (Harcourt 2001; Harcourt and Ludwig 2007; Fagan forthcoming).

To make a very brief summary at this point, the several essays outlined here assume the virtues of a stereotypic notion of order based roughly on middle-class ideas. This notion of order is an unexamined, unstated, and unquestioned baseline by which all other kinds of order should be judged. The police are to serve as proxies—the arbiters of such order and its presence or absence. The police are seen as responsible and in charge, as seen in the cliché that they alone can "take back the streets" (who lost them?). The broken-windows essay, as had Wilson earlier, simply dismissed some areas as beyond rescue and to be written off, while suggesting that other areas could be restored to orderliness with police intervention. The underlying idea was that if neighborhoods could be made places in which people could trust each other in public space, they could be restored to civility (my paraphrase).

REACTIONS TO THE ESSAYS

Several academics, at some distance and without a direct connection to the parade of self-congratulatory efforts that followed the early findings that suggested that disorder and crime were more closely related than was previously thought, began to unravel what was being claimed. Thacher (2001, 2003) has called this a "backlash" rather than a scholarly examination of widely touted and promoted claims. The logic connecting the officially registered, traceable aspects of policing disorder, since some are unknown and unknowable short of close observation of the process of order maintenance, was not specified in the original published materials (the essays of Wilson, Wilson and Kelling, and the Kelling and Coles book), if they are taken as a coherent set. There are a number of re-creations, imaginative logical reconstructions, that have been worked out and published by several researchers. The belief that it works was widely and enthusiastically accepted by police departments even as they claimed to be doing "community policing." Let us consider them.

1. Wesley Skogan (1990) first argued that the absence of arrests would lead to a decline in trust and informal controls that in turn could lead to more serious crimes.[7] This inferential post hoc statement was then published in *Disorder and Decline* and later cited by Kelling as "causal" proof of the BW thesis (as cited in Harcourt 2001). It did not, of course, establish causality, since the argument was a sample analyzed by a few correlations using ex post facto limited statistical controls. The sample itself was later challenged by Harcourt in his reanalysis of Skogan's work.

2. Other scholars claimed that the argument implied that if neighborhood trust was low or declining, criminals would encroach, and outsiders would escalate crime and disorder (this is stated in Wilson and Kelling 1982, 31–32). Thus,

crime would be a function of the intrusion of outsiders as well as those in the neighborhood responding to weakened social controls. This cannot, of course, be tested given the data available.

3. Another hypothesis advanced was, in a situation of low information about whether crime would be responded to, people took the best-available surrogate, the overt "broken windows" (a metaphor for a wide range of things, values, behaviors, and kinds of people), and committed more serious crimes (Cook and Gross 1996, cited in Harcourt 2001). This was an econometric data-free argument.

4. Yet another inference argument was advanced by Sampson and Raudenbush (1999). They argued that decreased trust may be a consequence of neighborhood decline. As reviewed above, this distrust is a function of the percentage of African Americans in an area, and this perception is heavily influenced by the very negative attitudes of Hispanics in Chicago. While their data show that both disorder and crime (robbery and burglary) are driven by disadvantage, the perceptions reported were not a function of the actual reported rates of crime in the area.

5. Several academic lawyers (Meares, Kahan, Sunstein, Ellickson, and Lessig), arguing from a modified rational choice model, claimed that local rules, if upheld locally, will do away with the need for crime-attack interventions. This in turn will encourage people to support the collective enterprise. They accept the BW thesis and argue for alternative responses to neighborhood decline.

6. Sousa and Kelling (2006, 79) suggest a number of reasons that the BW thesis might work. They conclude by dismissing the "root cause" ideology that had been "co-opted" by criminology. This is a dead end from a public-policy point of view, they claim (ibid., 92). The "real world," they assert, requires things that work, not scientific complexity. This is, of course, the reverse of the argument made throughout this book: that criminal justice (and policy makers) with a focus on "crime control" absent attention to the consequences of it on patterns of inequality and other matters of public service and trust building is politically, morally, and intellectually indefensible.

7. Pierre St. Jean, in a book (2005) based on his dissertation at the University of Chicago, outlines a model of the BW processes and elaborates upon it in provocative fashion. St. Jean focuses on a single police beat in Chicago and interviews police, residents, and criminals (robbers and drug dealers). His contribution to the debate is to point out that the "disorder" seen as indications that people do not care about the neighborhood is seen as a positive asset to criminals. These indications are useful to carry out the criminal activity—disorderly areas with commercial aspects bring together enablers who watch the stash or keep guns, attract people who might want to buy drugs or who can be robbed, and facilitate hiding and absconding. Non-robbery-based assaults also take place at these interactions and near commercial establishments. While physical disorder does not facilitate crime, social disorder (noise, traffic, activity), according to St. Jean, has a positive conducive effect. This is

consistent with the arguments of Wilson and Kelling about the attraction of disorderly areas to criminals. St. Jean clarifies with very detailed data that it is not the social or physical conditions that sustain crime or arrests but that all the participants—police, criminals, and others—know that crime in these areas is an elastic and endlessly expansive matter. As Moskos (2008) shows, this means that it is police knowledge and local knowledge about the social activity in these areas that produce the arrests and the reputation that these areas have. There is endless negotiation and bargaining among the enablers, criminals, and police. He does not speculate about how arrests for minor infractions and regulations reduce the arrest rate for more serious crime.

FURTHER RESEARCH FINDINGS

The thesis or the collected theses of this set of Wilson's BW papers, although it points to disorder, has been conceptualized as a matter of reducing crime, as measured by statistics, ORC for the most part. The most systematic research available on the crime drop in New York City, which was attributed by Kelling and Coles to the BW approach to policing taken by Bratton (Karmen 2000; Harcourt 2001; Levitt 2004), has not confirmed the loosely presented arguments of the article. Considering the broader question of the relationships between arrests for crimes and more serious crimes, although some evidence of the relationship between disorder and robbery in cross-sectional analysis is available (Sampson and Raudenbush 1999; Skogan 1990). Harcourt (2001) found Skogan's data did not stand up under reanalysis and like Sampson and associates determined that structural features of severely disadvantaged areas were the cause of both disorder and crime (burglary and robbery). Taylor, in a longitudinal study (2000), found more variation within neighborhoods on the effects of disorder on crime than across them (the argument made by Sampson and associates) and thus argued against a consistent policy of attacking disorder by arrests. Velez (2001), in a modification of the BW thesis, maintained that a positive attitude toward the police was correlated with increased CE, even in disadvantaged areas. Eck and Maguire (2000), in a rather breathless summary of a large number of cross-sectional studies, concluded that the BW thesis as they defined it in terms of reduced ORC could not be supported. St. John (2005, appx. B) summarized a variety of studies showing remarkably unclear and mixed results. Harcourt (2001), in a reanalysis of Kelling and Sousa's data, found that testing the thesis on the basis of arrests could not satisfactorily be done, in part because of regression to the mean in the areas targeted by the police for enforcement (perhaps a product of the decline in use of crack cocaine in robbery, assaults, and homicide). This argument is revisited by Harcourt and Ludwig (2007). Two recent studies published in 2008 also contributed to the question of the impact of policing on ORCS. Rosenfeld, Fornango, and Rengifo (2007) found a positive impact (reduction in the rates of homicide and robbery) as a result of order-maintenance policing in New York between 1988 and 2001. They speculated about why such patterns might have resulted (e.g., p. 377, about targeting disadvantaged communities; and p. 378, about record keeping). They did note that increased police personnel were allocated to disadvantaged areas and that these were areas where disorder was high or growing quickly (ibid., 370). They also noted in passing that those crackdowns that produce a sense of injustice or violations of rights might have negative effects they did not measure (ibid., 379). These inferences are consistent with the data of Parker, Stulz, and Rice (2005) concerning allocations of policing based on the racial composition of areas.

An article by Messner et al. also addressed the issues of the relationship between the homicide rate in New York City and policing tactics. They also found a negative relationship between misdemeanor arrests and the homicide rate during the 1990s. They admitted that they could not discern the meaning of the arrest tactics (2007, 406) and stated specifically: "Clarifying the precise mechanisms underlying the finding of a negative effect of misdemeanor arrests on homicide is an important challenge for future research." They also correctly pointed out that the processes related to crime, sociodemographic changes that were ongoing during the decade they studied, cannot be captured by census data alone They stated in a footnote, citing the work of Fagan, West, and Holland (2003), that the long-term negative consequences of arrest and incarceration, the product of BW policing, "might be contrary to its short term effect" (ibid.). Messner et al. speculated in conclusion that the negative and positive aspects of BW policing be weighed (ibid., 407). But this is impossible if the data used as the key test of the value of the tactic are police gathered, recorded, reviewed, and published and if alternative data on the consequences of such tactics on other matters of concern are not gathered. If the ways in which the measured dependent "variable" affects the independent variable are unknown, does a model showing correlations indicate an explanation? Is any brief reduction in ORCS an entirely positive matter to be welcomed uncritically?

Variations in arrests or the official rate of selected crimes have been used as surrogates for social order or the like without validation of their meaning, prevalence, or effects. Most notable in this regard is that the assessment of the consequences of BW policing lacks a feedback loop from arrests, enforcements, raids, and the like to the structural conditions conducive to crime—residential turnover, unemployment, reduced property values, abatements and evictions, divorce, and single-parent heads of households. *All the loops in the models presented (e.g., St. Jean, Meares and Kahan, and Skogan) do not address the feedback: the negative consequences on the structural conditions correlated with crime.*

Taylor's argument, reduced, is that the variation within areas is greater than the variation across the areas he studied, and that the impact of arrests is difficult to assess. The most powerful exploration of the thesis is found in Sampson and Raudenbush's "Seeing Disorder," in which they show, using survey interviews and crime data, that the primary correlates of perceived disorder were social structural, not actual observed disorder. The perception of disorder was based in large part on an implicit association of it with the presence of people of color. It is a stimulus. As the percentage of black residents increases in an area, the perception that disorder is increasing rises precipitously, and this is most marked for Hispanics. Respondents added to their cognitive knowledge with "prior beliefs" about "modern urban ghettos" (2004, 336). This research demonstrates that the perception of disorder and crime is associated with "blackness" and that this in turn reduces security and increases fear regardless of the actual level of crime and disorder in these areas.

As might be surmised from the above review of the focus and range of previous research, a series of observations about the BW thesis is possible. First, no research has combined qualitative data from refined and targeted observations within the specific neighborhoods studied with the quantitative data, although observational data on social and physical disorder were used by Sampson and associates and by Taylor and interviews are a fundamental part of Skogan et al.'s assessment (2006) of the Chicago Police Department's CAPS program. Second, no research has used time-series or time-based reinterview techniques to assess changes over time given a pattern of policing. The closest to this is the work of Katz, Webb, and Schaefer (2001) on gangs and litter that showed a modest change in disorder given community policing. Third, the confounding of perceptions, observations, calls for service (requests), attitudes, and practices makes it impossible to assess the direct and indirect effects of BW policing approaches or tactics. Calls to the police about disorder and calls about crime, which may be clarified or distinguished once an officer attends the scene, are impossible to differentiate on the basis of calls alone. Fourth, studies in alternations, up or down, in the posited matter of unity, community well-being, or CE have not been done. Broken-windows policing has been undertaken only in areas of deep disadvantage, and changes in well-being have not been measured. The concern has been with ORCS, and personnel has been used as a surrogate for police practices (Messner et al. 2007; Rosenfeld, Fornango, and Rengifo 2007). Finally, as Thacher (2003) goes to great lengths to point out, the direct impact of BW policing has been studied almost exclusively in respect to reduction in ORCS. This overlooks a variety of matters associated with disorder that may vary but are not measured. BW policing and its connection to innovation in policing are addressed in more detail in the following chapter. In short, of course, "deploying officers" as a variable is meaningless unless one has data on what they do while policing an area.

That the ideology or belief in the broken-windows thesis mobilizes a variety of police tactics, it would appear, indirectly reinforces the idea of threat from young male African Americans as the primary urban concern. The complex relationships between "white flight" and fear, black movements into new areas stripping previous black areas of middle-class people, and the violent crime that drives disorder, according to Sampson, confounds any clear depiction of how, on the one hand, policing disorder might increase community well-being or, on the other hand, whether policing disorder is peripheral to the deeper questions of crime and its impact on the quality of life. Bernard Harcourt, in perhaps the most detailed summary of the broken-windows thesis (2000, 2007), has argued that the underlying theme, not stated directly in "Broken Windows," is that poverty, lower-class lifestyles, and unemployment are themselves disorderly. The norm of orderliness, largely derived from a vague middle-class standard of order, lifestyle, dress, manners, and "civility," is implicitly used by Wilson and Kelling as the standard by which all citizens should be judged by police. As Harcourt shows (2001), when police in New York City ratcheted up arrests for minor crimes and misdemeanors in the 1990s, they arrested and jailed a strikingly disproportionate percentage of minorities.

A Reconsideration of the Arguments

Let us consider these BW arguments from a sociology of knowledge perspective. Whose interests are supported by these ideas, and what does the manifestation of their consequences support materially and intellectually? What are the academic sources of the ideas, and what are their broader intellectual commitments? Who gains from such ideas as they become governing notions, the touchstones of policing aesthetics? What is omitted from such considerations and the definition of what is relevant to control?

First, whose political interests are mirrored in the arguments? Let us not naively dismiss police views as differing from the Wilson-Kelling-Coles perceptions and attributions of causes and manifestations of crime and disorder. The ideas and their origins are well connected. The appeal of broken windows is precisely this: it rationalizes the prior operational assumptions of policing as usual in extremely disadvantaged areas. This is not a theory of police but a commonsense distillation of stereotypical beliefs about criminogenic places and groups. As is the case with any arrest-oriented crude and unexamined deterrence theory, it mirrors the police outlook. It could be said yet another way: what other modes have they refined and developed and made public over the past eighty-five years or so? The vested interests of the police are found in the defenses made. One police anti-intellectual position is that "liberal academics" believe that inequality causes crime. These "liberal academics" are wrong; because ORC can be reduced by police actions (Bratton and Kelling 2006). This argument in bare rudiments is that none of these social forces that cause crime are sufficient or in fact relevant to eradicating crime. The efforts of the Manhattan Institute and of Kelling in particular are directed in large part to encouraging police, sharpening their traditional practices, increasing the public knowledge of the front-stage rhetoric of police leaders such as William Bratton, elevating uncritically a conservative and conventional notion about policing, improving the quality of life in cities, and selectively demonizing and criminalizing lifestyles.

Second, no closely reasoned research can sort out directly the consequences of a growing economy, increased and focused police actions, high rates of jailing and incarceration, and declining birthrate and cohort effects (the heavy use of cocaine and the effects of the decimation of young blacks between fourteen and twenty-five over the past ten years via suicide, homicide, and incarceration. Fagan (forthcoming) found that for the year 2007 in New York City, the probability of a young African American aged eighteen to twenty-two being stopped in the disadvantaged areas in which police were most deployed was .90. Even the most cautious and thoughtful series of inferences by Harcourt (2001) and Levitt (2004) conclude that it is not possible to attribute decline in OCR directly to police actions, because the gap between macroeconomic factors, costs, and police practices cannot be closed. How these arrest tactics work, and what their consequences are, is unclear.

Third, no research, as will be discussed in the following chapter, has actually looked closely through interviews, observations, and persistent and repeated measures of impact to show how and why such actions affect the social organization of communities. This is quite clear. On the one hand, the research is focused on the likely effects of policing on OCR and very little else. On the other hand, ethnographic research takes time, effort, and patience and is often limited to specific places or microecologies and neighborhoods rather than comparisons of more than one area, police precinct, or city.[8] The work of economists (Cook and Gross), academic lawyers (Kahan and Meares, Lessig, Ellickson, and Sunstein), and political scientists (Fong and Skogan) relies heavily on "as if" arguments concerning hypothetical relations unspecified by local knowledge of any kind or inference from attitude surveys. No one reports what was said or done on the ground on a day-to-day basis that would illuminate the claim that police practices reduced "crime."

Fourth, the undefined nature of "community" in community policing as well as the implicit territorial-ecological notions used by Wilson and Kelling in the *Atlantic* essay make any clear delineation of the arguments difficult, if not impossible. The matter of undefined "community" remains a problem for the police, for researchers, and for community members. The implication of the first essay is that a single officer on a foot beat has a neighborhood, the outlines and boundaries of which are coterminous with (a) citizens' meanings and notions; (b) his beat; (c) the police areas as designated by the department; (d) social and ecological features that can be mapped, correlated, and measured consistently; and (e) census tracts. This narrowing of a focus means in turn that the broader forces of capitalism, development, urban decay and renewal, racial segregation de facto, income inequalities, and the rest are set aside, and the focus is now on an undefined "disorder," which is again a function of the officers' definitions and actions. In many ways, it sustains the ecological fallacy of attributing to individuals the characteristics of the areas, such as levels of crime and disorder, in which they live.

Let us examine this further.[9] Ideologies are circular in nature and confirm their premises. Consider the premises of policing. Given a notion that an area is disordered and in some state of decline, officers construct it as a place where they can find disorder and disorderly people. It is available to the naked eye. Summary caricatures of the social areas of any city are part of the oral culture, including the gossip, training, and early socialization of officers and the media's views and treatments of these areas. This means in common terms dramatizing areas on the basis of their visible disorder—the kind alluded to by Wilson and Kelling. Officers patrolling in these areas can act with full confidence of the validity of their perceptions, given the stereotypes and names given the areas and the people who live and work there (see Klinger 1997; and Herbert 1998). Sweeps and massive arrests can be carried out easily without protest given the powerlessness of the people and their lack of efficacy. Such arrests, ironically, can produce short-term relief—no more drug dealing on the street, no drug houses opening or operating, and fewer calls for service regarding drugs. Since the police view their job primarily as reacting to nineteenth-century crimes and delicts—robbery, assaults, burglaries, and street chaos—the broken-windows metaphor becomes an intellectual umbrella for their capture verbally their feelings and experiences. It is also a way to express their frustration with the deeply determined matters they encounter every day on the job. Since the majority of police officers now have some years attending college and often study criminal justice, they are all acquainted with the broad outline of BW ideas, can summarize it well, and use it as a justification for a wide range of actions and departmental policies.

The circularity of these arguments is perhaps obvious, since it captures the moral tapestry of urban policing—it deals with things that do not change much, and the tone and temper of much of police talk are that things are only getting worse, and their own powers and effects are severely limited. They are uninterested in things they cannot change. As many have noted, policing produces a great deal of cynicism, unmitigated by positive experiences, praise, and overt success. As an experiment, consider if the disorder in a community were defined by the levels of recreational drug use; cheating on tax obligations; adultery and clandestine sexual relations, especially by minors; domestic violence of a wide range; drunken driving; and attempted suicides (illegal in Massachusetts). These crimes are variously visible but committed across the class spectrum and not limited to the lower classes, the poor, the mentally ill, and the homeless. This again underscores that much of the broken-windows argument echoes class and racial biases about policing and what is taken to be "crime."

Fifth, who gains politically as a result of a reduction of reported, officially recognized crime? The auditing of police statistics is rare, and it is well understood that organizational decisions can easily alter the figures up or down. Police should be asked to show that these changes are not a result of changes in law, policies, organizational rules of thumb, or other matters, such as increased use of cell phones, number of operators or officers hired, alterations of the city boundaries, and the like not associated with the changes in behavior called crime. The argument asserts police power, and their surrogate measures of order claim that the concern of scholars and the public *should be* with order as they construe it. How these are related to order, well-being, quality of life, or even notionally "order" has been discussed only by Harcourt in a long discussion of the applicability of Foucault's ideas about ordering the subject-citizen. In effect, by creating a social object, "disorder," which is a surrogate or proxy for lower-class and particularly African American lifestyles or even presence, it spreads and blurs the mandate of the police, serves to demonize one segment of a population, intends to criminalize lifestyles, and perpetuates symbolic violence. Other scholars have pursued the false chimera that the connection between one kind of arrest and another is an accurate picture of the ways in which order is either created or restored. No study has addressed this, nor has any recent study actually looked closely at the process of sustaining neighborhood social control over time.[10]

Sixth, on what factual basis does one know this perspective on social order is valid? What evidence is presented outside standard police recorded and official data?

The circular nature of the arguments about misdemeanor arrests and more serious crime is contaminated by several well-known factors. The police of course are the gatherers and processors of these data, and there is no independent audit of their validity or reliability over time. (The probity of these statistics has been discussed in detail since they were invented as a political tool by J. Edgar Hoover.) In practice, controlling disorder is a matter of constructing evidence of a bad reputation among known young men. If, for example, a young man is stopped and arrested a number of times for misdemeanors, he builds up a reputation and is more and more likely to be arrested for a serious crime (Cicourel 1995). Kirk (2005) has shown that in Chicago in 1994–1995 the average number of arrests for young African American men at age eighteen is one. The tipping point from a misdemeanor arrest or two to a felony arrest is highly probable in Chicago, and so order is maintained. Furthermore, as Brodeur (forthcoming) has noted, a fact that can be established by examining the figures on the rearrests of individuals, those caught up in misdemeanor arrests are the same people who have been arrested previously for other crimes. What crime is reduced when the same people are rearrested now for minor crimes that are not included in national crime reports?

Seventh, what appeals does the BW framework have as the basis for police operational "policy"? Most police policy is not written but oral and takes place at roll calls, meetings, and press conferences. Most important, it would appear that the clarity of expression, the simplicity of the moralizing, the unspecified links between neighborhood informal controls and resultant disorder and crime, and the echoes of police notions about deterrence, control, and causation are factors in its wide appeal. It has academic appeal as well, given the frequent reprinting of the BW article in collections of articles intended for the academic market. As is perhaps obvious, it requires no problem solving, no retraining, no new tactics, no study or analysis, and no reorganization of standard modes of random patrol with the occasional intervention. Shifts in deployment of young officers are easily done in a big city. No additional supervision is needed.

Eighth, it is simple and popular. It set the terms of reference for debate for some twenty years, and had an especially wide popularity as a factor in the decline in crime in New York City in the early nineties.[11] It has occupied the high ground of discussions even as it has produced relatively little clear research support. It feeds into the conventional wisdom concerning the ability of the police to control and even dramatically suppress OCR; it plays into politicians' rhetoric and the public fears and disease with disorder. It provides an intellectual rationale for what is done every day on a practical level in every inner-city neighborhood in this country: manage order in some mixture of informal and formal ways of "keeping the peace." Whether this controls crime awaits further study. The incivilities thesis, as Taylor has titled it, has expanded the public mandate of the police so that the imagination that they have shown up to and including coercion is now argued as necessary. This is a radical reshaping of the argument of the police studies field in general, casting the job of the criminal justice system as one of regarding and avoiding the influence of "extralegal variables" while respecting the norms of legal procedure. This is held out as justice, and the influence of ethnicity, gender, age, and class are to be avoided. These are merely impediments to rational choice. The purpose of policing should be to protect order, not only to catch criminals. Wilson's careful bows in the direction of legal protections are just that, as the strong case made is the need to enforce order and avoid disorder more than to be too concerned with legal niceties. This is the music, if not the words.

Ninth, what is the observable impact of such general notions in reshaping any known police practice? The BW thesis in one sense was a radical effort toward redefining the public, known, permissible, and expected police practice. It admitted publicly and in print and later with the support in due course of police leaders such as William Bratton that policing was differential in given areas, times, places, and with people of different lifestyles. It argues that crackdowns and crime-focused policing in designated areas defined by the police, rather than policing broadly and equally to provide "service" across all areas, were not only done but should be done. This had not been the public police position, which previously was: we serve the public equally across time and space, and our duty is to "preserve and protect" all or most of the people all the time. Since most people are not threatened by actual criminal incidents, this is a truism. I have called this the responsiveness theme in late-twentieth-century policing—we are a 24/7 service agency ready to serve whenever called. BW, on the other hand, rationalized with intellectual support the unquestioned merit of employing different styles of policing in different parts of large cities. Further, it made clear publicly that officers could, should, and would (of course they did and had done) define order and apply coercion if needed, as they so judged. This position begged the question, of course, of what such definitions might be and their relationships to community priorities, the law, conventional local traditions, and differences within and between police forces policing the same areas (e.g., city, state, county, and federal agencies). It opened up the question of what policies, if any, might guide such "aggressive order maintenance." This tactical approach denies society's inequalities based on race and class as well as the severe social and economic problems associated with living in areas of severe disadvantage. The approach, superficial in nature, also possessed long-term possibilities of encouraging standing patterns of enforcement on the margins of the law—threatening, testing, and pushing the edges of acceptable police behavior. It certainly advocated net widening, raising the question of remedies—there were few available if the matter did not entail arrests or fines that could be appealed. Moreover, it is patently unclear how formal controls via arrest strengthen the informal norms within neighborhoods that grow from social structural disadvantage. In effect, as Sykes (1986) argued, policing becomes a laissez-faire operation. Given the present inequalities in society and the collective obligation to pay for order, laissez-faire policing increases inequalities and produces allocative justice, the opposite of what democracy requires.

Tenth, what was the value of BW for the prestige of the police? Policing since the 1920s has been seeking a rationalization for itself as an occupation. The scientific, quasi-militaristic model of policing, elaborated by Wilson and McLaren (1963), was in part an attempt to control the behavior of the lower participants and in part an appeal to public administration as a framework for police management or administration. It spoke silence to how policing was to accomplish lofty goals but reiterated the value of clear rules, good training, and bureaucratic attentiveness. The emergence of the broken-windows thesis post-1982 is remarkable for its influence, its data-free assertions, its implicit hegemony of police judgment about order, and its properties. Its ultimate consequence was not to change police behavior but to *rationalize* what had been and is being done every day in every large city in this country. Coincident with this was the absence of remedies for the cornucopia of police tactics huddled together as "broken-windows policing." It captured well the base notions of policing stated so elegantly by Bittner (1990)—intervene where needed or else it will get worse.

Eleventh, the cost-benefit analysis of the practices has not been undertaken. The costs of the actions guided by the application of the broken-windows policing style—and its justification as the source of drops in crime (Blumstein and Wallman 2005; Levitt 2004; Harcourt 2001)—have not been assessed:[12]

- Risks introduced to civil liberties, especially by those with few resources
- Rising complaints against the police
- A radical and unconscionable rise in misdemeanor arrests that are largely targeted at minorities and people of color (Harcourt and Ludwig 2007)
- Lower courts assailed with arrests for minor crimes
- Dramatic instances of police violence in a few well-known instances (Louima and Diallo in particular)
- Pitting in the media the "orderly" and "respectable" against the unnamed but demonized "disreputable"—the smelly, the drunk, the prostitute, and others who create disorder and produce fear (Wilson and Kelling 1982)

On the positive side, there may also be increases in the value of homes, reduced mortgage failure, increased feelings of collective efficacy, lower turnover in residency, or more active political participation. Evidence of these outcomes is not available.

Finally, what is most striking, given that policing is a craft, or set of practices, why have the *actual practices* associated with BW policing (if such a thing can be defined) not been studied carefully? Since "disorder" is a contextually defined matter, a kind of family of nuisances without a core dimension, it cannot be easily studied outside of careful observation of police practices (see Parks et al. 1999; and Thacher 2004, 391, 393, 396). This requires ethnographic observation. Measuring the effects of more police in an area, arrests made for minor crimes, or correlations between minor crime and major crime tells us little about what police do in the situations they confront.

In summary of these points, one can conclude that by focusing consistently, stridently, and narrowly on "arrests" and other aspects of ORC, the advocates of BW have failed to ask the question one must address to any policy and its advocates: what are the social, political, and material costs of such policies? The benefits associated with reduced ORC are arguable, but data on the costs have not been calculated. Of course, the benefits are not assessed other than by strident claims that crime drops as a result. What is their overall value when judged against the notional "benefits"? The long-term consequences have not been studied, the broader social costs have not been assessed, and the damage to collective life has been ignored. The present known effect, the subtle and troubling effect, of these changes is that it creates a climate of opinion that elevates order above all other considerations, "order" itself being a nominal, vague, variable politically loaded, ideologically charged, and undefined idea (Wilson and Kelling 1982; Thacher 2004); substitutes law enforcement for concern with collective efficacy and other modes of enhancing informal controls; and creates a subject, the other, who is deemed unworthy, categorically reified as the focus and target, and deprived of humanity, good sense, feelings, purpose, and viability.[13] The underlying idea that drives the perspective or approach is that order trumps all other concerns—justice, legal rights, collective obligations, and procedural guarantees— and that shifting the obligation for order to the police in fact diminishes collective obligations. This consequence is pointed out by Kahan and Meares (1998), Harcourt (2001), Kane (2003, 2006) and sociolegal theorists such as Lessig (1996) and Sunstein (1993). It should be emphasized finally that BW is a viewpoint, a simplification of vastly complex social processes, a deeply conservative moral and political position stated as a public policy, and a useful umbrella for policing as usual. It has made clear that policing is symbolic and dramaturgical as well as a "real" violent force; when it attempts to police lifestyles, feelings, potential, and or imagined delicts, it moves away from behavior. In this latter precise sense it is nondemocratic policing.

CONCLUSION

The chapter concerns the absence of theory in police studies and the consequences of this lack. The current renditions of policing revolve around crime control, crime prevention, and effectiveness and efficiency gauged against controlling crime. Theorizing is modest and aims at understanding the role of the police in the criminal justice system rather than as an organization in a contested position in an ecology of competing organizations and playing a role in social control more generally. The research and theory of policing are manifestations of *sociology for the police* and on their terms. This has handicapped the growth of a proper theory in which policing plays a role. The BW thesis, its origins and impacts, as well as the research it has generated, is a case in point of adapting a practitioner's ideas to guide research rather than developing a theory of policing based on principles. Changes in ORCS are only one indicator of performance and public expectations. The BW approach and criticisms thereof are outlined here because it constitutes one aspect of the broader panorama within which modest adjustments in police rhetoric and style (community policing, crime mapping/crime analysis hot-spot-based policing, and problem-oriented policing) have taken place. to this theme we return in the following chapter.

CHAPTER SEVEN

The Reform of Policing

The previous chapters have considered with evidence matters that bear on this question: what is policing good for? They have also addressed a narrower question: what is expected of democratic policing? Even a cursory review of research found in previous chapters reveals that the research reflects a commonsense view of the job developed and rationalized by the police. What passes for theory is not and reflects a sociology for the police. Conveniently, policing ignores much of what is known systematically about organizations, crime, and its patterning and causation. It resists innovation but accepts cosmetic and rhetorical changes, as do all occupations. This resistance to innovation is tied to the present mandate, a mandate shaped and sold to the public by police reformers and researchers. Crime control remains the public centerpiece.

This chapter first takes up some general programmatic changes in policing and then addresses specific reform efforts that have emerged in the past twenty-five or so years: *community policing, problem-solving policing, hot-spot policing,* and *crime mapping and crime analysis.* All these are essentially tactical modifications in resource deployment and thus require neither reorganization nor change in strategies. They require neither new resources nor resource reallocation. They do not require policy change or rethinking of standard operating procedures. They can be combined or paired, and since virtually every American police department claims to be doing community policing, any other innovation produces a working pair. They are on the surface quite significant attempts to reform, but no shifts, even in large and innovative departments, have been made in the fundamental random patrol, responses to 911 calls, and investigative functions (Maguire 2004; Weisburd and Braga 2006, final essay). Investigative work, subject of research in the 1970s, remains now outside any reform efforts.

THE SHAPE OF REFORM

By the 1990s, a new police reform movement, a combination of community policing, problem solving, and "managerialism," emerged. The rhetoric was redolent of
buzzwords taken uncritically from the business world: grandiose and general strategic
plans, euphemistic mission statements, management by objectives, and simulation
of business jargon. Policing rhetoric no longer resembled its early form and content
that was a mixture of liberal thought, optimism, and naïveté. Underlying this new
rhetoric was the firm conviction that the basic and essential role was crime suppression and that this was indicated solely by official numbers. The field, "police
studies" (see chapter 4), emerged, funding became consistent and abundant, and,
increasingly, top command was involved in and supportive of research consistent
with its own management aims.

The four approaches that emerged tantalized police administrators who ad-
mired reform. These four are most favored by police administrators and researchers
who are closely allied with foundations, government agencies, and private research
organizations such as the Institute of Law and Justice and the Urban Institute. Their
actual long-term success is seriously in doubt, even among those deeply involved and
funded to carry out the research (Weisburd and Eck 2004). These reforms are not
based on theories, have no academic history prior to being invented, and at best are
tactical approaches. What passes for a framework, broken windows, is tactical. It
should be emphasized that evaluations of effectiveness and efficiency focus entirely
on crime, even when words like *justice* and *fairness* are mentioned in the brief that
guides the assessment process (e.g., National Research Council 2004). Even those
approaches that speak of "partnerships" argue that their views are consistent with
the crime-control focus (Trojanowicz and Moore 1998). Because the concern has
not moved beyond "crime" as officially recorded or other official data such as calls
for service, the assessment leaves issues of justice and equal treatment unexamined
and relevant criteria unexplored. What are the police good for? Let now examine
these four programs or approaches to reform.

COMMUNITY POLICING

It is perhaps an overstatement to claim that in the early 1980s academics and police
top command began to question current police practices. This was the result of
liberal critiques of the police with respect to the "War on Drugs," the rising official crime rate, the still painful bloody rebellions of inner cities, and the absence
of change in the composition and function of police organizations (white males in
cars). Liberals and conservatives took public note of the failure to control crime,
the rising homicide rate, and the deterioration of the quality of life in large urban
centers. In due course, the notion that enforcement of local authority by officers, an
echo of the Wilson-Kelling thesis, could sustain trust and represent order emerged.
This was a perversion and elaboration of a past that never was, nor was as good as it

was remembered to be (Manning 1983). In many ways, this was a harking back to a nonexistent times and orderliness in which the American equivalent of the "bobby on the beat" was sanctified (Manning 1984, 1988; Walker 1984). Threads of ideas woven together in a semblance of order became a passionate rhetoric of nostalgia. Underlying it was the unseen potential that it would rationalize any attempt to change or transform policing and was a vague label that would encompass an as yet unforeseen endless number of tactics. Claimed to be a success before it was implemented, supported by a few studies of modest dimensions, it was soon touted by foundations, the National Institute of Justice, the Kennedy School, Harvard, and educated and sophisticated urban chiefs. Unlike any other major policy initiative in modern times, it was almost immediately deemed a complete success virtually everywhere with no supporting evidence.

The assumptions of this movement, most false and all misleading, were present in its *early manifestations* around 1983. Urban policing was not legitimate, strong, uncorrupt, and good prior to the mobilization and technological revolution post–World War II (Walker 1984). Reformers claimed, however, that there was now a single, general, good, and real "public," and they were the worthy customers of the police. Implicitly at least, victims of crime were not always worthy. This public, in turn (in general and especially the respectable people), yearned for more police; wanted them present, urged joint efforts, and missed the local nature of the police presence. It agreed that personalized, local authority should trump evenhanded policing that was consistent across districts, times, and places. It was also assumed that policing can sustain local order and enhance it and alter communities, making them both safer and more pleasant; police suggestively can deal with all manner of problems without regard to resource base; and policing is fair and just in operation in all parts of the city. The police, more than other agencies, are responsible for defending, defining, expanding, and shaping the common good of the community by active means (Manning 1983). This was a rhetorical effort to pin down the legitimacy of police claims as evidence mounted about the contradictions inherent in its claims (ibid.). The following claims arose to defend and sustain the movement under the shadow of public concerns. As I argued in *Police Work* (1997, 13–14), the movement's claims are flawed. Consider the following dubious claims:

- *Citizens are coproducers of order.* Scant evidence suggests that the selected citizens who are involved in meetings and crime-control activities are equals in power and authority. In any event, equality it is unlikely because the police value their autonomy and secrecy and guard their information (Skogan and Hartnett 1997; Skogan et al. 1999; Fung 2004).
- *Police are accountable to citizens.* Even when a "partnership" is respected, there is no accountability in the sense of altering the police practice. With a system of regular meetings (shown to exist nowhere but in Chicago), the police only take on problems they define and are resistant to citizen definitions of "problems." Most meetings do not find a problem on which to agree (Skogan et al. 1999).

- *Key police participants are the beat officers* (Skogan and Hartnett 1997; Skogan et al. 1999). Even when stability occurs for a time, transfers, seniority priorities in promotions, and retirements reduce continuity and familiarity of the public with officers assigned.
- *Citizens can shape deployment and targeting of the police.* Police organizations continue to maintain total control over allocation and deployment of officers. These practices in turn are almost entirely based on union contracts in cities outside the West. This permits "flooding areas" with new recruits to produce short-term decreases in recorded crime (Fagan forthcoming). On the other hand, when political pressure is brought by business owners, reallocation does occur (Lyons 1998; Herbert 2006).
- *Community policing is a success and is everywhere the practice.* The success of a beat officer and community policing in general is not measured by any public and known standard. The rewards are unclear to all involved. This stands in contrast to the public stance of the patrol officers and their supervisors who seize on and look for "activity" based on traditional ideas—traffic stops, gun seizures, arrests, and "keeping busy" while on patrol.
- *Community police officers are satisfied with their work.* In departments in which the activities are a separate division or unit, they are looked down upon as "not pulling their share" and as being "Ping Pong policemen" or "babysitters" uninterested in crime. Fielding (2005) has shown that nevertheless community police officers are unclear about what is expected of them and disappointed that they do not make arrests.
- *Community policing is combined with problem solving.* Problem solving, when carried out, is not linked consistently and systematically to community policing programs (Skogan 2006, 325). It becomes a name in search of a referent.
- *Police can and do increase the level of social control in areas.* There is no evidence of this in spite of police claims that policing measurably increases informal social control. At best this claim seems to hinge on reduced fear of crime in some cities (Skogan 1990).
- *Community policing is named as the policing strategy generally in the United States.* Close examination reveals that most of the visible changes are tactical, revealed in attempts to reduce social distance by foot patrol, bicycle patrol, community policing units, and public rhetoric.
- *Community policing has meant reorganization of modern police departments— they are now management driven, smart and lean, flexible and dynamic.* There has been no known change in the 911 reactive-responsiveness theme or the demand-solicitation strategy of sustaining political legitimacy. There is little reallocation of responsibilities on the ground.
- *Community policing is an overall policy and program.* Investigative work, one of the most important and profound sources of contact with citizens, and the public face of the police in disadvantaged communities, never had a role in CP, and resisted it at every point from the late seventies on (Sherman, Milton, and Kelly 1973). This is still the case. Detective work and proactive units such

as gang units, school units, and warrant-serving units act independently of community policing programs and initiatives. Their movements and raids are secretive and unannounced except at the last minute to patrol and community officers. They are not a part of the program and are not sanctioned for failure to comply.

As of 2009, after some twenty years of research and reflection, many in police studies have adopted a self-congratulatory pose.[1] While mailed and telephone surveys of departments report that changes in the direction of CP are in place (Zhao et al. 1996), the vague term and lack of definition suggest this is rather cosmetic in nature, perhaps capturing at best some shifts in tactics. While the evidence is ambiguous of the success of community policing in its several guises, it is now subject to fine-tuning (see, for example, the chapters in Skogan 2004). The pose is based on *claims* for massive change in police organizations, structural dedifferentiation and smart management, policies that change behaviors on the ground, and elegant new well-crafted strategies and tactics that penetrate the black heart of disorder and leave it exsanguinating on back streets (see the useful summary of Weisburd and Eck 2004, including some reservations concerning these claims). This vast theatrical curtain, hailed by the media and by few scholars, has been a rather handsome distraction. The facts on which it is based are thin, various, contradictory, and often troubling.

Community policing is now featured as in place in any and all large urban police departments. The conceptual problems are typically ignored: for example, the confusion and confounding of it with problem solving and Compstat; crime crackdowns based on analysis done by experts, not police; problem solving versus problem finding and defining; the relative importance of the role of the "community" and that of the police; and clarifications that associate it with tactics (Skogan and Hartnett 1997), a philosophy (Cordner 1999), four key features (specialization, open systems approach to the environment, technological sophistication, and dedifferentiation [Greene 2000]), and four other features roughly analogous (change in presentational strategies, reduced organizational complexity and formalism, changes in technology, and role changes [Greene 2004]). Some suggest the core features lie in differences between modes of patrol (more than motorized) and willingness of citizens to be engaged with the police (not whether they did anything together) (Reisig and Parks 2004, 213). Others claim it lies in distinctions within the approach involving philosophy, strategies, tactics, and organizational changes. Greene (2000) presents a list of some twelve dimensions useful in comparing traditional, community-oriented, problem-solving, and zero-tolerance policing. As Greene, in the most detailed and thoughtful reviews, has pointed out, these are ideal types, and no police department is solely one or the other, and all, in likelihood, practice some of each of the approaches over time. In many respects, the types are shorthand labels for officers' practices, not policies; police departments do not possess policies about how to police—they have modal practices (see, for example, Terrill and Mastrofski 2004 describing the differences between the Indianapolis Police Department and that of St. Petersburg in which officers' attitudes differed from the top commands' views and public statements). *Clearly, when there is no agreement on what is being defined, conceptualized, measured, and compared, no generalizations can be drawn. It cannot be evaluated as a program because it is not a program. Community policing is an ideal, not a program.*

Evidence gathered carefully since the late seventies in close analysis and case studies (Greene and Mastrofski 1988; Rosenbaum 1994; Thacher 2001; Skogan et al. 1999), ethnographic work (Herbert 2006; Lyons 1999; Manning 2003); well-designed sample surveys (Maguire 2002); observational studies (Sampson and Raudenbush 1999; Taylor 2000), and critical essays (Harcourt 2001) suggests the flawed claims of the movement. The most systematic and consistent reviews by Greene (2000, 2004) in the United States and Brodeur in Canada (2005) show little change in either matter (see also the useful review of research in Rosenbaum 1994), while Maguire (2003) found no change in structure, levels, or tactics and no dedifferentiation. In general, the findings are mixed, in favor of some change in organizational structure, knowledge, and process but a fast fade of effects (Rosenbaum and Wilkinson 1994). The most detailed studies of CP are the Skogan et al. project (Skogan 1990, 2004, 2006; Skogan and Hartnett 1991; Skogan et al. 1999) and the Fung study (2004) in Chicago. The Skogan project focuses on changes in tactics, meetings, and, in later publications, beat plans and structural correlates of social capital. Fong demonstrates that participation in neighborhoods already high in collective efficacy increases when an event stimulates public and police interest. In many respects the fine-tuning of community policing in Chicago involves making connections between beat plans, officer accountability on the ground, and required officer participation in neighborhood meetings. All of this hinges on the fact demonstrated early on by the work of Skogan and Hartnett: political support by local, state, and national elected officials and city (primarily) and budgetary provisions are essential to cultivating public trust in police and involvement in public affairs.

The most recent and rather pained review by Mastrofski summarizes the limited accomplishments of what he takes to be CP. He offers no definition, writing, "Community policing has remained multifaceted and diverse" (2006, 44). This, of course, should be the end of any serious discussion of the matter—if it cannot be defined operationally and precisely, it cannot be measured and systematically assessed. This should be the first serious objection to claims that CP has accomplished anything. Mastrofski identifies four areas in which to assess the accomplishments of community policing: changes in public expectations (little research has been done; none established change, but the hopeful, rather nostalgic, wish for policing as an available service remains), changes in police organization and performance (little change beyond modified tactics, but public mission statements and values are now generally paraded), changes in outcomes and services performed (what changes in the direction of more fair and less coercive policing practices exists, and there is considerable evidence of this, cannot be attributed to organizational or programmatic change, but may be due to other factors such as individual attitudes and preferences of officers), and police legitimacy (little research on this matter exists).

Mastrofski's very complete and perceptive review establishes another incontrovertible point: although changes in the public expectations and assessment of policing can be discovered, they cannot be directly attributed to CP as a program because the links between the organization, its leadership training and supervision, and the actions of officers have not been established and perhaps cannot be. The studies cited with some hopeful indications of change in every instance come from attitude studies, that is, observations of police officers; none of them deals with the systematic study of police organizations. The case studies of actual efforts to police in an altered fashion, the studies of Greene in Los Angeles, Lyons and Herbert in Seattle, Williams in Georgia, Manning in the Midwest, Rosenbaum and associates in three Illinois cities, and Mastrofski in Richmond, Indianapolis, and St. Petersburg, show little change and a brief soon-fading effect, if any. Maguire (2002) shows police departments in cities with more than 200,000 in population have not become less differentiated, less rule bound, or less stratified. As Mastrofski concludes (2006, 61–62), the Skogan studies are perhaps the only ones able to establish some change in the way policing is organized and some connection between policing and community involvement, fear of crime, and participation in problem solving. Mastrofski notes that few police organizations, when surveyed, even imagined in 1993, let alone carried out, the modest structural changes that Skogan et al. observed might be necessary to achieve positive effects.

These empirical studies demonstrate what has been well known for a considerable time: the present strategies and tactics, random patrol, response to 911, and investigative work built on the assumptions of "professional policing" are embedded in ritual, ideology, and myth. Current practices and attempts to change them are not based on evaluations, science, facts, or close scrutiny. While these strategies are a mollifying presence, rooted in ever-hopeful memory, they have changed policing little.

This is not to claim that all efforts at amelioration have had no noticeable impacts. However, the distinction should be drawn between aspects of community policing as an ideology or mini belief system; the sincere hope that policing will be transformed in some way to increase police legitimacy and respect, thus enhancing social control; a reorganization movement intending to reduce layers of management, improve supervision, and better deploy resources (Greene 2000; Maguire 2002; Mastrofski 2006); an organizational move toward reducing social distance between neighborhoods and police (Mastrofski, Reisig, and McCluskey 2002; Skogan and Hartnett 1997); and a collection of miscellaneous tactics and whimsical miscellany masquerading as innovation (e.g., officers on bicycles).

Community policing was always a blurred, undefined label in search of a social location. It was a solution searching for a problem. The implication of the fashionable political rhetoric was that it was not but would soon be current practice. It sucked in other attempts to innovate, became bloated with pregnant meanings, and eventually referred to everything and therefore nothing. The question remains whether the changes indicated by Mastrofski are sufficient to create a tipping point such that policing on the ground changes from the ground up rather than from the top down.

PROBLEM-SOLVING POLICING

In 1979 Herman Goldstein, who formerly served as an administrative assistant to O. W. Wilson, the commissioner of police in Chicago, argued in a brief article that rather than responding to calls for service seriatim, the police might better spend time analyzing *problems*. Rather than seeking to close calls and clean up any assignments by the end of a shift, Goldstein, then a professor at the University of Wisconsin School of Law, urged clustering and analyzing problems using a variety of data. By resolving the problem, the source of the calls would be identified and actions could be taken to reduce them. The relationship between the "natural event," or what stimulated the call, the call as processed, classified, and dispatched; what was done on the scene; and the underlying processes that produced each one of these had not been a matter of discussion among police. The idea was that intervention in some sense was to be preferred to reaction one at a time, case by case, as and when needed. In Goldstein's scheme, the call for service, the named incident, and the problem (often an underlying social, economic, or psychological matter) are analytically distinct. Goldstein wanted to move action toward analysis and ultimately to interventions that might mitigate the impacts of disorder and crime. Furthermore, there was a deeply conservative aim in his argument—to enable the police to sort out what they can and cannot do and to focus on what could be done. This is known in business as maintaining core values and functions and sloughing off the unnecessary and costly. Since policing's costs and benefits are unclear yet their necessity unquestioned, an examination of functions made sense.

For example, "prostitution" generates many calls and arrests every year. Solutions to "prostitution" could be seen as subject to arrests, sweeps, short-term harassment, undercover work, surveillance, or stings. These do nothing in the long run to reduce the supply or demand for sex, nor would these more than briefly remove the visible indicators. Calls and complaints would continue. "Prostitution" could be deconstructed. It could be seen as (1) a public health matter requiring education, use of condoms and needles, and police acting as educators; (2) a medical problem requiring medical expertise and referral by the police to hospitals and clinics (e.g., for AIDS or other sexually transmitted diseases); (3) a moral problem (unwanted pregnancies and violation of conventional sexual attitudes) in which police again are counselors or work with social workers to offer services; (4) a disorder problem (loitering, traffic obstruction, harassment) addressed by standard police tactics; (5) a business or commercial issue (maintaining convention business, keeping up the image of the city) in which the police would partner with the Chamber of Commerce or business associations; (6) a law enforcement problem (people breaking the law—both men and women) tackled by arrests and fines; or (7) a legal problem (outdated laws, unenforceable regulations) that should be changed by top command lobbying for change with the legislature or city council. Since the police view the job as doing something about the here and now as they see it, rather than "problem solving," they tend to repeat their practices without assessing the long-term consequences of such. Goldstein's later work (1989), presented in a textlike rendition, contained only hypotheticals, imagined examples, not actual problems. Goldstein worked diligently with the Madison police and the idea has become institutionalized in a Goldstein Award but has rarely shown results that appeal to street officers (Eck 2006) or top command.

In part this failure is accountable and well known and has been discussed previously as a product of one of the standard strategies of policing—responding to calls for service. This strategy has devolved into a staple of officers' standard work to rule and job-control ideology—also called "keeping a low profile" (Van Maanen 1975). The subtleties of police record-keeping practices have continued to maintain this ideology as reality. These practices (which have remained unchanged in spite of the problem-solving efforts) were the subtext of what Goldstein and others hoped to change. These practices mitigate against systematic problem solving, even when time is given and training undertaken. These are the driving forces in police work. It is conventional wisdom that officers do not patrol in their assigned areas more that 50 percent of the time (Reiss 1971). Officers "jump calls"—accepting them before another officer who has been called by the communications center to accept it or turning up on the scene anyway. This is usually associated with anticipating a "good call" that might include crime or action of some kind. This displaces cars from their usual beats and any routine assigned activity. While they are assigned beats and areas, officers wander and do not remain in their patrol areas. They accept calls themselves or as backup, which puts them in other districts or adjoining cities. They may voluntarily back up a fellow officer or respond to a violent or an unfolding major incident without announcing they are doing so. As a result, "rational allocation" based on proximity or "status" (in or out of service and the length of time in each status) has little value. Officers who are most active, a rewarded practice, are thus less likely to be working in their assigned districts. Because officers value their control of the job, its pacing (how quickly incidents are taken up), level (the number of incidents responded to), and intensity (the quality of the action or the time spent on each), they misrepresent their status (in an incident or out of it) and their location. Officers lie consistently about their locations and their current status and activities and keep record logs that support these lies (Meehan 1992, 1993, 2000; Moskos 2008). On the other hand, officers swarm or swing by locations indicated by "promising calls," to see what's happening, or to break up their boredom. They remain there until paperwork is done unless another call of interest arises. The job of the patrol officer in the occupational culture is defined by the incident, attending, clearing, and moving on in a routine fashion. The job does not entail concern for changing the forces shaping crime such as social structure, class vagaries, values, or the rest. As George Kelling once said (personal communication), policing is the only job where working and dealing with people is defined as "out of service." In service is driving around waiting for a call from central communications. The incidents and their content are not of equal interest to all officers, and some calls are avoided routinely. Officers have an informal and known division of labor concerning some calls that are preferred by their colleagues (e.g., those involving a possible arrest [Walsh 1986] and the related overtime). Job control is the most essential idea, iconic of the work. The restricted interest in problem solving comes directly from defining the job as "handling calls for service." Officers make diligent efforts to keep their workload modest, clearing, if possible, all the calls before the end of the shift, regardless of their complexity. They tend not to make arrests at the end of the shift if overtime is not available. The average workload even in big cities appears to be one to three calls an hour, hardly a demanding schedule (Moskos 2008, 11–13), but the ideology of overload remains. In fact, variations in workload by days of the week and time of day, for example, are assumed to occur, but the variations in time not taken up by assigned calls are used in "backup" of other officers' calls or random patrol without purpose or direction (see Famega 2005). When time is available, it is not used to systematically identify or work out solutions to problems that might be generating calls. Even efforts at allocating time to "directed patrol" are generally fruitless, in part because the matters of interest are in fact rare (e.g., driving around with a gun in the car and being stopped [Tien 1979; McGarrell et al. 2006]).

Shifting attention of officers to a specific object, purpose, or activity was attempted in the 1970s using the idea of directed patrol and revived as a crime-control tactic by research sponsored by the NIJ (see, for example, Tien 1978; McGarrell et al. 2001, 2002, 2006) with very modest results at best. These efforts were a marginal approach to "problem solving" by "solving" the problem in advance and simplifying it to "taking guns off the street" or PBJ—"putting butts in jail"—while reducing other call-answering obligations. It was a hopeful top down–command idea of organizing the work at the bottom by creating an imaginative puzzle standing outside the one-call-after-another notion that kept work in the control of the patrol officer.

An elaborate quasi–research ameliorative literature based on hypotheticals, imagined problem solving, individual officer initiatives, and solutions such as destroying a housing estate to prevent future crimes was publicized by the Police Foundation and the NIJ. The descriptive articles by Eck and Spelman (1987) based on work in Newport News, Virginia, were widely reprinted. This is largely smoke and mirrors, as the problem solving was done not by officers but by academics involved; the approach was never adopted and rewarded, and the outcomes were never evaluated as to their results based on any known standards.

An honest evaluation of the most sophisticated example of evaluating the effects of problem solving in Jersey City, New Jersey, was published by Braga et al. (1999). This could be considered as an example of hot-spot policing, as it claims to be based on police assessments and perceptions of problems. They first describe the imaginative experimental design with control and stimulus areas, measured treatments, and detailed measurement of outcomes. They note that "the complexities" of crime and disorder problems and the "difficulties encountered by the Jersey City officers" in implementing the problem-oriented approach led to limited problem analysis, because of "traditional law enforcement practices, reliance on situational responses that were often not directly linked to the violent crime problems at a place and a lack of community involvement" (ibid., 213). As described in the article, officers merely designated areas they knew were disorderly (mainly open drug-dealing areas in the city along main streets), comparable areas were designated by the researchers, and differential patrol and interventions were staged regularly. This is an elaborate method used to measure brief effects of routine and traditional tactics, not police problem solving. In fact, there was no discussion of what the problem was, only the apparent known manifestations of it. Modest changes in calls about incidents and reported crime were shown to be reduced in the matched areas policed closely.

Three cautions are to be observed. The actual practices of the police were not reported; they were only labeled "aggressive order maintenance" and "drug enforcement"—meaningless glosses on a range of practices that can be adopted. The authors admit they cannot identify the processes by which these practices were implemented in the target or treatment areas (ibid., 569, "Discussion"). In addition, there was no problem-solving process involved—the list of things were tactical actions (labeled "strategies" in table 2, which they are not), not "problems." These were never identified. For example, what is the problem identified by "required store owners to clean store fronts," and what was the resultant solution? (table 2). Reduction in the dependent variables cannot be associated with problem solving because it is undefined and left as obvious. The most telling aspect of this claim to be a study of problem solving is that the research had no explanation for why these results were found. The discussion and conclusion suggest a number of possibilities based on rational choice, situational crime prevention, and offender behavior, but include no data on any of these matters. It can be inferred that the actual research has no interest in exploring causal social factors, only evidence of change in the dependent variables. In what sense can one claim that policing of this sort has "effects"?

Problem solving, as it emerged in the dialogue with community policing, became a rhetorical facet, as did management reorganization such as Compstat and crime analysis and tactical actions with restricted and short-term effects, of current police practice in large cities (Roth et al. 1999; Eck 2004; Weisburd and Eck 2004). The connections between these operations in practice remain entangled, although Weisburd et al. (2002) show that Compstat-like approaches are tactical veneer on various forms of saturation-directed and focused patrol by uniformed officers in cars. They have had little or no impact on resource reallocation or organizational structure (Willis et al. 2004; Willis, Mastrofski, and Weisburd 2007). The imagined ideas have far outstripped the usufruct of problem solving. John Eck, one of the early advocates of problem solving while an employee of PERF, concludes after a systematic evaluation of problem-solving efforts (my paraphrase of Braga and Weisburd 2006, 149): there is no evidence it has worked extensively, that top-down creative and imaginative approaches such as imagined by Goldstein seem unlikely, and that the best thing to do is assume that low-level, conventional tactics applied to unreviewed "problems" and largely individual officers' efforts were the best bets. They conclude, "It is time for police practitioners and policymakers to set aside the fantasy of street level problem-oriented policing and embrace the reality of what they can expect from the beat officer in the development of crime prevention plans at the street level" (ibid., 14). This is what Braga's work with associates has reflected (Braga et al. 1999; Braga and Bond 2008).

A second example of the vague and misleading nature of problem-solving policing and crime prevention is yet another study by Braga (Braga and Bond 2008). The abstract states that there was no "crime displacement" found and that the "strongest crime-prevention gains were generated by situational prevention strategies rather than misdemeanor arrests or social service strategies" (ibid., 577–78). The article begins, "The available research evidence, however, does not demonstrate consistent connections between disorder and more serious crime.... Evaluations of the crime control effectiveness of policing disorder strategies also yield conflicting results" (ibid., 578). They then critique these studies, arguing that they are not randomized controlled experiments that provide more confidence in their findings and that "disorder" has been measured by surrogate measures (e.g., misdemeanor arrests) rather than by observation. The reported study used a randomized block experimental design to study crime prevention. They criticize earlier studies that did not support the crime-control arguments, including the previously discussed Braga et al. study, because the precise effects of the several "treatments" could not be separated as to effects. They argue there is a need for studies of "crime control effectiveness" (ibid., 582). Some information was gathered from officers about hot spots and from maps. Thirty-four "hot spots" (undefined) were split into seventeen experimental and seventeen control groups. In the experimental groups, treatments including social services, environmental changes, and efforts to reduce social disorder were provided and monitored by observation. The control groups or places were not provided with the same. Captains were held accountable for implementation of the program and reporting effects in Compstat-like meetings (ibid., 584). The problem activities were described as closely reflecting the problem-solving activities found in other research (in my view, shallow, and descriptive rather than abstract and analytic (see below on Cordner and Beibel). Nevertheless, they write that "situational strategies" were applied in each of the seventeen experimental places. These in term are described as "weak," accepting the visible signs as the problem and unrelated to the genesis of the crime problems (ibid., 585). These strategies included arrests, social services, and disorderly conditions. The captains did not know which the control and experimental groups were, so, according to the authors, only routine police work was applied in the control areas. They use the classified calls for service as the measure or indicator of crime. They claim these are less affected by police discretion than arrest and incident data and the best data collection modality for "criminal events" in the city (ibid., 586). They argue in conclusion that the efforts at "crime prevention" worked in the experimental areas because calls for service dropped 42 percent for robbery, 34 percent for nondomestic assault, 35 percent for burglary, and 14 percent for disorder (ibid., 592). Converting the distribution of these calls to a negative Poisson distribution enabled them to used parametric statistics to test the significance of the effects of the treatments on calls about crime and disorder. The paper ends with a series of speculations about why "crime," meaning calls for service as coded by police operators, uncorrected by whether actual service was rendered, was "prevented" (ibid., 598–99). Please refer to the above general critique of calls for service as an indicator or even surrogate. It is clearly a dummy variable analogous to those used by Katz, Webb, and Schaefer (2001).

Let us consider in light of this the only systematic study of how some officers actually did do some problem solving (see also Fung 2004; and Skogan et al. 1999). Cordner and Biebel, in their study of problem solving in the San Diego Police Department (2005), are rather generous in their review of the literature, as their work is the only systematic published study of problem solving of which I am aware. Their site is significant. San Diego has managed to move to the forefront of policing during the past ten years as a result of city council and mayoral support, innovative chiefs, and good fortune. This is intriguing insofar as San Diego some twenty years ago operated in the LAPD militaristic high-arrest "professional" mode and lavishly applied the criminal sanction to drunks, prostitutes, and other unworthies (McClure 1985). The history of the transformation of the SDPD has yet to be written. However, it has been a regular recipient of NIJ and COPS partnership grants, has hosted many researchers, and is seen as a progressive department.

Cordner and Biebel's essay notes the rare, thin character of problem solving on the ground. Some patrol officers, by attitude measures and by actions, make token gestures toward problem solving. They focus on a single incidents or places, use personal oral knowledge of outcomes and solutions, focus on arrest outcomes as evidence, and look into things rather superficially and briefly in any case. It might be good to note that the problem-solving movement has made its rhetorical march across the country. Case materials and observations suggest that researchers might best consider the extent of training and supervision of officers doing CP and training of supervisors in the evaluation of such activities and ask if sergeants routinely evaluate, what rewards are deployed for this work, how much time is devoted to CP, if the peer culture supports CP, if the organization provides time for activities other than responding to 911 calls, and if there are negative consequences for officers who refuse, finesse, obfuscate, or avoid problem solving and continue to patrol, respond to calls, and value short-term palliative responses. Cordner and Biebel set out plainly the operation of problem solving in a department with full commitment, during the tenure of several chiefs and deputies, to this approach. SDPD appears to have been supportive of the approach taken into account in promotion decisions and transfers and touted publicly its policies in this regard. Nevertheless, the authors show that the work done is largely illusory in consequence (unevaluated in any systematic fashion), labeling, and reconfiguring standard tactics and routines, unimaginative, based on superficial knowledge, and easily avoided without career damage. They conclude that it has been a modest success.

Problem solving, a creation of a police intellectual Herman Goldstein, used and employed and publicized by the Police Foundation and later the NIJ, became a device for labeling experimental studies that featured little or no "problem solving." The only full interview and observational study done in San Diego shows its appalling limitations as applied. Yet this approach is constantly repeated in texts in the field of criminal justice as present, well-done, successful, and widespread evidence of change in policing and in the transformation of its practices.

POLICING HOT SPOTS

The well-known cops' knowledge of the past—that crimes cluster in time and space and are done by repeat offenders—was in the 1980s transformed into a policy caricature. The process of concentrated policing based on calls for service, using arrests for crime suppression, and targeting clusters was now called hot-spot policing. It is simple: focus policing by targeting visible street crimes in lower-class neighborhoods.

The idea that particular areas or addresses, or places, or even broad locales or neighborhoods could be labeled by the number of calls for service they produced was in large part a consequence of Sherman's early work in Minneapolis. The clustering of calls and incidents—all of this before the invention and diffusion of mobile phones— at known public call centers, such as emergency rooms, hospitals, convenience stores, and bars became an intellectual find. This was and is commonsense wisdom known by every police officer in this country. This was part of a series of research projects carried out in Minneapolis by Sherman and associates with the encouragement of then chief Anthony Bouza. Sherman's research was predicated on reducing *calls for service* on the grounds that too many calls were a waste of police resources, that a focused and refined analytical basis could save money and time, and that reduced calls or demand would increase efficiency. Sherman and his research team sought to associate calls for service with addresses and demand questions. The discovery of clusters of reported crime in areas and crime-specific clusters via plotting and spatial representation of calls became more compelling with the advent of crime mapping. Hot spots were one feature of a crime map that could be seen, and their contours imagined, given knowledge of the particular areas of a city. Data were used to map what police officers in the city knew.[2]

In a major publication resulting from this study (Sherman, Gartin, and Buerger 1989), the authors argued that *telephone reports of crime* were concentrated in places (street addresses and places such as bars and malls); crime could be delineated as to place and shown to appear repeatedly in specific places. They argued that places perhaps had criminogenic properties, and that activities of places are more easily regulated than persons (ibid., 47–49). Places are criminogenic, they claimed, without providing a single shred of evidence of how or why a place causes crime (ibid., 47). These matters, however, stand apart from the sociological knowledge of crime causation and its correlates that are intrinsically necessary to understand if any lasting impact is to result.

This was a descriptive article proposing a focus on such patterning of crime. It was to foreshadow the scientific dehumanizing language that later appeared— focus on activities, not people; places, not social relations; reported crime, not quality of life; appearance, not underlying causation or dynamics. The definition of a place not only was misleading and trivial (a place is what can be seen with "one's naked eye" [ibid., 31]) but did not describe the places they listed as "hot spots"—"each address can include many apartments" (ibid., 41). The implied causes were routine activities of people unguarded with resources that are appealing to criminals, not sociocultural factors such as race, class, income, disadvantage, or police focus on such areas.

A companion to this effort was a small group of five officers who were to be dedicated to reducing calls for service from particular places in Minneapolis (Buerger 1994). It failed dramatically and did so because city agencies failed to cooperate, landlords failed to cooperate, city attorneys failed to cooperate, and the police department itself was divided in its commitment to the project. This illustrates a number of central points about the efforts at reform. When untrained officers encounter the structural features of the city, the rhetoric and practice prove inadequate; the problem to be dealt with was never defined outside the context of "call reduction" (this aim seemed to be associated with the claim made by Sherman that reduced calls would free up police to crush crime). On the other hand, since this activity does not require intrusiveness of the police into private relations and places or the application of their unique competence (Bittner 1990), police action is neither needed nor useful in solving the problems at hand.

Hot spots as a popular promoted tactic. Let us consider the impetus and popularity of hot-spot policing and research. The idea that such foci were productive and prevented crime grew in popularity among scholars, many of whom were associated with Sherman or Weisburd, both students of Albert J. Reiss Jr. at Yale, and the students of Weisburd at Rutgers (Green, Mazerolle, and Braga, among others). From this nexus of influence and funding (reviewed below) a number of well-written and -received papers were published between 1990 and 2005.[3] Although the idea had creative and imaginative aspects and moved attention from causation and sociocultural factors to those that could be counted and modified by police practices, it also was appealing for other reasons. Let us consider some of them.

The idea was *well promoted* internationally through the formation of the Campbell Coalition on Controlled Experiments, the *Journal of Experimental Criminology,* both of which were associated with hot spots and their consequences or correlates as the "dependent" variable to be modified by intervention, and the activities of productive scholars, who were well funded by the NIJ and later COPS. In short, good scholars were well funded.

The *looseness and elasticity of the concept* meant it could be applied variously without being subject to close criticism. The concept of a "hot spot" was never defined clearly in any publication in spite of the corpus of research on the topic. It made sense in that it suggested or implied some cluster of events, persons, incidents, crimes, reports of crime, actual disorder, actual victimization (reported by officers and recorded), or some such. Even calls of reported crime are themselves very distant surrogates for actual incidents (Warner and Pierce 1993). It had common sense—visibility, although what was actually suggested was something out of sight and merely reported. It could thus be easily relabeled as something police could control. It collapses, of course, the sensible, or what is felt, with the intelligible, or what we make of it.

It was popular because *it reified the police notion of real crime in real places*—not abstract social scientific statistics and tables, invisible crimes such as the most costly and serious crimes in regard to the public trust—fraud, white-collar crime or violations of trust, corruption, and pollution and violations of environmental law. It could be "seen" and responded to. Hot spots refer to "decent street crime"—what might be called the nineteenth-century model of crime and crime control—visible personal- or property-based crime "on the streets" subject to surveillance and reduction by police vigilance. It also amplifies one of the core values of police—crime control and crime suppression (viewed as arresting people if not putting them finally in jail or receiving punishment).

Ad hoc explanations for the results, especially the motivation of offenders, could be derived from currently popular explanations such as "rational choice," "routine grounds," and "deterrence doctrine" absent any evidence—ethnographic fieldwork, interviews, historical evidence, or close observations of offender behavior—that these matters did change as a result of police action. As observed in the previous chapter, such pragmatic, unreflective explanations are consistent with the ideology of the police and their lack of concern for processes outside their ambit of reflection and knowledge.

Hot-spot policing as publicized has *epistemological clout for police and policy makers.* Herbert (2006) suggests in a very powerful connected series of observations that the police filter the informational feedback to the public, which focuses the public on that which they can shape, not the structural impediments preventing change. Policing, because of public trust, is seen as attacking and controlling the relevant epistemological social reality. While they have little impact on economic conditions, the ecology of the city, its history or traditions, or its cultural heritage or practices and perhaps little impact on officially recorded crime, they can reify the presence of crime and their ability in the short term to reduce visible lower-class street crime.

The results of hot-spot policing when combined with crime mapping *can be easily shown and reshown.* This means that results are repeatedly demonstrated even when the "results" are of a single apprehension or solving a few vexing crimes. The mapping enterprise makes visible crime and disorder on a caselike basis when the spots are seen as "something done by someone about which something should be done" (to paraphrase Bittner 1972), and perhaps more mundanely, maps are stimulating: colorful, picturesque, at times animated or moving, rich in detail, or glaringly dramatic, they are easily combined with other kinds of data for display—pictures and links to other sites, pages, documents, pictures, maps, and drawings. They are both convincing and misleading.[4]

Recent work has suggested that some "positive displacement" takes place after hot spot–focused policing (Weisburd et al. 2004) or that displacement is minimal (Braga and Bond 2008) and that attrition of the effects is less rapid than previously thought.

Hot-spot policing is atheoretical. It also presents a muddled and confused sense of what is a problem, why it is a problem, and what might be done to reduce or control it. It has no contribution to the understanding of criminal behavior. The tactic when applied produces the rationale. Hot-spot arguments for intervention in short-term bursts of saturation patrol, undercover actions in drug-dealing areas, focus on disorder in small and controlled areas, surveillance, or concentrated patrol conceal deeper questions that remain unaddressed. The idea of space or place is left undefined—material? Phenomenological (what people see as dangerous place)? An activity, a process, a set of relations manifest publicly? A network or dealing coalition? The definition of an area itself, even in data terms, is problematic (block faces, all sides, principal streets, named places only?). The fundamental question of prevention itself is left unaddressed: how does a short-term reduction in arrests or visible behaviors mean something has been "prevented"?

As a pragmatic and programmatic matter it reifies police thinking without reflection. These experiments are crude behaviorism—try giving more uniformed police attention to an area and see if it changes any conventional measure. As Rosenbaum (2006), in an incisive summary of hot-spot policing, notes, many problems might be identified in an area. I would, echoing his suggestions, include such things as anger at landlords, underpolicing, lack of garbage removal and uneven city services, lack of informal social control or collective efficacy, profiling based on color, harassment of the young in disadvantaged areas, and rage at ongoing systemic inequalities (Weitzer 2000). Clearly, major problems of crime and exploitation of the collective will exist, and they are not place based or what might be called decent street crimes: terrorism, drug distribution networks, money laundering and economic crimes, and crimes of violation of trust more generally (Rosenbaum 2006, 247).

It should also be said that the concern of these studies is not strictly speaking to identify the logic or causation of crime but to identify the surface features that are readily at hand, visible, and measured sufficiently to note an impact of short-term police-based interventions using the criminal sanctions and any other means available. They draw indirectly on some rationalizing of police practice, such as "broken windows." This is not "prediction" in the usual statistical sense of predicting a given event or case or incident. It varies from chance given a Poisson distribution. It captures the sociological notion that routine, regular, systematic rates of crime in given places and at given times of the day, week, month, and over years occur and vary. The difference between sensitivity to neighborhood context and awareness of the general social conditions of a neighborhood might allow one to respond to an incident differently or manage it better. It does not imply crime suppression, crime eradication (a naive and impossible idea), or even a "zero-tolerance ideology" of appearing to control the marginal, the mentally ill, and the poor. It might move from here-and-now enforcement practice unguided by plan, evaluation, or impact to a concern for preventing, reducing, or managing crime, victims, offenders, or places. The point is quite simply that hot-spot policing takes no problem solving, no theory, no view of crime causation, no view of crime prevention, nor indeed any cogitation beyond "point and go" (Rosenbaum 2006; Manning 2008).

The data used to analyze the results of hot-spot policing are variously flawed if the inference is concerning the ongoing dynamics of crime in an area. Police notions about distribution, time and place, and variations in crime are suspiciously consistent and uncorroborated—there are known areas of crime and crime trouble, and these are reified by reference to incident, anecdotes, or experience that may span years and is not validated (Herbert 1998; Klinger 1997; Rubinstein 1972). In particular, media events and amplification have serious impact on police thinking about crime—its dynamics, location, threat, implications, causes, and solutions considered. GIS mapping or other software-based clustering still remains vague because of assigning incidents to block faces, multiple names for the same address, using calls as locations of crime rather than of the incident, using drug crime addresses as surrogates for actual crimes (Lum and Weisburd 2005), or police memories for charting drug sales (Braga et al. 1999) gangs (Braga, McDevitt, and Pierce 2006, in Lowell) or turfs (Braga et al. 1999) without independent validation.[5]

Calls for service are notoriously misleading as an indication of anything other than short-term responsiveness of areas. The data are deeply flawed and tendentious. The datum taken as the primary dependent variable in many studies is calls for service, edited and encoded to be a surrogate for behavior on the ground. Some research suggests this approach underreports crime (Klinger and Bridges 1997). It also reflects overreporting of some events (e.g., gunshots, loud parties, fires). There is ample evidence from reclassification studies (Nesbary 1998; Moskos 2008) that the point at which one gathers data alters the fundamental proportion of crime and other disorders reported and validated. CFS obviously is a crude indication of "crime," whether measured by investigator-founded crime, victim surveys of crime incidence and prevalence, case studies, or ethnographic work. While observations on the ground (e.g., Braga et al. 1999; Braga and Bond 2008) contain impressive direct measures, CFS is a very flawed surrogate for "crime" or disorder.

Limited and brief effects of crackdowns on officially recorded crime can be attributed to what police do, even if this is not described (Sherman 2005). The direct effects of policing tactics cannot be separated from other effects measured or unmeasured. While some "positive" results are reported that are consistent with the ameliorative frame (e.g., reduced gun crimes, reduced calls for service, reduced villains in place, and reduced problems in public housing as well as disorders), these studies are *limited* in many ways. The decay effects occur rapidly and admittedly (Sherman 1990, 1992). There is no answer to the degree to which displacement of activities to other areas is studied except by Weisburd et al. (2004, 2006) and Weisburd and Green (1995) and Weisburd and Mazerolle (2000). This, of course, implies that the underlying causes are neither of concern nor relevant to the stated purpose of reducing a given negatively defined matter for a short period of time. This tactical intervention modality is termed *crime control,* or *crime attack,* or one might say *attack on people* in areas where crime has been reported in the past (Sherman 1992). The secondary appeal is their almost entirely police-based tactical intervention mode as their "independent variable."

Citizens' views, citizen cooperation, partnerships, and changes in neighborhood security are not measured in hot-spot studies. A few studies are concerned with citizens' views, reduced disorder, and reduced reported problems, that is, what citizens or social scientists might expect of an intervention, but these are secondary (see below for any assessment of their effectiveness). This intervention tactic has little if any concern with public input, problem solving, or coproduction of order. Variations in public trust, concern, willingness to act and report crime, and satisfaction have not been measured in connection with these studies.

In sum, hot-spot policing fits well and neatly without controversy or complexity into the policing view of the world, what might be called its micro-ideology, and its relatively low cost and efficiency potential (production, reproduction, creation, distribution, and use) make it very useful to the police and attractive to city governments. In short, it is efficient in producing arrests (not reducing crime) in a short period of time. It is not fair in that it categorically targets some areas regardless of the actions of people who live there at the time of the sweep, raid, or crackdown. It is a hammer, and everything looks like a nail in the targeted area. This is sharply shown in the article written by Sherman, Gartin, and Buerger in which they speak of places and their activities, not people and their lives (1989, 47, 49).

CRIME MAPPING AND ANALYSIS

Prior to the electronic age, in which information is processed electronically by large mainframes (later servers and smaller computers) with rapid processing capacity and huge memories, crime was occasionally mapped using pin maps that showed the location of particular crimes for some selected period of time.[6] The idea was first used in the United States in the Department of Sociology at the University of Chicago by Ernest Burgess and colleagues (Faris 1966). The maps were hung on the wall, and colored dots marked crimes, juvenile offenses, and other social matters in the interest of characterizing the social areas of the city (as noted in previous chapters). This idea diffused to police departments and was adopted using pins placed at addresses and locations where crime clustered in a given period of time. The idea in theory was to chart crime and alert patrol officers to trends. There was of course no theory to rationalize the appearance or diffusion of crime, and no sense or notion of prevention. As now, if the crime did not continue over the next few weeks or months, it was viewed as having been "prevented." Though crime, like other socially relevant matters, had been shown spatially by geographers by drawing maps within the locations of crime incidents marked, or placing pins on maps mounted on cardboard, crime mapping became a feasible and practical tool between 1980 and 1990 as computers were adopted by police departments for dispatching, record keeping, and other managerial functions. In some combination with concerns for crime prevention and creating situational and ecological constraints on criminal opportunities, it was nurtured and made viable as a research technique by a generation of social scientists (Brantingham and Brantingham 1981; Rossmo

2000). In time, the technique evolved from a descriptive, geographically based way to present data spatially to a means by which data can be aggregated, displayed, and applied in practice. The burst of studies on crime and place has redirected and deployed officers to guide investigations. It was refashioned from a concern with theoretical and analytical aspects of spatial patterns to "practical" interventions designed to reduce disorder and crime.

An operating system of crime mapping as employed by the police in this country has a number of constitutive elements. As used in policing, crime mapping has a number of salient features. Crime mapping is a technique based on software (usually ERSI, ArcView, or MapInfo) that converts geo-coded addresses or locations (one set of files) so that maps, tables, and figures can be merged with them and maps created. These maps can display an array of signs on maps (tables, bar graphs, pictures, icons, or other figures) of a city or political area, and combined with pictures, sound, drawings, and diagrams. A wide range of facts can be included, such as fire risks, demographic characteristics, indexes of disorder and quality-of-life offenses, addresses of those on parole, registered sex offenders, and more conventional police-generated data concerning juvenile gangs, patterns of adult crime, and traffic. A range of other sorts of data has been added by some departments, such as addresses where restraining orders are to be enforced, turfs of gangs, as well as demographics of social areas in the city. Variations in density by location, types of crimes, or days of the week can be mapped, as can offenders' residences and patterns of co-offending (Bottoms and Wiles 1997). Anything that can be plotted spatially can be represented. In effect, almost by default, these displays have created a context for problem solving and reflection, what is loosely called crime analysis.

In policing, crime analysis covers a wide range of practices. At one level, it simply means examining the patterning of types of crime by time and space; its corollaries such as age, sex, and ethnicity; its temporal or episodic nature; and asking what can be done by the police, citizens, or other agencies to prevent, reduce, eradicate, or displace crime or disorder. Most of these analyses give rise to short-term interventions by police such as crackdowns, saturation patrol, or raids. More sophisticated versions of crime analysis may require models of the dynamics of areas including disorder, crime, and their correlates as a prelude to longer-term planning or interventions.

Crime analysis, and crime mapping as an adjunct, has at least four components that may or may not be present in a given police organization. The first is the *technical*—the software and knowledge needed to make tables, graphs, figures, and models. This is the job of the experts, the technicians, repair people, and often civilian analysts. It requires budgeting, serving, repairing, and maintaining the infrastructure. The second is the *implementation process,* the capacity to fit such materials into organizational planning, strategic plans, unit objectives, evaluations, and operating procedures. The third is command use of and *integration into daily police operations* of crime mapping. All of these must be examined in context to discover the effects of crime mapping and analysis. The fourth is the *sense-making activity* that must accompany the use of the maps: what do they mean, and how do they mean it in regard to imagined action? This latter issue has not been studied by scholars; most of the work has focused on the daily operations and modifications of standard police procedures.

Crime mapping and analysis in general has been used for fifteen years or so by police and criminologists to augment or refine police ideas (e.g., Sherman, Gartin, and Buerger 1989). As reviewed earlier regarding hot-spot policing, this mapping idea with increased memory of police computers permitted a more analytical approach to workload and the concentration of calls. Some key research reintroduced the idea of place to criminology and policing, although it has been central to the Chicago school's approach and refined in regard to crime by Thorsten Sellin in the 1930s (1938). Sherman's early work (Sherman, Gartin, and Buerger 1989) stimulated descriptive studies of the spatial distribution of repeat calls for service, clusters of crime, or other indexes of disorganization with the aim of reducing them on the grounds that they were burdensome. This later focus was refined into a series of studies designed to show that crime-attack tactics were much needed (Sherman 1990, 1992). Studies claiming to combine problem solving, spatial analysis, and crime reduction were published (see the entire issue of *Justice Quarterly* 12, no. 4 [1995]). In a useful and clear example of the application of experimental design to the reduction of disorder, Braga et al. (1999) used a variety of tactics including focused police saturation to reduce calls for service and reported (drug) crime. Some ex post facto statistical analyses of crime in places have been carried out to simulate experimental methods (Weisburd et al. 2004, 2006). This research, from Sherman's (1984, 1991) insights in Minneapolis through the series of works now featured in the *Journal of Experimental Criminology* (see www.springeronline.com), features increasingly elaborate statistical methods with a variety of remote, abstract, statistically based surrogate measures of the quality of life in neighborhoods. This technique has been refined to a concern for dynamics over time (Weisburd et al. 2004, 2006). Crime mapping and crime analysis have been readily adopted as described (Weisburd et al. 2003). They were rapidly accepted in the period between 1998 and 2004. Their featured use in Compstat, as applied, became a reification of hot-spot policing (see Weisburd et al. 2006; Wills, Mastrofski, and Weisburd 2005; and Manning 2008).

The advantages of crime mapping permit the demonstration of achievement, and competencies become more than anecdotal "canteen culture" stories; these achievements can be archived and memorialized and repeatedly shown. Collections of essentially little case studies based on descriptive work are published as evidence of the efficacy of crime mapping. They nevertheless make visible how the work was done for others. It is possible to use hot-spot tactics and mapping as purely descriptive, use them to "solve crimes" (that is, make arrests), and still have no underlying causal link between the maps, the incident, the motivation of the offenders, and the dynamics of crime or offending. Looking at a map and doing something require no theorizing. These studies are now the occasion for technical debates.[7]

The most visible, well-known, and evaluated studies of crime mapping are associated with the spawn of the management strategy called "Compstat" (reviewed below) but can exist independent of the overall management approach. It has been coupled with hot-spot policing, third-party policing (Buerger and Mazerolle 1998), and studies of crime displacement (Weisburd et al. 2006). With the appearance and development of what have come to be called "Compstat meetings" after the NYPD version (see Bratton 1998; Kelling and Coles 1998; Maple 1998; Silverman 1999; MacDonald 2002; Walsh 2001; and Henry 2003), presentation of crime and disorder data to police officials in order to press them into crime crusades, spatial analysis, and visual presentations were elevated to sacerdotal level. There was a hope that spatial analyses and problem solving would result in not only focused management to produce crime reduction using official police-generated figures but also a lean and "smart" police management style. It has been claimed to be the fundamental cause of the crime drop in New York City (Maple 1998; Bratton 1998; Kelling and Coles 1998; Manning 2001).

Crime mapping, when combined with meetings, has been studied as an innovation in policing by Weisburd, Mastrofski, and Willis and their colleagues in several important and comprehensive publications focused on the organizational features, implementation efforts, and operational effects of Compstat-like meetings and management approaches to policing (Weisburd et al. 2001, 2003; Willis et al. 2003; Willis, Mastrofski, and Weisburd 2004, 2007). According to Weisburd et al. (2003), in a theme that has been used in all subsequent publications from this research team, the Compstat model has some six major potentialities for reforming police practice: mission clarification, accountability, decentralized command, organizational flexibility, refined problem-solving tactics, and external information sharing. The core of their research, using three case studies, is the question of the extent to which this management approach truly reformed policing. They conclude that the elements as seen in the organizations are not making fundamental changes but merely making more visible and rational traditional tactics (see also Moore 2003). While each element was not present in all the organizations studied, the focus was not overwhelmingly crime-attack tactics and little modification in other aspects of management. No evaluation of the effects of the tactics was done in any of the reporting police departments in a previously mailed questionnaire. This survey and fieldwork carried out by Weisburd and colleagues in 2000–2001, and published subsequently (Weisburd et al. 2003; Willis, Mastrofski, and Weisburd 2004) found that the dominant and preferred use of crime mapping in most departments surveyed, and the three in which observations were made, was tactical, short term, and conventional: the departments reported deploying officers to an area for saturation patrol or undercover work. It had little effect on management, promotion, careful problem solving, or use of crime data except as indicators of unwanted spikes in known crimes. Crime analysis was seen as displays of simple clusters of crimes by area in a given time period. No problem solving was observed or reported.

Perhaps the most useful example of qualitative case-based research on Compstat-like meetings was done by the James Willis Lowell, Massachusetts, study (reported in Willis et al. 2004; and Willis, Mastrofski, and Weisburd 2004, 2007).

The authors were gentle with the police in reporting their findings. The infrastructure of support for the statistical and crime analysis was absent or severely lacking; the data were not in line, the chief had difficulty shifting officers in line with data not only because of a shortage of officers (too few available to shift to downtown foot patrol) but also because merchants complained if patrols did not concentrate in the city center, the maps were often unavailable to in districts, and it was extremely difficult to implement the approach even when goodwill and effort were present. ORC did not decrease; no other evaluation of the tactics was undertaken, that is, no feedback, and evaluation was used to shape future decisions as to potential effect. There is some question whether the program was actually implemented (see Manning 2008). The degree of external political influence, the field and the surroundings, has been underestimated in previous studies of technological change. Willis et al. (2004) showed that even with consistent efforts and most of the elements in place, resource deployment was rarely accomplished, and resistance remained among the patrol officers. The effects on management, crime, and organizational change were nugatory.

This study, as well as previous studies undertaken by Weisburd and colleagues, does not describe the content and sense-making processes within these meetings in any detail. The absence of these descriptions makes claims that such smart management altered practices, let alone had a consequences in crime and disorder, dubious at best:

- What kinds of things were defined as problems?
- Were they described in the meetings as problems prior to the analysis by staff or officers?
- How did these problems come to the attention of the meetings' participants?
- How were the problems nominally connected with the police actions planned or executed?
- How did officers present and others not present made sense of the maps and the crime data? What were they "thinking" as they discussed what to do?
- To what extent did officers merely do as they were told by captains in the districts? Did they apply these tactics by analogue to other problems? Where and how?
- Were other agencies alerted, informed, or made possible "partners" in the planned activities?
- What actions by whom (and where and why) were taken as a result of the meetings? Why?
- What were the results of the actions taken?
- Were these results recorded or available for others?
- Why were these actions taken and with what stated intention? What was their purpose?
- What are the consequences of these actions for future deployment of resources, strategies, and tactics? Did policy change as a result? Was the organization changed in any sense as a result of these meetings and crime mapping?

The authors were interested in the putative allocation of personnel resources and, having not deeply probed this matter, assume that the meaning of the maps and the problems discussed emerged in the course of the meetings that the infrastructure and traditional policing suffice to produce consensus, and that organizational intention or formal stated goals are needed to alter the environment and hold managers accountable. This is a bureaucratic mystery, as the processes by which the deciding is done are not explicated. Instead, an instrumental view obscures the diversity of social interactions taking place (and those not taking place) and the interplay between structural features of the meetings, process, and content.

A recent perceptive and penetrating article by Robert Behn suggests that these general observations hold for varieties of performance-based evaluation systems (my paraphrase) in which regular meetings are held to consider data relevant to the unit's performance to follow up on previous decisions to improve performance, establish next objectives, and examine the overall effectiveness of performance strategies (Behn 2008, 2). Now given that this definition excludes the workings of most such systems as described in the literature, and in my own work, Behn's essay is a matter of pointing out that some or all of these elements are missing in the organizations he studied. In fact, it would be easy to conclude that given his list of six common failures, none actually meets his definition. He describes with examples several flaws that he observed: no clear purpose, no specific assigned responsibilities as a result of the meetings, irregular meetings, no single person assigned to run the meetings, no dedicated analytical staff, and finally, the key in my view, no follow-up. The published work on Compstat and similar meetings cited above does not contain information on these dimensions, so it is difficult to determine what the role of such meetings could have been in controlling crime, solving problems, locating hot spots and reducing them, or enhancing the role of community policing.

THE PICTURE AGAIN: ADVANCES IN POLICING

These types of policing aim at very broad institutional reform. They intend to alter resource deployment, strategies, and tactics as well as to align functions with performance. Policing has changed, but in rather modest, incremental ways. In general, these have been technological in nature, but these technologies are fitted into traditional patterns and organizational functions. Maguire and King, in the most serious and careful review of changes in the organizational goals, boundaries, and activity systems in policing, conclude that "the police research industry is not currently organized or equipped to systematically detect and monitor change in policing. . . . As a result, we are unable to measure, detect, or explain major changes (or continuities) in policing with any scientific confidence" (2004, 34). The vast majority of research is reductionistic, individualistic, and outcome based and focuses on "police officers, police work, and police effectiveness" (ibid., 35). A similar conclusion is reached by Weisburd and Braga (2007) in the last chapter of their important summary volume on police innovation. As a result, the subtle changes in targeting groups and persons, maintaining surveillance on particular areas, systematic record keeping, and analysis at the organizational level are not detected across organizations and over time. The extent of transformation in police organizations might be revealed, as Maguire and King observe, by "comparative ethnographies of a [community policing implementation] in a cross-section of American police agencies" (2004, 34; my condensation). Nevertheless, some advances can be identified.

These advances are technologically driven. As new technology is adopted, embedded, and interlarded with traditional structures and processes, it amplifies the current practices and perhaps speeds them up (see also Dunworth 2000). Some hypotheses can be summarized as follows. The police are much better able to map, describe, track, and monitor those they consider persons of interest, "major players," felons, sex offenders, and the like. They are also better able, given this capacity, to make "sweeps," "operations," and other terrorist-like attacks on low-income areas under various labels of convenience: domestic violence, prostitution, drug dealing, gang activity, or simply serving backed-up warrants (see, for example, McGarrell et al. 2006). The number of electronically organized databases has increased, as has the capacity of the average officer to access and use them. The police can better sustain coherent and accessible electronic records and share these databases with others. Consider here the growth of several national databases, from the Federal Emergency Management Agency and Immigration and Customs Enforcement (ICE), the sharing of fingerprints and DNA electronically via the FBI, and the development of more than seventy-three Fusion regional centers (see Wikipedia) designed to develop partnerships, data sharing, and dialogue among local, state, and federal agencies (see Boston Police Department, annual report, 2003). Police can now develop cumulative records of patterns of crime given the mapping, crime analysis meetings, and dialogue across units such as gang units, school units, dynamic-entry and tactical squads, and patrol operations. The diffusion and popularity of such meetings have been rapid and national in scope. They have increased interest in applying data analysis to targeting and short-term interventions.

The police have shifted their rhetorical canon to include the capacity to reduce crime and bring safety to the streets (Kelling and Coles 1996) while not abandoning the community policing and visible officers "same cop, same beat" philosophy (Boston Police Department, annual report, 2003). As crime overall continues to decline from the high in the 1990s, spikes in violence become of greater media and police concern. On the other hand, the police continue to arm themselves with more and more powerful weapons (Kraska 2001) and equip themselves with more sophisticated equipment and matériel (body armor, hazmat suits, nonfatal weapons [especially tasers], sniffer dogs and robots for scanning premises, mobile and stationary surveillance cameras, pepper spray, and mobile digital terminals that function as in-car computers, and cell phones with cameras).

As has been reviewed above, local American police, under the guise zero-tolerance or broken-windows policing, have been more actively and publicly engaged in what has always been a stock in trade for police—the ways and means act (a facetious term used by English police to refer to police actions that stimulate a response, which in turn creates the justification for an arrest; it is not an actual law), the contempt of cop violations, and the fabricated excuse for doing the necessary when an office is convinced that someone needs a lesson, has been rude, is guilty of other crimes, is a known player, and so on. These tricks of the trade are now rationalized by reference to a kind of policy: encouraging officers to make stops and misdemeanor arrests to immobilize a wide variety of people who are the marginal, powerless, and demoralized populations of large American cities (see Quillian and Pager 2001). While they are justified as ways to get guns off the street, gather intelligence, or reduce felonies, none of these claims has been fully substantiated by research.

These observations on change in the "police industry," coupled with Maguire and King's astute and conservative assessment (2004) of change in policing—based on the research compilation funded by the National Research Council—are consistent with those of Weisburd and Braga (2006). These broad conclusions were drawn absent any detailed ethnographic or survey research on the perceptions, feelings, emotions, responses, or other assessment of what citizens think about policing and its practices. This is yet another mode of reinforcing the unreflective practices of modern policing.

CONCLUSION

Police studies emerged from the crisis of the late sixties. The field is based on a series of important research works. This research and related political forces spawned a reform movement aimed at some sort of transformation of policing—it was in some sense a challenge to the mobile, distant, crime-focused, and legalistic policing that emerged swiftly after World War II. This movement was a mixture of self-promotional activities, sincere hopes, and the efforts of foundations and government to reduce social distance between the police and the public. While the overt rhetoric was one of coproduction, mutual respect, and local concerns taken on board by the police, other forces were at work as well to direct policing. These less visible forces focused on moralizing, politically based ordering, and indirectly crime control, forming robust and visible SWAT teams, specialized paramilitary dynamic-entry and warrant-serving groups, hot-spot policing, and crime crackdowns. It is clear that some changes have taken place in policing, largely tactical and superficial, but some of these are oriented toward violent-crime control and some toward more benign community-oriented approaches. None of these approaches has raised the question "What are the police good for?" but make blurred reference to matters like "quality of life" (undefined except in the breach), "effectiveness" (implicitly crime reduction measured entirely by ORC), "efficiency" (undefined and unclear as to referent), and reform of the "industry" (see Christie's well-titled book *Crime Control as Industry* [2000]). It is perhaps fortunate that the misuse of the term, implying that it is a business producing some product with a market and a metric of success or failure, as mentioned above, also implies that it is a moneymaking organization with clear aims, products, goals, and "outcomes" and "outputs."

In reviewing the innovations attempted in the past twenty-plus years, it has been shown that these are modest and tactical, involve little alteration in resource deployment, and have been resisted. Even these tactical innovations fall on the sword of the patrol officers and their practices (see Cordner and Biebel 2006; Eck 2004; and the overview of Klinger 1997). In addition, some segments of the organization, detectives and specialized units such as the gang unit, warrant-serving units, and SWAT teams, are isolated from patrol routines and create their own "policies" and practices. This positioning of the agency in the surroundings of political forces, and in competition with a field of other agencies, allows it to oscillate between being a public agency ("You call, we haul," as one officer once told me) that builds community partnerships and serves metaphorically produced "customers" and a distant, violent, crime-focused "industry" without a product. This insulated organization is loosely coupled to other agencies (Weick 2000; Maguire and Katz 2002) and thus is able to sustain its practices.

The background of policing as localistic, locally funded, violent, and reactive is being replaced by a more rationalized force. Modern policing is mobile, technologically capable, responsive to the dominant political mood and concerns, and ever better armed and equipped. Having developed from a reactive organization of last resort that was to avoid interventions and certainly to remain outside private places and spaces, it has built a reputation as an active participant in shaping risks and trust throughout the urban world. Police are now expected to control and suppress crime, even crime taking place in complicity (drug use and sales, for example), in private (domestic violence, rape, most assaults), and rarely (homicide). There is some evidence that the growth in policing numbers municipally is related at least in part with increased fear (Stults and Baumer 2007) and reduced informal controls (Geis and Ross 1998), yet the approval of the police remains independent of particulars (figures). Much of what is done in the name of policing even now is tactical, various, generally decided upon quickly by individual officers, and subject neither to review nor to any broader evaluative procedures. It is rarely supervised, planned, or the result of policies. Yet these very exceptions are increasing their role and significance in modern policing in large cities. As the last chapter argued, attempts to reform the police have been modest in success, and this is perhaps because they do what they do adequately and that devolved craftlike actions are the most efficient use of resources. However, the past twenty years have seen the police dragged into a more intellectualized scrutiny of their practices, and these changes in rhetoric have nudged the police into a more proactive and preventive mode that is moving closer to a considered reassessment of deployment and its effects.

PART THREE

The Police As an Institution: Practice

CHAPTER EIGHT

Practice and Poesis

Tactical Poetry

The previous chapters develop a conception of policing that counters the current ideology and hopeful ameliorism of the field of criminology and police studies. At the root of this critique is the argument for criteria by which to judge democratic policing. These criteria are grounded in political philosophy—the philosophic conception of justice developed by John Rawls. The strategies of policing, now taken for granted, response to calls, random patrol, and reactive investigation, remain. Reform efforts have produced cosmetic changes, and crime control remains the justification for policing. Police practices are the ground against which the rest is background. I refer to the emotional aspect of police tactics as *poesis,* or tactical poetry. The enduring métier, police practice, is detailed in the next chapter. The principal consequences of this métier, or approach, are discussed in chapters 9 and 10.

WHAT ARE THE POLICE GOOD FOR?

What do the police do? What are they good for? What is just and fair about their actions? About this, we know less than we do about systematic crime-control efforts. Most of the ethnographies of policing are now dated, and a thin set of valuable and serious observational studies of policing is available.[1] What are the broader issues implied by policing as an institution in a democracy? They are rarely considered in the professional journals. No North American scholar, save Jean-Paul Brodeur, has argued with *The Report of the Independent Commission on Policing for Northern Ireland* (the Patten Commission 1999) that the aim of policing is to protect human rights: "The police should perform functions within the law and be respectful of human rights in both the technical sense and in the behavioural sense.... Technically, they should know the laws well and master policing skills, for example how to interview suspects so that they are less likely to be tempted to resort to unethical methods in order to get results. Behaviorally, they should perceive their jobs in terms of the protection of human rights. Respect for the human rights of all, including suspects, should be the instinct rather than a procedural point to be remembered" (Patten 1999, 21).

These propositions might be considered the outer limit of concern for social scientists, that is, a focus entirely on the civil liberties of individuals. On the other hand, a narrow concern with crime suppression or brief declines is begging the question of policing's function. Somewhere in between lies societal concern for security, the quality of collective life, and trust building. None of these provides a principle upon which to judge performance. This chapter argues that policing is a reflexive, situated practice that has been masterfully concealed behind the secrecy of bureaucratic rules and misrepresented by figures and media amplification. These misrepresentations, in turn, are the basis for most of the analyses in the field of police studies.

Policing by the Difference Principle

Recall now the accountability principles advanced by Rawls outlined in the preface and in chapter 3. They shape the assessment of policing. The principles hinge on assumptions made about citizens, the expectations of citizens of the polity, and conversely what the government "owes" its citizens. They rest also on the pursuit of the notion of "thick security" advanced by Loader and Walker (2007). Rawls's thesis requires making assumptions about citizens, their attachment to the institutions of government and their trust in them. Trust is the grounding of policing that relies fundamentally, even in authoritarian states, on a priori citizen trust and compliance. The *citizen* in a liberal democracy, Rawls argues, should have reasonable and rational trust (JF, 196; my paraphrase). Their personal interests are in theory obscured by the veil of ignorance. As stated previously, the citizen is assumed to have a capacity to be both reasonable and rational and a willingness to believe in the justness of institutions. This entails a belief that others are willing to do their parts as well. Citizens are held together by a reciprocated sense of trust: when others with evident intention do their part in just or fair institutions, then citizens tend to develop trust and confidence in them. This is a circular and reflexive trust and means a willingness to further invest trust. The trust and confidence grow stronger when a sense of cooperative arrangements is sustained, and when basic institutions framed to secure fundamental interests (for example, the basic rights and liberties) are more willingly and steadfastly recognized in public political life. Absent a generalized sense of trust by citizens of the state, no democratic polity can long operate. Recall also that the citizen has claims to basic justice and that inequalities that are to be sustained ought to benefit the least advantaged. These are stated clearly in JF (42–43). The propositions are that each person has the same indefeasible claim to a full, adequate scheme of equal basic liberties, which scheme is compatible with the same scheme of liberties for all. The social and economic inequalities that are to be sustained are to satisfy two conditions: first, they are to be attached to offices and positions open to all under conditions of fair equality of opportunity, and, second, they are to be to the greatest benefit of the least-advantaged members of society (the difference principle). These principles supply the conditions under which individual opportunities are maximized, given other constraints. Individual choices and actions are facilitated by supportive institutions within the Rawls scheme.

Justice as an aim, as Rawls has so eloquently stated, requires a distributive approach to resources and life chances, not a merely allocative approach that mirrors the current inequalities. To allocate further to those who already have abundant resources and indirect control on much more ultimately destroys the necessary commitment of citizens to work and sustain the economy. A core proposition that guides my analysis here and in the following chapters is that *policing is an allocative and reallocative agency in the sense that it shifts the burdens of those encountered, altering their life chances, opportunities for work, and attachment to society and, by inaction or tolerance, adding to the success of others.* Not only does policing disadvantage some, justly so, but it also advantages others who are more fortunate by virtue of their class, race, and gender. This latter issue is often overlooked, just as the indirect negative consequences of routine policing are ignored. The absence of policing as a direct force in altering behavior by negative sanction is an asset. Clearly, police assistance to victims and services delivered benefit all. Seen outside of this justice-allocative and reallocative function, it is a mere instrumentality of the state.

Recall also that chapter 3 contained principles to guide an assessment of democratic policing. These principles are secondary to the two main Rawlsian principles of equal opportunity and the difference principle. The absence of these in operation will mediate and mitigate attempts to alter the institution and practices of policing. It is possible, then, that if these secondary principles, more or less rules of thumb, are observed, we might expect of (domestic) democratic policing that it function as follows. They should strive to be constrained in dealing with citizens and fair in procedure. These dealings should entail a degree of civility in interactions and in police practices. This excludes under virtually all conditions torture; mass detentions; "round-ups" based on political beliefs, not behaviors; and lengthy suspensions of habeas corpus for citizens. This idea parallels in essence the message of the Hippocratic oath—do no harm. The police in a democracy policing democratically should be reactive to citizens' complaints—reticent in their actions rather than periodically and unpredictably intense. Most of all in this context, they should not be given to frequent secret, violent, proactive interventions; crackdowns; sweeps; and other militaristic "operations" that affect the innocent as well as those less innocent. While this is counterintuitive in some sense, since policing has modest resources and must husband them against the occasional massive and demanding event—whether natural or "man-made"—policing should in general attempt to be equal in its application of coercion to populations defined spatially and temporally. The level of coercion is based on minimalistic criteria, much like well-developed counterinsurgency tactics (Nagl 2008), rather than a mechanistic "use of force continuum."[2] Citizens have rights defined in law, whereas war is governed by conventions that limit violence to combatants; force cannot be easily rationalized. Given the first principle of fair hiring and evaluation, police should seek to be fair in hiring, internal evaluation, promotion and demotion, transfers, and disciplinary treatment of employees, whether sworn officers or civilians. While by tradition and law public police are the dominant force, they are in fact one among many policing agencies. They should acknowledge their position within a competitive organizational environment that includes private police, vigilante groups, posses, ad hoc policing under the guise of "self-help" and revenge, and, at times, the National Guard and armed services (army, navy, coast guard, and air force). Their apparent hegemony is thus embedded in a network of security forces, and they are a powerful node, perhaps the most powerful, but they are not always the center of the same. If these principles are applied routinely, police could be held accountable and responsible for their actions both individually and organizationally (Brodeur 1997). These principles might be considered a *tacit contract* between the police and the public. As such, it has noncontractual elements that are implied.

Agents of control, including the police, are implicitly bound up in this social contract no less than others and perhaps, although this is not Rawls's stated position, even more so. The idea of "more so" arises because police are trusted precisely to invigilate and assess the trustworthiness of other citizens on behalf of the collective well-being. They are expected to meet a higher standard. As Peter Moskos, who served for eighteen months as a police officer in Baltimore, writes, "We have no choice but to trust police officers and hold them responsible for their actions" (2008, 25). They are trust assessors. Police are expected to be suspicious of others in order to sustain citizens' trust.[3] They are distrustful in the service of trust. In many respects, this is embedded in the common law that permits police to question people they suspect of malevolence and to stand ready to respond if they are told of it.

In addition, in the Rawlsian world, agents of the law and those who create it are acting in good faith, attempting to clarify the meaning of rules, and treating crime as a criminal matter rather than as a proclivity and treating similar cases similarly.[4] In this sense, to expand a bit on the above principles, democratic policing would be that which does not violate these tacit assumptions or background expectations, because if such policing did so repeatedly, the necessary stability issuing from a shared sense of justice would be threatened (TJ, 453ff). Necessarily, the imposition of harsh laws, punishments, and regulative "net-widening" efforts that are attempts to humiliate and punish citizens cannot alone sustain stability based on justice. Categorical enforcement based on proclivity, putative "predictions" (Harcourt 2007), conflates behavior, the basis of a democratic enforcement system, with types of people, risks, the notional "others" who threaten. This ultimately strips citizens of their "sense" of inalienable rights. If, in addition, more burdens that result from arrest are levied on those who commit otherwise trivial offenses, those who are arrested for the place in which they act, not for their behavior per se, unfairness results. This in turn compounds a sense of unfairness and distrust of the police (see Harcourt and Ludwig 2007).[5] Further, if agents of the justice system repeatedly punish those who have not committed crimes, and these punishments are cumulative, the consequences serve to further undermine compliance. Since many arrests result not from crimes but from noncompliance or "contempt of cop," civility in the interest of compliance is essential (see Mastrofski, Reisig, and McCluskey 2002).

In effect, if democracy is predicated on efforts toward equality and the police are a redistributive mechanism that can radically alter the life chances of individuals and groups, then policing must be examined not only on the basis of its outcomes, reported data and official documents, but in respect to its practices. Here, the general principles can be linked to the proximate interactional face of the governmental authority. This can be glossed by calling them the practices of police in an institutional role. Practices are the interpersonal modes of coping with the vicissitudes of applied authority. Practices have meaning only in a "gamelike context." They are patterned by what the occupation views as necessary to sustain the front and teamwork necessary to accomplish policing. These might be called constitutive rules, tacit understandings, or the commonsense reality of policing. They have been developed earlier in Rawls's now classic paper, "Two Concepts of Rules" (1955).

Under the condition of constitutive rules, an action has meaning only in a given tacit context. Rawls uses the example of baseball, noting that only in that game can one do certain things such as "strike out" "steal a base," "make an error," "draw a walk," or "balk." They can only happen in a game, and be so described. As Rawls writes, only in a game of baseball would these terms operate: "No matter what a person did, what he did would not be described as stealing a base or striking out or drawing a walk unless he could also be described as playing baseball, and for him to be doing this presupposes the rule-like practice which constitutes the game. The practice is logically prior to the particular cases: unless there is the practice the terms referring to the actions specific by it lack a sense" (ibid., 25).

Order perhaps comes from step-by-step rule following, sort of a practice in action. Goffman's essays in *Interaction Ritual* (1967) suggest the relevance of self as found in the discussions of lines, deference to a line, failure in role claims that lead to embarrassment, and the emotional tone of risk. What is being claimed is that in situations, there is an object, "a self," created that has relevance to the action unfolding; this is not to say that the self is the driving force in the interaction; rather, it is one of the dynamic elements. Its place, role, salience, and the consequences of self-involvement are all in the situation decided. Even the use of the work *role* in these essays is itself indexical. Think again of the game of baseball. The self-involvement in the play, say, stealing a base or making a fielding play or hitting a home run, is all little determined by the self but in every way patterned by the *situation* of the games and its practices. As Garfinkel observed, the basic rules of play have nothing to do with personal desire, and motivation, although they can be inferred from the aesthetics of play. This is of course also a theme in Wittgenstein—emotion suffuses communication, but it is often unspoken or unseen.

These police practices are interactional modes of coping with situations that sustain order. They are constitutive, as in any game. Outcomes, on the other hand, as measured, for example, in official data of any kind, reflect *summary rules*. These are aggregations of many behaviors that omit and obscure variation in the practices that produced the visible and counted outcomes, such as arrests, traffic stops, convictions, sentences, and the like (Rawls 1955). These outputs are the basis of accounts or explanations that explain after-the-fact practices. Conversely, it is impossible to understand social control, its workings and failures, through a top-down sketch of what police or citizens, or police and citizens in interaction, *might* be doing to produce the statistics rendered. Ad hoc explanations abound.

Policing on the ground is a practice, that is, a set of routines intended to produce a degree of certainty in managing fundamentally problematic yet recurrent situations. Practices are focused on the concrete objects in the situation and reflect an understanding of both the material and the subjective constraints upon action. By orienting toward objects in subjective or phenomenological terms, police create the viable and recognizable matters that sustain their sense of control and accomplishment of the work. They are the stable core of cooperative, collective, and complex work directed to problem solving. At its best they contrast with technology and the technological conceit, and they support and enhance human capacities (Bittner 1983, 252). As Bittner points out, the Industrial Revolution produced a fundamental change in activity: "Technology makes visible and syntheses the earlier *bricolage* of diverse techniques into an independent, internally coherent, well-ordered body of principles" (ibid., 253). Policing in this sense is primitive or preindustrial in nature. It is not embedded deeply in technologies, but rather uses technology to support its practices. Its primary technologies are verbal and nonverbal activities, not other means of producing outputs or work. The complex, nuanced situations faced by officers do not have easily recognized scripts; the players are always changing and changeable, the settings various, and the outcomes unpredictable. This is a given in policing, even as the work must be done day in and day out. The outcomes reported and observed cannot be established independently of the informationally rich here and now and are thus produced by what Norton Long (1963) calls "acts of will." These are assertions of power in the face of *uncertainty* (unknown outcomes) and *risk* (the possibility of negative outcomes). Such activity cannot be ascribed to "habitus" (Bourdieu 1977) or highly socialized, unreflective actions reproducing past modes of strategizing because the socialization patterns, history, traditions, and understandings that pass for culture in industrialized societies cannot be glossed with such a generalized term. While repetitive patterns can be detected, they are the product of repeated ad hoc adjustments.

Let us extend this argument concerning the impact of policing a bit further. Let us consider it as a bureaucratically shaped blunt instrument. Here are some propositions: If through their practices, their interactions, they increase alienation and distrust, they are failing. If through systematic policies, not inadvertent accidents and miscues of justice, they are differentially applying coercion by area or category of person, they are failing. If they increase distrust and cynicism through misleading lies, they are failing. If they are applying laws and regulations differentially and systematically on the basis of local ethnic, class, or gender preferences, they are failing. If they increase inequalities in areas not directly regulated by criminal law, they are failing. Finally, if the long-term consequences of such practices produce vastly differential opportunities in respect to unemployment, incarceration, and further indexes of inequality, they are failing. These practices diminish, if not erode, the needed democratic context. In other words, if policing fixes on maintaining a stable level of crime control, ignoring some calls, responding rapidly to others, narrowing the vision of "success," dramatizing the rare gun arrest and crime-suppression tactic, and if it as a result fails to provide support and increases inequality by action as well inaction, policing is failing. This is true regardless of whatever else is done.

The present body of police research fails to illuminate these processes. It reflects the conventional wisdom about why and how policing works, what I call the police métier. It is a bundle of *practices* and ensembles of practices called *routines*. The research echoes the narrow research-for-the-police world that obscures more profound questions about the impact of policing.

SUSTAINING LEGITIMACY AND ACCOUNTING FOR POLICING

All occupations must define what they do and why they do it in order to carve out and defend an economic niche. Police are not an exception to this rule. The axial matter in this justification and accounting (in the sense of an explanation and rationalization [Mills 1940]) has been the officially reported crime statistics in spite of their frequent misuse by the police (e.g., Philadelphia, St. Louis, and Washington, D.C., as reported in Law Enforcement News 2005), balanced recently with emphasis on partnerships, improving quality of life, and reducing the social distance between the police and their publics. Since the latter activities have never been valued internally, there are no conventions for assessing and rewarding such practices. While since the 1920s the police have tied their legitimacy to the sciences, both laboratory and social, to their own managed and produced crime statistics, and to the dramatization of their essential role in public order and well-being, the ORCS are now more available, faster, and visually manifested. In order to understand the tension between crime control and nominally democratic policing, the *limits* of officially reported crime as a sole measure of policing's impact and value must be identified. This requires some groundwork.

The notions of efficiency and effectiveness cannot be applied usefully to policing because there are no conventional measures of such, and they are terms temporarily borrowed from industry. Police gauge their impact and their effectiveness by announcing variations in officially recorded crime statistics while ridiculing them and calling them misleading lies in private (Meehan 1998). *There is no body of data that is more consistently and brilliantly critiqued than officially gathered and processed crime data, yet it is repeatedly used without apology in every major journal that publishes work on crime and crime control.*[6] It is easy perhaps to plead that this is the next best, or best, approximation, yet the seduction of such data binds and blinds scholars to alternative conceptualizations of their discipline. The police by and large are the beneficiaries of such as they control the flow of data at the source with no auditing, accountability, or alternative sources of information. Such statistical representations became associated with policing in the reform era and have always functioned as a quasi-scientific surrogate for "effectiveness." They are of course the perfect foil, because if crime rises, more police are thought to be needed, and if it declines, more police are needed to keep up the momentum attributed (falsely) to police actions.[7]

Public service organizations, since they provide services generically to taxpayers in theory and do not charge on a unit-by-unit basis, must manage demand. Policing in fact is a public service, a public administration function the demand for which is in theory endlessly elastic. That is, the demand is open-ended and thus must be rationed and such rationing rationalized (Trebach 1973). The limits of policing are the limits of the resources available to monitor, watch, and track a subject population. This essential rationing takes place backstage because, of course, the public face is that policing is an always available—a twenty-four-hour operation. The actual rationing is not policy driven but emerges on a "case-by-case" basis. In general, approximately half of all calls for service are screened out at the source by operators and dispatchers. These are repeat calls for the same incident or block area, prank or nuisance calls, calls for nonpolice service or information, wrong numbers, untrusted callers, or calls lost in processing—hang-ups by operators or callers, unintelligible calls, or calls in a language the operators do not speak. Some cities have made efforts to shift some part of these calls to a city hall number or a 311 number without much success (Mazerolle et al. 2002). After classification, calls are dispatched, and most are answered, that is, accepted by officers on patrol. In practice, the rationing of police services, that is, what is "delivered" rather than what is received, is done on the ground and at the supervisory level. While several important studies have examined calls for service, most have simply described the distribution of calls by police categories, assuming their validity and relevance to what is done about them and with them. This is a severe mistake and misleading leap from classification to action (see Manning 1988). After accepting the call, officers redefine the nature of it by their feedback and relabeling (Maxfield, Lewis, and Szoc 1980; Meehan 1992, 1993, 2000; for a contrary view, see Pepinsky 1976). This is taken as the organizationally valid factual assignment even if the oral traditional (discussed below) rejects the paperwork version of policing.

Consider two penetrating examples of police work on the ground as officers redefine the nature of the call and the actions required in term of the occupational culture. The first is the insightful work of Moskos. Moskos (2008) shows that approximately 40 percent of those dispatched to officers in the eastern district of Baltimore were classified as "receiving but needing no police response," 35 percent resulted in some police action but "limited in scope," and 26 percent required written reports (crime, injured person, property damage, or domestic dispute). Officers reclassified after arrival about 39 percent as needing no response, about 33 percent as minor matters, and about 25 percent as requiring a written report. The 39 percent were unfounded by six codes, basically dismissing their connection to action. Moskos points out further that these categorical systems are overlaid with officers' definitions such that some are called "domestic" or not, depending on officers' assessment. Officers further divide calls in terms of their oral culture as "illegitimate" or "bullshit" depending on their personal assessment of the circumstances encountered when they arrive. Domestics constitute one-third to one-half of all written reports, and about half are not "founded" in the sense that officers decide they were not legitimate even though they are required to write a report. This means about 26 percent required a report, and 61 percent at least had been processed with some police service. Even in one of the most crime-ridden and busiest police districts, 50 percent of the calls were screened at communications, and another two-thirds were handled minimally. This leaves in Moskos's calculations about one call per hour per officer that is accepted, about 40 percent of which needed no police response. The rest of the time is spent driving around.

A second example comes from the work of Meehan. In several papers on policing gangs in two cities (1992, 1993, 2000), he shows that "gang" was a social construction, that is, a label that served to account for various practices consistent with "showing activity" (see also Rubinstein 1973, 44). By examining the logbooks of "gang cars" (renamed from "drinking cars" a few years earlier [2000, 343]), he shows that items were interpreted by officers based on their "readings" of the dispatchers' cues (the gang category was the third most commonly used by dispatchers [ibid.]); that logbooks were selective in both omitting and including certain information (ibid., 348–53); that official codes were used to obscure what was done on the ground (ibid., 352); that the ambiguity of citizens calls led to simple tactics of "brooming," which was a result of police deciding based on the political context of reducing the number of "gang arrests" (ibid., 356–58); and these actions also showed "activity" that did not raise the specter of increased gang arrests (ibid., 361). Meehan concludes clearly and persuasively: "The record keeping practices of the police easily accommodate and manage the various political and organizational pressures brought to bear upon them." (Meehan 2000, 364). Meehan concludes that the results of such practices are not variations that can be passed off as "measurement error." The records are the products of political and organizational features, not only officer "discretion." They are products based on organizational practices, from call handlers through supervisors and officers (my paraphrase of Meehan 2000, 364). As he emphasizes repeatedly, the labels for the incidents are police created and are only tangentially related on the one hand to "calls for service" and on the other the behavior observed.

As a result, the overt contradictory nature of policing (Manning 1998, 106–08)—that is, its public claims to justice, fairness, evenhandedness and the rest, given the here-and-now, craft-based nature of the work—cannot be understood fully by an exclusive examination of official records or data. As Weber wrote, the nature of bureaucracy is *secrecy*: "Every bureaucracy seeks to increase the superiority of the professionally informed by keeping their knowledge and intentions secret. Bureaucratic administration always tends to be an administration of 'secret sessions'; in so far as it can, it hides its knowledge and action from criticism" (1946, 233). What Weber subsequently wrote about Prussian statistics can be advanced as a general proposition: "In general [they] make public only what cannot do any harm to the intentions of the power-wielding bureaucracy" (ibid.). An early classic statement was made by Westley: "This study of one police force has shown that the maintenance of secrecy is a fundamental rule" (1955, 254). He notes later that the "successful policeman needs the full support of his partners in order to act in tricky situations" (ibid., 255). This of course sustains mutual in-group loyalty and is needed. He concludes, "The norm of secrecy emerges from the common occupational needs, is collectively supported and is considered of such importance that policemen will break the law to support it" (ibid., 257). This thesis about secrecy concerns the marginal activity that requires some "cover-up," but the occupational solidarity means this is a generalized rule about the work, not merely about those practices that are illegal or regarded as such. What the police do at one level is a reflection of their duty: they are to be available for whatever might require force (Bittner 1972), not to record all their actions in this regard (note that only 26 percent required a report in Baltimore). Officially recorded crime is just that: it is not solely a reflection of the behavior of those encountered but a complex mixture of that and the reactions and judgments of the agents of control. The part of this recording behavior that is called crime and processed as such grounds the conservative character of the police organization. *The question of what police do and how well, why, and when cannot be answered by what they choose to record and account for. They have no responsibility to record all that is seen, said, heard, or smelled.*[8] They are not after all routinely and independently audited by any agency for the accuracy of their records. As John Johnson observed as a result of his experience in the U.S. Navy, an observation that applies equally well to scholarship on policing, "Organizationally produced information does not report on facts or events, which are independent of the organizational culture and processes which produces them. Those who fail to observe this universal truth will ultimately be victimized by it" (2008, 334).

The police are not accountable for details. Moskos adds an additional point to the problem of reporting incidents: "creative writing." Like fiction, this entails what to leave in and what to leave out when reporting a response to a call or an arrest. *Creative writing* is the term for skillful editing and compressed summaries, covering your ass, as it is called elsewhere, but this is distinguished in the oral culture from lying (Hunt and Manning 1991). The line is vague but appears to be an ex post facto judgment, sometimes made after a sergeant calls for a rewrite of the report. When major incidents occur, crimes involving important people or children, media-produced scandals, or mass murders, care is taken to preserve detail, record it, make it consistent across the several sets of records, and ensure that careful detective work is undertaken (Corsianos 2001, 2003). These of course are the exceptions that prove the rule of differential fact reporting. The tricks of the trade, writing practices, as in all occupations, involve what to leave in and what to leave out when creating a written record of deciding. These are learned practices, sanctioned within the local culture and rewarded by status honor among one's peers. This is a part of the granted mandate, not secrecy alone.

Of course, not all police work is a response to "demand." Police-initiated work, such as vice and drug enforcement, is a function almost entirely of the resources allocated to carry it out (Manning 1979). Police clearances and related practices, with the possible exception of homicide investigations, are a function of local rules and regulations, the oral culture of detectives, and turgid practices (Waegel 1981).

Parsimony in reporting is a feature of all work, and as Weber reminds us, the primary concern of the worker is always control of the flow and level of effort.[9] Four matters are elegantly described by Moskos (2008) and Meehan (1992, 1993, 2000) and are relevant to the understanding of the processing of police data: "sitting on calls," "holding back incidents, "collars for dollars," and the "anything can be an arrest" rule.

Sitting on calls means that since the primary job is answering calls, time-out is needed for writing papers, finishing lunch, and so on. The problem is both overload and boredom, but when overload builds up (calls accepted by the officer but not yet responded to), officers may stretch out an incident, thus remaining "out of service." If a number of officers are assigned to a call, all assigned can remain on the scene until the paperwork is done. When the primary officer completes the paperwork on the call, this signals any other attending officers to return to service (see also Van Maanen 1988). This maintains job control and hegemony over the definition of the incident—it is in the hands of the primary officer (see above about classification and reclassification) and in effect is a "time-out" from the routine demands of answering calls or random patrol. As noted above, whatever that officer writes is what the incident is, not anything else unless later redefined by the sergeant or the prosecutor's office. On the other hand, officers expect that calls on their beat or area are closed out or otherwise serviced prior to the end of the shift. This has three consequences: officers are hesitant to take a call at the end of a shift that may mean paperwork or extended interactions, as in domestic violence or calls about loud parties; arrests are seldom made at the end of a shift; and every shift has a rhythm in part produced by the officers' style of answering or not answering calls. Meehan, Moskos, and Van Maanen emphasize that officers need to "show some activity" and hold back information on some of their activities until needed, or until under pressured to produce it. As Van Maanen shows in his creative work on the academy and through later socialization (1975), one of the fundamental rules of policing learned in the academy is "keep your head down" and avoid the attention of the sergeant. Less work is better for most officers. Sergeants' emphasis can temporally produce more arrests, but "collars for dollars" pressures impact only the few officers motivated for the overtime. Moskos (2008, 142–43) describes the memos that criticized officers who were under one arrest a month and later under two. This is consistent with officers' views that the higher administration is out of touch with the work and that their policies are arbitrary and capricious. In this sense, the police bureaucracy is a punishment-oriented bureaucracy (Gouldner 1954, 207–14; Manning 1977, 171–72). The production quotas were informal, but production was required. The officers observed by Moskos, as were the officers observed by Walsh some years ago (1986) varied in the number of arrests made per month, and these figures were based on those who wanted to go to court for overtime (in two-hour blocks usually requiring several appearances, even though the hearings were often canceled). It was clear that these were decisions made by officers rather than a manifestation of the level of crime in the district, since arrests could be made at any time. Moskos quotes officers as saying they can lock up anyone who walks away from an open-air dealing area (because this means they are in slang terms "dirty" or involved in the drug trade) or any white person in the area. As a summary rule he states, "You can always lock up someone" (2008, 55, 66) and in this area, "everybody's dirty" (ibid., 83). An officer can always do five traffics and lock up one or two drug offenders (ibid., 113). Standard "resource" charges used to make arrests are "loitering," which can be used on anyone who does not move on after a warning; curfew laws; failure to carry identification; or being there in a drug-free zone (ibid., 87–88). In this area of Baltimore, patrol is about officer safety, staying in the car (patrol is "car centered"), and making the occasional (more than one a month) drug arrest. Felony arrests, in Moskos's terms, are "stumbled upon." Clearly, misdemeanor arrests can be made daily and easily. As he writes (ibid., 138), one would expect that given race, demeanor, age, and so on that the rates of arrest by month would be roughly the same for officers in given areas, but it is not. Whenever arrest figures are disaggregated into districts and individual officers (Kane 2006), differentials in productivity by precinct, officer, and assignment (patrol or special units such as warrant-serving squads or drug units) are so striking that the fiction of a constant criminal base of behavior is difficult to sustain empirically if one does not locate the variation in the practices, not in the behavior, of offenders. *Thus, it is impossible to sort out the effect of given active officers from the behavior in question in a given area.* Finally, as Meehan (1992, 2000) shows dramatically, political pressures from elected officials can shape the focus of officers, their targets, and their record keeping. He shows, counter to some other research, that pressure can lead to *reduced* arrests and downgrading rather than increased arrests (see, in contrast, Beckett 1997; and Defleur 1975).

Let us make a more general claim: the volume of recorded output is variable and related to identifiable sources. Other variables that shape and produce variations in arrests or traffic stops within the same areas or districts have been reported by careful research. For instance, one variable is whether one or two officers are in a car (two run more plates and make more stops [Meehan 1998]). Two officers more than double the car output when working together. Younger officers, when paired, make more than similar older partnerships. Changes in supervision and enforcement of dispatching rules change the rates, up or down, depending on the supervisors' preferences (McCleary, Nienstedt, and Erven 1982). Policies on making proactive arrests and specific changes in policies within vice and narcotics units are very powerful influences on "production" and what is considered such (Defleur 1975) (e.g., the arrest of "johns" as well as solicitors for sex; shifts in the particular drugs, such as crack, other cocaine, heroin, or downers such as Oxycontin). Arrests for possession of marijuana, in the past primarily patrol officers' domain, are now rare unless a product of "zero tolerance" as a policy of enforcement. Broken-window and zero-tolerance policies that urge arrests for misdemeanors as a means to reduce officially recorded felonies can escalate misdemeanor arrests regardless of the base (Harcourt 2000; Sousa and Kelling 2006). Changes may be linked, of course, to changes in the law itself, as opposed to officers' practices. Changes in law, in particular the obligation to arrest on the allegation of domestic abuse (broadly defined), whether witnessed or not (Moskos 2008), in mandatory-arrest states, have a powerful effect of increasing arrests and dual arrests. Leadership in either local politics (Scheingold 1984) or changes in the chief of police (Seidman and Couzens 1973) are other variables. The specific interests of a chief in drunken driving, for example (Mastrofski, Ritti, and Hofmaster 1987), can affect arrest practices. Variations in the number of officers in a district, even if standardized by population (Messner et al. 2007), also alter arrests.

Policing is thus a flexible, situationally responsive organization that reflects not only the environment of events but also judgments about their meaning and consequence. It is in every way tertiary to other modes of control (informal, such as family, neighborhood, primary groups; and semiformal and associational, such as clubs, groups, business connections, and networks). Studies of variations in crime that compare crime rates across police organizations, cities, states, and over time assume that decisions on the ground, all decisions made and recorded, reflect some standardized "best guess" at the *actual distribution of crime*.[10] Practices are simply collapsed into outcomes. This is a seriously misleading reification. It might be better stated, as many have noted (Reiss and Bordua 1967; Black 1970; Meehan 1992, 1993, 2000), that police statistics measure primarily the level of police arrest activity in an area, rather than "crime," wherever the ratio of patrol officers to population. If this is true, then variations in arrest rates are simply variations in the productivity of officers, and doubtlessly a few officers in high-crime areas. It should not be overlooked that when the claim is made that police have reduced complaints, their own independent definitional work is obscured and the notion of crime as a standard, uniform matter is asserted.

Looking more closely at deciding, it is clear that deciding is a "situated" and occasioned practice. The pattern of available options and moves cannot be fully predetermined, and the actions of the public cannot be fully anticipated. Situated deciding is that which is done in the here and now, taking into account the cues available (age, ethnicity, gender, and the rest and verbal and nonverbal cues). This means *research that takes "arrests" to indicate consistent and invariant behavior on the part of citizens is false and misleading.* This has been known since the 1967 American Bar Association study that pointed out that arrests are made for many reasons, only a few of which are predicated on actual observed or witnessed behavior (LaFave 1965).

There are a set of assumptions about crime and its relationship to police records that I consider false and misleading that are as follows. The distribution of ORC associated with race, class, age, gender, name and place of incident, and those involved is assumed to be without public question an accurate approximation of the actual distribution of such events, incidents, and crimes in cities. They constitute the denominator for the percentages of this and that crime published. Thus, it is assumed that with large samples, tendencies for random error, noise, and multicollinearity tend to cancel out, and validity and reliability can be established. Or these can be established with ex post factor statistical controls. In such ways, *the chimera of constancy of "crime" as behavior in places and over time is maintained overtly and publicly.* This fiction is elaborated by gross studies that combine entire city districts (e.g., Messner et al. 2007; Sousa and Kelling 2006; Rosenfeld, Fornango, and Rengifo 2007) to aggregate the findings on "arrest" when the dynamics and patterns of enforcement in given districts are very different and the behavior of individual officers in reference to arrest production is variable.

The patterning of responses to incidents is not only department-wide but is also district specific. The constancy within and dubious comparisons across districts are in large part a function of several well-known matters: (1) periodic pressure placed on officers to produce statistics or activities that "count" (not all that can be counted actually), such as traffic stops, running plates, or checking sheets for stolen cars (Moskos 2008; Van Maanen 1988), or misdemeanor arrests under conditions of "zero tolerance"; (2) faux campaigns to "show the public" by reducing calls for service for given incidents (Meehan 1992, 2000), largely by relabeling the events and negotiating an orderly understanding; (3) the stability of stops, arrests, and searches routinely expected by the occupational culture of patrol in given places such as districts, neighborhoods, and beats (Klinger 1997, 298–300); (4) the understandings about what is not to be written up, responded to, up- or downgraded in a given district (Nesbary 1998; Moskos 2008); and (5) the local knowledge of police officers about the activities that characterize the districts or beat or sector they patrol, or the "normal deviance" there (Meehan 1992, 1993, 2000; Klinger 1997).

While the immediate and obvious impact of deploying more officers shows some effects in aggregated studies (Byrne 2008), these studies miss the fundamental fact of policing place: all specialized units—the gang squad, the school squad, the dynamic-entry or warrant-serving squad, the drug squad—at the district level and from central units, and other task forces, are always concentrated precisely in these areas. Thus, the roll-call assignment of uniformed officers is a misleading and in fact erroneous "variable" that distorts the actual numbers who could make an arrest, stop, or inquiry: specialized squads are not assigned to areas, and neither are detectives who work the same areas because the violent crimes are investigated in those districts. On the other hand, as Levitt (1998, 2004) argues, the sheer number of police added in a brief period of time—New York City added 12,000 officers in the early nineties—especially when deployed to disadvantaged areas, may slightly and temporarily reduce serious crime overall. It is not at all clear what the officers did or why they did it while in these high-crime areas that led to reduced crime. Such vague and disproven ideas as "deterrence" and "severe sanctions," if they have any purchase in reality, take place over time and in subtle and easy, not brief, periods. In the absence of observational evidence, the above arguments of this chapter would suggest that the hypothesis that the above-described practices pattern crime more than increased numbers would have to be accepted.

POETICS OF POLICING PRACTICE

There is a poetics at issue here as well. The standard product of policing is ironically a result of stylistic, poetic, quasi-aesthetic situated deciding. It is stylistic because it conforms to a set of well-known and learned tactics that are appreciated within the culture (Bayley and Garofolo 1989; Bayley and Bittner 1986; Klinger 1997). These tactics might be summarized (Bayley and Bittner 1986; Van Maanen 1973; Manning 1977; Moskos 2008) as concerning close-at-hand ideas as well as abstract goals set externally but translated and transformed poetically in the lower participants' social worlds.

These abstract goals vary widely. They may include meeting departmental goals—meaning whatever their supervisors expect them to show. This varies by current departmental concerns and the expectations of the supervisors. Periodic crackdowns are mounted in which the aim is to contain violence and control disorder by saturation patrols. This means once an intervention takes place, it must be controlled tactically in regard to entry and exit. In effect, tactics are goal statements because they hold regardless of the incident, whether it is traffic stops, domestic disputes, or juvenile policing. If the goal is to prevent crime, this means that insofar as it is possible, one wants to avoid repeat calls in a given shift. It has nothing to do with abstract efforts at intervening in the conditions that produced the event, only in reducing repeat calls. More proximate goals are explicit: avoiding injury. Moskos notes that both in the academy and at roll calls the emphasis was on the first goal—come home safe at the end of the shift. Moskos also notes the goal of avoiding provoking the public into retaliation that threatens their careers. This is what is commonly known as CYA, or "cover your ass": protect your own interests and make sure that what is written expresses the best-possible picture of the actions of the officer. This, of course, can also be a collective matter, as when squads cover up mistakes or supervisors are involved in complicity around corruption.

Policing as a practice also involves using generally accepted tactics. Bayley and Bittner (1986) emphasize three abstract stages in an encounter: contact, processing, and exit. At each stage they list a number of tactics for the two types they discuss, the domestic dispute[11] and the traffic stop. Maintaining a presence and controlling the incident is primary. Bayley and Bittner emphasize the necessary psychological alertness and calm to maintain control. To some degree, this is a combination of vigilance and apparent calm. Since any situation can unfold in an unexpected fashion, the drama of control must always be the primary concern. This presence may be physical or embodied or may be distant, as Moskos describes the police car–centered approach that emphasizes the stare and the polite request or confrontation.

Several points must be made about such tactics. They do not include that which is not done or recorded, even in interviews. They do not entail discussion of why some incidents are "blown off" (not attended at all), coded "rendered service," or described with other code words for having done nothing at the scene, or lied about what was done. Many dispatched calls are never attended, and no record is made therefore by the officer. They do not include the reclassification observed by Meehan. Some calls are simply neutered, as Moskos and Meehan both note. This happens when, for example, the address is not a good address, there is no citizen at the named address or place, or otherwise the incident is no longer viable. In these instances, reports that read "all quiet on arrival" or "services rendered" are used to gloss the incident. They are essentially neutral statements that will not "come back on you" and require further explanation. These lists elevate and dramatize the idealization of what should be done, not what is done. The vast majority of the time, even when in action, that is, responding to a call, there is no action (Moskos 2008). These labels are, in short, idealizations of the ebb and flow of complex organizationally accountable processes (Meehan 2000). By calling them poetic I mean to indicate that they are metonymical labels, appearing one after the other, but they must be seen as metaphoric, referring to various other things. A poem works because the words have meanings that may be contradictory but emotive. They play on linear logic, the law of the excluded middle, the rule of identity and contradiction set out by Aristotle. So do representations of police practices. They are understood as good enough within the police organization and mistakenly taken by many academics as indicative of a single aspect of a complex and contradictory reported situation.

THE PLAY OF EMOTIONS, THE CONCRETE, AND PRACTICES

What has been described using the metaphor of tactics is something like an idealized style, rhetorical and real, that is validated, reworded, talked about, and repeated, as are stories about its failures. This has been dramatized by the work of Shearing and Ericson (1991) using the notion that the occupational culture is in fact a configuration touched off and indicated by stories told and memorialized. It is also the essence of Waddington's classic evocation of the "canteen culture" (1999), that which is recalled in private, dramatized, selectively remembered, and used in large part to sustain the positive aspects of otherwise sometimes tedious and boring "dirty work." What is called the occupational culture is best seen as a series of loops that define what "works," on the one hand, via stories of success, and, on the other, what Hughes (1958) calls "cautionary tales" of failure and foul-ups. The point is that either way, the reflexive aspects remain: what is talked about conforms to the fuzzy goals, the inexact tactics, and the needed presence, since no uniform, consistent, neutral evidence is provided to correct "what works." The overall general rule is "You had to be there." If this holds as a criterion for proper demeanor and action, no one can state otherwise. That is not to say that bad police work, such as "bad shootings" and beatings, is not known and acknowledged (see Hunt and Manning 1992). These situations are known, however, after the fact.

The policing style at root is poetic in the sense of both responding to and shaping emotions (Wender 2008). It is not easily captured because it is poetic in the sense that it conforms to the function of poetry. According to *Webster's 9th Collegiate Dictionary,* poetry "formulates a concentrated imaginative awareness of experience in [ways] chosen and arranged to create a specific emotional response through meaning, sound and rhythm." It is, as argued above, aesthetic in that it issues from feelings and reproduces feelings in others over time and in repeated performances. Poetry communicates by what is omitted as well as what is said. It is a kind of metonymic metaphor.

This review of practices highlights the larger question: what do the police stand for, represent, and stimulate? The actions of policing, it should be remembered, are both the cause and the consequence of collective emotional feelings. Their effects are symbolic, that is, they shape the meanings and emotional context within which "crime" and "disorder" are viewed as well as instrumental in applying sanctions in everyday ordering situations. The socioemotional impact of policing cannot be denied, and this creates a forward-looking support as well as a backward-looking sting and resentment. Policing is not simply a governmentally supported instrumentality, a hidden social service, or a job, as much as this desiccated picture obtains in the criminology journals. Its instruments, crude and powerful, and often working behind the scenes and without public recognition, are perhaps less important than the emotions and catharsis it produces and amplifies. They are thus emotional repositories as other more visible sources of control and assurance—kinship, close religious ties, and neighborhood bonds—decline in salience.

Aristotle argues that art is something that produces an emotional effect in an audience. Policing is an art. Policing has an emotional effect, as do police officers. Policing is an aesthetic form. That is, it produces a response in audiences and in those who police, that is, it is sentimental and emotional in consequence. As an *aesthetic object* and a creator of aesthetic objects, criminals, and the other diverse objects of policing's attention, policing has a place in a larger political economy of emotions and energies that stimulate, simulate, animate, and consummate power relationships in a society. It is dramatic. Much of what policing does and produces is drama or the appearance of order and compliance with abstract, distant, unknown laws, regulations, and rules. The masterful turn of modern policing is connect law, abstract morality and propriety and convince the public that they are one, and that the police alone can respond to these complex matters of morality and justice. In a more general sense, it has long been the concern of theorists of mass society to point out that politics and aesthetics become fused in some fashion when direct material and class interests are blurred or misplaced. The spectacle of policing, what the media present, and the imagery that frames police actions replace the reality of its mundane actions. The politics of policing is rooted in a simple drama of good and evil reproduced daily on television. Policing reflects what a society expects of itself. It reflects on the taken-for-granted form of interpersonal conflicts and how they should be resolved. It is a reflexive operation, but it is not only reflexive; it is also cybernetic in the sense that it is a closed system of evaluation that keys off itself to differentiate internally.

CONCLUSION

The democratic polity depends on the trust of the citizens of each other and of the institutions of the society, and thus trust at best is reflexive and cumulative. The principles that should govern policing are two, of which the first is primary: the re-spect of the claim to equal liberties and to be subject to practices that do not increase the already-present inequalities. In order to assess to some degree the extent to which police have such operating principles, it is necessary to at least see how they define their mandate, what is central to it, and how its central theme, crime control, plays out in occupational actions. In accounting for their work, crime management and the official records police keep are dramatically center stage.

What are police good for? This question requires an examination of policing's organization, assumptions, and tools. Police act and react to that which society deems problematic, whatever its guise or appearances. Their targets, ends, and objectives are shifting, flexible, and often contradictory. The organization shifts targets, objectives, styles of enforcement, and outcome measures to reify the notion that it is producing order.

The police in the modern urban environment have developed a métier and a poetics. The métier is based on a conservative organizational structure, a multifaceted set of practices, rarely visible outside disadvantaged areas. It is composed of several interconnected threads, like strands of a rope. It has an aesthetic aspect and prosody, even though it resides in an ossified organizational structure that "overdetermines" the actions and practices that result; it has a recognizable set of tasks and routines; it operates territorially; and it is rationalized by top command. The sense making that takes place is localistic, patterned by shift, by district, and by current tactical fashions—bike and foot patrols, community policing units, sergeants' preferences for performance (Van Maanen 1983). It is based on deeply held assumptions about people, society, crime, and its causes. Police actions only reduce what might be worse; they cannot alter the causal factors—class, age, education, family, and school effects—that lie outside officers' control. The problems at hand are well known and well located (ask any police officer to take you on a ride along and see where the officers takes you and what you are shown). Policing's métier is reflexive, or reflective of its own practices, and self-defined. It is thus visibly and daily played out in disadvantaged areas. The métier reproduces itself: it responds to the known understandings of policing about where crime lies, in what areas of the city, carried out by what groups of people, and during what hours, days, and months of the year. The records kept sustain the validity of the practices because they are based on the same assumptions. The poetics are matters of style and aesthetics, part of both the management of appearances and the oral culture of the police.

Let us return finally to the six key *points* or expectations of democratic polic-ing raised at the beginning of the chapter. It would appear, as Moskos aptly writes, that "your constitutional rights depend on the neighborhood where you live" (2008, 31). Much of police work is reactive to "demand" or calls, but these are classified, reclassified, shaped, written about, and reported in line with the constraints of the occupation and the efficiency of the communication center. As Moskos has perhaps best captured and Alpert and Dunham (2004) have studied in detail, most policing does not involve much force or violence, and even arrests are usually based on compli-ance. In many respects, the policing even of high-crime and disorderly neighborhoods is overly benign; it is the constant surveillance, the concentrated disadvantage, the deployment of officers, and the tacit rules of controlling such populations that govern interactions, stops, and arrests. As Moskos (2008, 104) observes, the primary concern of the officer in disadvantaged areas is not so much controlling or suppressing crime, making arrests or stops, but maintaining their own credibility and sustaining parsimony of action. This is the dance of deference and respect.

This chapter does not discuss the treatment of officers internally and fairness in respect to promotion, hiring, and firing. The ways in which police cooperate or not across organizational boundaries is taken up in later chapters. The degree of accountability of police individually and organizationally is only suggested by the shadow of paramilitary supervision that obtains and its inconsistency with the craftlike nature of the work. These are, of course, inferences at an abstract level and must be considered as a series of hypotheses.

CHAPTER NINE

The Dynamics and Stability of Modern Policing

The pattern of democratic policing has emerged historically, and as it has grown in strength and reputation, it has crystallized a focus on crime control. This obscures many of the questions raised by an emphasis on the difference principle as a basis for evaluating policing. While it is commonly assumed that the police enforce the law, and their core tasks surround crime control, this does not capture what they do or why they do it. It does not evaluate the consequences of crime control, only the prima facie notion that what works is right. The police are a flexible and shifting device that responds to that which raises distrust. They are governed by situated actions deemed proper. While the targets of action are shifting and shaped by politics, the range of police tactics remains much the same, and the unstated purpose remains the same.

This shifting of targets and concerns is one side of a tension between stability and change. They are the two-sided topic of this chapter. On the one hand is the *dynamic side of policing*. The illusion of police necessity is sustained by identifying and controlling social objects that have a changing value and public concern. That is, as public concern and political issues change, police shift slightly their visible targets. These visible changes are only in part driven by legal change, and do not reveal the underlying stability of what is done.[1] The sources of stability in police practice, on the other hand, are discussed here as the *police métier*. The police have a stake in this stability and in the practices that reflect it.

The métier is revealed in repeated, somewhat routinized, practices. These practices are multiply determined or shaped by the organizational structure, ritualized interpersonal tactics, modes of deployment of resources, and rewards that characterize policing. A mirror into these practices is the incident—the police-citizen encounter. It is a kind of ceremonial locus that is a window into repeated practices reflecting the field of forces called policing. Rather than seeing these as "variables," "norms," or "values," they are seen as matters understood as having an overall resemblance to each other in the situation or incident, coherent yet unclear in precise connection, emergent over time, and reproductive of orderliness.

The idea here is to step back from the obvious labels and rhetoric and step closer to the patterning of policing. It is important to examine the actual practices of the police on the ground, rather than inferring these from aggregated data, and important to bear in mind that "crime" and crime control are not things, obdurate matters, but rather shifting *relational icons* that change in meaning and consequence by place, by time, by crime type, and as a result of changes in criminal and civil law. The métier reveals the deep patterning of police action regardless of the overt manifestations (e.g., records, rhetoric, press releases, and statistics).

THE SHIFTING TARGETS AND TASKS OF POLICING

Practices, institutionalized processes, sustain policing in the network of control agencies, not the isomorphism of organizations that are "rationalizing" (DiMaggio and Powell 1983). This is a tension evoked by the institutional analyses of DiMaggio and Powell, and others (Crank and Langworthy and later work by Weisburd, Mastrofski, and Willis). By focusing entirely on the organizational rhetoric and the "occupational culture" (meaning the public oral culture of the uniformed patrol officers), they overlook the work on the ground that has very little to do with myth, institutional norms and values, and accounts. *Policing is a situated practice* based on ritualized interpersonal tactics and reflects sense making. It is shaped by sociological processes that indirectly are reflected in the social reality of deciding. The politics of police organizations reveals multiple and competing rationalities that are seen in the ends chosen to be dramatized, the ways of achieving selected and competing ends, the relative emphasis on ends over means, and the differences in these within the various segments—top command, middle management, and the lower participants—within the organization. These segments are political arenas within which these contested rationalities are made visible (Espeland 1998). The institutional rhetoric is loosely coupled with the sense making of officers' deciding. Any generalization about the aims, goals, or mission of a police organization is a misleading chimera designed to sustain public legitimacy and generate institutional accounts or explanations for actions taken. It cannot guide deciding on the ground. While variable analysis can produce correlations, these are not explanations for deciding or the bases for them. In general, the error variance in such tables is larger than the variance explained. Let us reconsider why this is so.

First, recall that above all the police are ecologically separated from each other, and, for the most part, act alone, connected via radio, cell phones, and computers. They represent order and ordering, yet they apply violence, create disorder, arrest people, and put them in jail. They also supply a variety of social services. The police are the monitors of official violence, and while they create it, they also act to sustain the unequal distribution of violence that reflects the power and authority of a society.

While there is violence and disorder associated with disadvantaged areas, on balance, day after day, people conform. Given the vacillation of public concern about threats and disorderly matters and the changing labels for such, police are asked nevertheless to monitor some conception of order as well as to shift their attention to new items, abandoning the old, as their readings of society's concerns change. Ironically, as social and legal change occurs, the police adjust—they guard and underscore the constraints of the status quo, whatever that might be.

Second, as an organization or a field of ideas, holding material and symbolic capital, the police possess a mandate. The possession of a mandate, or the right to define the nature of the work, its scope and meaning (Hughes 1958), means that an occupation maintains the right to control its markets, conditions of work, and proper etiquette and conduct. The mandate and traditional strategies and tactics of the police, given public trust, enable them to *shift targets, dangers, and risks with considerable impunity.* They play by the rules, but carry them out with characteristic style. They have and actively protect their monopoly on definitions of crime and disorder and data on the same. The dangers that arise are not immutable, nor are they obvious; they are not seen, heard, and responded to every day by the various publics at large. We live in a secondhand, or mediated, world, amplified and distorted by the visual media, the Internet, and print outlets. The police mandate permits them to alter the terms of their concerns, and these are always symbolically elastic, defined, and redefined. While being responsive to political pressures and episodic media-amplified events, the police can on an everyday basis alter their current public focus on a wide variety of matters that represent risks. They hold slack resources for this purpose—at any given time less than a quarter of the available personnel are working (Ochteaque 2009). The risks identified may or may not be of current public concern. The risks noted reflect police interpretations of matters of public concern as well as their own analysis.

Third, undeniably, technology, or the means by which work is done, shapes practices. When technology expands its penetration into private spaces, matters such as pornography on the Internet, "stalking," "human trafficking," and "identity theft" are visited on the police. As drugs became seen as a problem in schools, DARE was created to teach children to "just say no." As Haggerty and Ericson point out (1997, 2000), and as is shown also in Maguire and King's review (2004), policing is a large sponge for peripheral functions, even as their core functions and values change little. The activities targeted at a given time are merely *representations* in various shifting and changing forms of acceptable behavior. The activities targeted by the police at a given time are merely miniature representations in various shifting and distorted forms of acceptable, conventional behavior. They are a distorted mirror of the dominant activities in a society. This means that a focus on "lawbreaking" and "crime" as an indication of specific identifiable behavior is only a partial truth. Crime, disorder, deviance, lifestyle offenses, "contempt of cop," and failure to defer to authority are all flexible and relatively available police resources.

The police stand as a kind of lightning rod for such conflicts, both as cause and effect. The shifting interests and targets of the police must not be seen entirely as manifestations of variations in the behavior of groups, rates of this or that, but a compromise circumstance, a bargain between police concerns, public concerns, and what is encountered. Even police-initiated crimes reflect politics in an indirect fashion.

THE DYNAMIC CYCLE

Police in effect produce an object of concern by their practices. When they direct attention to something, a social process, a place, a person, or a group, they highlight its salience for themselves. It becomes a matter of concern. They vary the content even as the form, the drama of control, remains. A drama of control is a symbolic process of identifying, bounding, classifying, and labeling. It can elevate or diminish the moral salience of the matter. Garfinkel (1956) has outlined such a process for constituting a negative reality—a degradation process for individual identities—but analogous processes occur for groups and places. The world as constituted by police is not the broad panorama imagined by the media, nor the idyllic imagery of the middle- and upper-middle classes punctuated by fear of crime and drugs as well as a touch of xenophobia. It is a focused slice of relevance supported by the oral culture; the field training; the local knowledge of areas, places, times, and people, and their potentiality for disorder; crime; boundary violation and incursion; and for "keeping up the numbers" (which is often linked to court time and overtime), if that is the officers' concern. The movements of police attention are dynamic and difficult to predict in advance, even given a rising or falling public concern.

These subtle changes in attention and action are not major movements of thought easily seen in major shifts in resources or "operations"—they are more subtle and representational, standing for deeper concerns. As Bourdieu (1977) has pointed out, the tacit agreement of people to their own subservience, even against their economic and political interests, is a characteristic of modern societies. Rather than beginning with processed, police-defined, semilegalistic definitions of the police role, it is more feasible to see that the police act out and act with a license, the specification of the mandate, to control and define order. Think of this as a form of collective behavior, seen more dramatically in the dynamics of crackdowns, "spikes" in reported crime, and what passes for public opinion in the tabloids, but also seen in everyday police work. In phenomenological terms, the subject and the object, the actor and the field of objects, are intertwined and relational.

Perhaps it is best to group or cluster these concerns to show how the police shift their attention. The following examples, presented in slightly epigrammatic fashion, are intended to illustrate how subtle changes in the regulation of moral life are accomplished as consistent dynamic faces of "law enforcement."

Cultural wars. Consider the broader question of cultural contests, or "wars," between religious- or belief-based segments of the population. These have led to public awareness of many diverse behaviors and lifestyles and to efforts to criminalize or decriminalize selectively activities carried out by some of the known populations at risk[2] (e.g., abortion, gay marriage, and prostitution, as well as "human trafficking") or to restrict public funding of them (e.g., prohibiting abortion and public moneys for stem cell research). These issues provide the broader political *surround* in which the police find and carve out their role. The application of such broad network laws as the Patriot Act and the RICO statues is guided as much by pragmatic interests in disruption of activities as by the intensity and risk of the activities targeted for investigation.

Drift and regulation of activities. When activities slip away from popularity among the middle and elite classes and drift "downward," they are redefined as criminal and subject to arrest and prosecution. This can be seen in analysis of making criminal bull baiting, cock fighting, various forms of gambling (and not others), changing modes of drug use, and sex. Activities associated originally with lower-class lifestyles or immigrant lifestyles that are not "adopted up" are made criminal (e.g., numbers gambling, dog fights, peyote use, and drinking homemade alcohol, or "moonshine"). On the other hand, activities or lifestyle preferences that diffuse, or move "up" from the lower classes to the middle and upper classes, are decriminalized, such as marijuana use (Massachusetts passed a law decriminalizing possession of small amounts of marijuana in 2008), gin drinking, cohabitation, and civil unions. Widespread activities once seen as deviant and then revealed as common among the middle and upper classes such as same-sex cohabitation and joint lives, money, and friends tend to become legalized and accepted. The many laws against selected sexual practices, between same- or opposite-gendered people, tend not to enforced at all or are used very selectively. Activities shared among classes and status groups are differentially sanctioned. When leisure patterns are shared by lower-class and middle-class people (e.g., sport gambling), the laws are enforced against betting parlors and barber shops that take bets, not country club "skin games" and other legalized gambling. Police do not raid card games and other gambling games and schemes. Online betting remains anomalous. Criminalization perhaps depends on establishing the social composition of the players. In action, in groups of diverse class or racial backgrounds, such as parties, the arrest sanction is typically applied to the lower classes or those seen as lower on the "racial ladder" (Beckett, Nyrop, and Pfingst 2006). Where the crimes are minor and the issue of race is mute, police comply with the wishes of the putative victim.

Media amplification. Media respond to brief spikes in reported activity, usually reported to the media by the police themselves, sustaining a "moral panic" about the reported activities and targeting the putative source of the crime. This is especially true of crime produced by police action without citizen complaint, such as drugs crimes. This is an inference from the work of Beckett (1997).

Social spaces and their occupants. As social spaces, such as shopping malls, parks, and recreation facilities, become associated with activities of lower-class groups, or more visibly people of color, they are policed by both public and private police with greater vigor. If such spaces, nominally public, become contested areas, enforcement, public and private, will target people of color rather than others for arrest, banishment, or harassment. This is a kind of boundary maintenance, since these are interactions of a potentially volatile sort. Within these local areas, as dress, hats, accessories, and accoutrements become signals of order or disorder, depending on context and visibility, they are differentially responded to and sanctioned. Think of the evolution of the meaning of baseball caps, depending on their color, texture, bill direction, tilt, and decoration from team wear, working-class wear, and middle-class wear to ambiguous association with "deviant lifestyles," black entertainment, and gang membership. Each nuance of color, style, tilt, and direction of the bill is read off as indicative of disorder. Spaces are differentially marked and dramatized in reference to those who traverse them. Where sacred areas exist, such as schools in particular, zones of transition are marked and criminalized such that "others"— truants, suspended students, nonstudents of various sorts—can be arrested for trespass on public property, or can be cited in a civil order to prohibit their existing in the zone of transition between the sacred, the school, and its boundaries and the secular world of everyday commerce. These are announced as "drug-free" zones, meaning the drugs of the suspects and their presence or either, taken as an indication of both. Spaces that produce intersections of middle-class and lower-class life, such as washing car windows for money at traffic lights, asking for money outside convenience stores, fixing a car on a public street, or allowing your dog to foul the street, can be converted from fines to quasi-criminal offenses. They can be sanctioned by arrest, issuing contempt-of-court summons, or urging jail time for failing to pay fines.[3] This is criminalizing lifestyles and in effect creating crime from miscellaneous delicts (see the following chapters). When applied with a vengeance, such as arrests of marijuana users in New York City, the differential impact of the enforcement becomes obvious (Harcourt and Ludwig 2007).

Police know the territory that is well known as a "drug-dealing area," high-crime area, or the worst part of the city. The ecology of the city, or more precisely, known, labeled niches and enclaves in cities, is significant in sustaining circular police practice. This is of course the premise in crackdowns and sweeps—police attempts to eradicate by miniwars the "disease" of crime by applying the proper dosage of the criminal sanction (Thacher 2003; Sherman 2005, 2007). Considerable research shows that police focus arrests efforts in a few selected well-known districts (Smith 1984; Herbert 1997; Klinger 1997) while their effects are both various and relatively absent in others (Venkatesh 2006, 2008; Kubrin and Weitzer 2003). For example, as noted in the previous chapter, research by Klinger (based on synthesizing a number of studies of policing and his personal experience as an officer) and Kane (2005, 2006) suggest the circularity of the effects of policing. Klinger (1997) argues that the workload, perceptions of victims (unworthy), and the frequency of visible crime tend to make officers *underenforce* in high-crime disadvantaged areas and conversely to *overenforce* in areas with less everyday violence. This argument is not substantiated by victimization or other independent measures of criminal activity. Kane argues in parallel fashion that the distribution of arrests for violent crime is inconsistent with the distribution of officers in precincts over the course of the year. In fact, relatively more officers per capita are patrolling low disadvantaged areas than in the more disadvantaged areas. He suggests that this is in part a function of distribution of officers and uneven, high variance in deployment of officers. "Officers are deployed in low disadvantaged areas for reasons other than violent crime" (2005, 483). That is, police patrol quiet suburban and wealthy city streets not for crime or "disorder" but to reassure the middle classes of the presence of the police, regardless of their indolence. Kane also found that the surge in arrests for robbery and burglary reduced crime briefly, but that there was a bounce back and increase in crime subsequently. Incidents of police misconduct predicted variations in future violent crime in high disadvantaged areas; in extreme disadvantaged areas, both overpolicing (arrests as a ratio of reported crimes) and police misconduct predicted future crimes. There was no relationship between these variables and crime in low disadvantaged areas of the city. What is taken to be true about policing is that which affirms the many assumptions outlined in the previous chapter about the police métier. These practices border on categorical enforcement since the presence of the police routinely makes incidents of reported crime more likely other things being equal.

Drugs. Consider the role of food, drink, and medicines. These are all drugs in that they act to alter the body's functions. If substances that are produced by legitimate purveyors such as painkillers, amphetamines, and stimulants are produced illegally, or diverted from the legitimate to the illegitimate market, regulatory force is converted into a criminal targeting of the (minority or marginal) users and the producers. Social control efforts move from regulation to eradication and shift in the social groups that are targeted. As Black correctly argues (1976), law, or governmental social control, acts against those at the lower end of cultural, social, and economic hierarchies. This becomes the context for regulatory deciding. Thus, modes of control, or tactics employed, shift according to the imposition of the known users of marginalized or illegal substances. DARE programs target all schoolchildren, but police focus on and arrest those who use "street drugs."

Conflict resolution. Private conflicts are handled using different strategies and tactics depending on the class and locale of the dispute. Paramilitary units and tactics are used for domestic disputes involving hostages in rural, marginal, or disadvantaged areas, but never in the middle-class ring of cities and suburbs. The frequency with which these produce violence and fatal shootings is increasing (Kraska, personal communication, April 2008).

Lifestyles and symbols. Overt dress and manner, including deference to and demeanor to the police, are cues taken by police as profound and indicative. Symbolizing dissent or group loyalty via lifestyles (e.g., dress) is differentially enforced and sanctioned. If an African American wears gold chains and a tipped-sideways cap and carries a beeper and cell phone, he is a suspected drug dealer and subject to questioning. If a plumber has a tattered American flag flying at the back of his truck (an illegal display, a federal crime, by flag position and state of repair), he will probably not be stopped. If a university student wears a bright American flag sewn on the rear of her sweatpants, or a middle-aged matron wears a flag plastered across her huge bosom, these are seen as patriotic acts and not enforced as violations of laws governing the respectful display of the flag. Lifestyles are differentially sanctioned. Leisure and toys are differentially evaluated. A real estate agent who drives a huge, grotesque Hummer (a small troop carrier developed originally for the army) with an expensive and loud stereo system and darkened windows to take clients to visit houses for sale is subject to vague approval, if not envy; a black man driving a Hummer or Cadillac Escalade is suspect and likely to be stopped.

Surveillance: audio, video, and personal.   Since particular persons, areas, or activities are less important than the principal aim, which is to control marginal populations, much effort is made in sustaining surveillance of known suspects, tracking their activities and scrutinizing field stops, previous arrests for misdemeanors, violations of curfew, and juvenile offenses. In this way, a critical mass of allegations and confirmed activities is built up and provides the leverage for eventual felony arrests (Cicourel 1995). This activity of tracking and watching known "key players" and "hot spots" has escalated in the past ten years with the widespread adaptation of descriptive crime-mapping techniques. While in the past the watching and arresting of known dealers, pimps, and "gang members" was localized and largely patterned by individual officer discretion (Meehan 1992, 2000), the department-wide capacity to map, label, and reify "gang activity" by maps permits an organizational memory that can become in time a centrally coordinated "operation" or militaristic attack on areas of the city. Gangs, an elusive and elastic concept that covers whatever the police say it covers, is a useful justification for specialized units and tactics. Systematic monitoring based on "operations" and assembling a network of control agents, parole officers, police, ministers, federal prosecutors, and others is reserved for lower-class youth who are seen as the cause of crime (Kennedy 1998). This is "pulling levers," a targeting and focus reserved for lower-class black men in disadvantaged areas. Levers are not pulled in high-status Massachusetts suburbs such as Brookline, Weston, Concord, or Lexington. Consistent with this surveillance is the notion that the existence of a visible small minority (percentage of the population) within the marginal-token range (5–10 percent of the population) increases the likelihood of arrest of that group over others even within the same population of potential arrestees (Beckett, Nyrop, and Pfingst 1994, 2006). The evidence about the relationship between high levels of residential segregation and arrests is mixed (but see the most convincing data-based argument that it is correlated in a positive direction—more segregation, more arrests, and more police per capita [Stults and Baumer 2007]).

In summary, this process of targeting activities and people is flexible, is endlessly elastic, and can include control of rising classes and their challenges to the status quo, such as new entrepreneurs who invent means to acquire wealth at the edges of the law (executives of Enron and Tyco, Michael Milliken, subprime-mortgage lenders), as well as marginalized or falling classes and status groups. The most vulnerable are of course illegal immigrants who have little recourse to law or procedures to avoid deportation. The criminalizing or decriminalizing lifestyle preferences is easily traced in any area of interest—sport, drinking, and leisure, depending on the class or social segment that practices these diversions. Absence of compliance with a rule provides yet another tool for sanctioning and constraining, regardless of the viability or logic of the rule itself. The constant redundant sanctioning envelops groups, limiting their options and increasing inequalities. It could be said that police practice sustains the social object they have created through their practices.

This is then what is overlooked by the police and overlooked by police researchers: there is an endlessly elastic sociopolitical context within which policing operates. This elasticity results in shifting targets, deployment of resources, and new rhetoric that shape the mandate over time. These changes are only partially a function of new laws and regulations. The mandate expands and contracts as a result of these forces. The political neutrality of policing (Beare and Murray 2007) is an important pose in democratic society in the sense that alterations in police strategies and tactics actually do alter life chances of groups by class, race, gender, and lifestyle. The active role of police in social control cannot be denied, yet it is when the idea that the behavior of individuals is the "cause" of crime and their arrest the source of its reduction. The police are part of the power balance in a society and select, dramatize, and elevate their perspective on disorder and crime. The police, in short, are an allocative and redistributive mechanism that changes life chances. What maintains the compromises that restrain the potential for open-ended surveillance and enforcement?

THE POLICE MÉTIER: THE STABILIZER

The police métier is a window into the ways in which policing shapes the social order in which it is located. This métier contrasts with how policing manages the mandate publicly. The term *shapes* can be only inferred from a number of studies of policing and its impacts as well as the available ethnographies and community studies of those policed.

The idea of a métier captures modes of action that are matters of practical logic. First, *assumptions* are made, as in any occupation, about the politics of the field, the etiquette of treating citizens, mistakes at work, and routines and performances required of the practitioners. This is the assumptive world in which the occupation operates. There is an assumed practical model or logic in action that informs choices made in line with these assumptions. These assumptions and connections are taken for granted as being in the nature of the work and how it is to be carried out. Police practices are verified with reference to the several compatible assumptions that produce them. The assumptions about policing are the context within which practices have a life and a social reality. They reflect the value of the assumptions, and the assumptions are the context within which the practices are lodged. They are mutually supportive and are logical and methodical. The sketch is one of valued practices and assumptions, something like Waddington's detailed sketch of the "police canteen culture," the oral culture of the patrol officer. The assumptions and practices form the métier.

- The police assume they know local areas, people, buildings, places, and their dynamics.
- The structural features of places, neighborhoods, corners, and niches, "pockets of crime," as St. Jean (2007) terms them, are largely immutable.
- The people found in problematic areas are incorrigible. If they are drug dealers, they are "always dirty" (Moskos 2008, 83) and have no rights because they have forfeited them (ibid., 43–45) and can always be arrested (ibid., 49).
- Long-term "prevention," "problem solving," or efforts to change the contours of such neighborhoods have no purchase on shaping policing reality.
- Disorder can be altered superficially by local and personalized "treatments" and pragmatic, order-based policing.
- It is only possible to disrupt, briefly deter, and make the occasional arrest as needed to maintain the essential authority of the officer.
- Policing is differential by targets, time, place, and persons.
- Policing should be personalized in the sense that officers identify with their district or beat.
- While it is democratic in the sense of being responsive, policing in local areas, or neighborhoods, is shaped by ethnicity, class, time of day, and the political context. There is little one can do to change the economy, schools, family life, or religious values; these rarely change.

Given the vagaries of social life and crime, the police organization sets out expected activities and rewards. These are viewed ambivalently: organizational records and "real police work" are distinguished. *Immediate and visible indicators are seen as adequate measures of matters of concern.* The results that come from everyday decisions, arrests, seizures, traffic stops, field interrogations, and warrant servings verify the practices used. For example, if heads of drug units are asked how they know that there is a drug problem in their city, they reply, "I know it because we make X number of arrests every month, year, and so on." The arrests indicate there is a problem, even though the number of arrests that can be made in any city is a function not of the number of users, dealers, level of use, market structure, or drugs of choice but rather of organizational features. These include: (a) the number of officers assigned to drug units; (b) units that are urged to make drug arrests or rewarded for doing so; (c) the resources necessary to make buys and pay informants and "front money" for bigger busts; (d) the equipment (e.g., cameras, videos, feeds, Internet-based software and connections) and capacity—skills—to use them; and (e) the percentage of minorities in the city (Beckett, Ning, and Ny- rop 2007). The organization places its efforts on results, and the results obtained verify the practices. Since no effort is made to otherwise measure or monitor the matters of concern, they establish the need to continue efforts or perhaps increase them if resources are available.

This everyday working conception of policing, its métier, is complemented by the ideology of the top command, which can be summarized in general as a belief in the need to show the flag; keep homicides down; punctuate everyday patrolling with crackdowns, warnings, threats, and shows of force; and pacify the troops and negotiate all changes as concessions in the contract terms (wages, overtime, and "details"—police work that is paid for at overtime rates by businesses—in Boston, and conditions of work). Spikes in crime may produce new "operations," press conferences, and shifts in a few officers and overtime, but all the rest—the random patrol, the job-control practices of patrol officers, the rationing of time and energy—remains. The core of the public rhetoric is crime control balanced with an emphasis on community policing. The emphases that arise are episodic, not policy driven, ad hoc, and temporary.

The following sketch, since it emphasizes the work practices of patrol officers, requires additional qualifications. The growing diversity of policing, the inclusion of people of color, and more varied gender orientation mean that the assumptions and practices have shades and variety, and the style of policing may vary even within the métier. Detective work and the detective subculture remain apart from the occupational subculture itself. While community policing has been the focus of reform in one guise or anther in the past thirty years, no successful effort has been made in any police department since the mid-1970s (Sherman, Milton, and Kelly 1973) to integrate detective work with patrol activities, produce teamwork, decentralize detective units, or change the evaluation process of investigators. The most entrenched of all units and divisions are the detectives: nothing has changed in this work since the introduction of the computer and enhanced, enlarged, and linked electronic databases. Problem solving, community policing, hot-spot policing, and the rest have had no effect whatsoever on detective work, and only one systematic study (Innes 2001) has been published in almost thirty years. The overwhelming bulk of police studies concerns the police patrol division in large cities. There are only a few studies of specialized units (Marks 2004; Katz 2001, 2003; Decker 2003), and almost none on top command and middle management (sergeants, lieutenants, and inspectors). Thus, the inferences about police work are disproportionately drawn from studies of those who chose not to be promoted to specialized units or investigative work, did not qualify or refused, or were demoted, resigned, or were transferred back to patrol from specialized units. While the patrol division, as seen in large urban forces, is the icon and the synecdoche for all of modern policing, it is a misleading literary trope.

THE INCIDENT FOCUS

Domestic everyday policing is grounded in what might be called the *cynosure of the incident* (see Manning 2008, 81–82). Here, the métier is displayed.

Figure 9.1 The dynamic aspects of the police métier. (This figure was developed in collaboration with Michael W. Raphael.)

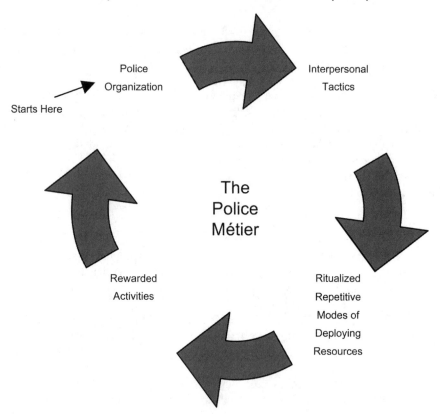

In the police world, the incident is a microcosm of sensible, thoughtful, rational individualistic choices. It is the sacred center of policing. The idealized concept of the police officer transcends the actual officer in everyday practice. The officer is idealized as exceptional—he or she stands apart from malice, emotion, prejudice, or distorted perceptions. The sacred status attributed to the officer is complemented in law by the "reasonable man" legal standard. To call actions within an incident sacred is to reaffirm the nature of these social facts—they are obdurate, external, and constraining. Incidents involving corruption, violence, or showing personal everyday flaws such as anger, exultation, or depression are seen as rare by the media and the police and fall under the category of "rotten apples" and exceptions that prove the overall integrity of the police as a body.

The incident is framed or viewed organizationally exclusively as the officer at the scene describes it unless otherwise known. As Moskos writes, "The chain of command is a myth. A sergeant cannot be in active command of five units simultaneously (2008, 112). Moskos captures the "you had to be there" rule: "While an officer may believe that another officer handles certain situations differently, the idea that officers should be allowed to make their own decisions is never in question. If these decisions are wrong, then the officers will face the legal, departmental or physical consequences" (ibid., 112–13). What is left unsaid here but revealed by the notion of absent supervision, creative writing, management of calls for service, and stops to avoid "trouble" is the rarity of actual information that might be seen as showing an officer was "wrong" in his or her decisions. "Otherwise known" refers to review later by supervisors, captured by the media or a citizen's camera, witnessed by third parties with an interest in the outcome, or observed as a result of the officer's request for advice or backup. Given that the theatrical core of policing is thought to be patrol work, the incident is seen in the context of responsiveness to citizen demand for order and showing activity to supervisors, but it is virtually always a low-visibility matter seen metaphorically through the eyes of the officer.

THE MÉTIER: POLICE PRACTICE

The métier is a name for police practices that are carried out routinely and determined by many forces.[4] As argued above, the incident or police-citizen encounter is the window into police practices and a kind of microcosm. It is shaped in the way that policing is organized—the *vertical and horizontal relationships* between segments are competitive, and rules are used in a punitive, coercive fashion. These features, when combined, are what scholars refer to as the "quasi-military" aspect of police organizations. But policing is not a military operation—it is a bundle of ecologically distributed entrepreneurial patrolling order (see the epilogue). The *resources* and how they are allocated, especially the deployment of the vast majority of personnel, matériel, and support to the patrol function, dramatize the métier. Also shaping the métier are the socialized *interpersonal tactics* that are sanctioned and warranted modes of controlling interactions. Finally, the rewards, both informal and formal, that are offered direct attention to and sustain the métier. These four forces are reaffirming, reinforcing, and repetitive. They reproduce the ways of doing policing seen every day in large cities in this country. Think of the incident as the center of the métier and each of the abstract forces shaping the métier and sustaining the ways of doing the job.

The first shaping force is the authoritative patterning of relationships called the organization. There is an abiding sense in which the work of the police is structured, that is institutionalized, routinized, unquestioned, done as if there was no other way to do it, taken for granted as to its effectiveness, purposes, and means. These constraints, social facts, make everyday work possible. They are valued up and down the hierarchy of the organization and in that sense are the *deep structures* that sustain meaning. The basic foundational assumption is that this organizing is functional and rational.

The organization is designed to allocate officers to randomly patrol mostly by automobile, to react and respond to calls, and to investigate "founded" (valid as a result of police investigation of the report). It is so structured and concentrates its resources at the bottom of the organization. The officers focus in the incident from whatever source to which they react. In this sense, "policy" is set on the ground by lower participants' situated practices. This kind of policy results from decisions made quasi independently and seriatum by loosely supervised officers.

The second shaping force is interpersonal tactics in the incident. These sanctioned *interpersonal tactics* of policing are those thought to guarantee successful asserting of authority, taking control, closing the incident in some fashion, and returning to service. These are learned on the job from other officers and especially field-training officers, as the academic aspects of the academy are viewed as irrelevant and even an impediment to doing good police work. (This is discussed above as "police tactics.") These constitute an aesthetic from which variation is permitted—a style—that has local departmentally shaped shadings.

The belief is that good policing, or a good piece of police work, has the following features. As a dramaturgical act, it requires:

- Sizing up the incident quickly (the police joke is that the officer is supposed to have it sized up *before* arriving)
- Dealing with the current situation in a parsimonious fashion
- Avoiding violence or extended arguments
- Deciding what to do and how to do it with dispatch
- Minimizing paperwork
- Producing solutions that facilitate returning to "service" (meaning becoming "available"—patrolling)
- Reducing cogitations about eventual guilt or innocence of the parties
- Eliminating remedies that are extensive, rehabilitative, educational, or transformative

The belief is that once framed by the officer and handled in accord with these features, the incident has the social reality attributed to it by the officer. It takes organizational shape as the officer defines and describes it. A protective epigram protects and elevates judgments made on the scene: "You had to be there" (to understand what was done, why it was done, and the results produced). This epigram rules the occupational culture. It protects the officer from criticism or punishment. It has a patently irrational element in that it attributes to officers that which no one possesses: endless patience, insight into human deception, deep penetration into character, a wariness combined with trust, and a moderated "wait-and-see" attitude. Even researchers seek the buried but obvious reasonableness that *must* characterize police deciding.[5] The idea that "distortions" are called upon suggests that the baseline of police deciding is of course reasonable, and somehow it must be shown by data that emotion, worry, guilt, anxiety, anger, and other mixed feelings exist in police shootings. This epigram and associated stereotype reinforce the inviolate and sacred center of the work—the reasonable, thoughtful, rational, cogitating individual officer on the street deciding things. It provides for flexibility of action and freedom from close supervision. The officer's account is virtually the rule of thumb in court as well: if the officer defines him- or herself as being in danger (or a police partner or member of the public), a shooting is considered prudent and legal (Hunt 1985). In addition, since the work is not defined in concrete terms or in terms of the content of the interactions involved, but rather is defined as a social form, what is done is open-ended and can be described using the conventional rhetoric sanctioned within the oral culture.

Consider, for example, the legal term *reasonable suspicion*. Grounds for reasonable suspicion are whatever the officer can articulate (Moskos 2008, 50–51). The written or verbal account for the work, or how it is explained, may arise from a current larger concern that frames the stop (e.g., immigration and homeland security), the political surroundings of the local area (e.g., crime as an election issue), dips and crescendos in official crime statistics, and internal matters such as contract negotiations and discipline. All these shape public dialogue about the contours, targets, and demands of policing (Scheingold 1984, 1991). The resultant institutional account offered for police action by the organization in press releases, press conferences, and media interviews is considered, on the one hand, pandering to the media. On the other hand, the reasons for the outcome of incidents are considered commonsensical and obvious to officers. In the vast majority of cases, even if there is gossip about a shooting, chase, or beating, the officers' views, condensed in the slogan "You had to be there," are considered true in the absence of additional evidence.

The deep grounding of police work in the incident is reinforced by other factors. These can be called the *tasks and routines* (sets of tasks) involved in the round of work for the patrol officer. An insight into these is the "tip of the iceberg," what is labeled activity in a police department. Most police attempt from time to time to show the numbers that are considered valuable and indicative of "activity." These may be traffic tickets, stops and searches, arrests, seizures, or warrants served, depending on the unit and emphases of the sergeant, but they are displaced surrogates for order that are useful to control and supervise the otherwise quite free officers on patrol. The particular emphasis can change from week to week or day to day, depending on the sergeants' concerns (Van Maanen 1988). The mini-ideology of the patrol segment is that they are overworked and overburdened chasing after calls, yet evidence suggests that the modal number of calls per hour is between one and three and that 40–50 percent of the time officers are driving around. The pressure of answering calls is always cited as the reason problem-solving and focused patrol activities are impossible.

These constraints on choice and action justify the here-and-now nature of the work; the absence of written policy and long-term planning and strategic "business plans" make close budgeting and accounting dubious. This focus is complemented by the flexible uses of overtime depending on the preferences of the top command and politicians. Major disasters and spikes in crime are powerful inducements to increasing overtime budgets. The incident focus undercuts systematic and generalizable modes of performance evaluation and analysis of long-term crime patterns. The continuing tension at the "bottom" is between the situated actions and deciding and its grounding in the tacit collectively sustained worlds of the patrol officer and the broader organizational rhetoric and public position of the top command.

Although police rarely identify with or live in the area they police, they are responsible during the day for the area they are assigned to patrol in and around. This is called in Baltimore (Moskos 2008) "post integrity," meaning that once an incident is closed, one should return to service and accept the next call dispatched. These patrolling operations lead to a boundary-maintaining manner of seeking activity relative to the area in which one is assigned (and may have been the result of a requested transfer), a division of labor among officers based on their skills and preferences (which vary from driving skills to traffic ticket skills to handling domestic violence), a differential focus on crime and arrests based on proactive policing (most common in high disadvantaged areas), and an ideology of defining some areas as dangerous, crime ridden, or full of criminals (usually elaborated with ideas about drugs, gangs, gunshots, and other commonsense indexes of violence potential). Rather than opening situations, police emphasize the importance of authority and control in interactions and place a premium on taking control of situations and manipulating compliance. Although the work does rarely involve crime control and suppression of crime, let alone arrests, the police in public employ the rhetoric of crime control.

These aspects of the interpersonal repertoire can be rendered in *narrative form*: effective policing is best carried out by random patrol by a few units differentially allocated to areas of the city based on workload (the past distribution of 911 calls that were processed and dispatched). This is most effectively accomplished not by direct territorial assignments based on citizens' local knowledge, socially defined enclaves, or neighborhoods but in police-defined districts or precincts, often shaped or constrained by natural areas, transportation lines, rivers, parks, lakes, highways and freeways, or railroad tracks. These roaming activities increase the chance of deterrence, visibility, and immediate response (the quicker the better) and via radio or phone communication resulting in encountering some subset of possible crimes to be investigated depending on time, energy, and overtime available to investigators. These activities in turn are rationalized (explained or accounted for) by a rhetoric of service and crime control and glossed with associations and symbols harking back to the military and medieval Christian standards of manliness (Keen 1984). These are truncated into slogans rather than spelled out publicly. These are very strongly held ideas, passionately defended if necessary. They embed the police in the past. The close examination of how such ideas are put into action reveals a different action pattern. The structure "overdetermines" the actions taken. While notionally officers are assigned to districts and beats within districts, the territorial assignment of officers is not enforced and could not be enforced (Reiss 1971; Jermeir and Berkes 1977).[6] This means an essentially semirandom wandering rather than a "patrol." This random patrol is punctuated by rushes to potentially engaging sites and calls, "the blue mice syndrome." Swarms to calls such as "Officer needs assistance" or "Crime in progress" are common. This sustains both the ideology that policing controls crime and the freedom of choice concerning time and effort. In part as a result of tradition about officer-defined random patrol and in part because supervisors rarely supervise, there is no directed patrol except in rare top down–mandated instances, such as "gun violence directed patrol" (McGarrell et al. 2001, 2002) or where overtime is used to pay officers to saturate an area. In general, then, specific guidance is not given and time is not allocated for specific activities, persons, places, or targets with specific assignments or for problem solving. Little training is given for these directed activities.

On the job, abstract programs, policies, philosophies, and rhetoric of management are eschewed and criticized. What is valued by most officers are the concrete rewards associated with keeping busy, responding to calls, and returning to service (meaning driving around awaiting the next call). Crime is a negligible part of it on a day-to-day basis, but it provides the excitement and tension that offset the boredom. Other officers value rank promotion, some value time off, and a few want the court and overtime rewards usually associated with arrests. Arrests and gun seizures are valued but also produce overtime since they require at least a single appearance at court and may require several. There are always a few officers who keep a low profile, do the minimum, and look forward to retirement. Since no specific concrete rewards—time off, promotion, overtime, public praise by top command—are given for variants of this street work, such as community policing activities, they are viewed cynically by the majority of officers (Fielding 1995).

The third shaping force is repetitive modes of deploying resources. This is partially structural and partially processual—a result of how officers patrol. The repetitive modes of deploying resources (by beats, districts, and other territorially based obligations) ground "order" and ordering in places and doings more than in categories of crime, law, or morality. Policing is about the control of territory and the symbolization of that control. These deployment modes are sensitized by the list (above) of shifting targets, places, and people. In disadvantaged areas especially, where policing is expected as required, policing is played out as reflexive cybernetic policing. It responds to the known understandings of policing about where crime lies, in what areas of the city, and carried out by what groups of people, and during what hours, days, and months of the year. The records kept sustain the validity of the practices because they are based on the same assumptions.

The fourth force is the cluster of rewarded activities. Any organization operates by inducements and their distribution. These inducements to perform policing as expected are based on assumptions about how the social world of work operates, as well as what practices are necessary to cope with this world. These generally revolve around stops, arrests, and other visible interventions in areas known as being full of that potential. As discussed above, the absence of rewards for other activities— problem solving, developing partnerships, working with community groups, excellence in organizational politics (other than rank promotion)—continues to tie the organization to its symbolic crime-control emphasis and ritual attachment to routine stops and "showing activity."

If we think of the incident as the window in which the practices are displayed, and these in turn being shaped by forces that are social facts, we can see that the incident is a ceremonial locus for repeating that which is valued and recognized as such in policing. In the incident the subjective and objective forces that govern the performance are mobilized. The activities have resemblance, coherence, and not a clear and obvious reality. Yet they are recognizable as "police work" in the here and now. The underlying continuity and resemblance between the actions may not be verbalized or described in nuance; the coherence is often assumed, not directly stated. The terms tied together by a fuzzy logic or like strands in a rope (Wittgenstein 1969) come to mind. They are known in spite of their emergent properties and complexity. These practices, and their existence as known properties of the incident, reproduce the modes of policing so frequently observed.

CONCLUSION

This chapter outlines the dynamic and stabilizing forces in policing as a practice. In the following chapter, chapter 10, the ripples and consequences of such policing are sketched, although little is well known about the impact of the police on the ongoing quality of life within disadvantaged areas.

CHAPTER TEN

Nondemocratic Policing

Democratic policing is a practice based on developments in Western industrial democracies. The series of chapters preceding this one are a kind of archaeology of development, permitting a kind of metaphoric "drilling down" to the actual here and now activities, the practices of American policing. While these are reflected in activities in the AADP countries, they are known through writings that reflect the interaction between the field of police studies and criminology, politics, and policing. The triangle that produces interaction and reflexivity among and between these points reifies a particular kind of concern and omits other matters. These omitted matters are of course the essential features of democratic policing. The previous chapter focused on the dynamics and stability of policing and the organizational structure, interpersonal tactics, resource deployment, and rewards that reflect the incident focus. It highlighted police practices—the police métier. This métier shapes the core of the current police ideology, and this ideology in effect is dramatized by the research enterprise.

What is known about the indirect and direct effects of policing, the effects on inequalities, in reference to the principles advanced in the preface and especially chapter 2? How does this shape the pattern of citizen trust that is essential in a democracy? What is known about the *experience of being policed* rather than what the police see as their role, their obligations, and how they account for them? What, other than *crime monitoring*, are police good for? As Rawls argues, a theory of justice must be reflexive and responsive, sensitive to constitutive rule and to changes in ideas. How can an organization invented in the early nineteenth century respond to the demands of postmodernity? In many respects, of course, the fundamental issues of policing, inclusion and exclusion, civility and just practice, remain vibrant and vivid.

The current climate of opinion, in the early days of the twenty-first century, is in striking contrast to the climate in the late 1960s (Sklansky 2007). Reform efforts directed toward policing in the aftermath of the riots of the late 1960s, seeking to reduce social distance and to co-opt minorities into "partnerships," were visible and important, but they were never designed to alter the pattern of inequality. In the end, a focus emerged: crime and the criminalization of lifestyles in the marginalized areas of large cities. *Changes in official crime and victimization rates have little altered the basic inequalities based on income, race, education, and region in this country.* It is not entirely clear how decline in the official reported rate of crime and other inequalities are related, but the question remains. The focus on "variables," a "drop in crime," or "attacks" on crime, suppressing crime briefly in selected "hot spots," obscures the ravages of high rates of incarceration, increased poverty, and high unemployment in large cities. These are dramaturgical efforts to persuade the public that brief alterations in the official rate has some bearing on the quality of life generally. Inequalities are not held constant by equations, and these variations do almost nothing to reduce the already abundant crime and disorder in these problematic areas. The consequences of the incarceration frenzy, not only in reintegration in large cities but in the impact on voting rights, democratic participation, and employment, have yet to be seen (Western 2007; Uggen and Mazden 2008).

What is known about the experience of violence, victimization, co-offending, and justice in disadvantaged areas? These areas are most police dependent and least able to mobilize informal controls to reduce the crimes and disorder about which they are concerned. Are these not the areas in which the obligation of policing is greatest? What is known about the consequences from the citizen perspective of most dramatic instances of police actions—the sweeps, the military-like operations, the crackdowns, some of them academically stimulated, sponsored, created, carried out, and evaluated—and the "controlled experiments" and related roundups? How does a decrease in variable, usually based on officially recorded crime figures for a brief time period or in a cross-sectional analysis, alter the life situation of those in disadvantaged areas? This chapter is an overview of the negative consequences of policing, policing that might be labeled nondemocratic.

TRUST AND LEGITIMACY

The basis of democracy is the trust in institutions that the public gives and the compliance that accompanies such trust. As is often said, but not heeded, the police are the public, and the public are the police. Absent trust, the magic that is attributed to the criminal justice system attenuates. Crime is an indicative but highly limited aspect of the larger aspects of trust in abstract ideas like "justice" and "fairness." Although many surveys have shown that trust in institutions, including the courts, prisons, and so on, and the police is higher among whites than people of color, among the older rather than the younger, and that local conditions alter the degree of trust in cities, these are rather grand concepts. Overall, trust in institutions is declining (Lafree 1998). Let us consider what is known about satisfaction with local police, fear of crime and responses to fear, people's sense of what policing is about, and cynicism about the criminal justice system and the availability of justice.

Satisfaction. With respect to evaluating the police on the basis of experience, it is well known that (1) satisfaction with policing is a rough indicator of satisfaction with community life generally; (2) policing is more negatively viewed as a function of experience—more experience, more negative views; (3) satisfaction and trust in police vary by neighborhood, even holding constant other socioeconomic and demographic factors; and (4) the most profound and consistent finding is that young African American men are treated most coercively, stopped most frequently, and experience consistent attention (Brunson 2007 summarizes this research in great and persuasive detail). They hold a symbolically conferred center stage, referred to by Elijah as "the anonymous black male," a kind of brutal dehumanizing shorthand recipe for threat (2003, 190). While Anderson surmises that this color coding is based on interactions, survey research based on interviews finds consistently that young black men as a category are perceived as symbolizing disorder and crime. It is unlikely that police do not share these tacit views. This perception of danger is *unrelated* to the actual reported crime rates in these areas (Chambliss 1994; Raudenbush 1999; Quinlan and Pager 2001). Perception trumps experience, data, and even positive media depictions of African Americans. This perceptual basis for risk of crime is argued by Sampson and Raudenbush (2004) to be based roughly on the percentage of young black men in the neighborhood as well as on reported perception, not the crime rate. On the other hand, young black men are the least trustful, most cynical about policing, emphasize what they see as its corrupt and violent character, and pay a high price for their part in the drama in respect to rates of arrest, conviction, incarceration, suicide, homicide, and accidental death (Fagan forthcoming, 2006).

Attitudinal data measuring citizen reactions to believed police deviance and policing in general gathered by the Sampson MacArthur project (work published with Earls, Raudenbush, and Morenoff) and others (the Comparative Neighborhood Study Project headed by suggest a high degree of variability in views of police by neighborhood and ethnicity [see Wilson and Taub 2006]). This includes data on collective efficacy (willingness to intervene) (also measured by Skogan et al. 1999) that shows it varies by neighborhoods and that it is inversely related to change and violence (both official and self-report). Trust and cynicism also vary by neighborhoods (low trust and high cynicism in areas of disadvantage, crime, welfare rates, single-person—mostly female—heads of households, turnover, immigration and percentage African American). These data show that police in inner cities are not trusted, and they are faced with cynicism that is structurally located and sustained. Neighborhoods, ethnicity, and age pattern both. Such attitudinal findings tell us little of what police do in these areas or why. The inference is perhaps possible that they have not produced trust in their daily visible operations.[1]

Fear and responses. Neighborhoods differ not only in demographic composition and fear of crime but also in their responses to it (Innes 2003; Weitzer 2000; Caravalho, Lewis, and Bursik 2005; Reisig and Parks 2000; Pattavina and Byrne 2006). This response is patterned by ethnicity and color. There is agreement in

Parks and Reisig's respondents (1998) about the crime level in neighborhoods, but blacks and whites differ in their views about how they cope and whether they are afraid (blacks are less afraid even in areas they agree are "high crime"). Weitzer's survey including interviews in three Washington, D.C., neighborhoods was revealing because he compares at the beginning of the article the generally positive view of policing in the city that does not discriminate by "race" (2000, 133). Yet three neighborhoods (one low-income black, one middle-income black, and one predominately white area) differed in their satisfaction with the police and most strikingly with this question: do police stop people in their neighborhoods without good reason? (Spartanburg 35 percent, Merrifield 5 percent, Cloverdale 11 percent), verbally abuse citizens (same order, 35 percent, 7 percent, 9 percent), and use excessive force against residents (28 percent, 4 percent, 6 percent). One-third of those interviewed in Spartanburg responded that people were frequently stopped without reason, verbally abused, and treated violently by the police. On the other hand, the data showed that all the neighborhoods agreed that blacks were treated differently than whites; the white neighborhood saw this as a result of the violence and the crime-prone nature of blacks and treatment handed out by the police as "rational discrimination" (ibid., 137). While black respondents accepted the differential treatment but argued that it was indiscriminate and based on the presumption of guilt. Black respondents in lower-class areas saw it as a form of repression. Middle-class blacks and whites felt that in their neighborhood police treated them about the same as other neighborhoods, while people in lower-class neighborhoods felt they were treated differentially—slow response time, insufficient police patrols, unwarranted stops, harassment, incivility, and brutality (ibid., 142). The quotes provided by Weitzer echo a consistent theme of racial perspective. Whites blame blacks, see them as crime prone and dangerous, and see the police as their allies and their neighborhoods as "safe" in part because blacks are not visible. The attitudes of suspicion and the exercise of brusque authority on the part of police are seen with ambivalence among black citizens. A similar ambivalence toward the police and the criminal justice system was found by Carr et al. (2007) in low-income areas of Philadelphia. Ironically, their respondents from low-income areas, black and white, were cynical about the criminal justice system and its workings, did not feel calling the police had much value, reported frequent unpleasant interactions, yet agreed that the police were the source of order and more were needed.

Encounters and experience. The few published observational studies on citizens' *sense* of policing are telling.[2] By "sense" I mean that the generalized feelings and cognitions that citizens take away from actual encounters with police, not generalized attitudes or phone-survey data. Data gathered in the POPIN studies and published by Mastrofski and associates (Mastrofski, Reisig, and McCluskey 2002) demonstrate through observation and inference that when officers observed civilities in addressing people, explained their procedures, and listened to them that citizens were more satisfied across levels of disadvantage, that is, they took from the encounter a sense of fairness. When looked at from the "police side," the view from more than forty years has been that the attitude of deference from the most troublesome segment of the population, youths between eighteen and twenty-four, has an uneven effect or arrest—it can be seen either as dissembling or compliance (Piliavin and Briar 1967). In a parallel finding, Mastrofski, Snipes, and Spina (2002) found that citizens' requests were deferred routinely in minor matters. Moskos (2008, 118) argues that explanation for an arrest or stop is irrelevant in the "ghetto" where he policed, arguing that after the handcuffs are on, an explanation is not needed. Nor did the Miranda warning have any bearing on the proceedings. His picture of the work suggests that the only time an officer gets out of a car is either to answer a call at a house or to arrest someone—otherwise, the work, warnings, stare-downs, deterrence by presence, and so on, is done from the car.

Perhaps the most insightful of the interview studies is a modest undertaking of Stoutland (2001). She carried out an interview study of trust that nicely complements the Braga et al. (1999) research on the effects of the "Boston gun project." Stoutland found residents in high-crime areas reported that police were viewed as competent (could make arrests and act against crime) and dependable (could respond in short term to crime) but had poor priorities (crackdowns that sweep innocent and suspects alike) and were not respectful. In particular, they felt the police were rude and dismissive. Those interviewed agreed that the police could not be trusted to act respectfully. The dependability of crime-control efforts came in direct contradiction to the lack of respect shown to residents. Their key concern was the absence of respect by police, and this had an erosive effect on citizens' willingness to inform, to support the police, to assist in their inquiries, and to be respectful in return. These views are echoed in the works of St. Jean (2008) and Venkatesh (2002, 2006, 2008) and are consistent with the general ideas about policing advanced by Klinger (1997) and Moskos (2008). That is, it is locally organized and orchestrated, reflects a deep cynicism about people in these areas, and is handled as a service to be controlled, restricted, and used as a tool to sustain police notions of "order." Of course, the surveillance process increases the probability of distrust prime facie. In disadvantaged areas, such as Boston's Dorchester and Roxbury, some seven modes of surveillance are applied daily: (1) visual (cameras—in ATMs and in shops and on some streets); (2) aural (shot detectors are anchored on telephone poles that transmit sounds to police communications center); (3) routine uniformed patrol (officers using all the relevant human senses—sight, sound, smell, touch); (4) specialized squads (gang, school, and dynamic-entry squads); (5) undercover agents from various specialized units; (6) helicopters; and (7) detectives of various units. In the surrounding more advantaged neighborhoods, even those nearby, even random patrol is light. Public outcry meant that surrounding lower-middle-class gentrifying areas of Boston were not included in the "experiment."

Cynicism. Generalized attitudes are reflected in such survey data, but the most powerful findings about trust and it role in police legitimacy are found in data gathered by Sampson and associates in Chicago. Sampson and Bartusch (1998), in a justifiably often-cited article, found that cynicism about the criminal justice system was one-third higher among blacks as whites, with Hispanics less cynical than blacks but more than whites. While all were intolerant of deviance and crime, their trust or lack thereof in the criminal justice system indicated the failure of police to equally serve and protect. This distrust is also found in research of Weitzer and Tuch (2004), patterned by age, ethnicity, and class. It is translated into a wish to reform police, and this is patterned also by ethnicity: blacks and Hispanics much more favor reform than whites. The negative attitudes of blacks (toward profiling, differential mistreatment of person and neighborhoods, police prejudice) are correlated with personal experience and knowledge of others' experience (information from others who have been mistreated). Experience and knowledge did not alter the beliefs of whites in the sample. They argue, following Blumer (1958), that the concept of race arises from feelings about a place in a social system of rankings and comparisons. Race arises from a sense of placement vis-à-vis other groups. Thus, the argument is that whites identify more with the police, overlook their misconduct, do not support reform of the police, and see them as acting in their interests. The opposite can be said about blacks, and Hispanics, although the views of Hispanics are less negative.

The availability of justice. It is perhaps redundant to note that the division by class and ethnicity between positive and negative opinions of the police, trust in the police, the fairness of the criminal justice system, and the belief in the availability of justice for people is large (Weitzer and Tuch 2004; Sampson and Bartusch 1998).[3] While whites of all classes have a positive view and consider the police fair, people of color are consistently and deeply more negative in their views. The irony of the racial-threat hypothesis is that not only do those "threatened" have little to do with the police, rarely see them, and maintain a general positive attitude, but evidence also suggests that they are responding more to the media than to the facts of crime and disorder (Beckett 199; Chiricos, Hogan, and Gertz 1997; Chiricos, Padgett, and Gertz 2000). Research also supports the idea that there is a correlation between size of minority population, fear of crime, the economic threat of minorities, and the ratio of police to the public (Brandl, Chamlin, and Frank 1995; Nalla, Lynch, and Leiber 1997; Stults and Baumer 2007). Parker, Stults, and Rice (2005), using 2000 census and arrest data, found that "urban disadvantage" influenced arrest rates for both blacks and whites. However, rates of blacks were higher; they were more likely to be arrested in these areas.[4] There is some suggestion that there is a tipping point for arrest behavior, as when the percentage black in a city reaches a certain level, arrests begin to decline (ibid., 1125), or increase when the percentage of Latinos increases in a police district (in this case, New York City [Kane 2003]). Again, as in other demographically based work, the inferences about how such numbers are produced are made absent any data on actual police actions and reactions; differential enforcement by areas, districts, and cities; the feedback resulting from differential treatment, arrests, or stops; and the actual ongoing dynamics, sociodemographic, political, or cultural, that produce such different rates. They cannot be ascribed to race alone.

THE RIPPLES OF THE MÉTIER:
INSTITUTIONALIZED MISRECOGNITION

The general perceptions and general attitudes of groups toward "police" as a category, the characterizations of areas policed, and trust of the police are quite well patterned and known. What is done in selected areas is less well known. What do police do in areas they consider problematic? What are their practices? In many respects, the absence of observational materials on practices is striking, given the volume of studies of attitudes toward the police. How is the "threat," economic or psychological, of a minority translated into action? What are the everyday work practices rather than the publicly stated policies of a secretive organization? The previous chapter has shown that the stability and dynamics of policing are a configuration with considerable durability. The assumptions and the practices are contextually linked in actions in managing incidents.

The police oral culture values stories and incidents that reflect and support the tacit assumptions about the job and its purposes. These punctuate and dramatize the otherwise mundane aspects of the work. Oral culture ritualizes and insulates police from alternative views of the work (e.g., that police are racist as seen in their traffic stops) and resolves contradictions (e.g., they do little with and about crime but are valued as a thin blue line protecting citizens against criminals). It sustains morale in the face of media and politicians' criticisms and binds together officers who otherwise experience rather isolated work, either working alone or in clerical capacities.

The social relationships between the police and the public are personalistic, and the patterns that emerge in places are based on a "top-down" notion of ordering and order. While familiarity obtains between the more visible street people in disadvantaged areas, they are seen almost entirely in their roles as past, present, or future offenders rather than in their many roles within the local network of relations (see, for example, Moskos 2008, chap. 3). This binary view of the world, rather typical of the public police stance, if not always in their practice, obscures the multiple roles played by those seen as criminal by the police (see Pattillo-McCoy 1997; and Venkatesh 1997, 2006, chap. 2). This blindness to complexity is reflected in the research on crime that reports only arrest or complaint data rather than the complex network of social relationships that obtain in these areas. Thus, while police view their actions as benign, given the structural conditions as they define them (Klinger 1997), their view of ordering excludes the complexity of illegal and legal activities and their links to visible crime. It also excludes the control of other matters that bear on crime, such as being a victim and offending, general patterns of lack of city service, illegal exploitation of the poor by each other, support of witnesses and connection of citizens, and minding disorder generally rather than making arrests.[5]

The drama of arrests and sweeps is not complemented by later information in the media or from the police about convictions, arrests thrown out of court, wrongful convictions, judges freeing arrestees, and the like. Neither the police nor the public is given systematic feedback about the *results* of the operations, campaigns, crackdowns, sweeps, or paramilitary activities of the police. The media report the operation, name the number arrested, and quote the police spokesperson about the virtues of the operation. The media may perhaps note the number of warrants served or arrests made, but never follow up on the consequences of such operations, those released immediately, those who were falsely arrested, or those charged and brought to trial, but officers involved are not informed of the outcomes. The offices of the U.S. attorneys, and local city and county district attorneys, communicate with those in the police concerned with prosecution, but officers are not informed of results unless they are asked to testify. This sustains two ideas—one that the operations were needed, required even, and apparently successful given the publicity and, on the other hand, that the same problems remain, the same areas produce calls for service, domestic violence, and everyday disorder and crime, and the same people are being stopped, warned, arrested, and jailed.

Given this, let us now review known data on the impacts of policing on the social organization of disadvantaged areas: those on indirect effects, those on deterrence, and those on direct effects including sweeps. The primary locus for analysis here is the reported and observed actions of the police in disadvantaged areas of large American cities, and other conurbations in the Anglo-American world. It is here that police spend most of their time; make the most stops, inquiries, and arrests; and believe crime and criminals flourish. Here, race/ethnicity and class intersect powerfully and visibly, and the indicia of disorganization or differential social organization are present. In many ways, modern urban policing is about patrolling the boundaries of such areas, and occasionally making militaristic entries. I conclude with some summary comments about the cybernetic reaffirmation of places and persons that edge close to tautology.

SOCIAL EFFECTS

There are three kinds of effects produced by the circular mode of policing: indirect, deterrent effects, and the effects of sweeps.

Indirect effects. Little is known about policing's direct and indirect impact on local social organization because ethnographies deal with police only incidentally, and policing research does not address the complex interaction between order, arrests, and complaints and services when they are provided (see the research of Stoutland and Venkatesh cited above). Research has replicated the commonsense police wisdom about crime, rather than social scientists' influencing policing away from a narrow notion of crime suppression. The ethnographies that describe life in disadvantaged areas provide some materials, but they are limited because their focus is not the police: the actions, thoughts, practices, and policies of the police are not a central part of their data gathering. Although police actions are salient, they are either cooperative or responsive and reactive rather than intrusive and proactive in the ethnographies. On the other hand, it perhaps suffices to say that of the many ethnographic studies of policing in the Anglo-American world, only a handful describe policing outside large urban areas, with a primary focus on the disadvantaged areas and their policing.[6] It is thus a "top-down" view, a view of the conventional society of those below them and a reflection of the general sympathetic view of policing in criminal justice and criminology.[7]

Little research is done by police researchers on the meaning of police practices to citizens at the interactional or even tactical level (as opposed to questions about trust and feelings of security). Since the interactions are global, involving personal relations as well as collective feelings and obligations, they echo throughout the locality and cannot be ascribed to attitudes alone or even to interactional sequence alone. In other words, major known negative experiences, both local and national, are known and talked about and are not restricted, especially in and around disadvantaged areas, to media-based conceptions of policing or those of whites alone (see May 2001, chaps. 3 and 4). In what May calls the "paradox" of racially homogeneous interactions, these interactions, especially in semipublic places, increase both the positive stereotypes of African Americans of themselves as well as "compounding negative impressions of those outside one's racial or ethnic group" (ibid., 163). This, as he shows, includes views of the police and police views of African Americans. May's analysis is consistent with Du Bois's views, in which the veil works both ways—to heighten stereotypes and to obscure both similarities and differences across racial groups.

However, an interesting attempt to assess the meaning of police actions is the Parks and Reisig research based on phone-survey data gathered in Indianapolis, Indiana, and St. Petersburg, Florida (2004). They argue that some police tactics played a role in people's approval of policing in their neighborhoods, and reduction in reported incivilities, but cannot discount the high correlation between trust in police and security and neighborhood attachment. One might argue that the sequence (which they did not and could not measure with a onetime cross-sectional design) runs from attachment to community to approval of police, not the other way around (note the misquote of Sampson and Raudenbush 1999, 638). They do not report what was actually done, where or why, nor any outcome measure of changes in actual levels of disorder or crime. There are no community voices in any of this research—no people, no names, no quotes, no observations on what is done. It is a lifeless litany.

Deterrence effects. Research claiming to focus on deterrence provides no evidence that it works. On the other hand, as the previous chapter demonstrated, when crackdowns and arrests are the focus of the research, using carefully crafted research designs, small variations are attributed to the experimental effects, and in addition, the short-term drops in officially recorded data on crime applauded as a direct consequence of policing interventions. This is all inferential, as the actual social processes that were altered or not are not described. It is *post hoc proper hoc* reasoning. Braga et al. (2001) emphasize that the key element in their research on the reduction in youth homicide in Boston was deterrence—young gang members were informed that they were targeted and that violence would not be tolerated. They were contacted by probation officers, police, and clergy, and notices were posted notifying gang members of the consequences of violence, gun possession, and gun use (Kennedy 1998, 2001). They argue for deterrence as the driving force behind the Boston Gun Project but note in the conclusion (Braga et al. 2001, 219) that they had no information on the dynamics of deterrence or how or why it shaped their data. The same argument is made in McGarrell et al. (2006), based on the same boilerplate discussion of the research. Research in the pulling-levers mode (see www.psn.gov) is inconclusive and weak, tenuous in conclusion, and largely based on inference rather than clear patterns of data (see, for example, Bynum and Varano 2003). The argument for deterrence based on the speculations of the researchers (Braga et al. 2001) can be illustrated in an examination of published research done in Lowell, Massachusetts (Braga, McDevitt, and Pierce 2006). The study is of "preventing" gang-related violence, but the key term, *gang,* is undefined and left to commonsense police notions, "a term of convenience," that is, it's whatever police say it is and who a member is (see footnotes 2 and 3 in Braga, McDevitt, and Pierce 2006; see also Meehan 2000). They write, "Developing a better notion of gang, ascertaining whether Lowell had gangs by this definition, and then determining whether these gangs were a problem—with the problem defined in some way that was independent from the existence of gangs as such—were beyond the scope of this inquiry" (Braga, McDevitt, and Pierce 2006, 32).

If the aim is to reduce gang-related crime, and "gang" is neither operationally defined nor measured, how can "experimental" data show "gang-related" crime has been reduced? This formulation of the problem suggests that the effort is to reduce official records of "gang-related crime" as the police, the sponsors of the research, define it. The homicide data were checked against the police department database (a product of police input and definitions) and a focus group (with members of the gang unit) and then refined to conclude that 70.5 percent of the homicides and 35.3 percent of the aggravated gun assault incidents were considered "gang related or gang related with a drug business nexus" (ibid.). The actions to deter violence (undefined) are entirely described in boilerplate language with no details as to what "treatments" were carried out in what depth, merely described in glittering generalities (ibid., 36–39), including a focus on "impact players," those who should be arrested because they were "carriers" (a term taken from virology and the spread of disease). Most significantly, they produce no evidence of the response of individuals, gang members or not, of the meaning of the actions to their choices, past or present. The "pulling levers" strategy was used with "Hispanic gangs," not with Lowell's Asian gangs (described on the basis of information from Los Angeles). Threats were made to known Asian gambling businesses, "delivery of a clear message": "When gang kids associated with you act violently, we will shut down your gambling business. When violence erupts, no one makes money" (ibid., 40). Is this the purpose of policing? Sustaining illegal businesses? This is, of course, a pretext for indirect categorical enforcement, based on behavior that is already known, illegal, and unconnected directly with gangs or gang activities (presumably these are parents or kin punished for their association, not their gambling). Thirty search warrants were served on "gambling dens," and one hundred gambling-related arrests were made. This program, these measures, not including any evidence, observed, reported, or derived from interviews, of their impact on the gang members, is argued to be or "seems to be preventing serious gun violence." "Seems to be" used in a research report? This "prevention" is stated as a 50 percent reduction in homicide in nine months (from four to two) and 24 percent reduction in gun assault incidents (from forty-nine to thirty-seven). They state that these are preliminary results (ibid., 41–42). The point is that one cannot claim deterrence is the factor based on the statistical evidence and programmatic actions described without observations, interviews, or other ethnographic data concerning the shaping of behavior as a result of the described tactics. The claim for deterrence is not proven.

As many have noted (W. Wilson 1987, 1997; Venkatesh 2002, 2006, 2008; Stoutland 1998; Rose and Clear 1998), the disadvantaged inner-city areas have the profound combination of families and neighborhoods with draining, complex, chronic, and overlapping multiple problems (legal, social, medical, economic); low and inadequate income; unemployment; and absent social services. These areas are isolated socially, culturally, and economically; the opportunities outside these areas are restricted cognitively, socially, and ecologically. In many respects, these areas are dependent on the goodwill of the police, emergency medical services, fire services, and volunteers and on their endless creativity in the face of adversity. The ambiguous and shifting role of the police as social service providers creates waves because they generate some goodwill, on the one hand, especially through community policing efforts and special units, yet, on the other, also periodically crack down from time to time (Venkatesh 2008, 270).

Sweeps. In targeted disadvantaged areas, sweeps are justified as one aspect of social services or opportunities for young men to get help (BPD 2003; Braga, McDevitt, and Pierce 2006), serving outstanding warrants, or dealing with open-air drug dealing (Nunn et al. 2006), part of a cycle of crackdown and let-up that reduces crime and adds positive deterrence (Weisburd et al. 2006) and displacement (Weisburd et al. 2004, 2006). These sweeps, or an onrush of officers, often state, local, and federal task force based) in early morning into a known high-crime area with warrants are categorical, that is, aimed at residents of a public housing estates (the former Robert Taylor Homes in Chicago or Grove Hall in Boston) or place based, not precisely focused on arresting a few known offenders. For example, the sweeps in Taylor Homes in 1993 were carried out without warrants (Venkatesh 2002, 254), were clearly illegal, and generated enormous ill-will. Such arrests of those wanted on outstanding warrants (sometimes proceeding by grand jury) are unlikely to "come back on you" in negative rejection of police requests and information needs. Many bases can be used to make the arrest—parole violation, outstanding warrants, violations of city regulations (e.g., parking tickets), contempt of court for failure to appear, violation of restraining orders, or merely refusing to move on, reacting with anger, running away, or carrying a weapon once frisked. Since these sweeps, in turn, net a large number of known offenders and previously arrested persons, they are deemed a success (Nunn et al. 2006). Of course, this is circular, since those arrested are already known to the police and could be arrested at any time. Yet, nevertheless, there is no standardized way of judging the success of the crackdowns; research interpretations are imagined, made up, or hypothesized, based on such fallacious and indirect indexes as calls for service, drugs calls being notoriously inexact (Moskos 2008), or brief dips in selected crime indexes (Sherman 1990, 1992). As noted above, even key terms such as *gangs* are not defined precisely and left to commonsensical and tautological definitions (it is what we say it is)—the officers' sense of what a gang is (Braga, McDevitt, and Pierce 2006, 32). These "successes" are predicated entirely on official police-sanctioned records and interpretations and are absent any data from the residents in such raided areas. The measures are measures of convenience. They ignore or bypass any alternative sources of interpretations in the areas inconsistent with the naive thesis that such sweeps produce "order" or "deterrence." This "crackdown" approach, dramatized and promoted by Sherman (1990, 1992) has no pretenses about order or ordering, no claims to long-term effects, and no claims to alter or minimize risks of crime or increase social order. It is about reducing officially recorded crime in selected areas for a short period of time at the expense of large amounts of police overtime and supervision called "experimental conditions." No announcement of failures, only of new initiatives (assumed to work). The underlying morality is that the matter targeted is worthy of intense police attention, whether it is truancy, gun carrying, or serious crime (see Sherman 1990). What is not included as effects are the unmeasured consequences of police crackdowns revealed in other research, although this is debatable point, given that police seem to be most effective in partnerships and the like in areas where the collective efficacy is already high (Skogan et al. 1999). The question arises, given these results, whether "crackdowns" have less to do with the effects imputed to police actions and more to do with the media response and the perceptions of those living outside these areas. They are neither reactive in nature nor designed to alter the conditions that produce arrests. As Wilson and Kelling once wrote, arrests and action by the police are considered matters of last resort (in Weisburd and Braga 2006, 79). Who are they intended to benefit? As Rosenbaum writes, in a statement that cannot be discounted, "We cannot avoid the fact that policing tactics and strategies vary by race and social class" (2006, 255). He might have added race as a social construction that indirectly guides policing actions. Even though "race" may overlap to a considerable degree with class and residential area, the survey data of Skogan 2006 and Weitzer and Tuch (2006) show that young black men's experience is singular and that the experience of African Americans with police stops, frisks, and street interrogations cannot be explained by "class."[8] Given the disproportionate resources denied such areas, why is the primary focus on known offenders in known places with known records?

Since most sweeps depend on surprise, secrecy is highly valued. Patrol officers on routine patrol will not be informed until shortly before the event, if at all; community police officers assigned to the area are not consulted or informed of the upcoming raid; and local community groups are left ignorant of the planned operation. The effects are seen later. When officers are involved in disadvantaged neighborhoods on an everyday basis, if we are to believe Venkatesh (2006, 2008), they are made aware of the criminal activities involved (e.g., drug dealing) and the complicity between the homeless, the gang leaders, and the shopkeepers to maintain order, and they forgo arrests in order to mediate, or avoid arrests on the ground, as those involved are perceived by police as "deserving victims." Thus, any sweep places them in a compromised position. The feedback from the community to those routinely involved is typically multifaceted—complaints as well as praise.

GENERALIZATIONS ABOUT EFFECTS

What are some generalizations that can be advanced, given the evidence, of the impact of such policing, an extension of the métier, circular policing? Those arrested are not merely those for whom warrants have been issued or the result of grand jury findings. The aim is to apply coercion in the interest of asserting police control in a named, known, and disreputable place. Sweeps have symbolic as well as instrumental effects. The sweeps and arrests of noncriminals, who are simply present, protest their innocence, or refuse access to their homes, are targets for police coercion, and illegitimate actions (Venkatesh 2008; Weitzer and Tuch 2006). The instrumental effects, regardless of the eventual outcome of the arrest, are significant. Known "players" who are arrested, even on minor charges, increase their "reputation" as key players in the eyes of the police and are seen as deserving of yet additional attention (Cicourel 1995; Braga and Bond 2008; Nunn et al. 2006).

While making abundant arrests for minor crimes have a temporary impact on serious crimes (perhaps reducing them [Formango and Rengifo 2007], perhaps increasing them [Kane 2005, 2006]), the consequences, the almost exclusive arrest of minorities, have a direct impact on the creation of "criminal careers," reputations as key players, and the building up or an arrest record toward a felony conviction. When top-down police-oriented research (e.g., Braga, McDevitt, and Pierce 2006; McGarrell et al. 2006; Nunn et al. 2006) lists the numbers of prior convictions of those arrested in sweeps and reduces arrested young black men as "lever pulling," it is evidence of such processes in operation. It is difficult, perhaps impossible, to distinguish reputation, known past record, and previous arrests from present culpability in the here-and-how situation, since the police are the sole judges at that time of the validity of their claims.

Bystanders are at risk of arrest, a fact that puts them at risk for another more serious offense when next they are stopped. Venkatesh writes about one such sweep and spot check, which led to "the arrest of a great many suspected drug dealers, including many young men who had nothing whatsoever to do with dealing drugs" (2008, 270).

People distrust police promises made in the form of community policing when such unannounced raids are made. Variation in tactics increases uncertainty and distrust within these areas. There is also wariness about when and where the police will appear, and divisions within areas between the "respectables" and others are blurred since some of the respectable and responsible members of the neighborhood may also be involved in the drug trade. Social control in these areas is not the result of a binary division but a shifting coalition of people who are linked into social networks of various degrees of intensity and contact (Venkatesh 1997; Pattillo-McCoy 2000; St. Jean 2007).

While the sweeps are periodic and dramatic, they have other effects as well. As Klinger (1997) and Venkatesh (2008, 270) point out, such invasions increase the number of arrests in areas that are otherwise areas of negotiated order in which many nonviolent crimes are overlooked and informal compromises are honored. The order is negotiated, has known routine aspects, and is the rule, not the exception.

In general, policing in high-crime areas is characterized by a degree of tolerance by police on the street and a rationing of everyday service. This includes downgrading calls, refusing to attend other calls, experiencing overload at peak hours, and using vague codes such as "service rendered" to reduce supervision and accountability (Moskos 2008). This produces an uncertainty effect in local populations. Uneven response produces a cynical view of police and an expectation in spite of numerous calls that assistance will not arrive (Venkatesh 2006, 2008). This shades into failure to enforce laws when the victims are "undeserving" (drug dealers, prostitutes, pimps) and a rise of informal means of reducing conflict (law, as Black [1983] reminds us, acts down, and "self-help" works horizontally and up). Venkatesh describes how routine patrols do not show up, problems raised in community meetings are not responded to, and bribes are required to secure services (Venkatesh 2006, 79–80ff).

Given the persistence of the problems addressed, such as drug dealing, these sweeps have only a temporary effect on the dealing structure, the number of dealers, the quality of the heroin, and the number of users (Nunn et al. 2006; St. Jean 2007; Venkatesh 2008). Net decreases in drug-related crime are short term and negligible when measured by actual arrests, seizures, and warrant servings, as these are surrogates for the actual level of dealing and use (see Nunn et al. 2006; cf. Manning 2003). Those arrested in drug sweeps are the more visible and younger dealers and assigned to more obvious spots to run errands and deliver the goods from a stash, so they are arrested more frequently than the managers and higher-level dealers (Jacobs 2000; Venkatesh 2008, 270). Higher-level dealers are elsewhere (St. Jean 2007) and are unlikely to be arrested because they are not street dealers or dealing in "open-air" contexts. Venkatesh, who witnessed these sweeps in Chicago and was closely monitoring the drug trade as part of his research, concludes: "The CHA sweeps were terribly ineffective, indeed that did little to deter gang activity and drug distribution" (2001, 198–200, quote at 254). Finally, interviews with offenders do not support the idea that they desist. On the other hand, the systematic criminal element is little affected by such police activities (Wright and Decker 1994, 1997; Jacobs 2000; Venkatesh 2002, chap. 5; St. Jean 2007) in part because they are known and in erstwhile cooperation with the police as informants and sometimes as witnesses.

Known negative consequences reverberate within the local area: violent retaliation among dealers for suspected snitching (Jacobs 1999, 2000); replacement effects with corollary violence (ibid.); and subsequent unwillingness to snitch (Carr et al. 2007; Silver and Miller 2004). Rosenbaum (2006), in part based on the arguments of Rose and Clear (1998), argues that considerable evidence exists that crackdowns weaken other forms of social control by neighborhoods (the anarchistic consequences of too much law [Black 1976]). Weaker informal social control results from absent wage earners arrested, family dependencies, and loss of social capital generally (Rose and Clear 1998). As legitimate income and sources of wages decrease as arrestees no longer contribute to family income, illegitimate sources of income and stability have new sources of respect and reward (Venkatesh 1997, 2008; Pattillo-McCoy 2000). Police raids and unpredictability in respect to victimization support the rise of alternative, semiformal means of control (e.g., drug dealers and those with gang ties [Venkatesh 1997, 2008, chap. 5] who provide services and protection in exchange for a "license" to deal within the area) (Venkatesh 1997, 136–38).

There is increased ambivalence among the "conventional" members of the neighborhood, as their belief in the police as sources of control and crime suppression is contrasted with their experiences and sense of powerlessness (Sampson and Bartusch 1998; Geis and Ross 1998; Carr et al. 2007).

The difference principle thus clearly applies here: crackdowns do not benefit the least advantaged. How, one might ask, do they benefit the others? The root causes of crime and disorder and social disorganization (as measured by Sampson and associates) remain unaffected, and perhaps are amplified by policing (St. Jean 2007). The models of the relationship between social conditions and crime and disorder in the work of Skogan, Sampson, and associates and Kelling and Sousa (2006) in a rethinking of BW policing, and the reformulations of Meares and Kahan (1998, 811), St. Jean (2007, 35, 45), and Moskos (2008, 182) do not include anticipated negative consequences of social control variables in the model. They omit unanticipated positive or negative consequences of police action or inaction and any indirect effects of policing. The focus is the ORCS, the final dependent variable, arrests, or crimes reported. The most obvious point derived from close studies of police behavior is that crime, ORCS, is shaped continuously by matters excluded from statistical analyses such as the social organizational processes within such crime dependent-areas and the bases for arrest other than and in addition to the criminal behavior subject to "reasonable suspicion"—offensive demeanor, routine loitering, running away from an open-air dealing scene—and, on the police side, a wish to get overtime through court appearances, maintain dignity and respect from those policed, keep up the numbers for supervisors, and so on. It is apparent that these short-term, or cross-sectional, research operations cannot comment on cause, but they certainly do not include the processes captured in historical, cultural factors and antecedent variables that shape the narrow slice of behavior studied. The point is not whether those arrested have engaged in criminal acts, whether they are "impact players," or whether they disrespected authority (not a crime in any case), but that the *focus* on such people produces yet more inequalities and produces in effect a categorical visible enforcement that in turn alters the life chances of others in the same area, and has no long-term effect on safety, security, or the quality of life. While this is a critique of research, it also dramatizes policing in a particular fashion to other researchers and to the police themselves.

The impacts of policing on social organization, within or without the arrest or crime focus, have not been well studied, and the inferences here are queries to be subjected to further rigorous research. In many respects, the detailed ethnographic work on policing shows only the work of the police, not the consequences outside their immediate purview, and work on the social organization of local communities sees policing at a distance, usually negatively, as do the citizens living there. With a few exceptions the recent studies are of moderately crime-free areas, that is, free of visible nineteenth-century street crimes.

EFFECTS ON POLICE OF SUCH POLICING

The more frequent the operations and "overpolicing" as measured by ratio of serious crime arrests over other arrests (Kane 2005), the more likelihood of a rise in official crime in the following months. The "boomerang effect" of long-term area-based arrest foci and crackdowns is likely to stimulate additional crime (Kane 2006) in the particular area policed as such.[9] Kane calls this "overpolicing" (violent crime arrests divided by the number of officers assigned to the precinct that year). In areas of high disadvantage and extreme disadvantage, these measures were correlated with a rise in violent crime in the coming year. There was no such correlation in low-disadvantaged areas. Kane has also argued that abuses and police misconduct are greatest in the most disadvantaged areas, those where crackdowns are targeted (Kane 2002). As and insofar as innocent or mere bystanders are arrested and detained in sweeps without explanation (Venkatesh 2008), they are less inclined to report crimes. As this is already true in disadvantaged areas, fewer reported crimes means fewer are investigated and cleared, adding to victims without the support an investigation might provide. This in turn means that witnesses are unwilling to respond, a common experience in Boston. The consequence is a low clearance rate for serious crimes that is dropping yearly. The bias of investigators is against "working" without witnesses, physical evidence, or confession, and thus absent witnesses, so cases that are reported are placed in the nonworking file and not investigated further (Waegel 1982). The clearance rate for homicides in Boston in 2005 was 35 percent. The homicides, victims and perpetrators, are concentrated in a few, overwhelmingly disadvantaged, sections of the city.

REFLECTIONS

Since the studies and related claims of the police-oriented researchers who have studied sweeps, crackdowns, and wars on drugs, Sherman, Weisburd, Mazerolle, and Braga and associates, are based entirely on premises, assumptions, and tentative analyses based on short-term interventions and brief controlled experiments, there is little evidence about how such interventions work or not, except from the official statistics and data gathered by the experimenters from nonethnographic sources (observation of selected cites and behaviors, telephone interviews, calls for service data, or official police reports or records). These methods continue to affirm and assert the police-focused, police-based notions about crime control and its consequences, positive and negative. They shift our attention to statistical correlations and to the variations in policies and actions that produce such temporal alternations, not social organization.

These new rationalized approaches to enforcement, based on the false idea of "prediction" (Harcourt 2007), that the past-recorded offenses are indicative of future behavior in the absence of other information, increase the burden on the visible, the public, and the less competent among those at risk (St. Jean 2007). As field research demonstrates repeatedly, such operations and most of the scholars using large databases and surveys who write about these operations demonstrate no understanding of the social dynamics of such low-income places and the impact of policing actions on citizens, those involved in illegal or legal activities. On the other hand, as close observers such as Venkatesh, St. Jean (2007), and Bruce Jacobs (1999, 2000) have spelled out in detail, these operations, when task forces combine to make arrests, using federal laws to prosecute and send large numbers of young black men to prison, served to reduce the market in crack cocaine in the late eighties and early nineties. This in turn shifted the focus of entrepreneurs in such areas to other modes of organized crime (Venkatesh 2008, chap. 2). When crime-dependent communities lose a form of income and are restricted systematically from other employment, new forms of crime emerge, and many forms of quasi-legitimate activities proliferate.

Thus, of course, these episodic interventions, federally funded and sponsored, such as the federally funded safe neighborhoods (www.psn.gov) and weed-and-seed programs, suggest that the scientific need is to examine not the outcomes of short-term interventions that escalate the arrest count and reduce serious crime briefly or disorder but the process by which this takes place and the "unintended" negative and positive consequences that result. These cannot be captured fully by arrest statistics claimed to be a product of imagined deterrence.

Crackdowns and other rational operations, sponsored externally (typically the National Institute of Justice) and guided by academic consultants, are inconsistent with the past traditional police practice when they involve task forces, federal prosecutors, use of federal laws and prisons, and the complicity of parole and social services in widening the net of possible violations (Kennedy 1998). They reify the notion that "crime" is equivalent to the visible street crime of the poor and the dispossessed in a few concentrated areas of large cities. In effect, from the view of citizens in disadvantaged areas the cycle of intervention and benign neglect, punctuated by a serious media-amplified incident, adds to their cynicism about social services in general (Venkatesh 2006). As Anderson (1992) most graphically shows, and other research illustrates, the anonymous black male is treated ambivalently, given mixed signals, treated as untrustworthy, and given constant attention in public places, especially those in which races and classes intersect. These places are often designated as "gang areas" since drug dealing draws people from outside, often white (see Jacobs 2000; St. Jean 2007; and Venkatesh 2006), and dealers "hang out" waiting.

These misconceptions lead to pressures for "gang-control laws" that outlaw "loiter-ing" by more than a few people (the numbers that make up a "gang" vary across the country in legal terms), and the application of RICO statutes to gangs that have the semblance, according to police experts, of corporate moneymaking structure and purposes.[10] These laws and their enforcement are, of course, categorical in ap-proach and do not relate to individual behavior and thus increase inequalities when enforced. They violate the difference principle. They are the equivalent in low-level law enforcement to suspension of habeas corpus. The notion behind these laws, that local arrests based on some social consensus about deviance might in the long run reduce the number of young black men in prison, is plausible but untested.

Some of the plausible direct and indirect effects of policing can be at least tentatively set forward. The primary concern of the police, beyond their job se-curity and personal safety and absent media amplification of a few homicides or a serial rapist or killer, is with negotiating and managing the consequences of known nineteenth-century visible street crimes: robbery, assault and battery, open and visible drug dealing, and to a lesser extent burglary and car theft. Since car theft (generally overreported) is covered almost entirely by insurance and is at best an inconvenience for most people, and burglary is virtually written off when no sus-pects are named, police work at the patrol level is about these nineteenth-century crimes and allegations of domestic violence. The importance of homicide and seri-ous sexual assault is acknowledged, and status given to arrests and visible trials, but since most crime is neither reported nor known to the media, the police concern is management of known crime. This implies that the level of known crime is far greater than that directly observed and investigated even on the street and that, as a result, petty criminals are known in disadvantaged areas. Routine offenders know they are known. They comport themselves with respect to this knowledge and are in that sense closer to the police than the average citizen (Young 1991, 189). The most visible, frequently encountered offender can be arrested at almost any time, given outstanding warrants, victims willing to report what was seen, known drug deals to informants known to the police and probate status. Endless accommodations are made in which minor crimes are overlooked, especially those of preferences in an area—public drinking and urinating, smoking marijuana, soliciting for sex, and public battery. Conversely, at any given time, many arrests can be made for miscel-laneous offenses or outstanding warrants (e.g., for child support, unpaid parking fines, contempt of court [failure to appear], and so forth). The balance in an area is constituted daily by compromises among good citizens, offenders, and the police (Pattillo-McCoy 1997; Venkatesh 1997; St. Jean 2007), and more important, perhaps, the order rests on these compromises, not on the police. Good citizens, enablers, as St. Jean calls them, recognize the essential character of crime in such areas. Struc-turally, external sociologic, demographic, and cultural factors create the conditions and opportunities for crime, and the deterrent effects of policing are brief (see the works of Sherman et al. summarized in Weisburd and Braga 2006; St. Jean 2007; and Wright and Decker 1994, 1997). This in turn suggests that the cycle of arrest and sweep may have a temporary impact of some value to those robbed, beaten, or otherwise victimized. In (relatively) efficacious areas, those with high CE according to St. Jean, for example, there is an effect on crime reduction and rates of official crime. Low CE areas are found to have high rates of crime. However, the imaginative research of St. Jean shows that within the high-CE areas, crime nevertheless takes place (he studied the district with one of the highest official rates of crime in the city of Chicago), in places that are most conducive socially to crime—those with social disorder. Interviews with criminals point very clearly to social considerations they find support crime—where they can easily move in and out of the situation; where they can stash goods and have enablers nearby; where people are distracted by noise, other people, and traffic and where there are available customers and or young helpers (I am summarizing across the three types of crime he studied). It is not disorder that causes the crime; it is that it is the context within which criminal behavior is facilitated in the absence of other factors (intervention by citizens, third parties, or police). The place in effect becomes seen as criminogenic (see Weisburd et al. 2007) when in fact the crimes known officially there are a function of behavior; intervention; absence of a concealing context; frequent patrols, sweeps, and interventions; and failure of the conditions of routine grounds of everyday activity (Garfinkel 1964). Officially recognized crime is the exception, not the rule.

CONCLUSION

There is here shown a failed imagery of policing and its functions. This is a double failure. This failure is first a failure to question the commonsense view of policing. This is a story involving good people making discretionary judgments that in turn provide safety and security. This view fails to see that policing deals with failures in social control and is a mechanism for applying force to marginalia. It must be emphasized that policing neither creates order nor restores it—it is in every way a tertiary remedy. The police are the beneficiaries of order, credited with maintaining it, yet they are called upon only when failure of other controls is intolerable to someone somewhere with a telephone ready at hand. The police act and react, but much of what they do is situated, occasioned, and unreviewed. The second failure is that this basic proposition has not enjoyed credibility in current research and writing about the police. The story is told "backwards" on the assumption that absent their work, order would never prevail—this is the "thin-blue-line story." The story is more than a story, of course; it is ultimately a self-serving myth. Thus, more than their crime regulation role is to be examined since it is a superficial gloss on the wide range of social services they provide. This is a cover story that conceals other important questions concerning the function of policing in a democratic society. The police may produce a veneer of order, but they also contribute systematically to chaos.

    The focus of policing is boundary maintenance, and in so doing the police reify the trust problem. By attending to the symbolic boundaries of inner cities, by proactive stops, traffic stops, warrant servings, sweeps, and other policy-driven initiatives termed "operations," they shift attention to the anonymous black man. This underlying yet unacknowledged force is behind crime-control initiatives. The faces of policing, "crime control," and "community policing" are motivated efforts to reduce social distance, on one hand, from the middle class in the form of crime control and deterrence and, on the other hand, from minority populations in disadvantaged areas in the form of community policing. In this way they segregate and divide audiences. As scholars became more aware of the deterioration in the quality of life in inner cities in this most wealthy nation, efforts were made to understand what the consequences of forms of policing are in disadvantaged areas. Sociolegal theorists approached it via sanctioning and legalistic tactics; social scientists gathered large data sets and developed portraits of violence, crime, and disorder in these places; and ethnographers sketched the dynamics of neighborhoods adjacent to the most seriously compromised areas in Chicago. These studies provide insights into the dynamics that lead to public concerns about crime, typically patterns of youth violence, and police operations, crackdowns, and sweeps. These illustrate the outer limits of democratic policing. They are not precisely targeted to individuals but to vague categories such as "gang members," "youth homicide or violence," or "hot spots or crime places," explained by vague motivations attributed by the media such as "senseless crime" or "drugs." These are not evaluated as to effect, or the measures used are indirect and dubious surrogates for the matter studied. They play on the notion of "showing the flag," "deterrence," or "sending a message" on the assumption that short-term criminal sanctioned–based actions will have some lasting effects on crime, disorder, drug use, or gangs. The focus on ORCS, of course, obscures the larger structural conditions of which "crime" is only a small part and modifications of which indicate more about police processing, the métier, than the level of criminal behavior in an area at any given time.

The police métier reviewed in this and the previous chapter is a product of the evolution of policing—its structure, its occupational cultures, its assumptions, and its now affirmed and sanctioned practices. Without question, the claims that crime has been substantially reduced by police actions, highlighted by the self-promotional efforts of those involved in the NYPD's work in the early nineties, have given renewed credibility to the claim to the impossible crime-control mandate beginning in the 1920s. The reform efforts outlined in chapter 7, taken in good faith, have not made measurable changes in policing, but they have been important in casting attention on the traditional practices and the extent to which they can be altered. When the impact of policing on community, setting aside the narrow and misleading arrest-based data (ORCS), is examined, whether it be attitude-based data, observational data or ethnographic studies, the picture is very mixed and would appear to be a function of the sociodemographic composition of the areas in interaction with the policing taking place there. The greatest impact would appear to be in those areas lacking strong organization based on traditional measures of advantage, and the least or perhaps negligible impact is found in the middle-class and advantaged areas of cities and surrounding suburbs. This perhaps more clearly raises the question of what the police are good for since in large part they are most trusted and respected in areas where they are least seen, do little, and are in a service and reactive mode when policing.

Finally, let's return to the six principles that constitute a shorthand for the matter of democratic policing. Policing's attention to civility and civil rights varies by area, time of day, shift, and local traditions of policing. Only recently have round-ups and categorical enforcement become public as a result of raids on factories employing immigrants (e.g. New Bedford, Massachusetts), efforts to question Arab Americans (Thacher 2003), and operations simulating the "pulling levers," net-widening threat, and federal crackdowns. The paramilitary trends noted and studied by Peter Kraska (2001) suggest the growing use of "military" operations and weaponry. While AADP policing is reactive, if not responsive to "demand," the unequal level of coercion applied, shootings, chases, beatings, and the like that are known in disadvantaged areas disproportionately involves African Americans. Thus, policing is not equal in its application of force and coercion across areas. While not discussed in the previous two chapters, the matter of acting within a network of organizational relations is addressed in the following chapter. In this realm, AADP policing is making notable and important progress. The degree of accountability of officers and police organizations varies widely across this country (Walker 2001, 2005).

PART FOUR

The Need for the Illusion of Justice

CHAPTER ELEVEN

Conclusion

The orienting question of this book is: what are the police as an organization good for? What does policing, functioning within a democratic framework of governance, accomplish? These questions were posed in the preface, a signpost on how to read this book. The questions cannot be answered outside a frame of reference, for as Wittgenstein once wrote, the truth of a proposition is a function of the framework within which we consider it. The required framework must account for the nature and character of democratic policing. What are the connections between democracy, democratic governance, and policing? An underling question by which policing should be construed is, what does it contribute to justice and a sense of justice? In some sense, justice is a good that cannot be precisely described or defined. Nevertheless, what criteria might be applied to assess policing in a democracy? In a general way, they are expected to support justice, enforce the law equally, and be guided by concerns for justice. It has been argued that the most fitting criteria must lie with political philosophy and the ethical side of that concern. In many respects the concept of justice is an illusion, a necessary illusion, since while it is a common belief, the experience of justice within the institutional system is uneven, disproportionately experienced, and evaluated negatively. It is, nevertheless, a necessary illusion. The core question is how justice is done or not. In some sense, it is necessary to deconstruct the illusion of justice to reveal its necessity. To draw on Durkheim and Mauss, policing is a form of magic in which the magician believes in the efficacy of what is being done in the name of justice.

The work of John Rawls, namely, his classic statement of political philosophy, *A Theory of Justice* (1970), contains a notion about the mutual trust of citizens as essential to democracy and that this sense is enhanced by instances of mutual trust. The assumptive criteria for justice are the first principle concerning equality and the second or difference principle that specifies that whatever should be done by policy should benefit the less advantaged. The police are an agency that distributes and redistributes social goods on behalf of the collectivity. This is in some sense their core function. Policy need not be a written and enforcement contract like statement. Given that police everyday act and shape life chances, they make policy (Gusfield 1975). As an institution, they shadow the citizenry literally and metaphorically. Using the Rawls position, I suggest that policing should not in their practices increase inequalities. Their ability to improve life is restricted to doing little harm. The police have indirect symbolic effects by what they are seen to do and expected to do; they have direct effects through their practices of surveillance, tracking, arresting, and serving the public, and these expectations and practices are reflexive and circular. That is, the actions of police are seen as examples of policing generally. Police believe they are acting on behalf of the whole. The features of democratic policing reflect the general consensus about what and why policing does what it does. A definition set out in chapter 2 and elaborated in chapter 3 is seen within the historical constraints outlined in chapter 3.

The study of policing arose in part because of the apparent failure of police to police fairly, and in part as a response to the more visible protests and challenges to law. The triangle of academics, government, and practicing police top command shaped and still does shape what is taken to be relevant and important research. This is research that is funded. The efforts to reform policing have failed. My point about the absence of reform and the absence of a theory of policing is not to blame the police for their wish to reform, to "professionalize," to be more scientific and respected.

The symbolic aspects of policing are largely ignored by scholars who focus on their instrumental and self-serving presentations of the mandate. In *Police Work* (1977) and later in *Policing Contingencies* (2003), I argued that policing is above all about the aesthetic and politics of appearances. The crime-control thesis advanced of late is inconsistent with evidence of direct police effect. *Variations in crime control are a function of many societal factors out of the control of the police, but the strongest evidence shows that police activity is the most important determinant of official recorded crime statistics.* One might pun and say that policing is risky, in that it takes on the burdens of others' risks on behalf of the collective. But the most important point is not that police work is dangerous or risky but rather that it is seen as a mode of order management and, as Black (1983) has reminded us, a means for conflict resolution. Consider the risky work of policing; the sacred aspect of this work; the close connection in policing between feelings, symbolization, and action; their axial role in generating reciprocity; and the violence associated with the role. These are invisible matters, that which is out of sight. It might be useful to think of the police in sequential terms. Police are risk assessors and stand in the breach between chaos and order, the sacred and the profane. While they are seen as "sacred," this is relative and compromised by many of their other features and practices that must of necessity remain backstage and out of sight. These are the practices that enable front-stage work and teamwork to go forward with the public (Goffman 1956). The police are feelings oriented in spite of their protestations— they enact poetic and aesthetic actions (Wender 2008). They enact tactical poetry.

That is, police play on the concatenation of feelings that are associated with their durable appearance; these emotions and sentiments are powerful and useful vehicles for the arousal of collective and individual sentiments such as trust, loyalty, excitement, fear, and the rest. The actions of police are not forgotten—they are memorialized, celebrated, recreated, reshaped, and brought to memory again and again in formal public ceremonies amplified by the media. In a sense, then, the police are accountable about what they do and to the public at large. Police are imagined as part of the collective memory of a society. While it is perhaps more central to collective memory in a more tightly integrated society such as England, and less so in a loosely articulated society such as the United States (Loader 1997), it remains a reliable indication of how a society looks after the well-being of its citizens. As memorable and as totems of broader order, the police are thematic of the habitual response to authority and are both interdicted and prohibited from proximity, that is, they are limited in their access to private places, conversations, and groups, as well as needed and sought out. The seeking and the finding are reciprocity based, and in this sense, policing is a form of reciprocated exchange that tends to be asymmetrical (Alpert and Dunham 2004), that is, police give more than they receive, they resist provocation, and the response of the other cannot always be anticipated. Yet a gift by police, in this sense tolerance and patience in the face of uncertainty, creates an obligation to reciprocate (Mauss 1990). However, it is a problematic pattern of exchange and reciprocity because the gift is invisible. As a social form, policing is tied to violence, and this is yet another indication of its symbolic power (Loader 1997, quoting Bourdieu 1977). Its powers arise in part because people fail to recognize the damage done to equality—they sustain what Bourdieu (1977) calls "institutional misrecognition." This is why their collective orientation is always ambivalent and why their mandate is always a contested one in a democracy. Police chew up the enemies of society. Police render and are the recipients of violence routinely, are killed in the line of duty, and are honored as a result. The honoring means they must be set apart, sacred in this context. The police as a uniformed paid, named force stand apart from everyday life, and they act with the power of collective sentiment as well as their own considerable firepower.

The role of policing, unfortunately, is ill-described in the basic works on democracy written by political scientists; the police act as background to the foreground of features of democracy such as voting, wide citizen participation, representative government, and so on. On the other hand, few social scientists have explored the role of democracy in policing and their interaction. The versions of the relationship between democracy and policing are variable in their focus. There are, however, at least seven versions of the relationship between policing and democracy reviewed in chapter 1. Unfortunately, in these detailed considerations there is no well-shaped definition of police. The historian Liang (1992) provides one building block in the pursuit of an outline of democratic practices. He argues for a legalistically guided police, one that does not damage civility, eschews torture and antiterrorism, and focuses on individual crimes, not categories of threats. Some five ways of defining police—historical, analytical, typological, contextual, and textbook versions—

exist. The most sophisticated and general approach and durable definition is that of Egon Bittner, whose ideas have shadowed and shaped ideas about policing since the publication of his *Functions of the Police.* The tensions in his definition arise from his devotion to a phenomenology of practice to the exclusion of the organizational nexus or institutional structures. "Policing" is an interactional process as well as an institution, and these two matters are often confused. He raises the question about what the police are good for and answers it by arguing they apply force as needed situationally. While this is a functional answer, the rise in education and reduced level of violence, as well as the shift in the nature of crime toward crimes of trust and away from crimes of violence, suggest policing may well become more a tracking and surveillance system and less a violence-applying device.

Nevertheless, the foundational definitions of police and policing remain debated in the field and subject to a number of efforts. While the work of Bittner is generally taken as primary as a basis for a definition of policing, the implications of his phenomenological and practice-based definition have not been grasped, and it is linked to broad, undefined ideas such as effectiveness and order, or left as in textbooks as a commonsense concept obvious in its character and implications. The police are in one sense a mode of applying coercion and are defined by practices as well as organizational features. Democratic policing developed as society differentiated and the economy grew. It is an extension of the state. To describe, compare, and contrast democratic policing, it is useful to set out *dimensions* along which they can be compared. There are some nine: the modes of emergence of central authority; the degree of democracy in the system; the extent of collective orientation; citizen perception of the organization; as fair and trustworthy and as a mixture of sacred and profane attributes; manifesting various degrees of centralization; imagined differently; in competition with other agencies; and possessing a valid mandate. Their functions tend to include both high politics of national security and low or domestic politics of crime and crime prevention.

Policing as a function should be guided by some working tenets or principles. These are derived from Rawls and reflect his concerns as well as the more concrete version of democratic policing advanced by Liang. These are rules of thumb that can guide evaluation and judgment of police functioning: procedurally fair and constrained in dealing with citizens; primarily reactive to citizen complaints and concerns; equal in application of coercion to populations defined spatially and temporally; fair in firing, hiring, and evaluation; in an acknowledged competitive environment; and are accountable. Here I have focused primarily on the first four as they are preeminent. The information on "fairness" within police departments is insufficient to make a judgment. The domain of control of local police is shrinking in the sense that they are becoming more competitive with citizens, federal and state agencies, and private police.

Policing is a broad function only part of which is carried out in democratic societies by the public police. Police then must include varieties of organizations, and the policing they do must be considered in reference to their practices. What is called the institution of police is composed of a set of practices, routines, recipe knowledge, and applied coercion. As I once wrote, *policing* is situationally justi-fied action. Its mandate defines the outer limits of acceptable practice. I define the police as follows: organizations in Anglo-American societies, constituted of many diverse agencies, that are authoritatively coordinated legitimate organizations with ideological grounding that stand ready to apply force up to and including fatal force in somewhat-specified political territories to sustain politically defined order and ordering via tracking, surveillance, and arrest. As such, they require compliance to request and command from lower personnel and fellow citizens. The several com-ponents of this definition are elaborated and explored in chapter 3.

The elaborations of the core definition deal with the fringe meanings that are a part of the core definition. Democratic policing is accountable, but largely in police terms; citizen demand exclusively cannot be the guiding rationale for policing; police play a symbolic role in society, whatever else they do; police are violent in a constrained and measure fashion; they are guardians of an increasingly blurred set of boundaries, nuances, and rules; they manage order but do not produce it; they are a "neutral" political force with an edge; loyalty of the police organization to the state is always problematic, and compliance is a negotiated matter; the loyalty of the force is assumed and rarely tested in democratic societies; policing is dangerous and honored for its production of collective goods, and police are being pushed toward surveillance, tracking, monitoring, and intelligence-lead activities in spite of their considered resistance.

These definitions and principles allow an examining of the police as an object of study. The field of police studies, emerging in the 1960s, created an object for due consideration: a *paradigm:*

- Imagining police duties as a function of statistical data
- Accepting uncritically data produced largely by the police for their own uses
- Assuming *only* positive consequences of policing
- Taking the police views of measurable and conventional viewpoints on such matters as crime, disorder, and service as valid
- Picturing policing from the top-down, the command version of police public rhetoric concerning the nature of their work, its problems, and practices

The result of accepting this paradigm is a conventional view of policing that is atheoretical and dominated by pragmatic concerns for what works. It is a shadow of the conventional wisdom that police talk about and believe, but it is not analyti-cally and theoretically derived or shaped. Furthermore, the field of police studies is technique driven and theorizing reduced to a few trivial citations at the opening paragraph of the article.

The institutional outlines of American policing, a variety of policing, are outlined in chapter 5. They are largely local, minimally federal, and dominated by local concerns. It is a locally funded and governed social service.

The absence of serious theory of policing has left a gap in academic thinking. Primary efforts to theorize policing are captured by the notion of broken-windows policing and its corollaries. It is, of course, at base simply a rationalizing of standard police practice. Reform efforts over the past thirty years, community policing, problem-solving policing, hot-spot policing, and crime analysis and crime mapping have had modest effects at best in part because the ideas are minor variations on current practices and have not altered the basic mandate, strategies, or tactics of policing. The deployment of resources—time, effort, personnel, and matériel—has remained relatively stable. This returns our attention to the difference principle and its relevance to assessing policing.

Police research in the paradigm reflects an acceptance as valid and reliable the police métier, or ways of doing things routinely. It is a *circular, reflective set of practices that are self-serving.* This métier flows from several sources. These include the social structure of the police organization; the interpersonal tactics of policing on the ground (asserting authority, taking control, making arrests, and returning to service quickly); the repetitive modes of deploying resources (by beats, districts, and other territorially based obligations) that grounds order in places rather than in categories of crime, law or morality (e.g., Internet crime, crimes of trust, pornography, abuse of authority); and the rewarded activities, based on assumptions about how the social world works, as well as what are the necessary practices to cope with this world. These generally revolve around stops, arrests, and other visible interventions in areas known as full of the potential for same and the funding and publication patterns that sustain the viability if this model in government, foundations, and academic life. This métier omits consideration of the wide range of effects of policing on those policed, the feedback loops that are sustained by these practices, and the effects of such policing on trust and police legitimacy. It envisions only the need to control, deter, and punish the visible and known contestants. While the valued outputs are called crime statistics, these are merely dramaturgical high points in an ongoing drama of control. Showing a decline in arrests does not mean crime otherwise measured has declined, but, more important, declines in ORCS are largely independent of other changes in the quality of life in cities.

The consequences of policing, then, are seen through the lens provided by this set of assumptions and practices called a métier. They are direct and indirect and redound not only to the citizens but to the police themselves. The most obvious efforts at crime control—crackdowns, sweeps, "operations"—are themselves seen only in a positive light, whereas the negative and other unanticipated consequences are not measured or publicly announced. While the direct effects of such policing are not known, the indirect effects on trust and legitimacy, especially among minority populations, are well known. The extent to which the police métier and their practices violates the difference principle remains to be closely measured and monitored with data other than the officially record crime statistics.

In *Justice as Fairness,* Rawls argues that the original position and the difference principle rest on the notion that inequalities within basic or "background institutions" should secure the basic equal liberties. The police are one of these background institutions and thus should be subject to reflection with reference to their performance in this regard. Each of the efforts at police reform (chapter 7) rests on the notion that crime control produces greater freedom and movement as well as increasing perception of the legitimacy of the police. In many respects, the "positive" consequences of crime control of all kinds, indicated by reduction in the official figures, is assumed to be a good, although this might be a jump in logic, and its negatives rarely explored. It fits with the notion of circular police practice and the métier. Not only is this an unexamined premise, but it is clear that crime has many positive economic and social consequences. Crime control is a *big* global industry (Christie 2000). On the other hand, the lack of reflection upon the consequences of crime control for inequalities means that the requirements of reflecting on the nature of justice and the illusion of justice are not being met.

A Motion to Reconsider the "Police" Signifier

Michael W. Raphael[1]

In a society where federal intelligence and law enforcement institutions like the CIA, FBI, IRS, ATF, and DEA have personnel designated as "agents" signifying persons as representatives of a particular organization where a slew of semiotic relations are attached (i.e., certain authority and powers), the designation of "police officer" has not been questioned. Given its historical etymology, the signifier of "police" has been taken for granted with its signifier, where its slew of semiotic relations provides several troubling connotating implications.

THE HISTORICAL ETYMOLOGY
OF THE "POLICE" SIGNIFIER

The term *police* is derived from the Latin term *politia,* meaning "civic administration," which itself developed from the ancient Greek πόλις, or *polis,* traditionally meaning "city-state" with reference to classical Athens. The semiotic reapplication from meaning "civic administration" to "administration of public order" allegedly occurred in 1716 from the French. The first force so-named in England was the Marine Police, set up in 1798 to protect merchandise at the Port of London.[2]

THE CAUTIOUSLY TROUBLING IMPLICATIONS

The first four letters in the *police* signifier, *poli,* may be perceived as a prefix associated with the terms *policy, political, politician, politicize, politic, politics,* and *polity* that all historically refer to "civic administration,"[3] which suggests that the departure to "administration of public order" seems faulty to maintain in contemporary American society given the fundamental structure of our government. As any criminal knows or should have figured out, the government is split into three branches, the branch that writes the law to be broken, the branch that catches the alleged violator, and the branch that judges whether one actually is a violator. These branches are also known as the legislative, executive, and judiciary. All eight listed terms with the perceived prefix *poli,* except *police,* have maintained strong semiotic relations, or stayed closely associated with, what is signified by "civic administration" and the legislative branch of American government. Leaving the signifier of *police* in with the rest of the aforementioned lot suggestively signifies that police are the pawns of politics and that the contemporary conventional associations connected to politics—inefficiency, corruption, and the like—apply. While some historical cases in terms of those associations come to mind, the idea that the police are pawns of politics is historically incorrect. In reality, it is actually the military that is the pawn of politics, and according to the Posse Comitatus Act, the military is prohibited from acting in a law enforcement capacity within the United States, except where expressly authorized by the Constitution or Congress except for the Coast Guard during peacetime.[4] Such historical concepts suggest that there can be only one pawn of politics and that the police cannot be that one.

Furthermore, given the term *civic,* more semiotic issues arise. Historical common law separates that which is civil from what is deemed criminal. Violations of civil law are referred to as torts, where a tort is any act that interrupts private order, while violations of criminal law are referred to as crimes, where a crime is any act that interrupts the public order. This classification is important since what work is typically done by those acting under the disputed signifier has relatively little to do with torts and a great deal to do with attempting to reduce crime and to maintain social homeostasis. The status of being "civic" also implicates being polite, upon which one deduces a full circle back to the *poli* prefix.

THE RESOLUTION OF THE CAUTIOUSLY TROUBLING IMPLICATIONS

While it would be easier to continue to refer to police as "police," it was John F. Kennedy who stated "we choose to do things … not because they are easy, but because they are hard, because that goal will serve to organize and measure the best of our energies and skills, because that challenge is one that we are willing to accept, one we are unwilling to postpone."[5] With this aforementioned argument, it is theoretically negligent to continue such significations. Thus, one must declare, by the power vested in the historically developed nature of semiotics and the English language, that from this day forward, "police" and its officers shall be referred to as agencies and agents, respectively, because they are agents of the people and their authority derives from the consent of the people governed and nowhere else. What they do derives not from civic administration or from the city-state as an institution but from, in theory, the people as a collective body consenting them the right, the agency, to patrol, to enforce, and to maintain order within society!

A Submotion on the Implications of the "Policing" Signifier

Once the word *police* is deleted from one's lexicon, *policing* must go as well. This provides the opportunity for the necessary resignification of its signified with a new signifier! Yet what can the signifier be? In order to deduce such, it must be known what the people's agents' primary responsibilities are. Ironically, despite the police's motto, "Protect and serve," the Supreme Court of the United States has ruled countless times since 1856 that law enforcement officers have no duty to protect any individual; it is their duty to enforce the law in general.[6] Thus, the main notion is given stronger ground in terms of the distinction between civil and criminal law. Furthermore, it is the tradition of common law that any citizen may participate in that maintenance of common order by means of filing a civil suit, whereas only an agent of the people may initiate criminal proceedings, thus widening the gap from "policing" being of a "civil" nature, for, based on the aforementioned premise, "civil" connotes that any citizen should have the capacity to do something that is contradictory. But no citizen, while having the legitimate capacity to make a citizen's arrest, enjoys the same legal protections as sworn officers. Additionally, any attempt to act in lieu of such an officer where an act has been solely reserved to sworn officers may constitute an act of vigilantism; even with good intentions, such acts have an ironic tendency toward disorder and the undermining and questioning of legitimate authority. Thus, for the sake of order, one must reconsider what an agent's duties are and how its signification is constructed, especially since there is no duty to protect any individual but a duty to maintain what is perceived as order in contemporary American society. Given the consideration of reported crime statistics, regardless of the margin of error, the agents certainly do not maintain order, although they do attempt to patrol order.

So, in actuality, to "police" or to take part in "policing" is to patrol order. To patrol order is to attempt to maintain order, where "order" is broadly understood to be a harmonious state of affairs. For the sake of this argument, a "crime" is any act that disrupts the harmonious state. In any capitalist democratic society, it is practically impossible for order to be maintained, since any single criminal act automatically disrupts harmony because in such a context crime will occur regardless, whether out of livable necessity or sociopolitical economic discourse. Given that crime is normal, as posited above and by Durkheim, such a harmonious state of affairs cannot be maintained but only patrolled. (The question of a disrupted harmonious state actually being harmonious given that crime is normal is a question for a different discussion.) Only by patrol can officers recognize that laws have yet to be generally enforced. Only upon such recognition can officers generally enforce the law and fulfill their duty as described by the U.S. Supreme Court.

Since what is patrolled is now more transparent, the significance of the term *patrol* and its various forms can be examined. To "patrol" empirically suggests what can be seen as three separate acts that merge into the one act that constitutes patrolling. Separately, these acts are observation, the gathering of information, and reaction. Together, officers observe, gather information from such observation (where "observation" and "gathering information" can suggest a wide array of methods, from conducting interviews to watching a street corner), and react to such observed information. Such reactions can entail anything from making an arrest to writing a traffic ticket. So how does one spell *patrol*? It's not with a *p* but by *observing informational gathering reactions! Patrol!*

CONSIDERATIONS OF FUTURE SIGNIFICANCE

Given that police do not "police" or conduct what is etymologically implied by "policing," civil administration, it seems negligent to continue the use of such a label. Although "agent," as previously suggested, seems to have a strong argument for becoming the new label, it is understandable that it might be desirable to avoid such federal implications, so consider alternate descriptively encompassing labels. Despite the fact that the label "patrol officer" is already used to describe a subset of officers, why not broaden its use? If not, then what?

Given Robert's Rules of Order, a motion to reconsider a previous question can only be made, and seconded, by a member on the prevailing side; considering the widespread use of both labels, society is the prevailing side. So here and now, before you, is a written motion to reconsider the previous question of the labels "police" and "policing." With such a motion on the floor, the issue of the replacing label is a separate question and should not have any merit on the present motion! While one could move to divide the question into a vote on each label individually, both labels are semiotically dependent on the other, and it is not advisable, especially since the chair is now asking society, "Is there any second?"

If such a motion were to pass, the next logical question to arrive on the floor would be one of the replacing label. After several written questions were presented and apparently rejected on this issue, one must wonder, "What motion would you second?"

Notes

NOTES FOR PREFACE

1. The central argument is elaborated and refined in *Political Liberalism* (1993), *Collected Papers* (1999), and *Law of Peoples* (1999).

2. The viability of rational choice theories and the even more bizarre adherence to the notion of deterrence via punishment seems quaint in an age of empirical social science (see Green and Shapiro 1994).

3. Whether they are or might be decreased is an entirely other matter. This position does not constrain the options that are usually covered by the vague term *discretion* as applied to everyday policing.

NOTES FOR CHAPTER 1

1. Professor Bayley took part in the implementation process following the acceptance of the "Patten Report" on the reform of policing in Northern Ireland.

2. This proliferation of policing has produced some reflective documents in regard to fostering democracy via policing abroad (Independent Commission for the Study of Policing in Northern Ireland [called the Patten Commission]) Patten 1999; Bayley 2001, 2005; Mayall 1996; Marenin, ed. 1995. The number and kinds of such policing ventures, policing as an export commodity (Brogden and P. Nijhar 2005), are vast and growing (see Haberfeld and Cerrah 2007). A critique of such ventures is outside the scope of this book.

3. I am not sure how equity is connected to efficiency, since police can be very efficient in serving a small coterie of the privileged or restrict work only to disadvantaged areas, delivering service very well to these targeted areas.

4. This was a written version of Shearing's verbal response and comment upon several of the papers given a conference at Eastern Kentucky University.

5. The difficulty in such a formulation, of course, is that the varying standards and lifestyles of a complex society will inevitably bring the forces of formal control against some and not others. This is why the police are expected to show judgment and constraint and be limited in their actions.

6. The inscrutability of the police is inconsistent with the claims of some that police should be transparent in their decisions (Newburn, Jones, and Smith 1996) and be able and willing to explain their decisions in public forums if necessary. This is a feature of the Patten Report (Mulcahy 2006, 155).

7. The concept of "high policing" has an interesting history. When working in London, I read Brian Chapman's book *The Police State* (1970) and found the term *high policing* a useful contrast to everyday low policing. The idea of the police state, Chapman argues, arose from a concern with the general welfare of the people, their entire thoughts, actions, and intentions, and that in totalitarian states it becomes an even more pervasive focus, with imagined wrongs, attributed stereotypes, and surveillance. Jean-Paul Brodeur published an article in *Social Problems* in 1983 that cited Chapman and me. Since that time the concept has been primarily associated with Brodeur, and citations refer almost exclusively to his work. He has published extensively on the idea, clarified its nuances, summarized historical sources of the idea in French thought and political practice, and illuminated the scholarly debate on the limits and scope of policing.

8. Some of these ideas are reworked from Manning 2003, 35–38, and an introduction I wrote to interviews with Professor Bittner carried out in 1999 by Jean-Paul Brodeur (cited as Brodeur 2007).

9. Bittner's primary data and examples are drawn from field studies of patrol officers regulating mental illness, the homeless, and drunkenness in large cities. He was a student of Harold Garfinkel at UCLA in the sixties.

10. I am indebted to Anne Rawls's formulation of these matters in Garfinkel's *Seeing Sociologically* (2005).

11. Michael Buerger's (1994) discussion of RECAP, an effort of a special unit within the Minneapolis Police Department to reduce repeat calls, describes a morass of frustration, inefficacy, bureaucratic nightmares, and consistent failure in part because the officers' skills, their core competence, bore no or little resemblance to what was needed to carry out the mission.

12. Other, somewhat peripheral, definitions are not dealt with here. They are less significant in this context because they are ideologically tinged; assume a few selective desirable functions, such as the alleged central or core role of the police as "peacekeeping," "exercising discretion," and "law enforcement"; and collapse complexity into simplicity. These labels confuse the means with the ends and implicitly connect matters that vary.

NOTES FOR CHAPTER 2

1. Exceptions to this generalization are the Christopher Commission (1992) that examined the Los Angeles riots and the Patten Commission on policing in Northern Ireland (1999). Previously, a series of commissions and judicial reports on policing in Northern Ireland, with one exception, the report of Lord Scarman (1972), concluded that police were acting properly and within the limits of their mandate. See also Philip Stenning's virtuoso chapter (2008) on the dubious political independence of the police in Canada and Brodeur and Viau (1994) on the Oka incident (a confrontation between the Sureté of Quebec, the Canadian military, and Mohawk tribal people near Montreal). The broader issues are taken up also in Beare and Murray 2007.

2. One of the most important scholars of police and democracy, David Bayley, credits Bruce (1949) and Raymond Fosdick (1915, 1920) with publishing the most insightful and consistent scholarship prior to the emergence of police studies as a discipline (see chapters 3 and 4 of this book). I would now add, as discussed above, Stanley Palmer's brilliant and enormously detailed consideration (1988) of the parallel developments in policing in Ireland and England between 1780 and 1850. A most important exposition and research-based work is Weitzer's study of policing (1996) in Northern Ireland (through 1990) that explores the edges of democratic policing. This "quasi-democratic" policing is discussed below. Marenin, in an important review article (1985), points out that the links among the state, democracy, and policing have not been well explored. This is still true, unfortunately.

3. Brogden (1987), in an original and important paper, has argued that the idea of policing called the Peel model originated in the eighteenth century to control colonials in Ireland and India and was then "exported back" to Great Britain.

4. Arendt distinguishes violence as a social instrumental action and force that she reserves for natural or physical actions—the release of energy called "accidents." She furthermore rejects the notion

that events can be predicted, arguing, in a point with which I profoundly agree, that events are known and labeled after they emerge from the stream of actions and interactions. The act of labeling them makes them events, and as such they cannot be "predicted" in advance.

5. The classic case for the dilemma of non-market-oriented organizations in a high capitalistic economy is outlined by (1967) in the form of an incisive set of propositions about organizational behavior. However, see Loader and Walker's incisive critique (2007, 146–51). With affluence, as the rise of private policing and war making suggests, changes in technology that expand the range of cheap goods to be sold collectively, thus changing demand, and the changing nature of property rights may make such justifications of security more tenuous than presently is the case.

6. In this regard, see the fascinating focus-group materials presented by Mulcahy (2003) and Innes (2003).

7. In each of the past three books I have included a long section on the sacred nature attributed to horses, dogs, robots, and other employed beasts. This section has been abandoned again in the current work.

NOTES FOR CHAPTER 3

1. Here I am referring to the scale that is used to train police officers in the use of force; it suggests a logical escalation based on the citizen's behavior. It rationalizes "self-defense," "threat," and "weapon" and leaves the definition of these to the officer.

2. This is a very subtle and important point made by Loader and Walker drawing on Bourdieu.

3. This proposition is discussed by Loader and Walker (2007, 99) as essential to the legitimacy of the state. Their position is a philosophical jurisprudential one, not a claim to empirical fact.

4. I have discussed this transition in a chapter on Nazi policing in "Aspects of Non-Democratic Policing" (Manning 2009).

NOTES FOR CHAPTER 4

1. An interesting figure in this regard is August Vollmer, who bridged academic and police life and created two quite notable careers (Vollmer 1936; Carte and Carte 1975). Vollmer's aim was to introduce science, technology, and careful and trained investigators in policing and thus bring public respect to policing. He aimed to make the occupation a respected profession. He was a successful academic entrepreneur, having a role in the creation of the School of Criminology at the University of California, Berkeley, and serving as chief of police in several cities. His protégé, O. W. Wilson, was the author of the first systemic book on what was then termed *police administration* (1950). Herman Goldstein, also one of the pioneer reformers, worked for Wilson in Chicago. The tradition of reform and social policy concerns remains a powerful influence in police studies.

2. Sklansky (2007) has argued that these events also reshaped sociolegal thinking and criminal law.

3. The revelations in May and June 2004 in Iraq, which reported torture of "detainees" by U.S. military police, private agents of the CIA, and the U.S. government, speak to the essential exclusion of torture, terrorism, and antiterrorism from democratic policing. They certainly demonstrate the consequences of the United States' rejection of the relevance of international treaties and law, including the Geneva Convention, and the wisdom of these conventions and treaties. The torture of prisoners (not of war) also speaks to blurring of the lines between "policing," "war," "anti-" or "counterterrorism," and "peacekeeping" by U.S. actions since 2003 in the Middle East. Later evidence established that this policy of torture that violated international law and conventions was supported and developed by the Bush administration including the secretary of defense and the vice president and their staff lawyers (Mayer 2008).

4. Cynthia Lum has suggested (personal communication, July 6, 2004) that it could be argued that "democratic policing" is policing within democratic nations, and that police research is research in democratic societies rather than research on democratic policing.

5. Brodeur's forthcoming book on policing correctly argues that the French version of policing is a complementary and parallel version of democratic policing (see also Emsley 1996). The notion of high policing is sourced in France, as the English resisted the notion of a secret police from the beginning (Radzinowicz 1968). On the other hand, as Brodeur (1983) points out, the actuality of secret and high police focused on national security has always been an essential feature of democratic policing.

6. Cannadine (2001) argues that British imperialism as high art and drama evolved most dramatically in countries with dominant non-Western populations. Conversely, democratic policing as a form emerged in the UK and subsequently in Canada, the United States, New Zealand, and Australia. These countries were settled by Anglo-Saxon peoples; the indigenous peoples were either massacred, placed in reservations through violence, or were nonexistent. In the British Empire outside these countries, three-tiered policing evolved with an indigenous local police, an armed constabulary for riotous conditions, and the army as a sustaining reserve force. The most important exception is the development in Ireland of the RUC as an occupying force and the high-policing continental style, fragments of which remain on the island (Brogden 1987; Mulcahy 2006; Ellison and Smyth 2000). It appears that both forces on the island, the Police Services of Northern Ireland and the Garda of the Republic of Ireland, have been so shaped by the British colonial occupation, the 1916 Easter revolution, and subsequent division as well as the more recent "troubles" that a kind of quasi-martial law has been a governing principle of security (Brewer et al. 1988).

7. The study of the impact of ethnicity ("race"), gender, and sexuality (gender identity) within the police organization has just begun to emerge in the past ten years. I do not review these studies here because I am not clear about how they bear on a general theory of democratic policing. The work of Holdaway (1996) and selected chapters in *The Oxford Handbook of Criminology* (Maguire, Morgan, and Reiner 2007) (e.g., by Heidensohn, Phillips, and Bowling and Gelsthorpe) and in the *Handbook of Policing* (Newburn 2003) (e.g., by Foster, Bowling, and Phillips and by Heidensohn) are relevant. Other than the Heidensohn chapters, none bears on the questions directly.

8. Jack Preiss was head of my Ph.D. committee at Duke University in the mid-1960s.

9. I include Punch's book on policing in Amsterdam in part because it shaped his oft-cited work on Anglo-American policing, including *Conduct Unbecoming* (1985).

10. Reiner has continued to revise his textbook, which is now in its third edition (2000).

11. The term *police* refers to the occupational and organizational features of this type, while *policing* refers to the practices, craftsmanship, and behaviors of those policing. See also the epilogue.

12. With apologies to my colleagues, I include only important exemplary sources, not their entire long and distinguished list of publications.

13. While rarely funding police research now, the NSF funded the ambitious work of Sykes, Brent, and Clark, published as Sykes and Brent (1983) and David Bayley's work (1985), while the NIMH sponsored and published Bittner's brilliant exposition (1972) on the functions of police in modern society.

14. In 1971, Michael Banton came to Michigan State, invited by Louis Radelet, for a several-day visit and a series of lectures and seminars. I met him and was further motivated to take my sabbatical in England. Later, in 1971, Stephen Brooks visited MSU from the "Met" on a bursarship and later sponsored me to a subdivision in the Met where I carried out the fieldwork in 1973 that led to *Police Work* ([1977] 1997*).*

15. I am much indebted to Tim Newburn's overviews (2003) of these matters in the UK and his impressive, detailed description of the intermingling of events, crime, and governmental policy toward the police since the late 1980s.

16. Taking this perspective, one can reflect on policing in the two countries. While its role has been reshaped, English policing remains a powerful icon representing to many people one of the best features of English society. This is not and could not be said of American policing, who are the police we deserve. Newburn, in ongoing research, has addressed the extent to which American politics has

led to an uncritical adaptation of "American policies," such as "three strikes" legislation, zero-tolerance policing, and "broken windows" community policing in the UK.

17. Here I include claims that the efforts of the NYPD through "smart management" drove down crime, that it is the best police force in the world, that "broken windows" is something of a theory (it is not), and that through the cooperation of Kelling and Bratton, practitioners now know how to best run a police department (Kelling and Corbett 2003). I also include claims about the generality of the assertions made in the "broken windows" essay. For important critiques of these points, see Harcourt 2001 and 2000. These matters are treated in more detail in chapter 6.

18. I include the use of the military as police postinvasions, the connections between "nation building" and policing, the "commodification" of "policing" as an export product, and problems associated with building a state-based police when it has not existed or has existed in a very weak form (see Singer 2003).

19. This narrowness during the Bush administration was part of American foreign policy, an aspect of what might be called the worldwide explosion of American power in many countries. It is both a commodity that is exported and established by military and economic power and a concept that has legitimated the development of nation-state policing (Bayley 2006).

20. At this point in the original journal article, "The Study of Policing" (2004), I discussed funding sources and their influence. This is omitted because my aim is to describe the relevance of the academic research to the matter of democratic policing.

21. Exceptions are the works of Sam Souryal (2003), Hickman, Piquero, and Greene (2004), and John Kleinig.

22. This argument, that policing was a concatenation of practices glossed by the rhetoric of management, was first proposed in *Police Work* (1977), chapter 8. In that chapter, the argument was couched in a critique of game-theoretical metaphors and following the brilliant analysis of Goffman (1970). See also Manning 2008.

23. This trend toward paramilitary domestic policing was first noticed in Great Britain in the late 1980s by Jefferson (1990). This tendency toward heavily armed teams, specialized units with high-powered automatic and semiautomatic weapons, armor, rapid transportation, and a variety of nonfatal weapons, has grown in the UK as well (Waddington 1991).

24. Clearly, there are other political positions at work in police studies. The most striking fact, however, is the absence of any stated value position combined with an implicit approval of police actions.

NOTES FOR CHAPTER 5

1. I have summarized these matters elsewhere (Manning 2003, 43–58).

2. Calls from cellular or mobile phones, because they do not produce an address shown on the 911 system, must be handled separately. I assume these calls will soon be classified in police departments on the basis of their origin using a GPS grid and satellite positioning.

3. For example, the Boston Police Department's computer system reallocates calls to an automatic answering system when a single city block of origin of the calls is the source of an overload. This happens in the event of a fire, gunshots, a loud multicar accident, or a power outage. These all attract attention and concern, and many people call the police about the same incident or sound.

4. The Office of Homeland Security was created in 2001, but the department was not formed and staffed until 2002. See Wikipedia.

5. In Boston and Cambridge, Massachusetts, for example, there are some four types of municipal police (housing, parks, municipal, and transportation system police called MBTA); at least seven university campus police forces; the Boston Police Department; state police; two county police departments (Middlesex and Suffolk), who do not regularly patrol but are present; and an unknown number of private security companies.

6. Unanswered by such research is the question of where this loyalty might lie in the case of a disaster, a coup d'état, or a civil war or internal rebellion that was not based on color. As is the case in Anglo-American societies other than the United Kingdom, neither an icon such as the Crown stands

as an object of loyalty nor the French or German idea that "race" or "blood" and state are sources of loyalty is present in the United States. This is being tested presently as immigration laws are reconsidered and immigration is being redefined and demonized.

7. Structural features affect the ratio of public to private police (de Waard 1999; Jones and Newburn 1998; Button 2002). It is likely that centralized state authority and the traditional acceptance of high policing in civil law countries reduce the growth of nonpublic policing.

8. This position is echoed in the most significant study of U.S. intelligence by Roberta Wohlstetter (1962). She examined the evidence of intelligence failure prior to and during the Japanese attack on Pearl Harbor in December 1941, using the thirty-nine volumes of congressional hearings on the matter.

9. These ideas are Patrick Healy's. We discussed them in Oxford in 1985–1986 and intended to publish a joint paper on regulation that was never realized.

Notes for Chapter 6

1. CE at best can be seen as the converse of the notion of disorganization, the capacity of a community to realize its values (Sampson et al. 1997, 2005). It has not been clearly defined and measured and remains an appealing but contested concept. The studies that show correlations between CE and policing are cross-sectional (e.g., Velez 2001) are based on attitudes, not performance or study of police practices bearing on CE.

2. Neither Wilson nor Kelling claimed that they were proposing a theory or presenting an empirically based research study (Sousa and Kelling 2006). They sought a policy change based on their political preferences. Later, when faced with researchers' questions, Sousa and Kelling (2006) presented a plausible set of relationships that might be entailed by such a formulation (see also the careful commentary in Eterno and Silverman 2006). The conceptual issues, measurement problems, and ramifying political implications of these provocative and conservative ideas, now twenty-seven years old, remain.

3. The relationship between a flexible labor pool such as those in prison or jail, immigrants, and the unemployed or underemployed and low wages and high profits is the implicit argument behind the warm reception of the incarceration frenzy. The actual relationship has been asserted often (Rusche and Kirchheimer 1939 [2003]) but never clearly established.

4. Wilson had written on organizational politics, participation of citizens in public policy in Chicago, and machine politics in big cities and published *Varieties of Police Behavior* (1968).

5. The primary fact, of course, is that there is little or no possible legal appeal for the persons subject to arbitrary controls in such undesirable neighborhoods. The word of an officer is law, to repeat a cliché.

6. Police uses of broken-windows notions to defend their practices are of course not the responsibility of Wilson and Kelling. However, Wilson repeatedly argues for the focused use of police to suppress crime and targeting and policy-based use of "meager [police] forces" (1985, 86). Perhaps as a result of Wilson's position on the board of the Police Foundation and Larry Sherman's role as director of research, more arrest- and crime-focused brief interventions were tried and evaluated in the 1980s, often using experimental methods. These are summarized in Sherman (1990, 1992, and more modestly in 2005).

7. This was not stated in any of the Wilson and colleagues' essays. It was an inference made by Skogan. His argument was first presented in a working paper at the "Measuring What Matters" seminar in Washington, D.C., sponsored by the NIJ. I attended this meeting with Skogan, Bratton, Kelling, and others.

8. However, see the work of ethnographers Anderson, Carr, Kefalas, Fong, and Small discussed in the next chapter and the paper of Rosenfeld and coauthors and Messner et al. reviewed above.

9. I am indebted to Jack McDevitt for his insights and this line of argument that he developed in personal communication with me in July 2007.

10. Two exceptions to this generalization discussed in following chapter are the study of the South End in Boston by Small (2004), who does not concern himself with crime, and McRoberts's study (2003) of the social impact of new ministries on the ecology of the Dorchester neighborhood of Boston. The police play no featured role in these studies, which are focused on how neighborhoods change and adopt to socioeconomic and political circumstances rather than to OCR.

11. Eterno and Silverman (2006) argue persuasively that the Compstat process and the BW approach were parallel developments within the NYPD. They opine that Compstat was a management innovation and the BW framework an ex post facto rationalization (Eterno and Silverman quoting Bratton on Maple's role in developing Compstat [2006, 220]). This is consistent with media attention that seized on the pair and intimates and attributed the drop in crime to the combination and by implication their close connection. It is quite true that using the Compstat process as a crime-focused technique requires no theory whatsoever. Silverman certainly links the two ideas in his book on the causes of reduction in officially recorded crime in New York City (1999). He reiterated the position years later (2007), even as crime was rising, Compstat had been refocused, and Bratton had moved to Los Angeles as police commissioner. See Harcourt's detailed citation of articles indicating the popular media's excited and uncritical initial view. This was especially true of writers based in New York working for the *Times,* the *New Yorker,* and *New York Magazine,* and those in Washington, D.C., writing for the *Washington Post.* There was, however, later questioning (see also Manning 2001). Malcolm Gladwell (2000) used the term *tipping point*—taken from Thomas Schelling and mentioned in the Wilson article—as a title for his best-selling pop–social science volume. Gladwell employs the idea as a vague gloss for patterns of diffusion and contagion, uses a simplified version of rational choice theory, and compares the control of crime to the popularity of Hush Puppy shoes.

12. See, however, Eterno and Silverman 2006 on concerns about costs.

13. The most systematic analysis of how such policing and social demonizing of a group of people occurs and the political and moral consequences is best found in the works of Hannah Arendt, especially her masterpiece, *The Origins of Totalitarianism* (1985). See also Evans 2004, 2005; and Manning (2009).

NOTES FOR CHAPTER 7

1. The following few pages on problem-solving policing are adopted from Manning 2005.

2. One component contributing to the popularity of crime mapping and analysis appears to be the fact that electronic representations, "electronic pin maps," simulate the ways in which police "encode" and perceive crime. They see it as being in places; done by unknown persons (but usually previous offenders); organized in territories, beats, districts, or regions (and the morality of cities into good and disreputable areas); and subject to deterrence and control primarily by threat, arrest, and direct sanctioning.

3. See Sherman 1990; Weisburd and Green 1995 (and other papers in this issue of *Justice Quarterly*); Braga et al. 1999; Mazerolle, Soole, and Rombouts 2006 on drugs and crime; and Weisburd and Lum 2005.

4. Mapping, noting, and responding to hot spots became one of the components of the Compstat model, as noted below.

5. Mapping does not solve the problem of independent validation of inferences made from maps. Maps can dramatize the existence of incidents if the colors, scale, icons, and range in the columns and rows of the original table from which the map is based are varied. The confidence intervals—that is, when a level of incidents exceeds "normal" and becomes a "hot spot" or matter of police concern—are arbitrary. Does 3–6 incidents known or recorded in some arbitrary time period produce a hot spot? What is the number above which it becomes problematic: 7–10? 11–20? 21–60? and so on. The sample size can be so small that a normal distribution cannot be assumed as the base against which the data mapped is shown. If, for example, there are two murders in a district in a year and three are recorded in the following year, this becomes a rise of one-third—but in actual fact, it is not a matter for concern

given the size of the base number of recorded homicides. On the other hand, lagged or time series data with large samples over time tend to reveal regression to the mean that will in effect cancel out the value of finding and responding to hot spots based on maps. In hot-spot policing, the focus is on finding and acting upon short-term spikes up (never down, as that is not a police concern). It could be argued, of course, that where crime is dropping, officers should be directed away from such areas and should focus their efforts elsewhere.

6. This is a summary of portions of the introduction and chapter 8 of my book *Technology's Ways* (New York: New York University Press, 2008).

7. In these works, there is no human presence, no active people, no life situations, no presentation of urban life as a moving, culturally embedded process. Urban life as mapped is police theater, a cartoon of methodological pretense.

NOTES FOR CHAPTER 8

1. I would include as important recent contributions to our understandings of policing on the ground the work of Steve Herbert (1997, 2006), George Rigakos (2002), Martin Innes (2003), Jonathan Wender (2008), Laura Huey (2007), Joe Hermer (2008), Ian Loader and Aogan Mulcahy (2003), and Peter Moskos (2008).

2. Here I am referring to the scale that is used to train police officers in the use of force; it suggests a logical escalation based on the citizen's behavior. It rationalizes "self-defense," "threat," and "weapon" and leaves the definition of these to the officer.

3. This proposition is consistent with the fact that those with more trust of the police are also less likely to see policing as racist, in need of reform, corrupt, and violent (Weitzer and Tuch 2006).

4. While Rawls does not consider in detail the criminal law and its role in justice, there is much implicit in his argument that requires these inferences. See also Dolovich 2004. Her primary concern in this working paper is with forms of punishment that are consistent with the Rawlsian ideas. This is implicit in Rawls's 1955 "Two Concepts of Rules" paper.

5. The argument raised by economists concerning targeting and arresting those who in the past have categorically been seen as "criminal" and arrested, even if this is based on suspicion, a pretext, categorical or place-based crackdowns or sweeps, therefore increasing efficiency, confuses economics with justice. There is no burden or obligation on the police to be efficient that could override the principle that requires that they be fair.

6. See, for one useful textbook summary of limitations of various measures of crime and victimization, Kauzlarich and Barlow 2009, 24–41.

7. This *idea,* that more police produce more order and less crime, has viability only in the United States. The results of such research are mixed, with the general opinion that they are marginal to other sociodemographic forces (Levitt, 1998, 2004). Even when this finding has marginal support, the ways in which this might occur are totally ignored or merely suggested (see the two key articles based on research data: Messner et al. 2007; and Rosenfeld, Fornango, and Rengifo 2007). In particular, the reduction in homicides due to the presence of more uniformed patrol officers remains a mystery. Adding more officers as a matter of course, year after year, is not the government position in Canada. In Canada, the ratio of police per capita has been declining slightly for the past ten-plus years (Rigakos 2001). This is actually true in the United States also, due to population growth.

8. Meehan's work (1992, 1993, 2000) in this regard is the most insightful and valid with respect to policing, but see also Wilson 1968; Garfinkel 1967; and Gardiner 1969.

9. Classics that demonstrate the centrality of worker control of all modes of production are Roy 1953, 1954, 2006; and Ditton 1977.

10. Alternative sources of information on crime—self-reports, organizational reports and insurance claims, and victimization surveys, both household and individual—reveal a consistent pattern that resembles but does not replicate the pattern by crime shown in the aggregated official data.

11. This article was first published in 1984, and changes in the law in the case of domestic violence have radically changed officers' tactics.

Notes for Chapter 9

1. It is possible that a Blackian sociology of law (1976) could generate propositions to explain such shifts. My list is a more modest effort at describing the dynamics rather than explaining the reasons behind the shifts. Furthermore, both are efforts at seeing "law" as governmental social control as being a dependent variable rather than an independent variable producing consequences.

2. I am making the perhaps obvious point that class and race shield the people in some groups carrying out the same activities—drug use, gambling, adultery, embezzlement, drunk driving, homosexual affairs, abortions—from visibility and that others are patently and continuously at risk for the same behavior. This is one extension of the idea that social control is active, not passive, in its choice of targets (Lemert 1972).

3. This strategy was adopted in New York City under Mayor Giuliani and Commissioner Bratton to neutralize and smash the putatively dangerous black "squeegee" men. The fine approach was adopted in Boston (*Boston Herald,* February 17, 2006).

4. The argument in this section has been much improved and sharpened by my conversations with Michael W. Raphael.

5. See the several articles on the subject of "perceptual distortions and police use of force" in *Criminology and Public Policy* 8, no. 1 (February 2009).

6. The policing done in Moskos's (2008) high-crime district in Baltimore, Maryland, appears to be an exception to this generalization. Moskos writes that officers were expected to remain in their districts and work only in their districts, and only in overload circumstances were officers from other districts called in to help. This rule would apply then to officers remaining only if called by the dispatcher to work outside their districts. Perhaps this is a result of the high-crime nature of the district and past traditions about one officer working a beat.

Notes for Chapter 10

1. This research is a cross-sectional study done in 1995 and does permit inferences about "causation," although since the variables measured are generally fairly stable, there is an inference that the data still are accurate representations of the neighborhoods in Chicago more than thirteen year later. Generalizations about homicide data that are lagged are reported in (Sampson 1987; Morenoff and Sampson 1997).

2. I do not review the work of Tyler (2006) and Tyler and Huo (2003) on trust in policing and the law because it is based on interview and attitudinal data, and is not observational in nature, nor grounded in any particular local area or city. This focus is a highly reductionistic approach to something that is profoundly social and collective in nature.

3. This is also the case in Northern Ireland (Mulcahy 2006). Weitzer (with data from a previous decade [1996]) suggests that when the threat of the minority reaches a certain level, police become the representative of the majority's perceptions of the police role vis-à-vis controlling minorities. How this works politically, aside from the increase in the sheer numbers of officers, is unclear. It is a fundamental question of the processes by which democratic policing is increased or compromised in the course of its development.

4. They ascribe this in a limp, offhand reference to the Marxian Bonger, advancing the idea that "the poor are less able to avoid arrest, and more likely to be seen as a threat, making them more vulnerable to formal social control" (Parker, Stults, and Rice 2005, 1125). How is it that people "avoid arrest" or are less able to do so since arrests in these areas are overwhelmingly for disorderly conduct, drugs, loitering, and other crimes reflecting departmental policies or officers' style of dealing will such disadvantaged areas rather than behavior in the moment (Moskos 2008; St. Jean 2007; Bynum and Varano 2003)?

5. Chicago under Mayor Daley has made a commitment to connecting the citizens and social services via the police (see Skogan and Hartnett 1997; and Skogan 2006) and is unique in this regard to my knowledge. On the other hand, the extent to which these services are broadly offered is an

empirical question. For example, in Carr's study (2003) of a working-class area in western Chicago's Bungalow Belt, the "graffiti blaster" was said to be dispatched "every day to clean up graffiti trouble spots." Carr notes that they were dispatched "as needed" in the area (2005, 88–89) in part because of the clout of the local alderman. Compare this pattern to Venkatesh's observation (2006) that the local alderman seemed unable to deliver services and that city services were lacking in and around the entirely African American area of Chicago he terms "Marquis Park."

6.   I would consider exceptions to this generalization Cain's work comparing urban and rural policing (1973); Banton's classic consideration (1964) of small town-rural policing in Scotland with some observations on Massachusetts; the work of Weisheit, Falcone, and Wells (1999) on policing small-town and rural Illinois; some work on the state police (Bechtel 1995); and historical studies of the Texas Rangers (Webb 1965; Utley 2002, 2007; Samora, Bernal, and Pena 1979). There are few studies of other policing modalities in rural America (e.g., slave patrols) (Hadden 2001), county sheriffs, and voluntary associations that police. In societies in transition, such as Ireland, the stark historically patterned differences between urban and rural economies and traditions pose problems to policing reform.

7.   By "sympathetic" I mean that there are few works with a demonstrably and consistently negative view of police and policing. I would include Sidney Harring's historical work (1983), Jock Young's on policing drugs (1971), Skolnick's *Justice without Trial* (1966) and Skolnick and Fyfe 1994, Rod Stark's *Police Riots* (1970), and perhaps William Westley's early work (1970). Important essays that are exceptions to this generalization are the works of Peter Kraska on the militarization of police (2001) and "Policing: A Minority View" by Hubert Williams and Pat Murphy (both former innovative police administrators) (in Kappeler 2006). On the other hand, the ironic and insightful fieldwork-based studies done by Egon Bittner, Jonathan Rubinstein, Malcolm Young, Richard Ericson, and Albert J. Reiss remain a rich source of ideas, hypotheses, and data for future generations. Studies of police deviance, on the whole, treat it as a produce of social forces, traditions, and pressures that envelop individual officers and, as such, do not appear as dismissive and condemnatory.

8.   W. J. Wilson (1987, 1996, 2009) is the most prominent advocate of the class-not-race thesis about disadvantage.

9.   I adapted the term *boomerang effect* from Dennis Rosenbaum's analysis (2006) of the negative and unanticipated effects of hot-spot policing.

10.   The most apt and competent advocate of such laws is Tracey Meares, who has written many law review articles and along with Dan Kahan has written persuasively on the topic (Meares and Kahan 1998). Her aim, in my view, is somewhat subtle, because such laws on the surface are antidemocratic and produce on-the-street inequalities of a cascading and spiraling sort. I believe her argument is that local-level agreements about enforcement, reflected in local regulations, civil codes, and criminal law (and their enforcement), could increase collective efficacy in neighborhoods, reduce crime in the long run, and provide tools that might reduce the impact of the court's application of severe sanctions to young black men.

NOTES FOR EPILOGUE

1.   Michael W. Raphael is a student at Northeastern University and the co-editor with Peter K. Manning and John Van Maanen of the forthcoming *Policing a View From the Streets* (2nd ed.).

2.   Douglas Harper, Online Etymology Dictionary, 2001, http://www.etymonline.com/index .php?search=police (accessed June 6, 2009).

3.   Ibid., http://www.etymonline.com/index.php?search=poli.

4.   1878, "Posse Comitatus Act § 1385," in U.S. Code, vol. *Title 18, United States of America.*

5.   "John F. Kennedy Moon Speech, Rice Stadium," 1962, http://er.jsc.nasa.gov/seh/ricetalk .htm (accessed June 6, 2009).

6.   Robert Cooper Grier, *South v. Maryland.* (59:369 [1855]).

Bibliography

Aas, K. F. 2007. *Globalization and crime.* Thousand Oaks, CA: Sage.

Abbott, A. 2005. Linked ecologies: States and universities as environments for professions. *Sociological Theory* 23 (3): 245–74.

Alpert, G. P., and R. G. Dunham. 2004. *Understanding police use of force: Officers, suspects, and reciprocity.* Cambridge: Cambridge University Press.

Anderson, B. 1983. *Imagined communities.* London: Verso Books.

Anderson, E. 1990. *StreetWise: Race, class, and change in an urban community.* Chicago: University of Chicago Press.

———. 2003. *A place on the corner.* Rev. ed. Chicago: University of Chicago Press.

———. 2008. *Code of the streets.* New York: W. W. Norton.

Angell, J. E. 1971. Toward an alternative to the classic police organizational arrangements: A democratic model. *Criminology* 9 (2–3): 185–206.

Arendt, H. 1970. *On violence.* New York: Harcourt Brace.

———. 1985. *The origins of totalitarianism.* New York: Harcourt Brace Jovanovich.

———. 1994. *Eichmann in Jerusalem: A report on the banality of evil.* New York: Penguin.

Bailey, W. G. 1995. *The encyclopedia of police science.* New York: Taylor and Francis.

Baldwin, R., and R. Kinsey. 1982. *Police powers and politics.* London: Quartet Books.

Bamford, J. 1983. *The puzzle palace: A report on America's most secret agency.* New York: Penguin.

———. 2001. *Body of secrets: Anatomy of the ultra-secret national security agency: From the cold war through the dawn of a new century.* New York: Doubleday.

———. 2004. *A pretext for war: 9/11, Iraq, and the abuse of America's intelligence agencies.* New York: Doubleday.

Banfield, E. 1958. *The moral basis of a backward society.* New York: Free Press.

Banton, M. 1964. *The policeman in the community.* London: Tavistock.

Barlow, H. D. 2009. *Introduction to criminology.* 9th ed. Lanham, MD: Rowman and Littlefield.

Bateson, G. 1958. *Naven: A survey of the problems suggested by a composite picture of the culture of a New Guinea tribe drawn from three points of view.* Stanford: Stanford University Press.

Baumann, Z. 1994. *Modernity and the Holocaust.* Cambridge: Polity Press.

Bayley, D. H. 1969. *The police and political development in India.* Princeton: Princeton University Press.

———. 1975. "The police and political development in Europe." *The Formation of National States in Western Europe,* ed. C. Tilly. Princeton: Princeton University Press, 328–79.

———. 1979. Police function, structure, and control in Western Europe and North America: comparative and historical studies. *Crime and Justice: A Review of Research* 1: 109.

———. 1985. *Patterns of policing: A comparative international analysis.* New Brunswick: Rutgers University Press.

———. 1991. *Forces of order: Policing modern Japan.* Berkeley and Los Angeles: University of California Press.

———. 1992. Comparative organization of the police in English-speaking countries. *Crime and Justice: A Review of Research* 15: 509.

———. 1994. *Police for the future.* New York: Oxford University Press.

———. 1996. Policing: The world stage. *Journal of Criminal Justice Education* 7: 241–48.

———. 2001. *Democratizing the police abroad: What to do and how to do it.* Washington, DC: U.S. Department of Justice, Office of Justice Programs, National Institute of Justice.

———. 2006. *Changing the guard: Developing democratic police abroad.* New York: Oxford University Press.

Bayley, D. H., and E. Bittner. 1986. The tactical choices of police patrol officers. *Journal of Criminal Justice* 14 (4): 329–48.

Bayley, D. H., and J. Garofalo. 1989. The management of violence by police patrol officers. *Criminology* 27 (1): 1–26.

Bayley, D. H., and C. D. Shearing. 1996. The future of policing. *Law and Society Review* 30: 585–606.

Beare, M. E., and T. Murray. 2007. *Police and government relations: Who's calling the shots?* Toronto: University of Toronto Press.

Bechtel, H. K. 1995. *State police in the United States: A socio-historical analysis.* Westport, CT: Greenwood.

Beck, U. 1992. *Risk society: Towards a new modernity.* Thousand Oaks, CA: Sage.

Becker, C. L. 1969. *The Declaration of Independence: A study in the history of political ideas.* New York: Alfred A. Knopf.

Becker, H. K., and D. L. Becker. 1986. *Handbook of the world's police.* Harrisburg, PA: Scarecrow Press.

Becker, H. S. 1958. Problems of inference and proof in participant observation. *American Sociological Review* 23 (6): 652–60.

Beckett, K. 1994. Setting the public agenda: "Street crime" and drug use in American politics. *Social Problems* 41 (3): 425–47.

Beckett, K., K. Nyrop, and L. Pfingst. 2006. Race, drugs, and policing: Understanding disparities in drug delivery arrests. *Criminology* 44 (1): 105–37.

Beckett, K., K. Nyrop, L. Pfingst, and M. Bowen. 2005. Drug use, drug possession arrests, and the question of race: Lessons from Seattle. *Social Problems* 52 (3): 419–41.

Behn, R. D. 2008. The seven big errors of PerformanceStat. *Policy Briefs* 2008 (February): 1–8.

Berkley, G. E. 1969. *The democratic policeman.* Boston: Beacon Press.

Bittner, E. 1967. The police on skid-row: A study of peace keeping. *American Sociological Review*: 699–715.

———. 1972. *The functions of the police in modern society: A review of background factors, current practices, and possible role models.* Washington, DC: National Institute of Mental Health.

———. 1974. Florence Nightingale in pursuit of Willie Sutton: A theory of the police. In *The potential for reform of criminal justice,* ed. H. Jacobs. Beverly Hills: Sage.

———. 1983. Technique and the conduct of life. *Social Problems* 30 (3): 249–61.

———. 1990. *Aspects of police work.* Boston: Northeastern University Press.

Black, D. J. 1970. Production of crime rates. *American Sociological Review* 35 (4): 733–48.

———. 1976. *The behavior of law.* New York: Academic Press.

———. 1980. *The manners and customs of the police.* New York: Academic Press.

———. 1983. Crime as social control. *American Sociological Review* 48 (1): 34–45.

Black, D. J., and A. J. Reiss Jr. 1969. Police control of juveniles. *American Sociological Review* 35 (1): 63–77.

Blackstock, N. 1976. *Cointelpro: The FBI's secret war on political freedom.* New York: Vintage Books.

Blumer, H. 1958. Race prejudice as a sense of group position. *Pacific Sociological Review* 1: 3–7.

Blumstein, A., and J. Wallman. 2000. *The crime drop in America.* Cambridge: Cambridge University Press.

Bogard, W. 1996. *The simulation of surveillance: Hypercontrol in telematic societies.* Cambridge: Cambridge University Press.

Bopp, W. J. 1971. *The police rebellion: A quest for blue power.* Springfield, IL: Thomas.

Bordua, D. J., ed. 1967. *The police: Six sociological essays.* New York: Wiley.

———. 1968. The police. *International encyclopedia of the social sciences,* ed. D. L. Sills. *Vol. 2.* New York: Macmillan.

Bordua, D. J., and A. J. Reiss Jr. 1966. Command, control, and charisma: Reflections on police bureaucracy. *American Journal of Sociology* 72 (1): 68–76.

———. 1967. Law enforcement. In *The Uses of Sociology,* eds. W. Sewell, H. Wilensky, and P. Lazerfeld. New York: Basic Books.

Bott, E. 2003. *Family and social network: Roles, norms, and external relationships in ordinary urban families.* London: Routledge.

Bottoms, A. E., and P. Wiles. 1997. Environmental criminology. In *The Oxford handbook of criminology,* ed. M. Maguire, R. Morgan, and R. Reiner. Oxford: Oxford University Press.

Bourdieu, P. 1977. *Outline of a theory of practice.* Cambridge: Cambridge University Press.

———. 1991. *Language and symbolic power.* Trans. G. Raymond and M. Adamson. London: Polity.

Bowling, B. 2006. Bobby, bond, and Babylon: Transnational policing in the contemporary Caribbean. Inaugural lecture, King's College, London.

Bowling, B., and J. Foster. 2002. Policing and the police. In *The Oxford handbook of criminology,* edited by M. Maguire, R. Morgan, and R. Reiner. Oxford: Oxford University Press.

Braga, A. A., and B. J. Bond. 2008. Policing crime and disorder hot spots: A randomized controlled trial. *Criminology* 46 (3): 577–607.

Braga, A. A., D. M. Kennedy, E. J. Waring, and A. M. Piehl. 2001. Problem-oriented policing, deterrence, and youth violence: An evaluation of Boston's Operation Ceasefire. *Journal of Research in Crime and Delinquency* 38 (3): 195–225.

Braga, A. A., J. McDevitt, and G. L. Pierce. 2006. Understanding and preventing gang violence: Problem analysis and response development in Lowell, Massachusetts. *Police Quarterly* 9 (1): 20–46.

Braga, A. A., D. L. Weisburd, E. J. Waring, L. G. Mazerolle, W. Spelman, and F. Gajewski. 1999. Problem-oriented policing in violent crime places: A randomized controlled experiment. *Criminology* 37 (3): 541–80.

Brandl, S. G., M. B. Chamlin, and J. Frank. 1995. Aggregation bias and the capacity for formal crime control: The determinants of total and disaggregated police force size in Milwaukee, 1934–1987. *Justice Quarterly* 12 (3): 543–62.

Brantingham, P. J., and P. L. Brantingham. 1981. *Environmental criminology.* Thousand Oaks, CA: Sage.

Bratton, W., and G. Kelling. 2006. There are no cracks in the broken windows. *National Review Online.*

Bratton, W., and P. Knobler. 1998. *Turnaround: How America's top cop reversed the crime epidemic.* New York: Random House.

Brewer, J. D., A. Guelke, I. Hume, E. Moxon-Browne, and R. Wilford. 1988. *The police, public order, and the state.* Oxford: Oxford University Press.

Brewer, J. D., and K. Magee. 1991. *Inside the RUC: Routine policing in a divided society.* New York: Oxford University Press.

Brinkley, D. 2006. *The great deluge: Hurricane Katrina, New Orleans, and the Mississippi Gulf Coast*. New York: William Morrow.

Brodeur, J. P. 1983. High policing and low policing: Remarks about the policing of political activities. *Social Problems* 30 (5): 507–20.

———. 1994. Policing appearances. *Critical Criminology* 5 (2): 58–83.

———. 1997. *Violence and racial prejudice in the context of peacekeeping: A study prepared for the commission of inquiry into the deployment of Canadian forces to Somalia*. Ottawa: Canadian Government Publication Centre.

———, ed. 1998. *How to recognize good policing: Problems and issues*. Thousand Oaks, CA: Sage.

———. 2000. Cops and spooks: The uneasy partnership. *Police Practice and Research* 1: 299–322.

———. 2007. An encounter with Egon Bittner. *Crime, Law, and Social Change* 48 (3): 105–12.

———. Forthcoming. *A treatise on policing*. Oxford: Oxford University Press.

Brodeur, J. P., and C. Shearing. 2005. Configuring security and justice. *European Journal of Criminology* 2 (4): 379–406.

Brodeur, J. P., and L. Viau. 1994. Police accountability in crisis situations. In *police powers in Canada: The evolution and practice of authority,* ed. R. C. Macleod and D. Schneiderman, 243–308. Toronto: University of Toronto Press.

Brogden, M. 1987. The emergence of the police: The colonial dimension. *British Journal of Criminology* 27 (1): 4–14.

———. 1991. *On the Mersey beat: Policing Liverpool between the wars*. Oxford: Oxford University Press.

Brogden, M., and P. Nijhar. 2005. *Community policing: National and international models and approaches*. Devon: Willan Publishing.

Brogden, M., and C. D. Shearing. 1993. *Policing for a new South Africa*. London: Routledge.

Brown, M. K. 1969. *Working the street*. New York: Russell Sage Foundation.

Browning, C. R. 1992. *Ordinary men: Reserve Police Battalion 101 and the final solution in Poland*. London: HarperCollins.

Brunson, R. K. 2007. Police don't like black people: African-American young men's accumulated police experiences. *Criminology and Public Policy* 6 (1): 71–101.

Buerger, M. E. 1994. Problems of problem-solving: Resistance, interdependencies, and conflicting interests. *American Journal of Police* 13: 1–36.

Buerger, M. E., and L. G. Mazerolle. 1998. Third-party policing: A theoretical analysis of an emerging trend. *Justice Quarterly* 15: 301–28.

Burke, K. 1965. *Permanence and change*. Indianapolis: Bobbs-Merrill.

Burns, T., and G. M. Stalker. 1961. *The management of innovation*. London: Tavistock.

Button, M. 2002. *Private policing*. Devon: Willan Publishing.

Bynum, T., and S. Varano. 2003. The anti-gang initiative in Detroit: An aggressive enforcement approach to gangs. In *Policing gangs and youth violence,* ed. S. Decker. Newbury Park, CA: Sage.

Cain, M. E. 1973. *Society and the policeman's role*. London: Routledge.

———. 1979. Trends in the sociology of police work. *International Journal of the Sociology of Law* 7 (2): 143–67.

Callil, C. 2007. *Bad faith: A forgotten history of family, fatherland, and Vichy France*. New York: Vintage Books.

Cannadine, D. 2001. *Ornamentalism: How the British saw their empire*. Oxford: Oxford University Press.

Carr, P. J. 2003. The new parochialism: The implications of the Beltway case for arguments concerning informal social control. *American Journal of Sociology* 108 (6): 1249–91.

———. 2004. *Clean streets: Crime, disorder, and social control in a Chicago neighborhood*. New York: New York University Press.

Carr, P. J., L. Napolitano, and J. Keating. 2007. We never call the cops and here is why: A qualitative examination on legal cynicism in three Philadelphia neighborhoods. *Criminology* 45 (2): 445–80.

Carruthers, B. G., and E. W. Nelson. 1991. Accounting for rationality: Double-entry bookkeeping and the rhetoric of economic rationality. *American Journal of Sociology* 97 (1): 31–69.

Carte, G. E., and E. H. Carte. 1975. *Police reform in the United States: The era of August Vollmer, 1905–1932.* Berkeley and Los Angeles: University of California Press.

Carvalho, I., D. A. Lewis. 2003. Beyond community: Reactions to crime and disorder among inner-city residents. *Criminology* 41 (3): 779–812.

Chambliss, W. J. 1994. Policing the ghetto underclass: The politics of law and law enforcement. *Social Problems* 41 (2): 177–94.

Chan, J. 1996. Changing police culture. *British Journal of Criminology* 36 (1): 109–34.

———. 1997. *Changing police culture: Policing in a multicultural society.* Cambridge: Cambridge University Press.

Chan, J., C. Devery, and S. Doran. 2003. *Fair cop: Learning the art of policing.* Toronto: University of Toronto Press.

Chapman, B. 1970. *Police state.* London: Pall Mall.

Chevigny, P. 1995. *Edge of the knife: Police violence in the Americas.* New York: New Press.

Chiricos, T., M. Hogan, and M. Gertz. 1997. Racial composition of neighborhood and fear of crime. *Criminology* 35: 107–32.

Chiricos, T., K. Padgett, and M. Gertz. 2000. Fear, TV news, and the reality of crime. *Criminology* 38 (3): 755–86.

Christie, N. 2000. *Crime control as industry: Towards gulags, Western style.* London: Routledge.

Christopher, W. 1998. *Report of the Independent Commission on the Los Angeles Police Department.* Los Angeles: The Commission.

Cicourel, A. V. 1995. *The social organization of juvenile justice.* New Brunswick: Transaction.

Clark, J. P. 1965. Isolation of the police: A comparison of the British and American situations. *Journal of Criminal Law and Criminology* 56: 307–19.

Clark, J. P., and R. Sykes. 1974. Some determinants of police organization and practice in a modern industrial democracy. In *Handbook of criminology,* ed. D. Glaser. Chicago: Rand McNally.

Clarke, R. V. G., and J. M. Hough, eds. 1980. *The effectiveness of policing.* Farnborough, UK: Gower.

———. 1984. *Crime and police effectiveness.* London: Her Majesty's Stationery Office.

Clear, T. R., D. R. Rose, E. Waring, and K. Scully. 2003. Coercive mobility and crime: A preliminary examination of concentrated incarceration and social disorganization. *Justice Quarterly* 20: 33–64.

Cohen, S. 1985. *Visions of social control.* Cambridge: Polity Press.

Collingwood, R. G. 1939. *An autobiography.* Oxford: Oxford University Press.

Colton, K. W., M. L. Brandeau, and J. M. Tien. 1983. *A national assessment of police command, control, and communications systems.* Washington, DC: U.S. Department of Justice, National Institute of Justice.

Cooley, D. 2005. *Re-imagining policing in Canada.* Toronto: University of Toronto Press.

Cooney, M. 1998. *Warriors and peacemakers: How third parties shape violence.* New York: New York University Press.

———. 2003. The privatization of violence. *Criminology* 41 (4): 1377–1406.

Cordner, G. 1999. Elements of community policing. In *Policing perspectives: An anthology,* eds. L. Gaines and G. Cordner. Los Angeles: Roxbury.

Cordner, G., and E. P. Biebel. 2005. Problem-oriented policing in practice. *Criminology and Public Policy* 4 (2): 155–80.

Corsianos, M. 2001. Conceptualizing "justice" in detectives' decision making. *International Journal of the Sociology of Law* 29 (2): 113–25.

———. 2003. Discretion in detectives' decision making and high-profile cases. *Police Practice and Research* 4 (3): 301–14.

Crank, J. P. 2003. Institutional theory of police: A review of the state of the art. *Policing: An International Journal of Police Strategies and Management* 26 (2): 186–207.

Crank, J. P., and R. Langworthy. 1992. Institutional perspective on policing. *Journal of Criminal Law and Criminology* 83: 338–63.

Crawford, A. 1998. *Crime prevention and community safety: Politics, policies, and practices.* London: Longman.

Crick, B. R. 2002. *Democracy: A very short introduction.* Oxford: Oxford University Press.

Crozier, M. 1964. *The bureaucratic phenomenon.* Chicago: University of Chicago Press.

Crozier, M., and E. Friedberg. 1980. *Actors and systems: The politics of collective action.* Chicago: University of Chicago Press.

Cumming, E., I. Cumming, and L. Edell. 1965. Policeman as philosopher, guide, and friend. *Social Problems* 12 (3): 276–86.

Cunningham, W., J. J. Strauchs, and C. Van Meter. 1991. The Hallcrest Report II: Private security trends, 1970 to 2000. *Journal of Security Administration* 14 (2): 3–22.

Cunningham, W., and T. Taylor. 1985. Private security and police in America (the Hallcrest Report).

Dahl, R. A. 2000. *On democracy.* New Haven: Yale University Press.

Dammer, H. R., E. Fairchild, and J. S. Albanese. 2006. *Comparative criminal justice.* Belmont, CA: Wadsworth.

Dawson, M. 1998. *The Mountie from dime novel to Disney.* Toronto: Between the Lines.

Decker, S. H. 2003. Gangs, youth violence, and policing: Where do we stand, where do we go from here? In *Policing gangs and youth violence,* ed. S. H. Decker. Newbury Park, CA: Sage.

Deflem, M. 2004. *Policing world society: Historical foundations of international police cooperation.* New York: Oxford University Press.

Defleur, L. B. 1975. Biasing influences on drug arrest records: Implications for deviance research. *American Sociological Review* 40 (1): 88–103.

de Waard, J. 1999. The private security industry in international perspective. *European Journal on Criminal Policy and Research* 7 (2): 143–74.

Diehl, J. M. 1977. *Paramilitary politics in Weimar Germany.* Bloomington: Indiana University Press.

DiMaggio, P. J., and W. W. Powell. 1983. The Iron Cage revisited: Institutional isomorphism and collective rationality. *American Sociological Review* 48 (2): 147–60.

Dolovich, S. 2004. Legitimate punishment in a liberal democracy. In *Public law and legal theory.* Los Angeles: UCLA Law School.

Donziger, S. 1996. *The real war on crime: The report of the National Criminal Justice Commission.* New York: Harper.

Douglas, J. D. 1971. *American social order: Social rules in a pluralistic society.* New York: Free Press.

Downs, A., and Rand Corporation. 1967. *Inside bureaucracy.* Boston: Little, Brown.

Dunworth, T. 2005. Information technology and the criminal justice system. In *Criminal Justice: 2000,* ed. J. Horney. Washington, DC: Department of Justice.

Dupont, B. 2000. Hacking the panopticon: Distributed online surveillance and resistance. *Sociology of Crime Law and Deviance* 10: 259–20.

———. 2002. *Construction et réformes d'une police: Le cas Australien.* Paris: L'Harmattan.

Dupont, B., P. Grabosky, and C. Shearing. 2003. The governance of security in weak and failing states. *Criminology and Criminal Justice* 3 (4): 331–49.

Durkheim, E. 1961. *The elementary forms of religious life.* London: Macmillan.

———. 1997. *The division of labor in society.* New York: Free Press.

Eck, J., and E. Maguire. 2000. Have changes in policing reduced violent crime? An assessment of the evidence. In *The crime drop in America,* eds. A. Blumstein and J. Wallman. New York: Cambridge University Press.

Eck, J. E., and W. Spelman. 1987. Solving problems: Problem-oriented policing in Newport News. Washington, DC.

Ellickson, R. C. 1991. *Order without law: How neighbors settle disputes.* Cambridge: Harvard University Press.

Ellison, G., and J. Smyth. 2000. *The crowned harp: Policing Northern Ireland.* London: Pluto Press.

Emsley, C. 1983. *Policing and its context, 1750–1870.* London: Macmillan.

———. 1996a. *The English police: A political and social history.* London: Longman.

———. 1996b. *Gendarmes and the state in nineteenth-century Europe.* Oxford: Oxford University Press.

Enloe, C. H. 1980a. *Ethnic soldiers: State security in divided societies.* Harmondsworth: Penguin.

———. 1980b. *Police, military, and ethnicity: Foundations of state power.* New Brunswick: Transaction.

Epstein, E. J. 1990. *Agency of fear: Opiates and political power in America.* London: Verso Books.

———. 2000. *News from nowhere: Television and the news.* Chicago: I. R. Dee.

Ericson, R. V. 1981. *Making crime: A study of detective work.* Toronto: Butterworths.

———. 1982. *Reproducing order: A study of police patrol work.* Toronto: University of Toronto Press.

Ericson, R. V., P. M. Baranek, and J. B. L. Chan. 1993. *Negotiating control: A study of news sources.* Toronto: University of Toronto Press.

Ericson, R. V., A. Doyle, and D. Barry. 2003. *Insurance as governance.* Toronto: University of Toronto Press.

Ericson, R. V., and K. D. Haggerty. 1997. *Policing the risk society.* Toronto: University of Toronto Press.

Espeland, W. N. 1998. *The struggle for water: Politics, rationality, and Identity in the American Southwest.* Chicago: University of Chicago Press.

Eterno, J. A., and E. B. Silverman. 2006. The New York City Police Department's Compstat: Dream or nightmare? *International Journal of Police Science and Management* 8 (3): 218–31.

Evans, R. J. 2004. *The coming of the Third Reich.* New York: Penguin Press.

———. 2005. *The Third Reich in power, 1933–1939.* London: Allen Lane.

Fagan, J., V. West, and J. Holland. 2003. Reciprocal effects of crime and incarceration in New York City neighborhoods. *Fordham Urban Law Journal* 30 (5): 1551–1602.

Fairchild, E. S. 1993. *Comparative criminal justice systems.* Belmont, CA: Wadsworth.

Famega, C. N., J. Frank, and L. Mazerolle. 2005. Managing police patrol time: The role of supervisor directives. *Justice Quarterly* 22 (4): 540–59.

Faris, R. E. L. 1970. *Chicago sociology, 1920–1932.* Chicago: University of Chicago Press.

Farrell, M. 1983. *Arming the Protestants.* London: Pluto Press.

Feeley, M. 1969. Coercion and compliance: A new look at an old problem. *Law and Society Review* 4: 505–20.

Feldman, M. S., and J. G. March. 1981. Information in organizations as signal and symbol. *Administrative Science Quarterly* 26 (2): 171–86.

Fielding, N. G. 1988. *Joining forces: Police training, socialization, and occupational competence.* London: Routledge.

———. 1995. *Community policing.* Oxford: Oxford University Press.

Flyvbjerg, B. 1998. *Rationality and power: Democracy in practice.* Chicago: University of Chicago Press.

Forcese, D. 1998. *Policing Canadian society.* Scarborough: Prentice-Hall Allyn.

Forst, B. 2000. The privatization and civilianization of policing. In *Boundary changes in criminal justice organizations,* ed. J. Horney. Washington, DC: Department of Justice.

———. 2008. *Terrorism, crime, and public policy.* Cambridge: Cambridge University Press.

Forst, B., and P. K. Manning. 1999. *The privatization of policing: Two views.* Washington, DC: Georgetown University Press.

Fosdick, R. B. 1915. European police systems. *Journal of Criminal Law and Criminology* 6: 28–38.

———. 1920. *American police systems.* Montclair, NJ: Patterson Smith.

Fung, A. 2004. *Empowered participation: Reinventing urban democracy.* Princeton: Princeton University Press.

Fyfe, J. J., J. R. Greene, W. F. Walsh, O. W. Wilson, and R. C. McLaren. 1997. *Police administration.* Vol. 5. New York: McGraw-Hill, 1950.

Gandy, O. H. 1993. *The panoptic sort: A political economy of personal information.* Boulder: Westview Press.

Gardiner, J. A. 1969. *Traffic and the police: Variations in law-enforcement policy.* Cambridge: Harvard University Press.

Garfinkel, H. 1963. A conception of, and experiments with, "trust" as a condition of stable concerted actions. In *Motivation and social interaction,* ed. O. J. Harvey. New York: Ronald.

———. 1964. Studies of the routine grounds of everyday activities. *Social Problems* 11 (3): 225–50.

———. 1967. *Studies in ethnomethodology.* Englewood Cliffs, NJ: Prentice-Hall.

Garfinkel, H., and A. W. Rawls. 2008. *Toward a sociological theory of information.* Boulder: Paradigm.

Garfinkel, H., A. W. Rawls, and C. C. Lemert. 2006. *Seeing sociologically: The routine grounds of social action.* Boulder: Paradigm.

Garland, D. 2001. *The culture of control.* Oxford: Oxford University Press.

Gau, J. M., and T. C. Pratt. 2008. Broken windows or window dressing: Citizens' (in)ability to tell the difference between disorder and crime. *Criminology and Public Policy* 7 (2): 163–94.

Geis, K. J., and C. E. Ross. 1998. A new look at urban alienation: The effect of neighborhood disorder on perceived powerlessness. *Social Psychology Quarterly* 61 (3): 232–46.

Geller, W. A., and N. Morris. 1992. Relations between federal and local police. In *Crime and justice: A review of research,* ed. M. N. M. Tonry. Chicago: University of Chicago Press.

Gerth, H. H., and C. W. Mills. 1948. *From Max Weber: Essays in sociology.* London: Routledge and Kegan Paul.

Gibbs, J. P. 1989. Conceptualization of terrorism. *American Sociological Review* 54 (3): 329–40.

Giddens, A. 1991. *Modernity and self-identity.* Cambridge: Polity Press.

Girard, R. 1977. *Violence and the sacred.* Baltimore: Johns Hopkins University Press.

Gladwell, M. 2000. *The tipping point: How little things can make a big difference.* Boston: Little, Brown.

Glaeser, A. 2000. *Divided in unity: Identity, Germany, and the Berlin police.* Chicago: University of Chicago Press.

Goffman, E. 1956. Deference and demeanor. *American Anthropologist* 58: 473–502.

———. 1959. *The presentation of self in everyday life.* New York: Doubleday.

———. 1963. *Behavior in public places.* New York: Free Press.

———. 1967. *Interaction ritual: Essays in face to face behavior.* Chicago: Aldine.

———. 1974. *Frame analysis: An essay on the organization of experience.* New York: Harper and Row.

Goldstein, H. 1990. *Problem-oriented policing.* New York: McGraw-Hill.

Gouldner, A. W. 1954. *Patterns of industrial bureaucracy (Glencoe, Ill.).* New York: Free Press.

Graham, H. D., and T. R. Gurr. 1969. *Violence in America: Historical and comparative perspectives.* New York: Bantam Books.

Green, D. P., and I. Shapiro. 1994. *Pathologies of rational choice theory: A critique of applications in political science.* New Haven: Yale University Press.

Greene, J. R. 2000. Community policing in America: Changing the nature, structure, and function of the police. In *Criminal Justice: 2000,* ed. J. Horney. Washington, DC: U.S. Department of Justice.

————. 2004. Community policing and organization change. In *Community policing: Can it work?* ed. W. Skogan. Belmont, CA: Wadsworth Thomson.

————. 2007. *The encyclopedia of police science.* London: Routledge.

Greene, J. R., and S. Mastrofski, eds. 1988. *Community policing: Rhetoric or reality?* New York: Praeger.

Gurr, T. R. 1989. *Violence in America.* Thousand Oaks, CA: Sage.

Gusfield, J. R. 1975. The (F)utility of knowledge? The relation of social science to public policy toward drugs. *The ANNALS of the American Academy of Political and Social Science* 417 (1): 1–15.

Guyot, D. 1979. Bending granite: Attempts to change the rank structure of American police departments. *Journal of Police Science and Administration* 7 (3): 253–84.

Haberfeld, M. R. 2006. *Police leadership.* Upper Saddle River, NJ: Pearson Prentice-Hall.

Haberfeld, M. R., and I. Cerrah. 2007. *Comparative policing: The struggle for democratization.* Thousand Oaks, CA: Sage.

Hadden, S. E. 2001. *Slave patrols: Law and violence in Virginia and the Carolinas.* Cambridge: Harvard University Press.

Hagan, J., and R. D. Peterson, eds. 1995. *Criminal inequality in America: Patterns and consequences, crime and inequality.* Stanford: Stanford University Press.

Haggerty, K. D., and R. V. Ericson. 1999. The militarization of policing in the information age. *Journal of Political and Military Sociology* 27 (2): 233–55.

————. 2000. The surveillant assemblage. *British Journal of Sociology* 51 (4): 605–22.

Hall, S., C. Critcher, J. Clarke, B. Roberts, and J. Tony. 1978. *Policing the crisis: Mugging, the state, and law and order.* London: Macmillan.

Harcourt, B. E. 2001. *Illusion of order: The false promise of broken windows policing.* Cambridge: Harvard University Press.

————. 2007. *Against prediction: Profiling, policing, and punishing in an actuarial age.* Chicago: University of Chicago Press.

Harcourt, B. E., and J. Ludwig. 2007. Reefer madness: Broken windows policing and misdemeanor marijuana arrests in New York City, 1989–2000. *Criminology and Public Policy* 6 (1): 165–81.

Harring, S. L. 1983. *Policing a class society: The experience of American cities, 1865–1915.* New Brunswick: Rutgers University Press.

Harris, C. H., III, and L. R. Sadler. 2007. *The Texas Rangers and the Mexican Revolution: The bloodiest decade, 1910–1920.* Albuquerque: University of New Mexico Press.

Heimer, C. A. 1985. *Reactive risk and rational action: Managing moral hazard in insurance contracts.* Berkeley and Los Angeles: University of California Press.

Henry, V. E. 2003. *Compstat: The emerging model of police management.* 2nd ed. Critical Issues in Crime and Justice. Thousand Oaks, CA: Sage.

Herbert, S. 1996. Morality in law enforcement: Chasing bad guys with the Los Angeles Police Department. *Law and Society Review* 30: 799–818.

————. 1997. *Policing space: Territoriality and the Los Angeles Police Department.* Minneapolis: University of Minnesota Press.

————. 1998. Police subculture reconsidered. *Criminology* 36 (2): 343–70.

―――. 2006. *Citizens, cops, and power: Recognizing the limits of community*. Chicago: University of Chicago Press.

Hermer, J., M. Kempa, C. Shearing, P. Stenning, and J. Wood. 2005. Policing in Canada in the twenty-first century: Directions for law reform. In *Re-imagining policing in Canada,* ed. D. Cooley. Toronto: University of Toronto Press.

Hersh, S. M. 2004. *Chain of command: The road from 9/11 to Abu Ghraib*. London: HarperCollins.

Hickman, M., A. R. Piquero, and J. R. Greene, eds. 2004. *Police integrity and ethics*. Belmont, CA: Wadsworth Thomson Learning.

Holdaway, S., ed. 1979. *The British police*. London: E. Arnold.

―――. 1983. *Inside the British police: A force at work*. Oxford: Blackwell.

―――. 1996. *The racialisation of British policing*. London: Macmillan.

Hoover, L. T. 2005. From police administration to police science: The development of a police academic establishment in the United States. *Police Quarterly* 8 (1): 8–22.

Horne, A. 2006. *A savage war of peace: Algeria, 1954–1962*. New York: New York Review of Books.

Horowitz, D. L. 1985. *Ethnic Groups in Conflict*. Berkeley and Los Angeles: University of California Press.

―――. 2000. *Ethnic Groups in Conflict*. 2nd ed. Berkeley and Los Angeles: University of California Press.

Hubert, H., and M. Mauss. 1964. *Sacrifice: Its nature and function*. Chicago: University of Chicago Press.

Huey, L. 2007. *Negotiating demands: The politics of skid row policing in Edinburgh, San Francisco, and Vancouver*. Toronto: University of Toronto Press.

Hughes, E. C. 1958. *Men and their work*. New York: Free Press.

Hunt, J. 1985. Police Accounts of Normal Force. *Journal of Contemporary Ethnography* 13(1): 315–341.

Hunt, J., and P. K. Manning. 1991. The social context of police lying. *Symbolic Interaction* 14 (1): 51–70.

Hunter, A. 1974. *Symbolic communities*. Chicago: University of Chicago Press.

Huntington, S. P. 1996. *The clash of civilizations and the remaking of world order*. Chicago: University of Chicago Press.

Innes, M. 2003. *Investigating murder: Detective work and the police response to criminal homicide*. New York: Oxford University Press.

Jackall, R. 2007. *Moral mazes: Bureaucracy and managerial work*. New York: Oxford University Press.

Jacobs, B. A. 1999. *Dealing crack: The social world of streetcorner selling*. Boston: Northeastern University Press.

―――. 2000. *Robbing drug dealers: Violence beyond the law*. New York: Aldine de Gruyter.

Jefferson, T. 1990. *The case against paramilitary policing*. Philadelphia: Open University Press.

Jermier, J. M., and L. J. Berkes. 1979. Leader behavior in a police command bureaucracy: A closer look at the quasi-military model. *Administrative Science Quarterly* 24 (1): 1–23.

Jermier, J. M., J. W. Slocum, L. W. Fry, and J. Gaines. 1991. Organizational subcultures in a soft bureaucracy: Resistance behind the myth and facade of an official culture. *Organization Science* 2 (2): 170–94.

Johnson, J. M., ed. 2008. *My short and happy life as a decorated war hero*. Ed. N. Denzin. Vol. 30, *Studies in symbolic interaction*. New York: Emerald Group.

Johnston, L. 1992. *The rebirth of private policing*. London: Routledge.

―――. 2003. From "pluralisation" to "the police extended family": Discourses on the governance of community policing in Britain. *International Journal of the Sociology of Law* 31 (3): 185–204.

———. 2005. From "community" to "neighbourhood" policing: Police community support officers and the "police extended family" in London. *Journal of Community and Applied Social Psychology* 15 (2005): 241–54.

Johnston, L., and C. D. Shearing. 2003. *Governing security: Explorations in policing and justice.* London: Routledge.

Jones, T., and T. Newburn. 2006. *Plural policing: A comparative perspective.* London: Routledge.

Jones, T., T. Newburn, and D. J. Smith. 1996. Policing and the idea of democracy. *British Journal of Criminology* 36 (2): 182–98.

Kakalik, J., and S. Wildhorn. 1971. *Private policing in the United States.* Washington, DC: U.S. Government Printing Office.

Kane, R. J. 2002. The social ecology of police misconduct. *Criminology* 40 (4): 867–96.

———. 2003. Social control in the metropolis: A community-level examination of the minority group-threat hypothesis. *Justice Quarterly* 20: 265–96.

———. 2005. Compromised police legitimacy as a predictor of violent crime in structurally disadvantaged communities. *Criminology* 43 (2): 469–98.

———. 2006. On the limits of social control: Structural deterrence and the policing of "suppressible" crimes. *Justice Quarterly* 23 (2): 186–213.

Kaplan, R. D. 2005. *Imperial grunts: The American military on the ground.* New York: Random House.

Kappeler, V. E. 2006. *Police and society: Touchstone readings.* 3rd ed. Prospect Heights, IL: Waveland Press.

Karmen, A. 2000. *New York murder mystery: The true story behind the crime crash of the 1990s.* New York: New York University Press.

Katz, C. M. 2001. The establishment of a police gang unit: An examination of organizational and environmental factors. *Criminology* 39: 37–74.

———. 2003. Issues in the production and dissemination of gang statistics: An ethnographic study of a large Midwestern police gang unit. *Crime and Delinquency* 49 (3): 485–516.

Katz, C. M., V. J. Webb, and D. S. Schaefer. 2001. An assessment of the impact of quality-of-life policing on crime and disorder. *Justice Quarterly* 18: 825–76.

Kaufman, H. 1960. *The forest ranger: A study in administrative behavior.* Baltimore: Johns Hopkins University Press, Resources for the Future.

Kean, T. H., and L. H. Hamilton. 2004. *The 9/11 Commission Report: Final report of the National Commission on Terrorist Attacks upon the United States.* New York: W. W. Norton.

Keane, J. 2004. *Violence and democracy.* Cambridge: Cambridge University Press.

Keegan, J. 2003. *Intelligence in war.* New York: Alfred A. Knopf.

Keen, M. H. 1984. *Chivalry.* New Haven: Yale University Press.

Kefalas, M. 2003. *Working-class heroes: Protecting home, community, and nation in a Chicago neighborhood.* Berkeley and Los Angeles: University of California Press.

Kelling, G. L. 1987. Acquiring a taste for order: The community and police. *Crime and Delinquency* 33 (1): 90–102.

———. 1995. How to run a police department. *City Journal* 5 (4): 34–44.

Kelling, G. L., and W. J. Bratton. 1997. Declining Crime Rates: Insiders' Views of the New York City Story. *Journal of Criminal Law and Criminology* 88: 1217–32.

Kelling, G. L., and C. M. Coles. 1998. *Fixing broken windows: Restoring order and reducing crime in our communities.* New York: Free Press.

Kelling, G. L., and R. P. Corbett Jr. 2003. This works: Preventing and reducing crime. *Civic Bulletin* 32.

Kellner, D. 1990. *Television and the crisis of democracy.* Boulder: Westview Press.

———. 1992. *The Persian Gulf TV war.* Boulder: Westview Press.

Kelsen, H. 1999. *General theory of law and state.* New Brunswick, NJ: Transaction.

Kennedy, D. 1998. Pulling levers: Getting deterrence right. *National Institute of Justice Journal* 236: 2–8.

Kennedy, D., A. Braga, A. M. Piehl, and E. J. Waring. 2001. Reducing gun violence: The Boston Gun Project's Operation Ceasefire. In *Research Report: National Institute of Justice.* Washington, DC: U.S. Department of Justice.

Kerik, B. B. 2002. *The lost son: A life in pursuit of justice.* London: HarperCollins.

Kerner, O., J. V. Lindsay, and F. R. Harris. 1968. *Report of the National Advisory Commission on civil disorders.* New York: New York Times Company.

Kessler, R. 1994. *The FBI: Inside the world's most powerful law enforcement agency.* New York: Pocket.

———. 2002. *The bureau: The secret history of the FBI.* New York: St. Martin's Press.

———. 2003. *The CIA at war: Inside the secret campaign against terror.* New York: St. Martin's Press.

Kinsey, R., J. Lea, and J. Young. 1986. *Losing the fight against crime.* Oxford: Blackwell.

Kitson, F. 2005. *Low intensity operations: Subversion, insurgency, peacekeeping.* New York: Hailer Publishing.

Kitson, S. 2008. *The hunt for Nazi spies: Fighting espionage in Vichy France.* Chicago: University of Chicago Press.

Klinger, D. A. 1997. Negotiating order in patrol work: An ecological theory of police response to deviance. *Criminology* 35 (2): 277–306.

Klinger, D. A., and G. S. Bridges. 1997. Measurement error in calls-for-service as an indicator of crime. *Criminology* 35 (4): 705–26.

Klockars, C. B. 1985. *The idea of police.* Thousand Oaks, CA: Sage.

———. 1996. A theory of excessive force and its control. In *Police violence: Understanding and controlling police abuse of force,* ed. W. H. T. Geller. New Haven: Yale University Press.

Klockars, C. B., S. K. Ivkovich, W. Harver, and M. R. Haberfeld. 2000. *The measurement of police integrity.* Washington, DC: National Institute of Justice.

Kraska, P. B. 2001. *Militarizing the American criminal justice system: The changing roles of the armed forces and the police.* Boston: Northeastern University Press.

———, ed. 2004. *Criminal justice as socially constructed reality: Theorizing criminal justice; eight essential orientations.* Prospect Heights, IL: Waveland.

Kraska, P. B., and L. J. Cubellis. 1997. Militarizing Mayberry and beyond: Making sense of American paramilitary policing. *Justice Quarterly* 14: 607–30.

Kraska, P. B., and V. E. Kappeler. 1997. Militarizing American police: The rise and normalization of paramilitary units. *Social Problems* 44 (1): 1–18.

Kubrin, C. E., and R. Weitzer. 2003. Retaliatory homicide: Concentrated disadvantage and neighborhood culture. *Social Problems* 50 (2): 157–80.

Kuhn, T. S. 1970. *The structure of scientific revolutions.* Chicago: University of Chicago Press.

LaFave, W. R. 1965. *Arrest: The decision to take a suspect into custody.* Boston: Little, Brown.

LaFree, G. 1998. *Losing legitimacy: Street crime and the decline of social institutions in America.* Boulder: Westview Press.

Lane, R. 1967. *Policing the city: Boston, 1822–1885.* Cambridge: Harvard University Press.

Langewiesche, W. 2003. *American ground.* New York: North Point Press.

Laurie, P. 1970. *Scotland Yard: A Study of the Metropolitan Police.* London: Bodley Head.

LaVigne, N. G., and J. Wartell. 2000. *Crime mapping case studies: Successes in the field.* Vol. 2. Washington, DC: U.S. Department of Justice, National Institute of Justice Crime Mapping Research Center.

Lawrence, R. G. 2000. *The politics of force: Media and the construction of police brutality.* Berkeley and Los Angeles: University of California Press.

Leishman, F., B. Loveday, and S. P. Savage. 2000. *Core issues in policing.* London: Longman.

Lemert, E. M. 1972. *Human deviance, social problems, and social control.* Englewood Cliffs, NJ: Prentice-Hall.

Lersch, K. M. 2008. *Space, time, and crime.* Durham, NC: Carolina Academic Press.

Levinson, D. 2002. *Encyclopedia of crime and punishment.* Thousand Oaks, CA: Sage.

Levitt, S. D. 1998. The relationship between crime reporting and police: Implications for the use of uniform crime reports. *Journal of Quantitative Criminology* 14 (1): 61–81.

———. 2004. Understanding why crime fell in the 1990s: Four factors that explain the decline and six that do not. *Journal of Economic Perspectives* 18 (1): 163–90.

Lia, B. 2006. *A police force without a state: A history of the Palestinian security forces in the West Bank and Gaza.* Reading, England: Ithaca Press.

Liang, H. 1970. *The Berlin police force in the Weimar Republic.* Berkeley and Los Angeles: University of California Press.

———. 1992. *The rise of modern police and the European state system from Metternich to the Second World War.* Cambridge: Cambridge University Press.

Loader, I. 1997. Policing and the social: Questions of symbolic power. *British Journal of Sociology* 48 (1): 1–18.

———. 2006. Policing, recognition, and belonging. *ANNALS of the American Academy of Political and Social Science* 605 (1): 202–21.

Loader, I., and A. Mulcahy. 2003. *Policing and the condition of England: Memory, politics, and culture.* New York: Oxford University Press.

Loader, I., and N. Walker. 2007. *Civilizing security.* Cambridge: Cambridge University Press.

Long, N. 1958. The local community as an ecology of games. *American Journal of Sociology* 64 (3): 251–61.

———. 1963. The political act as an act of will. *American Journal of Sociology*: 1–6.

Luhmann, N. 1979. *Trust and power: Two works.* New York: Wiley.

Lukes, S. 1977. *Essays in social theory.* London: Macmillan.

Lyon, D. 2001. *Surveillance society: Monitoring everyday life.* Philadelphia: Open University Press.

Lyons, W. 1999. *The politics of community policing: Rearranging the power to punish.* Ann Arbor: University of Michigan Press.

Macaulay, S. 1963. Non-contractual relations in business: A preliminary study. *American Sociological Review* 28 (1): 55–67.

Macleod, R. C. 1976. *The North-West Mounted Police and law enforcement, 1873–1905.* Toronto: University of Toronto Press.

Maguire, E. R. 1997. Structural change in large municipal police organizations during the community policing era. *Justice Quarterly* 14: 547–76.

———. 2003. *Organizational structure in American police agencies: Context, complexity, and control.* Albany: State University of New York Press.

Maguire, E. R., and C. M. Katz. 2002. Community policing, loose coupling, and sensemaking in American police agencies. *Justice Quarterly* 19: 503–36.

Maguire, E. R., and W. R. King. 2004. Trends in the policing industry. *ANNALS of the American Academy of Political and Social Science* 593 (1): 15–41.

Maguire, E. R., J. B. Snipes, C. D. Uchida, and M. Townsend. 1998. Counting cops: Estimating the number of police departments and police officers in the USA. *Policing: An International Journal of Police Strategies and Management* 21 (1): 97–120.

Maguire, M., R. Morgan, and R. Reiner, eds. 2007. *The Oxford handbook of criminology.* 4th ed. Oxford: Clarendon Press.

Manning, P. K. 1974. Dramatic aspects of policing: Selected propositions. *Sociology and Social Research* 59 (1): 21–29.

———. 1977. *Police work: The social organization of policing.* Cambridge: MIT Press.

———. 1979. The reflexivity and facticity of knowledge: Criminal justice research in the seventies. *American Behavioural Scientist* 22: 697–732.

———. 1983. Community policing. *American Journal of Police* 3: 205–27.

———. 1988. *Symbolic communication: Signifying calls and the police response.* Cambridge: MIT Press.

———. 1992. Information technologies and the police. In *Crime and Justice: A Review of Research,* ed. M. N. M. Tonry. Chicago: University of Chicago Press.

———. 1998. The police: Mandate, strategies, and appearances. In *Policing: A view from the street,* edited by P. K. Manning and J. Van Maanen. New York: Random House.

———. 2001. Theorizing policing: The drama and myth of crime control in the NYPD. *Theoretical Criminology* 5 (3): 315–44.

———. 2003. *Policing contingencies.* Chicago: University of Chicago Press.

———. 2005. The study of policing. *Police Quarterly* 8 (1): 23–43.

———. 2008. *The technology of policing: Crime mapping, information technology, and the rationality of crime control.* New York: New York University Press.

———. 2009. Aspects of non-democratic policing: The rise of the Nazi policing system. In *New perspectives on criminal justice,* ed. A. Sarat. London: Emerald.

Manning, P. K., and L. J. Redlinger. 1977. Invitational edges of corruption: Some consequences of narcotic law enforcement. In *Drugs and Politics,* ed. A. Trebach. New Brunswick: Rutgers University Press.

Manning, P. K., and J. Van Maanen, eds. 1978. *Policing: A View from the Street.* Santa Monica, CA: Goodyear Publishing.

Manza, J., and C. Uggen. 2006. *Locked Out: Felon Disenfranchisement and American Democracy.* New York: Oxford University Press.

Maple, J. 1999. *The crime fighter: How you can make your community crime free.* New York: Broadway.

March, J. G., and H. A. Simon. 1958. *Organizations.* New York: John Wiley.

Marenin, O. 1996. *Policing change, changing police: International perspectives.* London: Routledge.

Marrus, M. R., and R. O. Paxton. 1995. *Vichy France and the Jews.* Stanford: Stanford University Press.

Martin, J. P., and G. Wilson. 1969. *The police: A study in manpower.* London: Heinemann.

Massey, D., and N. Denton. 1993. *American apartheid: Segregation and the making of the American underclass.* Cambridge: Harvard University Press.

Mastrofski, S. D. 2004. Controlling street-level police discretion. *ANNALS of the American Academy of Political and Social Science* 593 (1): 100–118.

Mastrofski, S. D., M. D. Reisig, and J. D. McCluskey. 2002. Police disrespect toward the public: An encounter-based analysis. *Criminology* 40 (3): 519–52.

Mastrofski, S. D., and R. R. Ritti. 2000. Making sense of community policing: A theory-based analysis. *Police Practice and Research* 1: 183–210.

Mastrofski, S. D., R. R. Ritti, and D. Hoffmaster. 1987. Organizational determinants of police discretion: The case of drinking-driving. *Journal of Criminal Justice* 15 (5): 387–402.

Mastrofski, S. D., R. R. Ritti, and J. B. Snipes. 1994. Expectancy theory and police productivity in DUI enforcement. *Law and Society Review* 28: 113–48.

Mastrofski, S. D., J. B. Snipes, R. B. Parks, and C. D. Maxwell. 2000. The helping hand of the law: Policing control of citizens on request. *Criminology* 38 (2): 307–42.

Mastrofski, S. D., J. B. Snipes, and A. E. Supina. 1996. Compliance on demand: The public's response to specific police requests. *Journal of Research in Crime and Delinquency* 33 (3): 269–305.

Mastrofski, S. D., R. E. Worden, and J. B. Snipes. 1995. Law enforcement in a time of community policing. *Criminology* 33 (4): 539–63.

Mauss, M. 1990. *The gift: The form and reason for exchange in archaic societies.* London: Routledge.

Mawby, R. C. 2002. *Policing images: Policing, communication, and legitimacy.* Devon: Willan.

Mawby, R. I. 1990. *Comparative policing issues: The British and American experience in international perspective.* London: Unwin Hyman.

———. 1999. *Policing across the world: Issues for the twenty-first century.* London: UCL Press.

———. 2003. Models of policing. In *Handbook of policing,* ed. T. Newburn. Devon: Willan.

Maxfield, M. G., D. A. Lewis, and R. Szoc. 1980. Producing official crimes: Verified crime reports as measures of police output. *Social Science Quarterly* 61 (2): 221–36.

May, R. A. B. 2001. *Talking at Trena's: Everyday conversations at an African American tavern.* New York: New York University Press.

Mayall, J. 1996. *The new interventionism, 1991–1994: United Nations experience in Cambodia, Former Yugoslavia, and Somalia.* Cambridge: Cambridge University Press.

Mazerolle, L., D. W. Soole, and S. Rombouts. 2006. Street-level drug law enforcement: A meta-analytical review. *Journal of Experimental Criminology* 2 (4): 409–35.

———. 2007. Drug law enforcement: A review of the evaluation literature. *Police Quarterly* 10 (2): 115–53.

McCleary, R., B. C. Nienstedt, and J. M. Erven. 1982. Uniform crime reports as organizational outcomes: Three time series experiments. *Social Problems* 29 (4): 361–72.

McClure, J. 1985. *Cop world: Inside an American police force.* New York: Pantheon Books.

McDevitt, J., A. A. Braga, D. Nurge, and M. Buerger. 2003. Boston's youth violence prevention program: A comprehensive community-wide approach. In *Policing Gangs and Youth Violence,* ed. S. H. Decker. Belmont, CA: Wadsworth.

McDonald, P. P., S. Greenberg, and W. J. Bratton. 2002. *Managing police operations: Implementing the New York crime control model Compstat.* Belmont, CA: Wadsworth.

McGarrell, E. F., S. M. Chermak, A. Weiss, and National Institute of Justice. 2002. *Reducing gun violence: Evaluation of the Indianapolis Police Department's directed patrol project.* Washington, DC: U.S. Department of Justice, Office of Justice Programs, National Institute of Justice.

McGarrell, E. F., S. Chermak, A. Weiss, and J. Wilson. 2001. Reducing firearms violence through directed policing patrol. *Criminology and Public Policy* 1 (1): 119–48.

McGarrell, E. F., S. Chermak, J. M. Wilson, and N. Corsaro. 2006. Reducing homicide through a "lever-pulling" strategy. *Justice Quarterly* 23 (2): 214–31.

Meares, T. L., and D. M. Kahan. 1998. Law and (norms of) order in the inner city. *Law and Society Review* 32 (4): 805–38.

Meehan, A. J. 1992. "I don't prevent crime, I prevent calls": Policing as a negotiated order. *Symbolic Interaction* 15 (4): 455–80.

———. 1993. Internal police records and the control of juveniles: Politics and policing in a suburban town. *British Journal of Criminology* 33 (4): 504–24.

———. 1998. The impact of mobile data terminal (MDT) information technology on communication and recordkeeping in patrol work. *Qualitative Sociology* 21 (3): 225–54.

———. 2000. The organizational career of gang statistics: The politics of policing gangs. *Sociological Quarterly* 41 (3): 337–70.

Meehan, A. J., and M. C. Ponder. 2002. Race and place: The ecology of racial profiling African American motorists. *Justice Quarterly* 19: 399–430.

Merelman, R. M. 1998. On legitimalaise in the United States: A Weberian analysis. *Sociological Quarterly* 39: 351–68.

Merkl, P. H. 1975. *Political violence under the swastika: 581 early Nazis.* Princeton: Princeton University Press.

Messner, S. F., S. Galea, K. J. Tardiff, M. Tracy, A. Bucciarelli, T. M. Piper, V. Frye, and D. Vlahov. 2007. Policing, drugs, and the homicide decline in New York City in the 1990s. *Criminology* 45 (2): 385–414.

Meyer, J. W., and B. Rowan. 1977. Institutionalized organizations: Formal structure as myth and ceremony. *American Journal of Sociology* 83 (2): 340–63.

Miller, J. G. 1996. *Search and destroy: African-American males in the criminal justice system.* Cambridge: Cambridge University Press.

Miller, W. R. 1977. *Cops and bobbies: Police authority in New York and London, 1830–1870.* Chicago: University of Chicago Press.

Mills, C. W. 1940. Situated actions and vocabularies of motive. *American Sociological Review* 5 (6): 904–13.

———. 2000. *The sociological imagination.* New York: Oxford University Press.

Monkkonen, E. H. 1981. *Police in urban America, 1860–1920.* Cambridge: Cambridge University Press.

———. 1992. History of urban police. In *Modern Policing,* ed. M. Tonry and N. Morris. Chicago: University of Chicago Press.

Moore, M. H. 1977. *Buy and bust: The effective regulation of an illicit market in heroin.* Lexington, MA: Lexington Books.

———. 1995. *Creating public value: Strategic management in government.* Cambridge: Harvard University Press.

———. 2003. Sizing up Compstat: An important administrative innovation in policing. *Criminology and Public Policy* 2 (3): 469–94.

Moore, M. H., G. L. Kelling, R. C. Trojanowicz, Policy Harvard University Program in Criminal Justice and Management. 1988. *Crime and policing.* Cambridge: John F. Kennedy School of Government, Harvard University.

Morenoff, J. D., and R. J. Sampson. 1997. Violent crime and the spatial dynamics of neighborhood transition: Chicago, 1970–1990. *Social Forces* 76: 31–64.

Morenoff, J. D., R. J. Sampson, and S. W. Raudenbush. 2001. Neighborhood inequality, collective efficacy, and the spatial dynamics of urban violence. *Criminology* 39 (3): 517–58.

Moskos, P. 2008. *Cop in the hood: My year policing Baltimore's Eastern District.* Princeton: Princeton University Press.

Mulcahy, A. 2006. *Policing Northern Ireland: Conflict, legitimacy, and reform.* Devon: Willan Publishing.

Murphy, C. 1998. Policing postmodern Canada. *Canadian Journal of Law and Society* 13: 1–25.

Nadelmann, E. A. 1993. *Cops across borders: The internationalization of U.S. criminal law enforcement.* University Park: Pennsylvania State University Press.

Nagl, J. A. 2005. *Learning to eat soup with a knife.* Chicago: University of Chicago Press.

Nalla, M., M. J. Lynch, and M. J. Leiber. 1997. Determinants of police growth in Phoenix, 1950–1988. *Justice Quarterly* 14: 115–44.

Nalla, M., and G. Newman. 1990. *Primer in private security.* Albany: Harrow and Hudson.

National Advisory Commission on Criminal Justice, Standards, Goals, and United States. 1972. Progress report of the National Advisory Commission on Criminal Justice Standards and Goals, May 1972. Executive summary.

National Research Council. 2004. *Fairness and effectiveness in policing: The evidence.* Washington, DC: National Research Council.

Nesbary, D. K. 1998. Handling emergency calls for service: Organizational production of crime statistics. *Policing: An International Journal of Police Strategies and Management* 21: 576–99.

Newburn, T., ed. 2003. *Handbook of policing.* Devon: Willan Publishing.

Newburn, T., T. Williamson, and A. Wright, eds. 2007. *Handbook of criminal investigation.* Devon: Willan Publishing.

Niederhoffer, A. 1967. *Behind the shield: The police in urban society.* New York: Doubleday.

Nunn, S., K. Quinet, K. Rowe, and D. Christ. 2006. Interdiction day: Covert surveillance operations, drugs, and serious crime in an inner-city neighborhood. *Police Quarterly* 9 (1): 73–99.

Odom, W. E. 2004. *Fixing intelligence: For a more secure America.* New Haven: Yale University Press.

O'Toole, K. 2007. *Report of the Garda Siochana Inspectorate.* Dublin, Ireland.

Ousby, I. 1998. *Occupation: The ordeal of France, 1940–1944.* New York: St. Martin's Press.

Palmer, S. H. 1988. *Police and protest in England and Ireland, 1780–1850.* Cambridge: Cambridge University Press.

Parker, K. F., B. J. Stults, and S. K. Rice. 2005. Racial threat, concentrated disadvantage, and social control: Considering the macro-level sources of variation in arrests. *Criminology* 43: 1111–34.

Parks, R. B., S. D. Mastrofski, C. Dejong, and M. K. Gray. 1999. How officers spend their time with the community. *Justice Quarterly* 16: 483–518.

Pattavina, A., J. M. Byrne, and L. Garcia. 2006. An examination of citizen involvement in crime prevention in high-risk versus low- to moderate-risk neighborhoods. *Crime and Delinquency* 52 (2): 203–31.

Patten, C. 1999. *A new beginning: Policing in Northern Ireland.* Belfast: Independent Commission on Policing for Northern Ireland.

Pattillo-McCoy, M. E. 1997. Sweet mothers and gangbangers: Managing crime in a black middle-class neighborhood. *Social Forces* 76: 747–74.

———. 2000. *Black picket fences: Privilege and peril among the black middle class.* Chicago: University of Chicago Press.

———. 2007. *Black on the block: The politics of race and class in the city.* Chicago: University of Chicago Press.

Paxton, R., and M. Marrus. 1981. *Vichy France and the Jews.* New York: Basic Books.

Pepinsky, H. E. 1976. Police patrolmen's offense-reporting behavior. *Journal of Research in Crime and Delinquency* 13: 33–47.

Pepper, S. C. 1972. *World hypotheses: A study in evidence.* Berkeley and Los Angeles: University of California Press.

Perrow, C. 1984. *Normal accidents: Living with high-risk technology.* New York: Basic Books.

Piliavin, I., and S. Briar. 1964. Police encounters with juveniles. *American Journal of Sociology* 70 (2): 206–14.

Pino, N., and M. D. Wiatrowski. 2006. *Democratic policing in transitional and developing countries.* Burlington, VT: Ashgate.

Powers, T. 2004. *Intelligence wars: American secret history from Hitler to Al-Qaeda.* New York: New York Review of Books.

Preiss, J. J., and H. J. Ehrlich. 1966. *An examination of role theory: The case of the state police.* Lincoln: University of Nebraska Press.

President's Commission on Law Enforcement and Administration of Justice. 1967. *The challenge of crime in a free society.* Washington, DC: U.S. Government Printing Office.

Punch, M. 1979. *Policing the inner city.* London: Macmillan.

———. 1983. *Control in the police organization.* Cambridge: MIT Press.

———. 1985. *Conduct unbecoming: The social construction of police deviance and control.* London: Tavistock.

———. 2007. *Zero-tolerance policing.* Amsterdam: Policy Press.

Quillian, L., and D. Pager. 2001. Black neighbors, higher crime? The role of racial stereotypes in evaluations of neighborhood crime. *American Journal of Sociology* 107 (3): 717–67.

Radzinowicz, L. 1968. *A history of English criminal law: Grappling for control.* Vol. 4. London: Stevens.

Radzinowicz, L., and R. G. Hood. 1948. *A history of English criminal law and its administration from 1750.* 3 vols. London: Stevens.

Rafter, N. 2000. *Encyclopedia of women and crime.* Phoenix: Oryx Press.

Rawlings, P. 1995. The idea of policing: A history. *Policing and Society* 5 (2): 129–49.

———. 2002. *Policing: A short history.* Devon: Willan Publishing.

Rawls, A. W. 1987. The interaction order sui generis: Goffman's contribution to social theory. *Sociological Theory* 5 (2): 136–49.

———. 1996. Durkheim's epistemology: The neglected argument. *American Journal of Sociology* 102 (2): 430–82.

Rawls, J. 1955. Two concepts of rules. *Philosophical Review* 64 (1): 3–32.

———. 1993. *Political liberalism.* New York: Columbia University Press.

———. 1999. *A theory of justice.* Oxford: Oxford University Press.

———. 2000. *Lectures on the history of moral philosophy.* Cambridge: Harvard University Press.

Rawls, J., and E. Kelly. 2001. *Justice as fairness: A restatement.* Cambridge: Harvard University Press.

Reaves, B., M. J. Hickman, United States, and Bureau of Justice Statistics. 2002. *Census of state and local law enforcement agencies, 2000.* Washington, DC: U.S. Department of Justice, Office of Justice Programs.

Reichel, P. L. 1988. Southern slave patrols as a transitional police type. *American Journal of Police* 7: 51–78.

Reiner, R. 1978. *The blue-coated worker: A sociological study of police unionism.* Cambridge: Cambridge University Press.

———. 1991. *Chief constables: Bobbies, bosses, or bureaucrats?* Oxford: Oxford University Press.

———. 2000. *The politics of the police.* 3rd ed. Oxford: Oxford University Press.

Reisig, M. D., J. D. McCluskey, S. D. Mastrofski, and W. Terrill. 2004. Suspect Disrespect toward the Police. *Justice Quarterly* 21: 241–68.

Reisig, M. D., and R. B. Parks. 2000. Experience, quality of life, and neighborhood context: A hierarchical analysis of satisfaction with police. *Justice Quarterly* 17: 607–30.

———. 2004. Can community policing help the truly disadvantaged? *Journal of Research in Crime and Delinquency* 50 (2): 139–67.

Reiss, A. J., Jr. 1971. *The police and the public.* New Haven: Yale University Press.

———. 1974. Discretionary justice. In *Handbook of criminology,* ed. D. Glaser. Chicago: Rand-McNally.

———. 1992. Police organization in the 20th century. In *Modern policing: Crime and justice; a review of research,* edited by M. Tonry and N. Morris. Chicago: University of Chicago

———. 1995. The role of the police in crime prevention. In *Integrating crime prevention strategies: Propensity and opportunity.* Stockholm: Scandinavian Criminological Society.

Reiss, A. J., Jr., and D. Bordua. 1967. Environment and organization: A perspective on the police. In *The police: Six sociological essays,* ed. D. Bordua. New York: John Wiley.

Reppetto, T. A. 1978. *The blue parade.* New York: Free Press.

Rex, J., and R. Moore. 1967. *Race, community, and conflict: A study of Sparkbrook.* Oxford: Oxford University Press.

Reynolds, G. W., and A. Judge. 1968. *The night the police went on strike.* Worthing, UK: Little-hampton Book Services.

Richardson, J. F. 1970. *The New York police, colonial times to 1901.* Oxford: Oxford University Press.

———. 1974. *Urban police in the United States.* New York: Kennikat Press.

Richman, D. C. 2000. The changing boundaries between federal and local law enforcement. In *Criminal Justice: 2000,* ed. J. Horney. Washington, DC: U.S. Department of Justice.

Rigakos, G. 2002. *The new parapolice: Risk markets and commodified social control.* Toronto: University of Toronto Press.

Rigakos, G., Commission du droit Canada, and Law Commission of Canada. 2001. *In search of security: The roles of public police and private agencies.* Ottawa: Law Commission of Canada.

Robinson, C. D., and R. Scaglion. 1987. The origin and evolution of the police function in society: Notes toward a theory. *Law and Society Review* 21: 109–53.

Robinson, C. M. 2000. *The men who wear the star: The story of the Texas Rangers.* New York: Random House.

Romney, M. 2007. *Turnaround: Crisis, leadership, and the Olympic Games.* Washington, DC: Regnery Publishing.

Rose, D. R., and T. R. Clear. 1998. Incarceration, social capital, and crime: Implications for social disorganization theory. *Criminology* 36 (3): 441–80.

Rosenbaum, D., ed. 1994. *The challenge of community policing: Testing the promises.* Newbury Park, CA: Sage.

Rosenbaum, D., and D. Wilkinson. 2004. Can police adapt? Tracking the effects of organizational reform over six years. In *Community policing: Can it work,* ed. D. Rosenbaum. Thousand Oaks, CA: Sage.

Rosenfeld, R., R. Fornango, and A. F. Rengifo. 2007. The impact of order-maintenance on New York City homicide and robbery rates, 1988–2001. *Criminology* 45 (2): 355–84.

Rossmo, D. K. 2000. *Geographic profiling.* Boca Raton: CRC Press.

Rousseau, J. J. 1920. *The social contract, and discourses.* New York: E. P. Dutton.

———. 1999. *Discourse on the origin of inequality.* Oxford: Oxford University Press.

Roy, D. 1953. Work satisfaction and social reward in quota achievement: An analysis of piecework incentive. *American Sociological Review* 18 (5): 507–14.

———. 1954. Efficiency and "the fix": Informal intergroup relations in a piecework machine shop. *American Journal of Sociology* 60 (3): 255–66.

———. 1959. "Banana time": Job satisfaction and informal interaction. *Human Organization* 18: 158–68.

———. 2006. Cooperation and conflict in the factory: Some observations and questions regarding conceptualization of intergroup relations within bureaucratic social structures. *Qualitative Sociology* 29 (1): 59–85.

Rubinstein, J. 1973. *City police.* New York: Farrar, Straus, and Giroux.

Russell, F. 1975. *A city in terror: The Boston police strike.* New York: Viking.

Ryan, A., ed. 1993. *Justice.* Oxford: Oxford University Press.

St. Jean, P. 2007. *Pockets of crime.* Chicago: University of Chicago Press.

Samora, J., J. Bernal, and A. Peña. 1979. *Gunpowder justice: A reassessment of the Texas Rangers.* Notre Dame: University of Notre Dame Press.

Sampson, R. J. 1987. Urban black violence: The effect of male joblessness and family disruption. *American Journal of Sociology* 93 (2): 348–82.

———. 2002. Transcending tradition: New directions in community research, Chicago style. *Criminology* 40 (2): 213–30.

Sampson, R. J., and D. J. Bartusch. 1998. Legal cynicism and (subcultural) tolerance of deviance: The neighborhood context of racial difference. *Law and Society Review* 32: 777–804.

Sampson, R. J., and W. B. Groves. 1989. Community structure and crime: Testing social-disorganization theory. *American Journal of Sociology* 94 (4): 774–802.

Sampson, R. J., D. McAdam, H. MacIndoe, and S. Weffer-Elizondo. 2005. Civil society reconsidered: The durable nature and community structure of collective civic action. *American Journal of Sociology* 111 (3): 673–714.

Sampson, R. J., and S. W. Raudenbush. 1999. Systematic social observation of public spaces: A new look at disorder in urban neighborhoods. *American Journal of Sociology* 105 (3): 603–51.

————. 2004. Seeing disorder: Neighborhood stigma and the social construction of "broken windows." *Social Psychology Quarterly* 67 (4): 319–42.

Sampson, R. J., S. W. Raudenbush, and F. Earls. 1997. Neighborhoods and violent crime: A multilevel study of collective efficacy. *Science* 277 (5328): 918–24.

Sampson, R. J., and W. J. Wilson. 1995. Toward a theory of race, crime, and urban inequality. In *Crime and Inequality,* eds. J. Hagan and R. Peterson. Stanford: Stanford University Press.

Scahill, J. 2007. *Blackwater: The rise of the world's most powerful mercenary army.* New York: Nation Books.

Scarman, Lord, and Justice. 1972. Violence and civil disturbance in Northern Ireland in 1969. London.

Scheingold, S. A. 1984. *The politics of law and order: Street crime and public policy.* London: Longman.

————. 1991. *The politics of street crime: Criminal process and cultural obsession.* Philadelphia: Temple University Press.

Schmitt, C. 1986. *Political Romanticism.* Trans. Guy Oakes. Cambridge: MIT Press.

Schwartz, R. D., and J. C. Miller. 1964. Legal evolution and societal complexity. *American Journal of Sociology* 70 (2): 159–69.

Scott, J. C. 1990. *Domination and the arts of resistance: Hidden transcripts.* New Haven: Yale University Press.

————. 1998. *Seeing like a state: How certain schemes to improve the human condition have failed.* New Haven: Yale University Press.

Scott, R. F., and L. Huxley. 1914. *Scott's Last Expedition.* New York: Smith, Elder.

Sebald, W. G. 2003. *On the natural history of destruction.* New York: Random House.

Seidman, D., and M. Couzens. 1973. Getting the crime rate down: Political pressure and crime reporting. *Law and Society Review* 8: 457–94.

Sellen, A., and R. Harper. 2003. *The myth of the paperless office.* Cambridge: MIT Press.

Sellin, T. 1938. Culture, conflict, and crime. *American Journal of Sociology* 44 (1): 97–103.

Shearing, C. D. 1992. Relation between public and private policing. In *Crime and justice: A review of research,* ed. M. N. M. Tonry. Chicago: University of Chicago Press.

————. 2005. Nodal security. *Police Quarterly* 8 (1): 57–63.

Shearing, C. D., and R. V. Ericson. 1991. Culture as figurative action. *British Journal of Sociology* 42 (4): 481–506.

Shearing, C. D., and P. C. Stenning. 1983a. Private security: Implications for social control. *Social Problems* 30 (5): 493–506.

Shearing, C. D., and P. C. Stenning, eds. 1983b. *Private security: Its growth and implications.* Vol. 3, *Crime and Justice: An Annual Review of Research.* Chicago: University of Chicago Press.

Sheptycki, J. W. E. 2000. *Issues in transnational policing.* London: Routledge.

Sherman, L. W. 1978a. Introduction: Towards a sociological theory of police corruption. In *Police corruption,* ed. L. Sherman. New York: Anchor Press/Doubleday.

————. 1978b. *The quality of police education.* San Francisco: Jossey-Bass Publishers.

————. 1980. Causes of police behavior: The current state of quantitative research. *Journal of Research in Crime and Delinquency* 17 (1): 69–100.

————. 1990. Police crackdowns: Initial and residual deterrence. In *Crime and justice: A review of research,* eds. M. Tonry and N. Morris. Chicago: University of Chicago Press.

————. 1992. Attacking crime: Police and crime control. In *Crime and justice: A review of research,* eds. M. Tonry and N. Morris. Chicago: University of Chicago Press.

————. 2005. The use and usefulness of criminology, 1751–2005: Enlightened justice and its failures. *ANNALS of the American Academy of Political and Social Science* 600 (1): 115–35.

————. 2007. The power few: Experimental criminology and the reduction of harm. *Journal of Experimental Criminology* 3 (4): 299–321.

Sherman, L. W., and R. A. Berk. 1984. The specific deterrent effects of arrest for domestic assault. *American Sociological Review*: 261–72.

Sherman, L. W., P. R. Gartin, and M. E. Buerger. 1989. Hot spots of predatory crime: Routine activities and the criminology of place. *Criminology* 27 (1): 27–56.

Sherman, L. W., C. H. Milton, and T. Kelly. 1973. *Team policing: Seven case studies*. Washington, DC: Police Foundation.

Sherman, L. W., J. D. Schmidt, D. P. Rogan, P. R. Gartin, E. G. Cohn, D. J. Collins, and A. R. Bacich. 1991. From initial deterrence to long-term escalation: Short-custody arrest for poverty ghetto domestic violence. *Criminology* 29 (4): 821–50.

Short, J. F. 1984. The social fabric at risk: Toward the social transformation of risk analysis. *American Sociological Review* 49 (6): 711–25.

Siegel, L. J. 2006. *Criminology*. Belmont, CA: Wadsworth Thomson.

Silver, A. 1967. The demand for order. In *The police: Six sociological essays,* ed. D. J. Bordua. New York: Wiley.

Silver, E., and L. L. Miller. 2004. Sources of informal social control in Chicago neighborhoods. *Criminology* 42 (3): 551–84.

Silverman, E. B. 1999. *NYPD battles crime: Innovative strategies in policing*. Boston. Northeastern University Press.

Simon, J. 2007. *Governing through crime: How the war on crime transformed American democracy and created a culture of fear*. New York: Oxford University Press.

Singer, P. W. 2004. *Corporate warriors: The rise of the privatized military industry*. Ithaca: Cornell University Press.

Sklansky, D. A. 2005. Police and democracy. *Michigan Law Review* 103: 1699.

———. 2007. *Democracy and the police*. Stanford: Stanford University Press.

Skogan, W. G. 1990. *Disorder and decline: Crime and the spiral of decay in American neighborhoods*. New York: Free Press.

———. 1994. The impact of community policing on neighborhood residents: A cross-site analysis. In *The challenge of community policing: Testing the promises,* ed. D. P. Rosenbaum. Thousand Oaks, CA: Sage.

———, ed. 2004. *Community policing: Can it work?* Boulder: Westview.

———. 2006. *Police and community in Chicago: A tale of three cities*. New York: Oxford University Press.

Skogan, W. G., and S. M. Hartnett. 1997. *Community policing, Chicago style*. New York: Oxford University Press.

Skogan, W. G., S. M. Hartnett, J. DuBois, J. T. Comey, M. Kaiser, and J. H. Lovig. 1999. *On the beat: Police and community problem solving*. Boulder: Westview Press.

Skogan, W. G., and T. L. Meares. 2004. Lawful policing. *ANNALS of the American Academy of Political and Social Science* 593 (1): 66–83.

Skolnick, J. H. 1966. *Justice without trial: Law enforcement in democratic society*. New York: Wiley.

———. 1969. *The politics of protest*. New York: Simon and Schuster.

Skolnick, J. H., and J. J. Fyfe. 1994. *Above the law: Police and the excessive use of force*. New York: Free Press.

Small, M. L. 2006. *Villa Victoria: The transformation of social capital in a Boston barrio*. Chicago: University of Chicago Press.

Smith, B. 1949. *Police systems in the United States*. New York: Harper and Brothers.

———. 1969. *The state police*. Montclair, NJ: Patterson Smith.

Smith, D. A. 1986. The neighborhood context of police behavior. In *Crime and justice,* ed. T. Morris. Chicago: University of Chicago Press.

Smith, D. J., S. Small, and J. Gray. 1983. *Police and people in London*. London: Policy Studies Institute.

Sometimes the numbers crunch back. 2005. *Law Enforcement News* 31 (628).

Souryal, S. S. 2003. *Ethics in criminal justice.* 3rd ed. Cincinnati: Anderson.

Sousa, W. H., and G. L. Kelling. 2006. Of "broken windows," criminology, and criminal justice. In *Police innovation: Contrasting perspectives,* eds. D. Weisburd and A. Braga. New York: Cambridge University Press.

Stalker, J. 1988. *The Stalker affair.* New York: Viking Press.

Staples, W. G. 2000. *Everyday surveillance: Vigilance and visibility in postmodern life.* Lanham, MD: Rowman and Littlefield.

Stark, R. 1972. *Police riots: Collective violence and law enforcement.* Belmont, CA: Wadsworth.

Stenning, P. C. 1994. Police and politics: There and back and there again? In *Police powers in Canada: The evolution and practice of authority,* ed. D. S. R. C. Macleod. Toronto: University of Toronto Press.

———, ed. 1995. *Accountability for criminal justice.* Toronto: University of Toronto Press.

———. 2008. Brief encounters: A tales of two commissioners. In *Honouring social justice,* ed. M. Beare. Toronto: University of Toronto Press.

Stenning, P. C., and C. D. Shearing. 1981. Modern private security: Its growth and implications. In *Crime and Justice: A Review of Research.* Chicago: University of Chicago Press.

———. 1991. Policing. In *Criminology: A reader's guide,* ed. E. Fattah. Toronto: Canadian Criminal Justice Association.

Storch, R. 1975. The plague of blue locusts: Police reform and popular resistance in northern England, 1840–1857. *International Review of Social History* 20 (1): 61–90.

Stoutland, S. E. 2001. The multiple dimensions of trust in resident/police relations in Boston. *Journal of Research in Crime and Delinquency* 38 (3): 226–56.

Stults, B. J., and E. P. Baumer. 2007. Racial context and police force size: Evaluating the empirical validity of the minority threat perspective. *American Journal of Sociology* 113 (2): 507–46.

Sullivan, L. E., M. S. Rosen, M. R. Haberfeld, and D. M. Schulz. 2005. *Encyclopedia of law enforcement.* Thousand Oaks, CA: Sage.

Sunstein, C. 1992. On analogical reasoning. *Harvard Law Review* 106: 741–91.

Sykes, G. W. 1986. Street justice: A moral defense of order maintenance policing. *Justice Quarterly* 3: 497–512.

Sykes, R. E., and E. E. Brent. 1983. *Policing, a social behaviorist perspective: A social behaviorist perspective.* New Brunswick: Rutgers University Press.

Taylor, P. 1980. *Beating the terrorists? Interrogation at Omagh, Gough, and Castlereagh.* Middlesex: Penguin Books.

Taylor, R. B. 2000. *Breaking away from broken windows: Evidence from Baltimore neighborhoods and the nationwide fight against crime, grime, fear, and decline.* Boulder: Westview Press.

Terrill, W., and S. D. Mastrofski. 2002. Situational and officer-based determinations of police coercion. *Justice Quarterly* 19: 215–48.

Terrill, W., E. A. Paoline, and P. K. Manning. 2003. Police culture and coercion. *Criminology* 41 (4): 1003–34.

Thacher, D. 2001. Conflicting values in community policing. *Law and Society Review* 35: 765–98.

———. 2003. Order maintenance reconsidered: Moving beyond strong causal reasoning. *Journal of Criminal Law and Criminology* 94: 381–414.

Thompson, J. D. 2003. *Organizations in action: Social science bases of administrative theory.* New Brunswick, NJ: Transaction.

Tien, J. M., J. W. Simon, and R. C. Larson. 1978. An alternative approach in police patrol: The Wilmington split-force experiment. In *Washington, D.C.: National Institute of Law Enforcement and Criminal Justice.* Washington, DC.

Tita, G., National Institute of Justice , and Corporation Rand. 2005. *Reducing gun violence:*

Operation Ceasefire in Los Angeles. Washington, DC: U.S. Department of Justice, Office of Justice Programs, National Institute of Justice.

Tonry, M. 1995. *Malign neglect: Race, crime, and punishment in America.* Oxford: Oxford University Press.

Tonry, M., and N. Morris. 1992. *Modern policing: Crime and justice.* Chicago: University of Chicago Press.

Trebach, A. S., ed. 1970. *The rationing of justice.* New Brunswick: Rutgers University Press.

Trojanowicz, R. C., and B. Bucqueroux. 1990. *Community policing: A contemporary perspective.* Cincinnati: Anderson.

Tuch, S. A., and R. Weitzer. 1997. Trends: Racial differences in attitudes toward the police. *Public Opinion Quarterly* 61 (4): 642–63.

Turk, A. T. 1969. *Criminality and legal order.* Chicago: Rand McNally.

Tyler, T. R. 2006. *Why people obey the law.* Princeton: Princeton University Press.

Tyler, T. R., and Y. J. Huo. 2002. *Trust in the law: Encouraging public cooperation with the police and courts.* New York: Russell Sage Foundation.

Utley, R. M. 2002. *Lone Star justice: The first century of the Texas Rangers.* New York: Oxford University Press.

———. 2007. *Lone Star lawmen: The second century of the Texas Rangers.* New York: Oxford University Press.

Van Maanen, J. 1973a. Observations on the making of policemen. *Human Organization* 32 (4): 407–18.

———. 1973b. Working the street: A developmental view of police behavior. In *Annals of criminal justice,* ed. H. Jacobs. Beverly Hills: Sage.

———. 1975. Police socialization: A longitudinal examination of job attitudes in an urban police department. *Administrative Science Quarterly* 20 (2): 207–28.

———. 1978. The asshole. In *Policing: A view from the street,* ed. P. J. Manning and J. J. E. Van Maanen. New York: Random House.

———. 1983. The boss: First-line supervision in an American police agency. In *Control in the police organization,* ed. M. Punch. Cambridge: MIT Press.

———. 1984. Making rank: Becoming an American police sergeant. *Journal of Contemporary Ethnography* 13 (2): 155–76.

———. 1988. *Tales of the field: On writing ethnography.* Chicago: University of Chicago Press.

Velez, M. B. 2001. The role of public social control in urban neighborhoods: A multilevel analysis of victimization risk. *Criminology* 39 (4): 837–64.

Venkatesh, S. A. 1997. The social organization of street gang activity in an urban ghetto. *American Journal of Sociology* 103 (1): 82–111.

———. 2002. *American project: The rise and fall of a modern ghetto.* Cambridge: Harvard University Press.

———. 2006. *Off the books: The underground economy of the urban poor.* Cambridge: Harvard University Press.

———. 2008. *Gang leader for a day: A rogue sociologist takes to the streets.* New York: Penguin Press.

Vinen, R. 2006. *The unfree French.* New Haven: Yale University Press.

Vold, G. B., T. J. Bernard, and J. B. Snipes. 1958. *Theoretical criminology.* New York: Oxford University Press.

Vollmer, A. 1936. *The police and modern society.* Montclair, NJ: Patterson Smith.

Waddington, P. A. J. 1991. *The strong arm of the law: Armed and public order policing.* New York: Oxford University Press.

———. 1999. Police (canteen) sub-culture: An appreciation. *British Journal of Criminology* 39 (2): 287–309.

Waegel, W. B. 1981. Case routinization in investigative police work. *Social Problems* 28 (3): 263–75.

Waegel, W. E. 1982. Patterns of police investigation of urban crimes. *Journal of Police Science and Administration* 10: 452–65.

Wakefield, A. 2003. *Selling security: The private policing of public space.* Devon: Willan Publishing.

Wakeman, F. 1995. *Policing Shanghai, 1927–1937.* Berkeley and Los Angeles: University of California Press.

———. 2002. *The Shanghai badlands: Wartime terrorism and urban crime, 1937–1941.* Cambridge: Cambridge University Press.

Walker, D. 1968. *Rights in conflict: Chicago's 7 brutal days.* New York: Grosset and Dunlap.

Walker, S. 1984. Broken windows and fractured history: The use and misuse of history in recent police patrol analysis. *Justice Quarterly* 1: 75–90.

———. 2001. *Police accountability.* Belmont, CA: Wadsworth Thomson Learning.

———. 2005. *The new world of police accountability.* Thousand Oaks, CA: Sage.

Walker, S., and C. M. Katz. 2005. *The police in America.* 4th ed. New York: McGraw-Hill.

Walsh, W. F. 1986. Patrol officer arrest rates: A study of the social organization of police work. *Justice Quarterly* 3: 271–90.

———. 2001. Compstat: An analysis of an emerging police managerial paradigm. *Policing: An International Journal of Police Strategies and Management* 24 (3): 347–62.

Waring, E. J., and D. Weisburd, eds. 2001. *Crime and social organization.* New Brunswick, NJ: Transaction.

Warner, B. D. 1997. Community characteristics and the recording of crime: Police recording of citizens' complaints of burglary and assault. *Justice Quarterly* 14: 631–50.

———. 2003. The role of attenuated culture in social disorganization theory. *Criminology* 41 (1): 73–98.

———. 2007. Directly intervene or call the authorities? A study of forms of neighborhood social control within a social disorganization framework. *Criminology* 45 (1): 99–129.

Warner, B. D., and G. L. Pierce. 1993. Reexamining social disorganization theory using calls to the police as a measure of crime. *Criminology* 31 (4): 493–517.

Weatheritt, M. 1986. *Innovations in policing.* New York: Croom Helm in association with the Police Foundation.

Webb, W. P., F. MacMurray, J. Oakie, U. Pictures, and P. Pictures. 1965. *The Texas Rangers: A century of frontier defense.* Austin: University of Texas Press.

Weber, M. 1947. *The theory of economic and social organization.* Trans. T. Parsons. New York: Oxford University Press.

Weick, K. E. 2000. *Sensemaking in organizations.* Thousand Oaks, CA: Sage.

———. 2001. *Making sense of the organization.* Oxford: Blackwell.

Weisburd, D., and A. Braga, eds. 2006. *Police innovation.* Cambridge Studies in Criminology. Cambridge: Cambridge University Press.

Weisburd, D., S. Bushway, C. Lum, and S. Yang. 2004. Trajectories of crime at places: A longitudinal study of street segments in the city of Seattle. *Criminology* 42 (2): 283–322.

Weisburd, D., and J. E. Eck. 2004. What can police do to reduce crime, disorder, and fear? *ANNALS of the American Academy of Political and Social Science* 593 (1): 242–65.

Weisburd, D., and L. Green. 1995. Policing drug hot spots: The Jersey City drug market analysis experiment. *Justice Quarterly* 12: 711–36.

Weisburd, D., and C. Lum. 2005. The diffusion of computerized crime mapping in policing: Linking research and practice. *Police Practice and Research* 6 (5): 419–34.

Weisburd, D., S. D. Mastrofski, A. McNally, R. Greenspan, and J. J. Willis. 2003. Reforming to Preserve: Compstat and strategic problem solving in American policing. *Criminology and Public Policy* 2 (3): 421–56.

Weisburd, D., and L. G. Mazerolle. 2000. Crime and disorder in drug hot spots: Implications for theory and practice in policing. *Police Quarterly* 3 (3): 331–49.

Weisburd, D., L. A. Wyckoff, J. Ready, J. E. Eck, J. C. Hinkle, and F. Gajewski. 2006. Does crime just move around the corner? A controlled study of spatial displacement and diffusion of crime control benefits in two crime hot spots. *Criminology* 44 (3): 549–92.

Weisheit, R. A., D. N. Falcone, and L. E. Wells. 1999. *Crime and policing in rural and small town America.* Prospect Heights, IL: Waveland Press.

Weitzer, R. 1990. *Transforming settler states: Communal conflict and internal security in Northern Ireland and Zimbabwe.* Berkeley and Los Angeles: University of California Press.

———. 1995. *Policing under fire: Ethnic conflict and police-community relations in Northern Ireland.* Albany: State University of New York Press.

———. 1999. Citizens' perceptions of police misconduct: Race and neighborhood context. *Justice Quarterly* 16: 819–46.

———. 2000. Racialized policing: Residents' perceptions in three neighborhoods. *Law and Society Review* 34 (1): 129–55.

Weitzer, R., and S. A. Tuch. 1999. Race, class, and perceptions of discrimination by the police. *Crime and Delinquency* 45 (4): 494–507.

———. 2002. Perceptions of racial profiling: Race, class, and personal experience. *Criminology* 40 (2): 435–56.

———. 2004a. Race and perceptions of police misconduct. *Social Problems* 51 (3): 305–25.

———. 2004b. Racially biased policing: Determinants of citizen perceptions. *Social Forces* 83: 1009–30.

———. 2004c. Reforming the police: Radical differences in public support for change. *Criminology* 42 (2): 391–416.

———. 2006. *Race and police in America.* New York: Cambridge University Press.

Wender, Jonathon. 2008. *Policing and the poetics of everyday life.* Urbana: University of Illinois Press.

Westermann, E. B., and D. E. Showalter. 2005. *Hitler's police battalions: Enforcing racial war in the East.* Lawrence: University Press of Kansas.

Western, B. 2007. *Punishment and inequality in America.* New York: Russell Sage Foundation.

Westley, W. A. 1953. Violence and the police. *American Journal of Sociology* 59 (1): 34–41.

———. 1955. Secrecy and the police. *Social Forces* 34: 254–57.

———. 1970. *Violence and the police: A sociological study of law, custom, and morality.* Cambridge: MIT Press.

Wilkinson, D. L., and D. P. Rosenbaum. 1994. The effects of organizational structure on community policing. In *The challenge of community policing: Testing the promises,* ed. D. Rosenbaum. Thousand Oaks, CA: Sage.

Williams, H., and P. Murphy. 1990. *The evolving strategy of police: A minority view.* Vol. 13, *Perspectives of Policing.* Washington, DC: National Institute of Justice.

Willis, J., S. D. Mastrofski, and D. Weisburd. 2004. Compstat and bureaucracy: A case study of challenges and opportunities for change. *Justice Quarterly* 21: 463–96.

———. 2007. Making sense of Compstat: A theory-based analysis of organizational change in three police departments. *Law and Society Review* 41 (1): 147–88.

Willis, J., S. D. Mastrofski, D. Weisburd, and R. Greenspan. 2003. *Compstat and organizational change: Intensive site visits report.* Washington, DC: Police Foundation.

———. 2004. Compstat and organizational change in the Lowell Police Department: Challenges and opportunities. Washington, DC.

Willis, J. J., D. Weisburd, and S. D. Mastrofski. 2003. *Compstat in practice: An in-depth analysis of three cities.* Washington, DC: Police Foundation.

Wilson, J. Q. 1968a. Dilemmas of police administration. *Public Administration Review* 28 (5): 407–17.

———. 1968b. *Varieties of police behavior.* Cambridge: Harvard University Press.

———. 1975. *Thinking about crime.* New York: Basic Books.

———. 1985. *Thinking about crime.* Rev. ed. New York: Vintage Books.

Wilson, J. Q., and G. Kelling. 1982. The police and neighborhood safety: Broken windows. *Atlantic Monthly* 249 (3): 29–38.

Wilson, O. W., and R. McLaren. 1963. *Police administration.* 3rd ed. New York: McGraw-Hill.

Wilson, W. J. 1987. *The truly disadvantaged: The inner city, the underclass, and public policy.* Chicago: University of Chicago Press.

———. 1996. *When work disappears: The world of the new urban poor.* New York: Vintage Books.

———. 2006. *The declining significance of race.* Chicago: University of Chicago Press.

Wilson, W. J., and R. P. Taub. 2006. *There goes the neighborhood: Racial, ethnic, and class tensions in four Chicago neighborhoods and their meaning for America.* New York: Alfred A. Knopf.

Wittgenstein, L. 1969. *The blue and brown books.* Oxford: Blackwell.

Wohlstetter, R. 1962. *Pearl Harbor: Warning and decision.* Stanford: Stanford University Press.

Woods, Arthur. 1919. *The policeman and the public.* New Haven: Yale University Press.

Wright, R., and S. H. Decker. 1994. *Burglars on the job: Streetlife and residential break-ins.* Boston: Northeastern University Press.

———. 1997. *Armed robbers in action: Stickups and street culture.* Boston: Northeastern University Press.

Yoo, J. 2005. *The powers of war and peace: The Constitution and foreign affairs after 9/11.* Chicago: University of Chicago Press.

Young, J. 1971. *The drugtakers: The social meaning of drug use.* London: HarperCollins.

Young, M. 1991. *An inside job.* Oxford: Clarendon Press.

Zhao, J. 1996. *Why police organizations change: A study of community-oriented policing.* Washington, DC: Police Executive Research Forum.

Zhao, J. H., M. C. Scheider, and Q. Thurman. 2002. Funding community policing to reduce crime: Have cops grants made a difference? *Criminology and Public Policy* 2 (1): 7–32.

Zhao, J. S., N. He, and N. P. Lovrich. 2003. Community policing: Did it change the basic functions of policing in the 1990s; a national follow-up study. *Justice Quarterly* 20: 697–720.

Index

About the Author

Peter K. Manning (Ph.D. Duke, 1966, MA Oxon. 1982) holds the Elmer V. H. and Eileen M. Brooks Chair in the College of Criminal Justice at Northeastern University, Boston, MA. He has been a Fellow of the National Institute of Justice, Balliol and Wolfson Colleges, Oxford; the American Bar Foundation; the Rockefeller Villa (Bellagio); and the Centre for Socio-Legal Studies, Wolfson College, Oxford. Listed in *Who's Who in America* and *Who's Who in the World,* he has been awarded many contracts and grants, the Bruce W. Smith and the O. W. Wilson Awards from the Academy of Criminal Justice Sciences, and the Charles Horton Cooley Award from the Michigan Sociological Association. The author and editor of some nineteen books, his research interests include democratic policing, uses of information technology, and qualitative methods. His most recent books are *Policing Contingencies* (University of Chicago Press 2003) and *The Technology of Policing* (NYU Press 2008). His current research concerns information technologies in policing and the transformation of the policing of Ireland in both the Republic and in Northern Ireland since the Patten report of 1999.